BUYERS' REMEDIES IN INTERNATIONAL SALES LAW

An authoritative, in-depth examination of remedies in international sales of manufactured goods, this book provides a detailed analysis of the remedies available to a commercial buyer.

The book concentrates on four prominent legal regimes, namely the UK sales law, the United Nations Convention on Contracts for the International Sale of Goods 1980 (CISG), the American Uniform Commercial Code (UCC), and the UNIDROIT Principles of International Commercial Contracts 2016 (UPICC).

It surveys the remedies available to a commercial buyer in the event that a seller fails to fulfil the contractual obligations stipulated by an international sales transaction of manufactured goods. The remedies investigated are self-help remedies, including suspension of performance and termination; monetary remedies, including damages and price reduction; and performance remedies including specific performance and the right to cure.

Providing access to, and analysis of, cases and arbitral decisions from all over the world, the book scrutinises the strengths and weaknesses of buyers' remedies through comparative and normative examination.

Buyers' Remedies in International Sales Law

A Comparative Study

Reza Beheshti

•HART•

OXFORD • LONDON • NEW YORK • NEW DELHI • SYDNEY

HART PUBLISHING

Bloomsbury Publishing Plc

Kemp House, Chawley Park, Cumnor Hill, Oxford, OX2 9PH, UK

1385 Broadway, New York, NY 10018, USA

29 Earlsfort Terrace, Dublin 2, Ireland

HART PUBLISHING, the Hart/Stag logo, BLOOMSBURY and the Diana logo are trademarks of Bloomsbury Publishing Plc

First published in Great Britain 2024

A catalogue record for this book is available from the British Library.

A catalogue record for this book is available from the Library of Congress.

Library of Congress Control Number: 2023950829

ISBN: HB: 978-1-50994-046-2
ePDF: 978-1-50994-048-6
ePub: 978-1-50994-047-9

Typeset by Compuscript Ltd, Shannon

FOREWORD

This book tackles the important topic of 'relational contracting' through a comparative and international lens, and the author is to be congratulated for drawing attention to it. Although widely discussed in academic circles for over 50 years, 'relational contracting' or relational contract theory as a notion is still highly divisive. In addition, aside from the recognition in *Bates v Post Office Ltd* (2019) of 'relational contracts' as a formal category, its contours are still undefined and the notion is yet to be formally accepted by higher courts. In spite of this, comments and studies highlighting the limits of the English law of contract as a tool lacking flexibility,[1] academic critiques of classical law theories[2] or the critical appraisal of the resurgence of formalism leading to the decline of the role of contract law as a governance tool for relations[3] are still ongoing. Within this wider background and with similar conversations taking place in the commercial law realm, this book is therefore of the utmost importance and its international and comparative setting is a crucial lens through which commercial contracts can be considered. Indeed, as the author himself reasserts throughout the book, English law is still the law of choice in many international disputes, and the discussion of its continued relevance is therefore particularly timely. Within that context, of great interest is the focus on the law of remedies through the lens of four significant legal regimes governing international sales transactions and the examination of those regimes through a novel normative framework inspired by the relational theory of contract. These regimes allow for a more 'contextualised view' of English law rules and principles and their application within the necessary wider context. The tone used throughout the book is both academic and pragmatic, and it is interesting to analyse which methods used by these regimes allow for greater cooperative behaviour.

To conclude, this book is a useful and very welcome addition to anyone wishing to learn more about how commercial contracts really work in practice.

Séverine Saintier
Professor of Commercial Law School of Law and Politics Cardiff Unversity
November 2023

[1] See in particular the British Institute of International and Comparative Law, 'Breathing Space – Concept Notes on the effect of the pandemic on commercial contracts' at www.biicl.org/projects/breathing-space-concept-notes-on-the-effect-of-the-pandemic-on-commercial-contracts.

[2] D Campbell, *Contractual Relations: A Contribution to the Critique of the Classical Law of Contract* (Oxford University Press, 2022).

[3] C Mitchell, *Vanishing Contract Law* (Cambridge University Press, 2022).

ACKNOWLEDGEMENTS

This book is dedicated to my beloved son Nikan and my wonderful wife Narjes, whose encouragement and patience throughout the most difficult and insurmountable moments of this venture have been a constant source of inspiration. I would like to express my sincere gratitude to my parents and my sister, whose unwavering support and encouragement fuelled the creative process behind this book.

The support of the Hart Publishing team played a pivotal role in bringing this project to fruition, and I am thankful for their guidance. Last but not least, I owe special thanks to the Law School, University of Nottingham for granting me sabbatical leave and providing me with adequate facilities for writing this book.

I also want to thank the readers – your curiosity and engagement inspire me. This book is as much yours as it is mine.

CONTENTS

TABLE OF CASES

Belgium

Canada

China

Denmark

Estonia

France

Finland

Germany

Greece

Italy

Netherlands

Poland

Russia

Spain

Sweden

Switzerland

United Kingdom

United States of America

Uruguay

1

Introduction

1. General Description of the Book

An authoritative, in-depth study of remedies in international sales of manufactured goods, this book provides detailed analyses of the remedies available to a commercial buyer. It surveys the remedies available to commercial buyers in the event that a seller fails to fulfil the contractual obligations stipulated by an international sales contract for manufactured goods. These remedies fall under four legal regimes, namely: (1) the English Sale of Goods Act 1979 (SGA); (2) the American Uniform Commercial Code (UCC); (3) the United Nations Convention on Contracts for the International Sale of Goods 1980 (CISG); and (4) the UNIDROIT Principles of International Commercial Contracts 2010 (UPICC). The remedies made available in these regimes will be scrutinised on the basis of an evaluative framework grounded on 'commercial needs and expectations' and inspired by the norms of 'relational theory of contracts', with a view to determining which of these regimes provide the most appropriate array of remedies for commercial buyers. The remedies investigated will be self-help remedies (suspension of performance, rejection and termination), compensatory remedies (damages, set-off and price reduction) and performance remedies (specific performance, the seller's right to cure). Findings will be presented to show which of these regimes provides the array of remedies that most effectively fulfils the needs of commercial buyers involved in international sales transactions, as ascertained by the evaluative framework.

The book does not investigate sellers' remedies, which are mainly specific performance (action for the price) and damages, due to their limited number and their lower degree of complexity. In contrast, a buyer has a wider array of remedies, some of which, for example, price reduction, can only be used by an injured buyer. Therefore, only buyers' remedies are scrutinised in order to rigorously analyse a wider range of relevant doctrines so that a more profound theoretical evaluation of this particular area of law can be provided.

A. International Sale of Manufactured Goods

An international sales transaction is a 'contract of sale' which involves the movement of goods from one state to another.[1] The goods move from one legal regime to another, even if the seller and the buyer have their places of business in the same state.[2] However, another approach is to consider the places of business of the parties. This approach regards a transaction as international where the place of business of the seller is different from the place of business of the buyer.[3] The latter approach has been taken in CISG Article 1.[4] This book considers both approaches, in order to cover a comprehensive range of transactions and relevant legal instruments.

There are two significant types of goods in international sales transactions.[5] One group is commodities, such as agricultural products, fuels, mining products, wheat, grain and rice. The other group is manufactured goods, such as iron and steel, chemicals, telecommunication products, automatic products, textiles, and clothing. Manufactured goods constitute the most important segment of international trade in terms of value. According to the website of the World Trade Organisation (WTO), international sales of manufactured goods comprise around 70 per cent of all international trade, while international sales of commodities amount to 30 per cent.[6] Moreover, trade in manufactured goods arguably requires access to a wider range of buyers' remedies than international commodity sales, because in the latter, the parties are often mere links in a chain of transactions with no need for any cooperation. The breach of commodity sales contracts can only be satisfactorily covered by monetary remedies due to the fungible nature of this sort of goods. Therefore, if the book focused on commodity sales, it would run the risk of analysing a range of remedies that is too narrow to take account of a very important segment of international trade. The chosen focus on the sale of manufactured goods consequently has the advantage of justifying and enabling coverage of the whole array of remedies that are likely to be important to buyers in

[1] SGA s 2(1) states that 'A contract by which the seller transfers or agrees to transfer the property in goods to the buyer for a money consideration, called the price'; see also UCC ss 2-106 and 2-401, which offer similar definition to SGA.

[2] E McKendrick, *Goode and McKendrick on Commercial Law*, 6th edn (Penguin Books, 2020) 941.

[3] ibid.

[4] CISG Article 1: 'This Convention applies to contracts of sale of goods between parties whose places of business are in different States.'

[5] On the World Trade Organisation website goods are classified under three groups: (1) agricultural products, (2) fuels and mining products, and (3) manufactured goods. See www.wto.org/english/res_e/statis_e/its2011_e/its11_merch_trade_product_e.htm.

On the website of the European Commission, goods in international trade are classified as follows: Machinery and transport equipment; other manufactured goods; chemicals and related products; mineral fuels and lubricants; foods, drinks and tobacco; and raw materials. See www.wto.org/english/res_e/statis_e/its2011_e/its11_merch_trade_product_e.htm.

[6] World Trade Organization, World Trade Statistical Review, 2022, see www.wto.org/english/res_e/publications_e/wtsr_2022_e.htm.

international sales transactions, whether these concern commodities or manufactured goods. A final reason for adopting this focus is that the CISG is excluded by some associations and oil companies involved in the trade of commodities, such as the Grain and Feed Trade Association (GAFTA)[7] and the Federation of Oils, Seeds and Fats Associations (FOSFA).[8] For the most part, traders of commodities choose the English law as the applicable law for their contracts. For all of these reasons, focusing on the international sale of manufactured goods enables the book to investigate a broader range of legal regimes.

B. Four Legal Regimes

An important reason for choosing the four legal regimes of SGA, UCC, CISG and UPICC is their historical development. SGA is essentially a replication of the Sale of Goods Act 1893, which was the first statutory framework in English law for the sale of goods.[9] UCC, which to a large extent developed on the common law grounds, was officially written in 1962 and would be valuable to explore whether and to what extent it has followed the English sale of goods in terms of providing remedies for commercial buyers. CISG came into force on 1 January 1988 after being ratified by the requisite number of states. UPICC is the newest legal regime governing international commercial contracts, having been originally written in 1994 and revised in 2016, which thus represents the latest approaches in this area. The consideration of these four legal regimes helps to contextualise the historical development of buyers' remedies over the years. Such development can contribute to a more coherent evaluation of this area of law, thus enabling a clearer understanding of both the necessity and content of legal reform.

English sales law and in particular SGA are applicable to both domestic and international contracts of sale and it governs business-to-business contracts. Although the SGA is part of English law, it has become a universally acceptable legal instrument for governing international commodity sales transactions. English sales law governs the standard form contracts of commodity associations, including GAFTA and FOSFA, as well as of major oil companies such as BP and Shell. This legal regime can also apply to non-commodity sales transactions. An empirical study of more than 4,400 international contracts shows that English law has been chosen by parties three times more than their closest competitors, such as US State, French or German contract law.[10] This signifies that English law plays

[7] See GAFTA, Contract No 100 (2022): clause 28 states that: 'The following shall not apply to this contract: The United Nations Convention on Contracts for the International Sale of Goods of 1980

[8] See FOSFA Contract No 53.

[9] MG Bridge (ed), *Benjamin's Sale of Goods*, 11th edn (Sweet & Maxwell, 2022) 3; C Twigg-Flesner and R Canavan, *Atiyah and Adams' Sale of Goods*, 14th edn (Pearson Education Limited, 2020) 3–4.

[10] G Cuniberti, 'The international market for contracts, the most attractive contract laws' (2014) 34 *Northwestern Journal of International Law & Business* 455, 459.

an important role in international trade. Accordingly, it is essential to examine this legal regime to ascertain whether this legal regime is truly capable of satisfying the needs of commercial buyers in the event of a breach of contract.

The American Uniform Commercial Code (UCC) is the third legal regime considered in this book. This instrument has been designed and developed under the sponsorship of the American Law Institute and the National Conference of Commissioners on Uniform State Laws. The Code is claimed to be the most extensive piece of legislation ever undertaken at anytime, anywhere.[11] It has also been featured quite prominently at the international level.[12] The focus will be on Article 2 dealing with Sales, which has been described by the New York Revision Commission as an 'intelligent and workable commercial law', and would render commercial law and practice 'clear, sane and safe'.[13] Drafted in the realist tradition, Article 2 is grounded on a broad definition of agreement and a collection of flexible standards rather than rules to engage the particular sale with the surrounding business context.[14] It is, therefore, essential to examine this important legal instrument as well as its related case law to realise whether they have been sufficiently developed to be widely applied at the international level.

The United Nations Convention on Contracts for the International Sale of Goods 1980 (CISG) is the second regime examined here. The CISG deals specifically with non-consumer international sales transactions and its purpose is to make it easier and more economical to buy and sell raw materials, commodities and manufactured goods in international commerce.[15] The CISG contains rules governing the designing and interpretation of international contracts for the sale of goods and rules concerning the obligations of the parties to such transactions as well as the remedies available to them in the event of breach. It has been claimed that this legal regime is 'the most successful substantive private law convention in history': a claim which is lent credence by the fact that 97 countries, as of

[11] 'The proposed Uniform Commercial Code – a symposium' (1949) 5(1) *The Business Lawyer* 156, 159; K Llewellyn, 'Why We Need the Uniform Commercial Code' (1957) 10 *University of Florida Law Review* 367; WD Malcolm, 'The Proposed Commercial Code, a report on developments from May 1950 through February 1951' (1951) 6 *The Business Lawyer* 113, 126.

[12] See generally Cuniberti (n 10) 455.

[13] State of New York Law Revision Committee Report, *Hearing on the Uniform Commercial Code* (1954) 113; see also S Williston, *The Law Governing Sales of Goods at Common Law and Under the Uniform Sales Act* (Baker, Voorhis & Company, 1924).

[14] RE Speidel, 'The Revision of UCC Article 2, Sales in Light of United Nations Convention on Contracts for the International Sale of Goods' (1996) 16 *Northwestern Journal of International Law & Business* 165, 168; R Hillman, 'The Crises in Modern Contract Theory (1988) 67 *Tulane Law Review* 103.

[15] Preamble of the CISG available at: uncitral.un.org/sites/uncitral.un.org/files/media-documents/uncitral/en/cisg-commonwealth.pdf; see also J Lookofsky, 'The 1980 United Nations Convention on Contracts for the International Sale of Goods' in R Blanpain (ed), *International Encyclopaedia of Laws – Contracts* (Kluwer Law International, 2000); I Schwenzer and P Hachem, 'The CISG – Successes and Pitfalls' (2009) 57 *The American Journal of Comparative Law* 457.

September 2023, have adopted the regime; while the UK[16] and India, as significant trading nations, have yet failed to accede to it.[17] Additionally, it has already governed a large volume of international commercial transactions with more than 4,500 decisions to date by state courts and arbitral tribunals.[18] Thus it is necessary to consider this legal regime in order to provide a comprehensive analysis of buyers' remedies.

The final legal regime covered in this book is the UNIDROIT Principles of International Commercial Contracts (UPICC). These principles were published by the International Institute for the Unification of Private Law in 1994 and subsequently revised in 2004, 2010 and 2016.[19] The book only surveys the latest version of these principles, as it is the most updated version and includes the official comments prepared by the Governing Council of UNIDROIT.[20] The objective of the UNIDROIT Principles is 'to establish a balanced set of rules designed for use throughout the world irrespective of the legal traditions and the economic and political conditions of the countries in which they are to be applied'.[21] There are several reasons for analysing this legal regime. First, it is a transnational legal instrument which is based on the idea of 'common origin', ie, not reflecting the principles of any particular national legal order but rather being detached from any national legal context.[22] Second, 'the UPICC provides a simple neutral set of

[16] See B Hayward, B Zeller and CB Andersen, 'The CISG and the United Kingdom – exploring coherency and private international law' (2018) 67 *International and Comparative Law Quarterly* 607.

[17] See the website of United Nations Commission on International Trade Law at www.uncitral.org/uncitral/en/uncitral_texts/sale_goods/1980CISG_status.html; United Nations Treaty Collections at treaties.un.org/; see also LA DiMatteo, 'Harmonization of International Sales Law' in LA DiMatteo, Q Zhou, S Saintier and K Rowley, *Commercial Contract Law, Transatlantic Perspectives* (Cambridge University Press, 2013) 560; see also Schwenzer and Hachem (n 15) 457, 457–58; MJ Bonell, 'The CISG, European Contract Law and the Development of a World Contract Law' (2008) 56 *The American Journal of Comparative Law* 1, 1–2; H Kronke, 'The UN Sales Convention, the UNIDROIT contract principles and the way beyond' (2004) 9 *Uniform Law Review* 758; F Ferrari, 'What sources of law for contracts for the international sale of goods? Why one has to look beyond the CISG' (2005) 5 *Internationales Handelsrecht* 314, 314–17; J Felemegas, 'The United Nations Convention on Contracts for the International Sale of Goods: article 7 and uniform interpretation' in *Pace Review of the Convention on Contracts for the International Sale of Goods* (Kluwer Law International, 2000–2001) 115; MJ Bonell, 'The UNIDROIT Principles of International Commercial Contracts and CISG – alternatives or complementary instruments?' (1996) 1 *Uniform Law Review* 26; the website of United Nations Commission on International Trade Law at www.uncitral.org/uncitral/en/uncitral_texts/sale_goods/1980CISG_status.html.

[18] UNICTRAL Digest of Case law on the United Nations Convention on the International Sale of Goods' (2016), see uncitral.un.org/sites/uncitral.un.org/files/media-documents/uncitral/en/cisg_digest_2016.pdf; and CISG-online at cisg-online.org/home.

[19] International Institute for the Unification of Private Law, see www.unidroit.org/; see also UNILEX Website at www.unilex.info/dynasite.cfm?dssid=2377&dsmid=14311; and scholarship.law.duke.edu/cgi/viewcontent.cgi?article=6058&context=faculty_scholarship.

[20] Hereinafter, the 'UPICC' refers to the UPICC 2016.

[21] The Governing Council of UNIDROIT, 'Introduction to the UNIDROIT Principles', Rome, 1994. See www.unilex.info/dynasite.cfm?dssid=2377&dsmid=14311.

[22] MJ Bonell, 'The law governing international commercial contracts and the actual role of the UNIDROIT Principles' (2018) 23 *Uniform Law Review* 15; JH Dalhuisen, 'Some realism about a

well-organised parameters to govern international contracts that are rarely found in domestic legislations'.[23] An empirical study shows that the application of the UPICC in international commercial contracts is growing, and on the UNILEX database, there are currently 558 cases that have referred to the UPICC in different ways.[24] For these reasons, it is essential to consider this legal regime in order to test the appropriateness of its approach towards buyers' remedies in international sales of manufactured goods.

2. Rationale for the Book

There is a significant amount of literature covering both: (a) comparisons of the remedies made available by each of the four legal regimes discussed in this book,[25] and (b) the specific advantages and disadvantages of various remedies for breach of contract.[26] However, both sets of literature have limitations and gaps.

Common European Sales Law' (2013) 24 *European Business Law Review* 299, 301; G Baron, 'Do the UNIDROIT Principles of International Commercial Contracts form a new lex mercatoria?' (1999) 2 *Arbitration International* 115; MJ Bonell, 'The UNIDROIT Principles of International Commercial Contracts and the Harmonisation of International Sales Law' (2002) 36 *Revue Juridique Themis* 335; MJ Bonell, 'The UNIDROIT Principles of International Commercial Contracts and the Principles of European Contract Law: Similar Rules for the Same Purposes?' (1996) 26 *Uniform Law Review* 229.

[23] S Lake, 'An empirical study of the UNIDROIT principles- International and British responses' (2011) 16(3) *Uniform Law Review* 669, 672; see also MJ Bonell, *An International Restatement of Contract Law, The UNIDROT Principles of International Commercial Contracts*, 3rd edn (Transnational Publishers, 2005) 7.

[24] UNILEX UNIDROIT Principles, see www.unilex.info/dynasite.cfm?dssid=2377&dsmid=13618&x=1; S Lake, 'An empirical study of the UNIDROIT principles – International and British responses' (2011) 16 *Uniform Law Review* 669; see also N O'Malley and LB Nieuwveld, 'The UNIDROIT Principles: Are They Law?' (2007) 11 *Vindobona Journal of International Commercial Law and Arbitration* 229.

[25] See PA Piliounis, 'The Remedies of Specific Performance, Price Reduction and Additional Time (Nachfrist) under the CISG: Are these worthwhile changes or additions to English Sales Law?' (2000) 12 *Pace International Law Review* 1; A Gartner, 'Britain and the CISG: The Case for Ratification – A Comparative Analysis with Special Reference to German Law' in *Review of the Convention on Contracts for the International Sale of Goods* (Kluwer Law International, 2001) 59; R Feltkamp and F Vanbossele, 'The Optional Common European Sales Law: better buyer's remedies for seller's non-performance in sales of goods? (2011) 6 *European Review of Private Law* 873; MBM Loos and HN Schelhaas, 'Commercial sales: the Common European Sales Law compared to the Vienna Sales Convention' (2013) 21 *European Review of Private Law* 105; G Virgo and S Worthington, *Commercial Remedies: Resolving Controversies* (Cambridge University Press, 2017) in which only one chapter deals with remedies in international cases; R Halson and D Campbell, *Research Handbook on Remedies in Private Law* (Edward Elgar Publishing, 2019).

[26] A prominent example is S Rowan, *Remedies for Breach of Contract, A Comparative Analysis of Protection of Performance* (Oxford University Press, 2012), which compares remedies under English law, French law and the Draft Common Frame of Reference (DCFR) on the basis of protecting the performance interest. Rowan's book mostly focuses on domestic legal regimes and analyses the existing approaches of remedies for consumers, whereas this thesis covers international commercial transactions. W Bishop, 'The choice of remedy for breach of contract' (1985) 14 *The Journal of Legal Studies* 299; AH Kastley, 'The Right to Require Performance in International Sales: Towards an International Interpretation of the Vienna Convention' (1988) 63 *Washington Law Review* 607; MG Bridge, 'A law for international sales' (2007) 37 *Hong Kong Law Journal* 17; F Ferrari, 'Fundamental Breach of Contract Under the UN Sales Convention, 25 Years Article 25 CISG' (2005) 3 *International Business Law*

The existing literature does not enable us to answer the questions of which legal regime's approach to buyers' remedies is best suited to satisfying the needs of international commercial buyers of manufactured goods, and which would commercial actors be best advised to select to govern their international contracts of sale. In particular, the comparative analyses which have previously been carried out of remedies under these four legal regimes mostly focus on divergences in the application of remedies, and the remedies have not been seriously examined on the basis of specific and integrated normative criteria.[27] Indeed, it has been suggested that there is no clear criterion for evaluating remedies: 'The suggestion is to adopt fixed and clear criteria that permit derogation from the rule. The criteria must be based on a country's needs and economic conditions, not on the basis that certain rules inherited from the past should never be challenged.'[28]

There are, however, more general studies discussing the suitability of remedies for breach of contract. One prominent strand consists of the economic analysis of contracts. Such examinations have tried to provide theoretical insight (though not necessarily comparative) into remedies using the normative criterion of efficiency. Economic analysts attempt to examine the law of damages, specific performance and the duty to mitigate on the basis of efficiency.[29] The core issue for contract remedies under economic theory is creating 'a system that both avoids breaches of contracts that are worth performing and avoids performances of contracts that are not worth the cost.'[30] It seems that the purpose of contract remedies under economic theory is to encourage the parties to act efficiently. The law of remedies can influence the behaviour of parties in different ways, yet the economic analysis of remedies has focused on two decisions: 'the promisee's decision to rely and the promisor's decision to breach.'[31] Moreover, most of the economic literature about remedies has focused only on two remedies: damages and specific performance. Other remedies, such as price reduction and buyers' right to cure, have tended to

Journal 389; T Plate, 'The Buyer's Remedy of Avoidance under the CISG: Acceptable from a Common Law Perspective?' (2002) 6 *Vindobona Journal of International Commercial Law and Arbitration* 57; B Zeller, *Damages under the Convention on Contracts for the International Sale of Goods*, 3rd edn (Oxford University Press, 2018); D Saidov (ed), *Research Handbook on International and Comparative Sale of Goods Law* (Edward Elgar Publishing, 2019).

[27] The article by Piliounis is a clear example of a comparative analysis of remedies which has not provided any clear criteria for assessing the divergences between the laws of remedies of the CISG and the SGA: Piliounis (n 25) 1.

[28] N Boghossian, 'A comparative study of specific performance provisions in the United Nations Convention on Contracts for the International Sale of Goods' in *Review of the Convention on Contracts for the International Sale of Goods* (Kluwer Law International, 2000) 75.

[29] LA Kornhauser, 'An introduction to the economic analysis of contract remedies' (1985–1986) 57 *University of Colorado Law Review* 683; see also AT Kronman 'Specific performance' (1978) 45 *University of Chicago Law Review* 351; A Schwartz, 'The case for specific performance' (1979) 89 *Yale Law Journal* 271; S Shavell, 'Damage measures for breach of contract' (1980) 11 *The Bell Journal of Economics* 466; TS Ulen, 'The efficiency of specific performance: toward a unified theory of contract remedies' (1984–1985) 83 *Michigan Law Review* 341.

[30] Bishop (n 26) 299, 301.

[31] Kornhauser (n 29) 683, 694.

be ignored. As Ulen stated, 'the bulk of the scholarship on efficient remedies has concerned the award of damages, and a consensus has been reached that damages are most likely to promote economic efficiency'.[32]

Another theory for evaluating the appropriateness of remedies is the relational theory of contract. Notwithstanding the remarkable development of relational theory since the initial works of Macaulay and Macneil, the law of remedies has not been rigorously considered in the literature.[33] According to Macneil, contracts represent 'relations among people who have exchanged, are exchanging, or expect to be exchanging in the future; in other words, contract is exchange of relations'.[34] This theory focuses on informal devices for the regulation of long term contractual relations, for example, consensual adjustment of primary contractual arrangements in light of changing circumstances, informal incentives for performance and cooperation, the tendency to avoid relying on formal rights and duties and the frequent use of alternative dispute resolution mechanisms.[35] English law appears to embrace relational ways of thinking more prominently than other legal regimes. The recognition that not all the obligations between the parties can be precisely determined at the formation stage of contract and that flexible approaches to consideration in renegotiated contracts is needed was, for instance, reflected in the decision of *Williams v Roffey Brothers and Nicholls (Contractors) Ltd*.[36] Additionally, in the remarkable case of *Bristol Groundschool Ltd v Intelligent Data Capture Ltd*, the parties agreed to collaborate to provide training manuals for pilots.[37] One party provided the content and the other converted them into

[32] Ulen (n 29) 341, 343.

[33] S Macaulay, 'Non-contractual relations in business: a preliminary study' (1963) 28 *American Sociological Review* 1; S Macaulay, 'Changing a continuing relationship between a large corporation and those who deal with it: automobile manufacturers, their dealers, and the legal system, law and society' (1965) 483 *Wisconsin Law Review* 2; IR Macneil, 'Contracts: adjustment of long-term economic relations under classic, neoclassical, and relational contract law' (1977–1978) 72 *Northwestern University Law Review* 854; IR Macneil, *The New Social Contract: An Inquiry into Modern Contractual Relations* (Yale University Press, 1981); IR Macneil, 'Values in contract: internal and external' (1983) 78 *Northwestern University Law Review* 340; V Goldberg, 'Relational Exchange: Economics and Complex Contracts' (1980) 23 *American Behavioural Scientist* 337; CJ Goetz and RE Scott, 'Principles of Relational Contracts' (1981) 69 *Virginia Law Review* 1089; RE Speidel, 'The Characteristics and Challenges of Relational Contracts' (2000) 94(3) *Northwestern University Law Review* 823; D Campbell, 'Good Faith and the Ubiquity of the "Relational" Contract' (2014) 77 *Modern Law Review* 460; Z Xing Tan, 'Disrupting doctrine? Revisiting the doctrinal impact of relational contract theory' (2018) 39 *Legal Studies* 98; D Christie, S Saintier and J Viven-Wilksch, 'Industry led standards, relational contracts and good faith: are the UK and Australia setting the pace in (construction) contract law?' (2022) 43 *Liverpool Law Review* 287.

[34] Macneil, 'Values in contract: internal and external' (n 33) 340, 344; see also IR Macneil, 'Economic analysis of contractual relations: its shortfalls and the need for a rich classificatory apparatus' (1980–1981) 75 *Northwestern University Law Review* 1018, 1020.

[35] See generally: D Campbell, 'The relational constitution of remedy: co-operation as the implicit second principle of remedies for breach of contract' (2004–2005) 11 *Texas Wesleyan Law Review* 455; D Kimel, 'The choice of paradigm for theory of contract: reflections on the relational model' (2007) 27 *Oxford Journal of Legal Studies* 233; Y Adar and M Gelbard, 'The role of remedies in the relational theory of contract' (2011) 7 *European Review of Contract Law* 399.

[36] [1991] 1 QB 1 (CA).

[37] [2014] EWHC 2145 (Ch).

an electronic application, which was jointly published and marketed. Following the parties' conflict, one of them secretly accessed the other party's database and downloaded materials, later using this downloaded material to continue selling electronic training manuals. One issue was whether the secret access and download of the materials was a breach of contract. There was no express term of the contract which prohibited it. The court described the joint venture agreement as a relational contract and decided that there was an implied term of the contract requiring good faith in its performance. The defendant had breached that term by engaging in conduct that 'would be regarded as commercially unacceptable by reasonable and honest people'.[38]

It has been argued that 'under the traditional view, legal rules in general and formal rules of remedies in particular, play a marginal role in factual settings that fall under the purview of a relational contract'.[39] This is because 'informal, non-legal understandings' are more often the basis of business activities, especially conflict resolution.[40] The reason for this might be that legal remedies hinder cooperation and negotiation between the parties, according to proponents of this theory.[41] There appears to be a tendency to abstain from resorting to formal rights and duties, and therefore, remedies, especially judicial remedies, have not been seriously taken into account. There are some publications analysing only the self-help remedies, probably because they do not require any formal litigation: 'These remedies might open the way to further negotiation and cooperation between the parties.'[42] The existing literature assessing remedies thus does not present a comprehensive analysis of remedies; rather, they have mostly focused on the domestic application of the relational theory without exploring it in the context of international sales. There is a need for more in-depth exploration of remedies for international sales transactions in light of the relational theory. The more general literature on remedies for breach of contract holds much potential for filling the gaps left by the literature on international sales transactions, in particular by providing more rigorous criteria for the assessment of remedies. Nevertheless, sufficient attention has not been given to remedies and commercial needs that are more prominent in international commercial transactions.

These limitations in both the literature dealing specifically with the legal regimes governing international sales and the more general literature on remedies

[38] ibid, para 144; see also *Mackie Motors (Brechin) Ltd v RCI Financial Services Ltd* [2023] EWCA Civ 476, where most recently the Court of Appeals in the context of long-term car dealership arrangements dealt with the implication of good faith doctrine in contracts with relational nature.

[39] Adar and Gelbard (n 35) 399, 403; see also E McKendrick, 'The regulation of long-term contracts in English law' in J Beatson and D Friedmann, *Good Faith and Fault in Contract Law* (Oxford University Press, 1995).

[40] Campbell (n 35) 455, 469.

[41] D Harris, David Campbell and R Halson, Remedies in Contract and Tort, 2nd edn (Butterworths LexisNexis, 2002) 34; S Macaulay, 'Renegotiations and settlements: Dr. Pangloss's notes on the margins of David Campbell's papers' (2007–2008) 29 *Cardozo Law Review* 261, 265.

[42] Harris, Campbell and Halson (n 41) 44.

for breach of contract make it essential to develop and apply a clear evaluative framework that bridges the gap between them. This book takes up the task of developing integrated and coherent criteria that can be applied in order to examine accurately the available remedies for buyers under those four legal regimes. The book will not only expose the theoretical and doctrinal operation of contract remedies but will also examine them in the relational context in which they are employed. This proves to be difficult, since not much work has yet been written on this juncture, where four prominent legal regimes are scrutinised against an innovative normative framework.

It is questionable whether any coherent set of 'commercial needs and expectations', shared by all commercial contractors, actually exists to be satisfied by a legal regime. There are also serious doubts whether there is any alignment between contract law doctrines and commercial contracting behaviour.[43] This book attempts to make a modest contribution in identifying a set of coherent criteria reflecting the likely preferences of commercial contractors in transactional process. The evaluative framework employed in this book draws on the insights of 'relational theory of contract' in order to develop criteria that are specifically designed in light of the commercial realities and needs of international sales transactions. This framework will then be applied to the significant range of buyers' remedies made available by those four legal regimes.

Lord Justice Legatt in *Yem Seng Pte Ltd v International Trade Corp Ltd* argued that many commercial contracts involve a long-term relationship between the parties, in which they are likely to make a substantial commitment.[44] It is, indeed, a mistake to draw an outright dichotomy between relationships giving rise to fiduciary duties and other contractual relationships, which leads to this erroneous conceptualisation of treating the latter all alike.[45] There could be a category of contract in which the parties are committed to collaborating with each other, typically on a long term basis, in ways which show regard to the spirit and objectives of their venture. However, they have not tried to determine, and which it may be impossible to determine, exhaustively in a written contract. Such 'relational' contracts involve a different kind of trust and confidence from that involved in fiduciary relationships. The nature of this trust cannot be described as the loyal subordination by one party of its own interests to those of another. The necessary trust for this category of contract is that parties will conduct with integrity and in a spirit of cooperation. In particular, the international sales of manufactured goods normally formed between commercial parties need a high degree of communication, co-operation and predictable performance based on mutual trust and confidence, which are not legislated for in the express terms of the contract. Where manufactured goods are specific goods (which may be unique or rare), they

[43] C Mitchell, 'Remedies and reality in the law of contract' in Halson and Campbell (n 25) 68–69.
[44] [2013] EWHC 111 (QB), para 171.
[45] ibid, para 142.

need to be made to the buyer's special requirements, which are not necessarily reflected in the contract terms. They are rather implicit in the parties' understanding and necessary to give business efficacy to the arrangements. This compliance is likely to be achieved through regular negotiation and communication between the parties before the ultimate performance of the contract. Even after this point, the parties need to cooperate with each other to correct any deficiency relating to the goods. In addition, commercial parties are likely to have interests beyond the short-term, formally written transaction: they wish to conduct business again with each other or with others. Therefore, the need to keep their reputation is a more significant incentive than proper performance, and the risk of losing business a more significant sanction against default, than any legal remedy. This does not mean that the provision of remedies in these legal regimes are irrelevant: not all commercial parties have such long-term interests, or the interests may not be sufficiently powerful to avoid some risk of default. However, the significance of maintaining the commercial relationship between firms and manufacturers becomes significantly more evident when a sizeable investment is at stake, which is specific to the contemplated transactions. Such investments may take various forms: a supplier may prepare its equipment to meet the buyer's particular requirements and human resources may be trained in building up a bespoke working relationship responsive to each other's needs and expectations.

In light of the above illustration, two norms inspired by the relational theory of contract will be employed in this book. First is the 'preservation of relation', which is an expansion of contractual solidarity and involves the maintenance of particular relationships at both the individual and collective levels.[46] 'Solidarity' identified by Macneil reflects the fact that individuals necessarily have relations with each other in order to satisfy their needs, while preservation of relation signifies that particular membership is optimal for expanding the relationship.[47] The 'preservation of relation' seeks to analyse whether the remedial principles enable parties to extend the period of performance. Sales of manufactured goods are likely to become more meaningful for both parties as time passes. A commercial buyer may prefer to maintain its relationship with a particular manufacturer because it is inconvenient to move manufacturers, or because they prefer the service and fear worse service elsewhere. Greater stability is derived from such long-term relations than from short-term ones, and thus planning is easier.

The second norm of 'conformity of extended relations with commercial matrix', which complements the first norm, seeks to realise whether an extended relationship is economically and financially sustainable and whether the parties should maintain such a relationship. This norm expounds that the more the commercial parties have organised their relations in accordance with commercial reality and efficient contractual behaviour, the more likely the relation is to survive over

[46] ibid, para 222.
[47] ibid, para 223.

a long period that would be profitable to both parties. An important feature of relational, long-term contracts concerns the nature and extent of the investment made by the parties. More specifically, the nature and extent of the initial investment made by each of the parties to the transaction (or the one each party undertakes to make in the future) make the costs of withdrawing from it prohibitively high. As a consequence, the parties may be regarded as being effectively 'locked into the relationship', as they realise that a complete withdrawal from the bargain will be harmful to both parties. Therefore, this norm examines whether those legal regimes freely entitle the parties to end hostile, economically detrimental relationships, or whether they encourage them to use less drastic remedies such as price reduction or the right to withhold performance.

Undertaking analytical research in light of the normative framework established in this book necessitates the adoption of a sound method. Comparative analysis will be employed at two levels in this book. First, the theoretical-descriptive form of this method will be used.[48] Here, the aim will be to provide expository explanations of remedial principles in order to illuminate the similarities and differences. The purpose of this form is to present symmetrical information relating to each particular type of remedy in the four legal regimes. Second, this study will provide a critical comparative analysis. This method is adopted for a very specific purpose: identifying the legal regime which provides the best array of remedies for a commercial buyer. To that end, the significant differences discovered in each category of buyers' remedies will be highlighted and analysed, as these differences might lead to different solutions, and therefore, they have to be scrutinised rigorously to determine the best legal regime. At the stage of critical analysis, the novel normative framework described above will be used to evaluate those discovered significant differences in order to ascertain which remedial rule in which legal regime most effectively satisfies the criteria of the framework. The assessment will be based on the important distinctions found amongst the provisions for a particular remedy in each of the four legal regimes. Accordingly, in this book, each substantive chapter will take this format: first, there are expositions of the remedial principles under the four legal regimes, followed by an analysis drawing upon the similarities and significant differences. Second, the differences will be assessed against the evaluative framework.

[48] For further explanation about the descriptive form of comparative analysis, see O Kahn-Freund, 'Comparative Law as an Academic Subject' (1966) 82 *Law Quarterly Review* 40, 45; HC Gutteridge, *Comparative Law, An Introduction to the Comparative Method of Legal Study & Research*, 2nd edn (Cambridge University Press, 1971) 8; O Kahn-Freund, 'On Uses and Misuses of Comparative Law' (1974) 37 *Modern Law Review* 1, 7; G Frankenberg, 'Critical comparisons: rethinking comparative law' (1985) 26 Harvard International Law Journal 411, 412; B Markesinis, 'Comparative Law – A Subject in Search of an Audience' (1990) 53 *Modern Law Review* 1, 8; P Legrand, 'Comparative Legal Studies and Commitment to Theory' (1995) 58 *Modern Law Review* 262, 267; K Zweigert and H Kotz, *Introduction to Comparative Law*, 3rd edn (Oxford University Press, 1998) 39; P Legrand and RJC Munday, *Comparative Legal Studies: Traditions and Transitions* (Cambridge University Press, 2003) 33; G Samuel, *An Introduction to Comparative Law Theory and Method* (Hart Publishing, 2014) 44.

3. Structure of the Book

This book has five substantive chapters. Following the conclusion of the sales transaction, the buyer may find grounds for concern that the seller will not fulfil its obligations. Such grounds can range from a clear expression of intention to non-performance of similar contracts by the seller. The seller should have behaved in a way that the buyer, on the balance of probabilities, could have drawn an inference that the seller is likely to commit a breach when the time for performance arrives. However, to realise whether there are reasonable grounds for insecurity, many factors, including the seller's exact words or conduct, the course of dealing or performance between the parties involved, and the nature of the industry should be taken into account. Chapter two will analyse the solutions provided in these legal regimes to such reasonable concerns. In particular, the law concerning withholding performance, anticipatory breach and adequate assurance will be examined. Chapter three aims to compare the law of price reduction with the law of set-off. The reason for their inclusion in this chapter lies in the fact that both are self-help remedies and provide monetary remedies to an injured buyer. The remedy of price reduction is not prescribed under SGA and UPICC. This exclusion will be explored. There will be analysis of the law of set-off under SGA, UPICC and UCC. It is debatable whether this remedy is available under CISG. The doctrine of set-off is solely considered within the context of buyers' remedies in international sales transactions when it is used as a buyer's defence against the seller's claim for the contract price. Chapter four will explore damages under the four legal regimes. Given the range of issues concerning damages that could be examined to this end, this chapter is necessarily selective, focusing on the central aspects of damages. The doctrines governing damages under CISG and UPICC will be described together, as the relevant provisions have considerable textual uniformity. However, those doctrines and principles under SGA and UCC appear to be distinctive, and they will be surveyed separately. Chapter five will analyse the law relating to the remedies directed at bringing about performance, including specific performance and the seller's right to cure, under the four legal regimes on the basis of the evaluative framework developed in chapter one. In this chapter, the salient divergence of common law and civil law towards specific remedies will be taken into account in an attempt to realise and evaluate the existing discrepancies between the four legal regimes. The chief difference lies in the secondary nature of specific performance under SGA and UCC, as opposed to other regimes where specific performance is available as a general buyer's entitlement. Chapter six focuses on termination under the four legal regimes. Termination is investigated in this chapter as a remedy available to the buyer who has not received or will not receive the promised performance, thus entitling them to end a contract otherwise fulfilled properly. The grounds for termination, the limitation on the buyer's right to terminate and effects of termination of the contract are three key issues that will be comparatively investigated in this chapter.

2

Insecurity before Performance is Due

1. Introduction

Following the conclusion of the sales transaction, the commercial buyer may find grounds for concern that the seller will not fulfil their obligations. Such grounds can range from a clear expression of intention to non-performance of similar contracts by the seller. The seller should have behaved in a way that the buyer, on the balance of probabilities, could have drawn an inference that the seller is likely to commit a breach when the time for performance arrives. However, to realise whether there are reasonable grounds for insecurity, many factors, including the seller's exact words or conduct, the course of dealing or performance between the parties involved, and the nature of the industry should be taken into account. This chapter analyses the solutions and remedies provided by those four legal regimes to such reasonable concerns. In particular, the right to withhold performance, anticipatory breach of contract and request for an adequate assurance will be examined.

2. Theoretical Foundation of Withholding Performance of Contract

There is no doubt that an international sale of goods contract is a bilateral or reciprocal contract in nature. The synallagmatic nature of such contracts means not only that each party undertakes an obligation but has the feature that the performance promised by one party is to be exchanged for that of the other.[1] However, there is risk in performance of these obligations. A party who is willing and ready to perform has a significant interest in performing provided that the other party will perform and thus reciprocate. When the party willing to perform lacks confidence in the other party's willingness and ability, they will face an uneasy decision. On the one hand, failure to perform may amount to a breach of contract and on the other hand performance exposes them to considerable risks. The law should therefore offer a sensible and practical solution. The civil law systems recognising the good

[1] GH Treitel, *Remedies for Breach of Contract: A Comparative Account* (Oxford University Press, 1988) 236; R Zimmermann, *The Law of Obligations: Roman Foundations of the Civilian Tradition* (Clarendon, 1996) Part IV (II).

faith principle furnishes the parties with the defence known as the *exception non adimpleti contractus*: the buyer, as the willing and able party, suspends payment, the seller sues, claiming that the suspension constitutes a breach of contract, and the buyer defends, citing the *exceptio*.[2] A functional characteristic of synallagmatic contracts is that failure by a seller to perform their part of the promised exchange will justify the buyer's refusal to pay.[3] Suspension of performance, as a self-help remedy, is premised on the *exceptio* principle and is employed to force the seller or debtor to clarify the situation by either performing the contract or renouncing their obligations. The buyer, who faces a potential non-performance, can take a temporary action by withholding their performance and potentially preventing disputes without official assistance of a governmental official or disinterested third parties.[4]

While the *exceptio* is unknown in the common law systems, Professor Treitel has suggested that 'analogies can be drawn [to it], though they are far from precise'.[5] From a general contract law perspective, common law systems approach the issue differently to civil law. To start with, common law adopts an 'all-or-nothing approach', in that one party's breach does not automatically give rise to a right to suspend the performance.[6] Rather, an optimal solution for the innocent party is to escape their obligations by avoiding the contract, provided that the breach is sufficiently serious to justify avoidance. However, the remedy of suspension of performance can be analysed in the context of the occurrence or performance of a 'condition'.[7] Whether explicitly stated in an agreement or implied by law, 'conditions' determine the content of a party's obligations and the effects of their breach. This term is employed in a variety of senses in Anglo-American contract law.[8] A particularly accepted sense refers to a kind of term, which specifies an event on which a party's obligation depends. In the context of sale of goods contracts that event is prima facie the due performance of the other party's undertaking. The parties' performances are envisaged to be 'concurrent conditions' where a simultaneous exchange is expected.[9] The buyer is not bound to pay unless the seller is willing and prepared to deliver the goods. This follows that no actual tender of performance is necessary to satisfy this rule: an expression of willingness to perform is sufficient, on the condition that it is 'accompanied with manifested present ability to make it good'.[10] Of course these prototypical situations may be freely varied or excluded by a contrary agreement. The significance of concurrent

[2] Treitel (n 1) 188.

[3] ibid, 248.

[4] For a full analysis of the nature of self-help remedies see CR Taylor, 'Self-help in contract law: an exploration and proposal' (1998) 33 *Wake Forest Law Review* 839.

[5] Treitel (n 1) 306.

[6] JW Carter, 'Suspending Contract Performance for Breach' in J Beatson and D Friedman, *Good Faith and Fault in Contract Law* (Oxford University Press, 1997) 487.

[7] Treitel (n 1) 194.

[8] ibid.

[9] ibid 278; see SGA section 28.

[10] USA Restatement (Second) of Contracts (1981) section 238, Comment B; see also *MoonScoop SAS v American Greetings Corp* (2012) United States Court of Appeals, 489 Fed.Appx. 95.

conditions to suspension of performance is that non-performance by one party does not justify the other party's performance being excused. In other words, the buyer's obligation to pay never materialises without the seller's performance. Such characterisation of conditions in the common law systems establishes the conceptual link to the civil law principle of '*exceptio*' and provides the theoretical ground for the availability of suspension of performance as one of the buyer's remedies.

3. Suspension of Performance

A. UPICC

UPICC has formally recognised the general right to suspend performance. Article 7.1.3 states that 'where the parties are to perform simultaneously, either party may withhold performance until the other party tenders [their] performance'. This article is applied in conjunction with Article 6.1.4, which imposes the presumption of simultaneous performance of obligations only when that simultaneous performance can possibly be made. This means that if one party is not yet obliged to perform, withholding performance by the other party is premature and does not serve any purpose. But this presumption can be disregarded where one of the party's performances is to be rendered over time and the other party is deemed to perform first. The wording of this article indicates that the right to withhold is a temporary remedy and can only be exercised during the period in which the other party does not perform.[11] If the failure to perform takes a long time, which may not be commercially reasonable, the party suspending the performance lawfully may no longer wait for the performance. Instead, they resort to the drastic remedy of termination in order to be released from their contractual obligations.

UPICC Article 7.1.3, corresponding in effect to the *exceptio non adimpleti contractus*, implies that the right to suspend is generally permitted in case of total non-performance by the other party.[12] Under UPICC, a party does not require to show fundamental or substantial non-performance in order to exercise their right to withhold performance. Since it is a general principle of law to withhold performance, it is questionable whether such right can be exercised in the events of defective or partial performance. UPICC fails to address this uncertainty. The Official Commentary to this article, which is quite succinct, indicates that in cases of partial performance 'the party entitled to receive performance may be entitled to withhold performance but only where in normal circumstances this is consonant with good faith and fair dealing'. The overriding requirement of good faith, operating as a proportionality

[11] UPICC Official Comments Article 7.1.3. para 3.

[12] See *Bulgarian-Greek ULIS sales contract case* (1999), ICC International Court of Arbitration (Paris), CISG-online 2601: it was held that the right to withhold performance can be regarded as a general principle of law, with reference to UPICC Official Comments Article 7.1.3.

mechanism, effectively restricts the application of the right to withhold in cases of partial performance. This means that the performance suspended must not be wholly disproportionate to the obligation breached. In other words, a party is not permitted to invoke the right to withhold for each and every partial performance, however trifling.[13] For instance, in divisible sale of goods contracts or where goods are delivered in instalments, the buyer may make part payment in exchange for the part of the goods, conforming with the contract, received in due time. The buyer is then entitled to hold payment for the part not received or defectively received. The buyer's right to withhold partial payment lasts, as long as the seller fails to cure their deficient performance or indeed delivers the remaining goods. As such, there is the possibility of suspension for minor and even nonreciprocal obligations, subject to the requirements of good faith and fair dealing.

B. CISG

Contrary to UPICC, CISG does not explicitly state a general right to withhold performance. CISG Article 71 provides that a party has the right to suspend when it becomes apparent that a substantial part of the other party's obligation will not be performed as a result of: (a) a serious deficiency in the other party's ability to perform or in their creditworthiness; or (b) their conduct in preparing to perform or in performing the contract.[14] These two situations appear to be so comprehensive, which would arguably cover all causes of future disturbances. The reference to serious deficiency in part (a) is concerned not only with factual difficulties in performance, such as strike or loss of production facilities by fire, but also covers legal obstacles.[15] If the suspension is not justified, the party suspending performance will breach the contract when they fail to perform their obligations.[16]

Literally interpreting this article, the buyer's right of suspension seems to be restricted to the situation in which performance has not yet become due. This indicates that the wording of the provision provides the buyer no general right to withhold performance after the seller's performance has materialised. Once the date for performance has arrived the injured party must seek to invoke other remedies under the Convention. Where the seller provides adequate assurance of due performance, the buyer suspending their payment obligation 'must continue with performance'.[17] Nevertheless, it can be deduced that CISG

[13] UPICC Official Comments Article 7.1.3. para 27.

[14] Similar to this provision can be found in UPICC Official Comments Article 7.3.4.

[15] CM Bianca and MJ Bonell, *Commentary on the International Sales Law, The 1980 Vienna Sales Convention* (Giuffre, 1987) Article 71, para 2.6; P Schlechtriem and L Schwenzer, *Commentary on the UN Convention on the International Sale of Goods*, 5th edn (Oxford University Press, 2022) 1240.

[16] *Italian Shoes case V* (1991) Local Court Frankfurt am Main, Germany, CISG-online 34: in this case, the buyer was entitled to damages because seller failed to give immediate notice that it was suspending delivery.

[17] Article 71(3); adequate assurance will be explained in detail in section 5 below.

recognises a general right to withhold performance even after the seller has performed their obligation, but unsatisfactorily and non-conforming with the contract.[18] The general right to withhold performance lies on the principle of simultaneous exchange of performances, which is derived from several CISG provisions.[19] Article 58 (1) stipulates that the payment of the price becomes due only when the goods delivered to the buyer are in conformity with the contract. Thus, when the seller fails to deliver the goods in due time, the buyer is permitted to refuse payment of the price, since pursuant to this article the price is due only when the goods have been delivered and placed at the buyer's disposal. There is, however, no clear indication under CISG on what placing at the buyer's disposal requires. An autonomous interpretation of CISG suggest the basic requirements of identifying the goods to the contract and giving notice to the buyer that the goods are available for collection. In addition, when the goods delivered are defective, the buyer may wish to request repair or substitute delivery of the goods, in pursuance to Articles 46 (2) or (3). In so doing, the buyer must accept delivery of the defective goods. The buyer may rather decide to invoke Article 58(3), which establishes that 'the buyer is not bound to pay the price until he has had an opportunity to examine the goods', unless otherwise agreed. This article implies that by suspending their payment obligation, the buyer would have the chance to examine the goods and ensure that they are confirming. Therefore, the right to examine the goods would be meaningless if the buyer needed to pay the price following examination of the goods and realising that the goods were non-conforming.[20] The general right to withhold performance is supported in several cases. For instance, the buyer was held to be entitled to suspend payment of the purchase price when the delivered machines were defective.[21] In another case the buyer was held to be allowed to revoke the letter of credit because of defective goods delivered under two previous contracts between the same parties.[22] However, in a case decided by a Spanish court, the buyer who retained the purchase price due the malfunctioning of the water dispensers, was held not to be entitled to withhold their obligation, as they needed to immediately request enforcement of the manufacturer's warranty.[23]

[18] Schlechtriem and Schwenzer (n 15) 1235; CISG Advisory Council, 'The buyer's right to avoid the contract in case of non-conforming goods or documents' (2005) Opinion n 5, para 4.18; P Schlechtriem, 'Interpretation, Gap-Filling and Further Development of the U.N. Sales Convention' (2004) 16 *Pace International Law Review* 279, 303; MG Bridge, 'Avoidance for fundamental breach of contract under the UN Convention on the International Sale of Goods' (2010) *International & Comparative Law Quarterly* 911, 938.

[19] Schlechtriem and Schwenzer (n 15) 948.

[20] This view is also reflected in CISG Advisory Council, 'The buyer's right to avoid the contract in case of non-conforming goods or documents' (2005) Opinion n 5, para 4.20.

[21] *Glass Recycling Machine case* (2005) Austrian Supreme Court, CISG-online 1156.

[22] *Balance Industry Co. Ltd v Cixi Chenyang Package Co. Ltd* (2011) *Zhe Shang Wai Zhong Zi* No. 11 Civil Judgment.

[23] *Elkay Manufacturing Co. v Compañía de Aguas Belnature, SL* (2000) Court of Appeal Navarra, Spain, CISG-online 575.

The first uncertainty in applying CISG Article 71 lies in determining what constitutes 'a substantial part of obligations'. A German judgment provides the only guideline that a future failure to perform 'substantial part of the obligations does not have to amount to a 'fundamental breach' as defined in CISG Article 25.[24] It thus provides for a buyer to suspend performance where the seller's breach, while substantial, may not be sufficiently fundamental to justify termination. If a seller declares that they will not perform their duty, the buyer is entitled to withhold performance.[25] The wording of this article shows a slight departure from the *exeptio* principle, in that the suspended performance need not be the mirror image of the other party's obligation. This indicates that CISG permits a party with a reasonable fear of not receiving future performance to suspend their performance until that fear is overcome. To decide about a 'substantial part of obligations', the contract must be considered as a whole to determine the extent to which parties attach importance to a particular obligation. Considering CISG Article 8(1) and (2), it seems logical to assume that such determination may not depend on one party's subjective intentions and state of mind. It rather depends on an objective interpretation as to whether it becomes apparent to a reasonable person in the same position as the party suspending their performance that a failure to perform a substantial part will happen.[26] Nevertheless, case by case analysis is inevitable for such determination. Some relevant factors are the parties' negotiations, past dealings, trade usage and the size of the prospective breach relative to the contract as a whole.[27] For instance, it was held in a case that the defective delivery of 420 kg of frozen bacon out of the entire quantity of 22,400 kg to be delivered in several instalments was only a minor part of one instalment.[28] The buyer was therefore not permitted to suspend their own performance in regards to the future instalments.

Suspension is only allowed when 'it becomes apparent' that the other party will not perform a substantial part of their obligations. The probability standard employed in this article should be interpreted objectively to prevent the right of suspension from being exercised on the basis of purely subjective fears of one party.[29] In several cases, despite buyer's attempts, the seller failed to communicate clearly when delivery takes place and thus the buyer was entitled to suspend the payment.[30] Also, in an ICC arbitral case, the seller was delayed in delivery of

[24] *Italian Shoes case XV* (1994) District Court Berlin, Germany, CISG-online 399.

[25] *Glass Bottles case* (2007) German Supreme Court, CISG-online 1617: in this case, a party insisting on payment of supplemental consulting fees, to which they were not entitled, gave an indication that they would not perform their obligations.

[26] S Kroll, L Mistelis and PP Viscasillas, *UN Convention on Contracts for the International Sale of Goods (CISG) Commentary* (Hart Publishing, 2011) 899.

[27] ibid.

[28] *Bacon case I*, (1992) Court of Appeal Hamm, Germany, CISG-online 57.

[29] JO Honnold and HM Flechtner, *Honnold's Uniform Law for International Sales under the 1980 United Nations Convention*, 5th edn (Wolters Kluwer Law and Business, 2021) 726; see also Kroll, Mistelis and Viscasillas (n 26) 892.

[30] *Machine case* (2003) Court of First Instance Appenzell Ausserrhoden, Switzerland, CISG-online 852; *Belarusian Coniferous Timber case II* (2019) Supreme Court of the Republic of Belarus, CISG-online 4819.

samples to be approved by the buyer, as required by the contract, which became apparent that the seller was unable to manufacture and deliver the goods on time.[31] If the risk of future breach of contract could have reasonably been assumed prior to the conclusion of the contract, the right of suspension is unavailable.[32] Whether and when the risk of future breach 'becomes apparent' must be determined objectively. Common knowledge, information and relevant trade usage will be assumed to be imputed on the creditor.[33] The language used in this article should be contrasted with Article 72, which emphasises that avoidance is permitted only when 'it is clear that a party will commit a fundamental breach of contract'. This deliberate linguistic difference shows that greater certainty of future breach is required in order to justify avoidance of the contract than is required for the remedy of suspension. The flexible requirement laid down in the first part of this article is also aligned with the purpose of the self-help remedy of suspension of purpose, which strives to preserve a fair balance between the parties' interests and promote a cooperative behaviour between them.

C. UCC

UCC has clearly established the right to withhold performance. Section 2-609 holds that a sale of goods contract imposes an obligation on each party that the other's expectation of receiving due performance will not be impaired. This section was intended to protect the 'essential purpose of the bargain, which is performance itself'.[34] An implied duty is therefore imposed on the parties not to injure each other's expectations that a contract will be performed.[35] The origin of this implied duty lies in the doctrine of 'constructive concurrent conditions' upheld in UCC and more generally in American contract law.[36] By virtue of this doctrine, each party's performance or tender is a constructive or implied condition to the other's party obligation to perform, on the basis that the performances must have been intended as the price or consideration for one another and that 'justice requires a concurrent exchange'.[37] In one leading American case, which involved a contractor's failure to render payments to a subcontractor due to the subcontractor's alleged failure to perform a part of the work, the court held that the modern rule of contract law, which may have a universal application, is that 'there is a presumption that mutual promises in a contract are dependent and are

[31] *Clothing case* (1997) ICC International Court of Arbitration, Zurich, CISG-online 749.

[32] Kroll, Mistelis and Viscasillas (n 26) 893.

[33] Schlechtriem and Schwenzer (n 15) 1012.

[34] LT Garvin, 'Adequate assurance of performance: of risk, duress and cognition' (1988) *University of Colorado Law Review* 71, 93.

[35] D Saidov, 'Anticipatory non-performance and underlying values of the UNIDRPOIT principles' (2006) 11 *Uniform Law Review* 795, 797.

[36] EW Patterson, 'Constructive Conditions in Contracts' (1942) 42 *Columbia Law Review* 903, 905.

[37] USA Restatement (Second) of Contracts (1981), section 234.

to be so regarded, whenever possible'.[38] When parties make agreements entailing an exchange of promises, they not only consider the promises as the subject of an exchange, but they also intend that the performances of those promises shall subsequently be exchanged for each other.[39] More precisely, a concurrent condition is indeed a special type of condition precedent, which involves conditions on both sides of a bilateral contract and each of which must be fulfilled to trigger the other party's obligation.[40] Both obligations are of course capable of being simultaneously fulfilled so that each is regarded as a condition precedent to the other party's obligation.

The simultaneous performance of obligations offers both parties maximum protection against disappointment of their expectations of a subsequent exchange of performances. The maximum protection can be achieved by allowing each party to suspend their own performance until it has been assured that the other will perform.[41] In a sale of goods contract where parties exchange promises, there is usually every reason to presume that they contracted on the basis of the expectation of receiving the other party's performance; otherwise, the exchange of promises would have little value. UCC recognises that buyer's payment and seller's relinquishment of full possession of goods are 'concurrent conditions'.[42] Section 2-507 provides that seller's proper tender of delivery entitles it to 'payment according to the contract'.[43] In other words, tender of delivery is a condition to the buyer's obligation to accept the goods and more importantly a condition to the buyer's obligation to pay for the goods. Section 2-511 also stipulates that tender of payment is a condition to the seller's obligation to tender and fulfil delivery of the goods. In addition, section 2-310 (a) stipulates that 'payment is due at the time and place at which the buyer is to receive the goods even though the place of shipment is the place of delivery'. These UCC sections as well as the general approach under the US Restatement of Contract show that a continuing sense of confidence and security that the promised performance will be forthcoming according to contract is a significant feature of sale of goods contracts. If either party's willingness or the ability to perform declines substantively between the time of contracting and the time for performance, the other party is justified to fear for the loss of a substantial part of what they have bargained for. For instance, a buyer who thinks that the seller's deliveries have become uncertain is not expected to wait for the due date of performance when they need materials for their ongoing manufacturing.

UCC section 2-609 has adopted three measures to protect the needs and interests of a buyer who faces with difficulties in performance by the seller. First, the

[38] *K & G Const. Co. v Harris*, (1960) Court of Appeals of Maryland 223 Md. 305.
[39] USA Restatement (Second) of Contracts (1981), section 231.
[40] RA Lord, *Williston on Contracts*, 4th edn (Thomson Reuters, 2023) para 38:8.
[41] USA Restatement (Second) of Contracts (1981) section 238.
[42] *Spikes v Baur* (1981) Court of Appeals of Kansas, 626 P.2d 816.
[43] *Montgomery Ward, LLC & Montgomery Ward LLC v Wiseknit Factory Ltd* (2003) United States Bankruptcy Court, Delaware, 292 B.R. 49.

right to withhold performance can be exercised by the buyer in the case of reasonable insecurity as to the seller's performance. Second, the injured party is given the right to require adequate assurance that the other party will perform in accordance with contractual stipulations. Third, the injured party can invoke the principle of anticipatory breach of contract. They may terminate the contract if their reasonable grounds for insecurity are not addressed sufficiently within a reasonable time. The latter two measures will be explained later.

The party withholding performance enjoys an excuse for any consequential necessary delay, until the situation is clarified by the seller.[44] Because in a sale of goods contracts, the performances are supposed to be exchanged and fulfilled simultaneously under an exchange of promises, each party is entitled to refuse to proceed with that simultaneous exchange until the other party performs, or they are assured that the other party will perform at the same time. As established already, there is a presumption in bilateral sale of goods contracts that each party's expectation of receiving due performance should not be prejudiced. When reasonable grounds for insecurity arise in relation to the seller's performance, the buyer can hold up the payment until the seller clarifies the situation by for example providing a commercially reasonable assurance that the performance will unduly forthcoming. In *US Salt Inc v Broken Arrow Inc*, the buyer who agreed to purchase salt from a reputable seller, was faced with reasonable grounds for insecurity.[45] The seller stopped providing salt to the buyer for certain period of time. The seller then stated that they could not continue to deliver the goods unless the buyer and other customers made early payments. The buyer was held to be entitled to suspend their payment until the situation was clarified. However, a contrary decision was made in the recent case of *Cambridge Valley Machining Inc v Hudson MFG LLC*, where a buyer who contracted to purchase firearm components from a manufacturer, failed to pay for parts that they accepted.[46] The buyer, who faced with seller's failure in timely production and thus delivery of products according to contract, sent emails asking whether the seller needed anything further to be able to hit production targets and whether the seller was confident they would meet release schedules. The seller failed to respond satisfactorily to those emails but delivered products with delay. While the buyer received and accepted the goods for nearly a year, they failed to make a payment. Their right to repudiate the contract was not upheld by the court, as they should have notified the seller of their intention to suspend payment following their request for adequate assurance. As shown, UCC permits the buyer suspicious of seller's prospective performance to suspend their payment obligation until the seller clarifies the situation.

[44] USA Restatement (Second) of Contracts (1981) section 237; JD Calamari and JM Perillo, *The Law of Contracts*, 3rd edn (West Group, 1987) § 11-17.

[45] (2009) US Court of Appeals, 8th Circuit, 563 F.3d 687; see also *Smyers v Quartz Works Corp.* (1995) US District Court, Kansas, 880 F. Supp. 1425; *BRC Rubber & Plastics Inc v Continental Carbon Company* (2018) US Court of Appeals, 7th Circuit, 900 F.3d 529.

[46] *Cambridge Valley Machining Inc v Hudson MFG LLC* (2020) United States District Court, New York, 470 F.Supp. 3d 230.

D. SGA

It is questionable whether the right to withhold performance is officially recognised in English law. While *Channel Tunnel Group Ltd* v *Balfour Beatty Construction Ltd* is not a case concerning a sale of goods contract, it has re-emphasised the English law's position concerning the right to withhold performance.[47] In this case, one of the parties suspended performance of their contractual obligations and accused the other party of breach of contract. The parties were not able to settle on a price for a variation in their contract. The Court of Appeal, in an *obiter*, held that it is well established in English law that if one party is in serious breach, the other can treat the contract as altogether at an end.[48] The Court then maintained that it is not yet any established doctrine of English law that entitles either party to suspend performance, keeping the contract alive.[49]

English law seems to be generally hostile to the notion of 'suspension' of a contract, partly because it can lead to 'an undesirable degree of uncertainty'.[50] The uncertainty lies on the lack of clarity concerning the time span a party may withhold performance due to the other party's non-performance or defective performance. Another reason stems from the traditional approach, holding that the innocent party has only two choices when the repudiation occurs after the time for performance arrives.[51] Similar to the situation of anticipatory breach, when an innocent party encounters a contractual repudiation, they enjoy two choices of either affirming the contract by treating it as still in force or they may treat it as finally and conclusively discharged.[52] The binary choices open to the innocent party represents the all or nothing approach under the English common law, which is likely to be inconsistent with the common commercial norms and practices.[53] A buyer receiving defective goods may wish to keep the goods and ask the seller to repair or replace them. The binary choices favoured under English law disregards this practical option open to the buyer. In other words, the buyer may decide to reject the performance tendered but keep the contract alive for performance on the condition that a proper performance is tendered within a reasonable time. Lord Ackner in the significant case of *The Simona* opined that it is true that there is no '... third choice, as a sort of via media, to affirm the contract and yet be absolved from tendering further

[47] *Channel Tunnel Group Ltd and Another v Balfour Beatty Construction Ltd and Others* [1992] QB 656.
[48] ibid, 670.
[49] ibid.
[50] Treitel (n 1) 405.
[51] ibid.
[52] E Peel, *Treitel on The Law of Contract*, 15th edn (Sweet & Maxwell, 2020) 942.
[53] R Goode, H Kronke and E McKendrick, *Transnational Commercial Law: Text, Cases and Materials*, 2nd edn (Oxford University Press, 2016) 140; see also JW Carter and W Courtney, '"Ready and willing to perform": discharge for breach and damages' (2020) 1 *Lloyd's Maritime and Commercial Law Quarterly* 251.

performance unless and until [the guilty party] gives reasonable notice that he is once again able and willing to perform.'[54]

Lord Ackner's statement can easily be misread. His explanation concerns the innocent party's duty to continue performance following their affirmation of the contract. He does not propose the same ruling for the innocent party facing with repudiation not yet accepted. There is no doubt that following a repudiatory breach a middle ground between acceptance of repudiation and affirmation of the contract can be envisaged. The middle ground lies in the period when the innocent party should decide about what do to. They may wish to give another chance to the guilty party to reconsider their situation and to provide an appropriate performance without being treated as having thereby affirmed the contract.[55] In *Edge Tools & Equipment Limited v Greatstar Europe Limited, G2 Products Limited*, the innocent party who gained knowledge of the guilty party's repudiatory breach was permitted a reasonable period of time to make up their mind.[56] Determining 'a reasonable period' depends on the facts of the case.[57] During the stage when the innocent party decides about their options and possibly negotiating with the other party, they are not obliged to continue with their own performance and can thus suspend it.

In addition, the innocent party is entitled to simply withhold performance of their own obligation until the other party renders their obligation under the contract. Such entitlement depends on the interdependence of the parties' obligations. SGA section 28, reflecting the *exceptio non adimpleti contractus* principle, stipulates that 'unless otherwise agreed, delivery of the goods and payment of the price are concurrent conditions'.[58] This indicates that there is a presumption that delivery and payment are mutual and concurrent. The seller must be ready and willing to give possession of the goods to the buyer in exchange for the price and the buyer must be ready and willing to pay the price in exchange for possession of the goods. This principle was examined in *Astrazeneca UK Ltd v Albemarle International Corp*, where it was held that where the parties have not explicitly agreed on the order of contractual performance in general, performance of one obligation is considered a condition precedent to the other obligation only where either the first obligation must for practical reasons clearly be fulfilled before the

[54] *Fercometal SARL v Mediterranean Shipping Co SA* [1989] AC 788, 801.

[55] *Stocznia Gdanska SA v Latvian Shipping Co (No.2)* [2002] EWCA Civ 889, [2002] 2 Lloyd's Rep 436; see also *Astea (UK) Ltd v Time Group Ltd* [2003] EWHC 725 (TCC), [2003] All ER (D) 212 (Apr).

[56] *Edge Tools & Equipment Limited v Greatstar Europe Limited, G2 Products Limited* [2018] EWHC 170 (QB), 2018 WL 00691621; see also *Force India Formula One Team Ltd v Etihad Airways PJSC* [2010] EWCA Civ 1051; *White Rosebay Shipping SA v Hong Kong Chain Glory Shipping Ltd* [2013] 2 All ER (Comm) 449.

[57] *Edge Tools & Equipment Limited v Greatstar Europe Limited, G2 Products Limited.* [2018] EWHC 170 (QB).

[58] See *Mooney v Lipka* [1926] 4 DLR 647 (Can.); *Astrazeneca UK Ltd v Albemarle International Corp* [2011] EWHC 1574; *Doherty v Fannigan Holdings Ltd* [2018] EWCA Civ 1615.

second obligation can come into effect.[59] In this case, the buyer had to provide the means of transport in order for the seller to be able to deliver to the carrier as the buyer's agent.[60] Another possibility is that the second obligation is the direct pro quo of the first obligation, in the sense that only performance of the first reinforces the second obligation.[61] It can thus be inferred that since the buyer's obligation to pay depends on the seller's ability and willingness to deliver conforming goods, the buyer has the right to suspend payment when the seller indicates inability or unwillingness to perform.[62] The paradigm example is perhaps that of a CIF seller who is liable to forward the bills of lading to their buyer within a reasonable time.[63] Suspension of performance by the buyer is characterised by Treitel not as a remedy but as 'the practical consequence' of the seller's default in performing a concurrent condition, or a condition precedent to, the buyer's obligation to pay.[64] Default in performance, either defective delivery or delay in performance, should however not be sufficiently serious to justify termination. By choosing to withhold performance, the obligations of the parties are effectively in halt until the seller performs. Contrary to the previous legal regimes, the right to request for adequate assurance is not recognised in English law. Therefore, the party suspending performance will have to either reasonably await proper tender of performance or seek to terminate the contract.

4. Anticipatory Breach of Contract

A. SGA and UCC

The concept of anticipatory breach of contract originates in English law and was first coherently prescribed in terms of legal principles in *Hochster v De la Tour*[65] in England and *Howie v Anderson*[66] in Scotland. An anticipatory breach of contract emerges when the promisor renounces the contract or disables themselves from performing their obligations before the time for performance arrives.[67]

[59] [2011] EWHC 1574 (Comm); [2011] 2 C.L.C. 252 at para 250.

[60] *Astrazeneca UK Ltd v Albemarle International Corp* [2011] EWHC 1574; see also *Doherty v Fannigan Holdings Ltd* [2018] EWCA Civ 1615.

[61] *Astrazeneca UK Ltd v Albemarle International Corp* [2011] EWHC 1574, 1579.

[62] ibid, 1582.

[63] *Sanders v Maclean* (1883) 11 QBD 327.

[64] Treitel (n 1) 405.

[65] (1853) 2 El & Bl 678; 118 ER 922.

[66] (1848) 10 D 355.

[67] MG Bridge (ed), *Benjamin's Sale of Goods*, 11th edn (Sweet & Maxwell, 2022), para 12.021; HG Beale (ed), *Chitty on Contracts, vol 1*, 34th edn (Sweet & Maxwell, 2022), para 24.022; Treitel (n 1) 379; S Rowan, *Remedies for Breach of Contract, A Comparative Analysis of Protection of Performance* (Oxford University Press, 2012) 75; R Bradgate and F White, 'Rejection and termination in contracts for the sale of goods' in J Birds, R Bradgate and C Villiers, *Termination of Contracts* (John Wiley & Sons, 2005) 20.

'A renunciation of a contract occurs when one party, by words or conduct, evinces an intention not to perform, or expressly declares that he is or will be unable to perform his obligations under the contract in some essential respect.'[68] Adopting the English law doctrine of anticipatory breach, UCC section 2-610 states that:

> When either party repudiates the contract with respect to a performance not yet due the loss of which will substantially impair the value of the contract to the other, the aggrieved party may (a) for a commercially reasonable time await performance by the repudiating party; (b) resort to any remedy for breach, even though he has notified the repudiating party that he would await the latter's performance and has urged retracting.

Under English law, determining whether a renunciatory conduct exists depends upon the objective appearance of renunciation coupled with the promisee's subjective belief that the promises intended to renounce the contract.[69] UCC Section 2-610 is rather centred objectively on an overt communication of intention or a behaviour which renders performance impossible, which clearly demonstrates a determination not to continue with performance. According to the UCC Official Comments, it is not even necessary for repudiation that performance be made utterly impossible.[70] Repudiation may result from behaviour reasonably indicating a rejection of the continuing obligation. In other words, a contract is considered breached due to an anticipatory repudiation, when the seller without justification and before they have committed a breach, makes a positive statement to the buyer indicating that they will not or cannot substantially perform their contractual duties.[71]

In the context of sale of goods, to confer the right to terminate on the basis of an anticipatory breach of contract, it should be reasonably inferred that there will be a prospective fundamental breach by the seller.[72] Such inquiry is therefore constituted of two aspects. First, it should examine the intention of the seller to infer whether they will fail to perform their obligations.[73] A reasonable inference is essential to the establishment of an anticipatory breach: this requirement is considered one of 'the most distinctive features of an anticipatory breach'.[74] This is so because 'an anticipatory breach is inferential in nature'.[75] The seller

[68] Beale (n 67), para 27.048; See also Bridge (n 67), para 12.019; *Mersey Steel and Iron Co Ltd v Naylor, Benzon & Co* (1884) 9 App. Cas. 434; *Bradley v H Newsom Sons & Co* [1919] AC 16; *Cehave NV v Bremer Handelsgesellschaft mbH (The Hansa Nord)* [1976] QB 44 (CA); *Brinkibon v Stahag Stahl und Stahlwarenhandels GmbH* [1980] 2 Lloyd's Rep 556 (CA).

[69] *Forslind v Bechely-Crundall* (1992) S.C. (HL) 173; *SK Shipping (S) Pte Ltd v Petroexport Ltd* [2009] EWHC 2974 (Comm); [2010] 2 Lloyd's Rep 158 at 89–97.

[70] UCC Official Comments, section 2-610, para 2.

[71] *Gold Mining & Water Co. v Swinerton* (1943) Supreme Court of California, 142 P.2d 22; *Combs v International Ins. Co.* (2004) United States Court of Appeals, 6th Circuit, 354 F.3d 568; Lord (n 40) para 63.30.

[72] Q Liu, *Anticipatory Breach* (Hart Publishing, 2011) 73.

[73] ibid.

[74] ibid.

[75] ibid, 75.

should have behaved in a way that the buyer, on the balance of probabilities, could have drawn an inference that the seller is likely to commit a breach when the time for performance arrives.[76] In other words, 'a party's present words or conduct are recognised as a contractual wrong precisely because they give rise to an inference that the future obligation will not be duly performed when due'.[77] It was held by the English Court of Appeal in the *Hermosa* case that the claimant's termination was unjustified 'not because the breach which [the claimant] anticipated was insubstantial, but because the conduct of [the defendant] and the owners did not justify a firm inference that there would be a further breach'.[78] Similarly, in *Dingley v Older*, decided by the USA's Supreme Court, the court refused to find a repudiation, where a seller failed to deliver ice to the buyer due to an increase in the market price, but instead suggested two alternative courses of action.[79] The court argued that the seller's failure to ship the goods is accompanied with the expression of alternative shipment arrangement, which seemed far from being a positive, unconditional, and unequivocal declaration of fixed purpose not to perform the contract in future.[80]

Second, it should be examined whether the prospective breach of contract satisfies the criterion of a fundamental breach.[81] UCC has employed the different term of 'substantial impairment of the value of the contract to the other', which connotes the same underlying concept as English law. The UCC Official Comments states that the test chosen to justify an injured party's action is the most useful test of substantial value, which seeks to determine whether material inconvenience or injustice will result if the injured buyer is forced to wait and receive an ultimate tender minus the part or aspect repudiated.[82] This signifies that the buyer's right to terminate on the basis of anticipatory breach can only be exercised when the requirement of serious detriment is satisfied. Under English law, 'the buyer's right to terminate a contract will arise only if the prospective effects of the anticipatory breach are such as to satisfy the requirement of substantial failure in performance'.[83] Lord Diplock stated that 'it is to fundamental breaches alone that the doctrine of anticipatory breach is applicable'.[84] For instance, an anticipatory breach happened

[76] For instance, in *Leeson v North British Oil and Candle Co Ltd* (1874) Ir. R. 8 C.L. 309, seller informed buyer they cannot deliver balance of instalments; see also UCC Official Comments, section 2-610:1, para 2.

[77] Liu (n 72) 36.

[78] *Chilean Nitrate Sales Corporation v Pansuiza Compania de Navegacion SA and Marine Transportation Co Ltd ('The Hermosa')* [1982] WL 961199 (CA) para 30.

[79] (1886) Supreme Court of the United States, 117 U.S. 490.

[80] ibid, 853–54; see also *Management Capital, L.L.C. v F.A.F., Inc.* (2019) Supreme Court of Rhode Island, 209 A.3d 1162; *Homeland Energy Solutions, LLC v Retterath*, (2020) Supreme Court of Iowa, 938 N.W.2d 664.

[81] *Afovos Shipping Co SA v R Pagnan & Fratelli (The Afovos)* [1983] 1 WLR 195 (HL) 203; see also *Universal Cargo Carriers Corp v Citati (No 1)* [1957] 2 QB 401 (QB).

[82] UCC Official Comments, section 2-610:1, para 3.

[83] Peel (n 52) 844; see also Liu (n 72) 70–71.

[84] *Afovos Shipping Company S.A. v R Pagnan and F. lli* [1983] 1 WLR 195 (HL) 203.

in the English case of *Fleming & Wendeln GmbH*, where the seller was in breach of his obligation to declare loading places and silos, 'which was a main obligation that was fundamental to the performance of the contract'.[85] Similarly, in *Cargill, Inc. v Storms Agri Enterprises, Inc*, governed by UCC, the buyer's repudiation of 14 out of 17 cottonseed loads substantially damaged the value of contract to the seller, thus entitling the latter to terminate the contract and claim for damages. As such, under both English law and UCC, the question of 'fundamental breach' or 'substantial impairment', is a question of fact.

The most significant factors in realising whether the breach is of sufficient gravity in the context of long-term sale of goods transactions, where goods are delivered by instalments, has been said to be 'first, the ratio quantitively which the breach bears to the whole, and secondly the degree of probability or improbability that such a breach will be repeated'.[86] In *AstraZeneca UK Ltd v Albemarle International Corp*, decided by English law, the parties were involved in a supply of goods contract with a minimum duration of three years.[87] The contract had a long-term nature due to the fact that selection and actual sourcing of pharmaceutical materials in question took place for around three years. Such time was essential for AstraZeneca to obtain regulatory approval of potential suppliers and their products worldwide. Against this commercial background, the parties had included clauses indicating their intention to establish and maintain a long-term contract.[88] The selected supplier failed to honour the trust and confidence required in preserving long-term contract, when they failed to deliver all the agreed quantity of goods in their first delivery. It was questionable whether the supplier's short delivery of goods constituted a repudiatory breach of contract, allowing the buyer to terminate the entire contract. The buyer argued that the fulfilment of the supplier's delivery obligation was so essential to the nature of the sale and supply agreements of pharmaceutical materials that their non-performance of that obligation amounted to a substantial failure to perform the contract at all. Nevertheless, the court held that in the context of a three-year contract of this kind, non-delivery of one purchase order or possibly even two were unlikely to be categorised as a repudiatory breach, which deprived the buyer of substantially the whole benefit of the contract.[89]

When an anticipatory breach occurs, the buyer has a choice thereafter. Under both English law and UCC, the buyer may affirm the contract despite the professed repudiation, thereby keeping the contract alive, and continue to insist

[85] *Fleming & Wendeln GmbH & Co v Sanofi SA/AG* [2003] EWHC 561 (Comm), [2003] 2 CLC 774, 780.
[86] *Maple Flock Co Ltd v Universal Furniture Products (Wembley) Ltd* [1934] 1 K.B. 148 at 157.
[87] [2011] EWHC 1574 (Comm); [2011] 2 C.L.C. 252, 261.
[88] One of their clauses, showing such intention, is Clause H of the contract, which states: 'In the event that at any time BUYER reformulates or otherwise changes its Diprivan brand to substitute propofol for the PRODUCT, BUYER will so notify SELLER and will give SELLER the first opportunity and right of first refusal to supply propofol to BUYER under mutually acceptable terms and conditions'.
[89] [2011] EWHC 1574 (Comm); [2011] 2 C.L.C. 252 at para 261.

on performance.[90] Otherwise, they may wish to accept the renunciation, treat the contract as discharged immediately, and claim for damages.[91] UCC also entitles the buyer to suspend their own performance while negotiates with the seller.[92] When the buyer accepts the breach, 'the general principle is that their remedies become available at once, i.e. even though performance from the defaulting party has not yet become due'.[93] For acceptance to be valid, there is no formality attaching to acceptance and no need for any express statement of acceptance.[94] If they accept the breach, they are relieved from further performance of their obligations under the contract. The buyer has to communicate with the seller in order to inform them about their decision, however, 'in some cases failure to perform may signify to a repudiating party an election by the aggrieved party to treat the contract as at an end'.[95] When the buyer chooses to affirm the contract, which has been communicated to the seller, the choice becomes irrevocable.[96] The doctrine of election 'rest on the basis of informed choice'.[97] If a buyer has a choice between two contradictory courses of action and unequivocally communicates their decision to pursue one of them, they are not permitted to pursue the other. The doctrine of election thus requires an unambiguous communication of decisions for effective functioning.

There are divergent viewpoints under the English law on whether there is a 'middle way' or 'third choice' open to the buyer. Rix LJ expressed his controversial opinion in *Stocznia Gdanska SA v Latvian Shipping Co (No 3)* that 'in my judgment, there is of course a middle ground between acceptance of repudiation and affirmation of the contract, and that is the period when the innocent party is making up his mind what to do'.[98] However, the courts have been reluctant to recognise any third choice for an innocent buyer. In *Fercometal SARL v Mediterranean Shipping Co SA (The Simona)*, Lord Ackner opined that that there is no 'third choice, as a sort of via media, to affirm the contract and yet be absolved from tendering further performance unless and until the breaching party gives reasonable notice that he is once again able and willing to perform'.[99] Similarly,

[90] *Fercometal SARL v Mediterranean Shipping Co SA* [1989] AC 788; UCC Official Comments, section 2-610:1, para 1.

[91] A Burrows, *English Private Law, Oxford Principles of English Law* (Oxford University Press, 2013) 600–601.

[92] UCC Official Comments, section 2-610:1, para 1.

[93] Treitel (n 1) 379; Bridge (n 67), para 12-021; see also UCC Official Comments, section 2-610 1, para 1.

[94] *Suisse Atlantique Société d'Armement Maritime SA v NV Rotterdamsche Kolen Centrale* [1967] 1 AC 361, 398; *Peyman v Lanjani* [1985] Ch. 457; *Tele2 International Card Co SA v Kub 2 Technology Ltd* [2009] EWCA Civ 9, [2009] All ER (D) 144 (Jan).

[95] Bridge (n 67), para 12-021; see for example: *Johnstone v Milling* (1886) 16 QBD 460 (CA) 467; *Vitol SA v Norelf Ltd (The Sant Clara)* [1996] AC 800 (HL) 811.

[96] Bridge (n 67), para 27-057.

[97] *Force India Formula One Team Ltd v Aerolab SRL* [2013] EWCA Civ 780, [2013] RPC 36, [37] [Lewison LJ].

[98] [2002] 2 Lloyd's Rep 436, 452.

[99] [1989] AC 788, 801.

Higgins J stated in *Bowes v Chaleyer* that 'a door must be either open or shut; a contract must either subsist or be at an end'.[100] If the buyer stays idle and does nothing for too long, the law may treat them as having affirmed the contract. They may also run the risk, in the sense that their right to terminate the contract and claim for damage could be prejudiced by frustration of contract or even their own breach. However, it may be logical to argue that there is a middle way available to the innocent buyer and that they may be given a reasonable period to make up their minds on what choice they may elect in their response to the breach. The length of the period afforded to the innocent buyer very much depends on the facts of the case. In long term contracts, characterised by flexibility and cooperative behaviour, the buyers may enjoy a lengthy period, depending on when their obligations would fall due for performance. It is worth mentioning that UCC appears reluctant in affording a third choice to the innocent buyer. The Official Code Commentary states that if the buyer awaits performance beyond 'a commercial reasonable time he cannot recover resulting damage which [they] should have avoided'.[101] An anticipatory breach of contract, therefore, entitles the buyer to exercise appropriate contractual remedies, including termination of contract, even though the time for performance has not yet arrived.[102]

B. CISG and UPICC

The notion of anticipatory breach of contract under CISG is taken from the English doctrine of anticipatory breach, as enunciated in the landmark case of *Hochster v de la Tour*.[103] Anticipatory breach of contract is promulgated under CISG Article 72. UPICC has laid down the doctrine of anticipatory breach of contract under Article 7.3.3, which is identical to CISG.[104] An anticipatory breach of contract can be illustrated by two examples provided by the UPICC Official Commentary: first, 'where one party declares that it will not perform the contract; however, the circumstances also may indicate that there will be a fundamental

[100] [1923] 32 CLR 159, 190.

[101] UCC Official Comments, section 2-610:1, para 1.

[102] For elaborate discussions concerning the underlying reasons for such a striking entitlement, see R Beheshti, 'Anticipatory Breach of Contract and the Necessity of Adequate Assurance under English Law and The Uniform Commercial Code' [2018] *Lloyd's Maritime and Commercial Law Quarterly* 276.

[103] (1853) 2 El & Bl 678; see also MG Bridge, *The International Sale of Goods*, 4th edn (Oxford University Press, 2017) para 12-17; Schlechtriem and Schwenzer (n 15) 1024; M Vanwijck-Alexandre, 'Anticipatory breach and instalment contracts in the CISG' (2001) 3 *International Business Law Journal* 353, 355.

[104] MAD Silveira, 'Anticipatory breach under the United Nations Convention on Contracts for the International Sale of Goods' (2005) 2 *Nordic Journal of Commercial Law* 1, 17; see also Scottish Law Commission, 'Discussion paper on remedies for breach of contract' Discussion paper n 109 (April 1999) para 2.07.

non-performance'.[105] The second one involves the case where the delivery date is of the essence under the transaction:

> A promises to deliver oil to B by M/S Paul at the terminal in country X on 3 February. On 25 January M/S Paul is still 2,000 kilometres from the terminal. At the speed it is making it will not arrive on 3 February, but at the earliest on 8 February. As time is of the essence, a substantial delay is to be expected, and B may terminate the contract before 3 February.

The innocent buyer can invoke CISG Article 72 where the very essence of the contract is endangered, either because the seller refuses performance of their obligations or because there are other objective reasons showing a prospective fundamental breach of contract. Similarly, under UPICC, 'it is necessary that the non-performance be fundamental and that the party who is to receive performance give notice of termination'.[106] Both legal regimes entitle the buyer to avoid the contract, without the need to wait until the breach materialises on the date when performance is due, if it is clear that the seller will commit a fundamental breach of contract.[107] '[A] suspicion, even a well-founded one, is not sufficient.'[108] Understanding and applying both the standard of 'being clear' and that of 'fundamental breach' requires objective interpretation of the parties' intentions in light of the circumstances. For assessing whether the breach will be fundamental, the standard of CISG Article 25 applies,[109] which stipulates that the future breach must be of such a serious nature as to substantially deprive the buyer of what they were entitled to expect under the contract.[110] In addition, the seriousness of the future breach must have been foreseeable by the seller. The standard of 'when it is clear' employed in both CISG Article 72 and UPICC Article 7.3.3. is, ironically, vague. '"Clear" emphasises the need for a high degree of probability that a breach will actually occur', and there is no need to show absolute certainty.[111] A seller announcing that they will not perform their obligations satisfies this precondition.[112] In one case, it was argued that the future occurrence of a fundamental breach must be 'obvious to everybody' to provide the necessary ground for avoidance of a contract under Article 72(1).[113] There are some circumstances which are

[105] UPICC Official Comments Article 7.3.3.
[106] ibid.
[107] Silveira (n 104) 1; see also S Vogenauer, *Commentary on the UNIDROIT Principles of International Commercial Contracts*, 2nd edn (Oxford University Press, 2015) 846; see also Saidov (n 35) 795, 803.
[108] UPICC Official Comments Article 7.3.3.
[109] UPICC Official Comments Article 7.3.1.(2) has also adopted very similar terms to CISG Article 25 in explaining 'fundamental non-performance of the contract'.
[110] See Article 6.2.3(i).
[111] Schlechtriem and Schwenzer (n 15) 973.
[112] See *Sunflower seed* case decided by the Court of Appeals of Lamia, Greece. 2006 (docket No. 63/2006).
[113] *Italian Shoes case VIII* (1992) District Court Berlin, Germany, CISG-online 70; see also *BSC Footwear Supplies, Ltd. v Brumby, SL* (2000) Court of Appeal Alicante, Spain, CISG-online 1318; *Cooling Machine case* (2002) Austrian Supreme Court, CISG-online 643; *Sizing Machine case* (2002) Commercial Court

clear that the future performance will be impossible, such as 'the destruction of the seller's plant by fire or the imposition of an embargo or monetary controls'.[114] Also, the future fundamental breach is likely to become clear when, as a result of the seller's previous delivery of non-conforming goods, it appears that the seller will not be able to deliver conforming goods in the future.[115] In one case, a seller, a Russian firm, due to some changes in their corporate structure, decided to stop all deliveries of raw aluminium to a buyer.[116] During the course of their negotiations, the buyer warned that they would suffer substantial prejudices if the goods would not be supplied in a timely manner. The Arbitral Tribunal held that the seller's interruption of deliveries clearly indicated non-performance of future instalments, thus satisfying the future fundamental breach requirement. It has also been claimed that when the seller fails to provide adequate assurance of their performance, this 'may make it clear' that they will fail to perform his obligations.[117] The failure to provide such assurance is an indication that the seller is unwilling to continue their commitment to their contractual obligation. Should they be genuinely willing to perform their obligations, providing an adequate assurance would not be onerous.

The buyer, who intends to declare the contract avoided, must give a notice to the seller. The purpose of CISG Article 72(2) is to give the seller, as the debtor, a chance to dispel doubts about their commitment to the contract by providing adequate assurance.[118] Article 72 (2) is thus an instrument of 'forced communication', which seeks to bring about clarity and prevents the buyer from prematurely terminating the contract.[119] Two requirements in relation to this duty must be satisfied. First, the buyer must give notice in a manner that is reasonable in the circumstances. Reasonableness of the buyer's notice relates to the form, content and procedure of giving it.[120] Reasonableness requirement aims to give the seller sufficient time to be able to provide adequate assurances.[121] It remains unclear what the consequences of failure to give reasonable and sufficient notice would be. It can be argued that the failure to provide notice should not prevent avoidance of the contract. The only effect of a lack of notice could be that it should invoke a duty to account for damages. This interpretation of the notice requirement is not persuasive. The duty to give notice in Article 72(2) is clearly a precondition for contract avoidance.[122] If it is rendered insufficiently or unreasonably, the right

Canton St Gall, Switzerland, CISG-online 727; *YPF S.A. v AES Urugaiana Emprendimientos S.A. et al.* (2013) ICC International Court of Arbitration, Montevideo, Uruguay, CISG-online 4558.

[114] UNCITRAL Digest of Case Law on the United Nations Convention on Contracts for the International Sale of Goods (2016) Article 72, para 2.

[115] *Skin Care Products case* (1998) Helsinki Court of Appeal, Finland, CISG-online 1304.

[116] *Soinco SACI et al v NKAP* (1996) Zürich Arbitration proceeding, Switzerland, CISG-online 1291.

[117] Honnold and Flechtner (n 29) 741; Kroll, Mistelis and Viscasillas (n 26) 962.

[118] ibid; the notice requirement under UPICC is emanated from Article 7.3.2(1) which should be interpreted as applying to all instances of a right to terminate.

[119] See *Skin Care Products case* (1998) Helsinki Court of Appeal, Finland, CISG-online 1304.

[120] Kroll, Mistelis and Viscasillas (n 26) 960.

[121] ibid.

[122] Schlechtriem and Schwenzer (n 15) 1031; see also Kroll, Mistelis and Viscasillas (n 26) 927.

of avoidance is undermined. The whole purpose of the notice requirement is to grant the seller a chance to maintain the contract to give an adequate assurance.[123] If the contract could be terminated despite the lack of notice, the seller would be deprived of this very chance, whereby the parties could cooperate to preserve the contract. However, there is no duty to give notice where the seller has announced that they refuse to perform under CISG Article 72(3). It is pointless to give a seller who declared that they will not perform the contract the opportunity to prevent avoidance of the contract, since they are evidently unwilling to fulfil their contractual obligation.[124]

The second requirement relating to the duty to give notice is 'if time allows'. This time requirement must be read and applied alongside the requirement that the notice be reasonable. The purpose of the notice requirement is to allow the seller to show their willingness and ability to perform by affording assurance. The notice must thus be relatively substantiated. The question of whether 'time allows' needs to be decided by reference to the reasonable person standard.[125] The party in breach may be awarded damages if they can show that the innocent party's failure to give notice was unreasonable.[126] With rapid development of modern communications, situations where time will not allow for a notice to be given are likely to be rare.[127] Yet, there might be situations where there is insufficient time for a notice. For instance, where there is a highly fluctuating market for the goods in question and the buyer should promptly enter a substitute transaction, or, when there are short periods of delivery and the buyer has to find alternative supplier of complex machinery in order to deliver to their customers on time.[128]

5. Doctrine of Adequate Assurance of Contract

A. UCC

Notwithstanding the reasons underlying the buyer's entitlement to remedies prior to the time for performance of a contract, anticipatory breach can be a trap. An innocent buyer may misinterpret signals from an ostensibly underperforming seller as repudiation. The seller may also show highly ambiguous and frequently inconsistent expressions, raising doubts as to whether they will perform the

[123] Schlechtriem and Schwenzer (n 15) 1031; see also M Bridge, 'Issues arising under Articles 64, 72 and 73 of the United Nations Convention on Contracts for the International Sale of Goods' (2005–2006) *Journal of Law and Commerce* 405, 419.

[124] Schlechtriem and Schwenzer (n 15) 1031; see also Honnold and Flechtner (n 29) 525.

[125] Kroll, Mistelis and Viscasillas (n 26) 927.

[126] MG Strub, 'The Convention on the International Sale of Goods: Anticipatory repudiation provisions and developing countries' (1989) 38 *International & Comparative Law Quarterly* 475, 498.

[127] Bianca and Bonell (n 15) 528.

[128] ibid, 976.

contract. This would create a dubious and uncertain situation for the buyer. The doctrine of anticipatory breach, as it currently stands in English contract law, fails to effectively rescue a promisee who faces uncertain circumstances. As will be shown in the rest of this chapter, the other legal regimes, proving themselves to be more realistic, modified certain rules of this doctrine which have remained rigid in English law. These legal regimes supplemented the doctrine by introducing the buyer's right to demand adequate assurance that the contractual obligations will be fulfilled. This chapter also seeks to offer a response to the normative question of whether the right to demand adequate assurance should be introduced into English law.

The concept of adequate assurance was one of the innovations that drafters introduced into UCC.[129] It has even been claimed that the right to request adequate assurance constitutes 'the most innovative and commercially sensible development in contract law in the twentieth century'.[130] The UCC drafters believed that law is an instrument to achieve social ends which should be constantly examined in terms of its purpose and its effect to gauge whether it fits the society it purports to serve.[131] In this regard, they endeavoured to design a set of rules which took group practices and their prevailing norms as its central principle.[132] As part of their attempt to modernise the law of sales, they introduced the doctrine of adequate assurance into the Uniform Commercial Code. This doctrine represents their attempt to establish properly adjusted rules for commercial transactions.[133] As already explained, the doctrine of anticipatory breach of contract may lead to difficult and blurred situations for promises, and for this book's purpose 'buyers',

[129] See generally Garvin (n 34) 71; TM Campbell, 'The Right to Assurance of Performance under UCC § 2-609: Toward a Uniform Rule of Contract Law' (1982) 5 *Fordham Law Review* 1292; GS Crespi, 'The Adequate Assurance Doctrine after UCC § 2-609: A Test of the Efficiency of the Common Law' (1993) 38 *Villanova Law Review* 179.

[130] RJ Robertson, 'The right to demand adequate assurance of due performance: Uniform Commercial Code Section 2–609 and Restatement (Second) of Contracts section 251' (1988–89) 38 *Drake Law Review* 305, 353.

[131] K Llewellyn, *The Common Law Tradition: Deciding Appeals* (Little Brown, 1960) 122; K Llewellyn, 'Some Realism about Realism – Responding to Dean Pound' (1931) 44 *Harvard Law Review* 1222, 1265; K Llewellyn, 'Why We Need the Uniform Commercial Code' (1957) 10 *University of Florida Law Review* 367, 371.

[132] State of New York Law Revision Committee Report, *Hearing on the Uniform Commercial Code* (1954), 108. See also J Whitman, 'Commercial Law and the American Volk: A Note on Llewellyn's German Sources for the Uniform Commercial Code' (1987) 97 *Yale Law Journal* 156, 163; AR Kamp, 'Between-the-wars social thought: Karl Llewellyn, legal realism, and the Uniform Commercial Code in context' (1995) 59 *Albany Law Review* 325, 339; W Twining, *Karl Llewellyn and the Realist Movement* (Weidenfeld & Nicolson, 1973) 316.

[133] UCC, Article 2 contains the following provisions designed particularly for merchants: section 2-103(l)(b) (good faith); section 2-201(2) (statute of frauds 'between merchants'); section 2-205 (firm offer); section 2-207(2) (additional terms in acceptance 'between merchants'); section 2-209(2) (modification, rescission and waiver 'between merchants'); section 2-312(3) (warranty of title and against infringement); section 2-314(1) (implied warranty of merchantability); section 2-327(l)(c) (sale on approval); section 2-402(2) (rights of seller's creditors); section 2-403(2) (entrusting); 2-509(3) (risk of loss); section 2-603(1) (rightful rejection); section 2-605(l)(b) (waiver of buyer's objections by failure to particularise); and section 2-609(2) (adequate assurance of performance).

especially when sellers behave inconsistently. These buyers require a mechanism by which such blurred situations would be clarified, thus enabling them to make decisions with sufficient confidence. Adequate assurance is likely to address this legitimate concern of buyers by obliging sellers to confirm future fulfilment of their contractual duty. The right to adequate assurance was first prescribed in UCC section 2-609. This provision highlights the importance of a continuing sense of reliance and security that the promised performance will be forthcoming.[134] To protect this interest, the buyer may demand adequate assurance of performance when there are reasonable grounds for insecurity regarding the other party's willingness or ability to perform. Adequate assurance is considered a form of self-help and thus a non-judicial mechanism.[135] It envisages the buyer's immediate reaction to a perceived problem and would render it unnecessary to resort to judicial remedies or third party intervention.[136] After demanding an assurance, the buyer is entitled to suspend their performance. If reasonably adequate assurance is not received, the buyer may treat the failure to provide assurance as a material breach justifying termination of contract, as indicated in UCC § 2-609 (3).

Although the UCC provision exposing the doctrine of adequate assurance is relatively clear, the provision entails a few vague terms that require explanation. The major sources of uncertainty in section 2-609 are the terms of 'adequate assurance' and 'reasonable grounds for insecurity'. UCC has provided no clear guideline for interpreting them, although the official commentary has striven to clarify these obscure terms.[137] The drafters of UCC intended business standards to be applicable, which may be varied in different scenarios.[138] UCC thus requires objective factual grounds to assess the adequacy or inadequacy of assurance, just as for the determination of reasonable grounds for insecurity.

It seems unpredictable for the buyer to figure out what reasonable grounds constitute sufficient insecurity to allow them to demand an adequate assurance. To realise whether there are reasonable grounds for insecurity, many factors, including the seller's exact words or conduct, the course of dealing or performance between the parties involved, and the nature of the industry should all be taken into account.[139] Insolvency is perhaps the most significant cause of insecurity.

[134] UCC Official Comments, section 2-609, para 1.

[135] MJ Borden, 'The Promissory Character of Adequate Assurances of Performance' (2010) 76 *Brooklyn Law Review* 167, 206; see also MW Sargis, 'The Uniform Commercial Code Section 2-609: a Return to Certainty' (1980) 14 *John Marshall Law Review* 113, 120; MP Gergen, 'A Theory of Self-help Remedies in Contract' (2009) 89 *Boston University Law Review* 1397, 1447.

[136] D Harris, David Campbell and R Halson, *Remedies in Contract and Tort*, 2nd edn (Butterworths LexisNexis, 2002) 62; see also DI Brandon, ML Cooper, JH Greshin, AL Harris and JM Head, 'Self-Help: Extrajudicial Rights, Privileges and Remedies in Contemporary American Society' (1984) 37 *Vanderbilt Law Review* 845, 913.

[137] See UCC Official Comments, section 2-609.

[138] PR Tepper, *The Law of Contracts and the Uniform Commercial Code*, 3rd edn (Cengage Learning, 2014) 452.

[139] UCC Official Comments, section 2-609, para 2; see also *Wildwood Industries, Inc. v Genuine Machine Design, Inc* (2008) 587 F. Supp. 2d 1035, 1047; Sargis (n 135) 113, 124.

In *Atwood-Kellogg v Nickeson Farms*, farmers entered into a contract to sell corn and soybeans to Farmers Elevator Company of Eden (FEC).[140] Atwood-Kellogg provided financing to FEC and maintained a security interest in FEC's accounts receivables and contract rights. After concluding the contract, FEC fell into serious financial difficulties and became insolvent. FEC's insolvency was undisputed by the parties. Although it was clear that the buyer was unable to fulfil his contract duties, the farmers requested adequate assurance that the finance company would pay them the specified amount. The finance company could not provide sufficient documentation showing adequate assurance of future payment by the buyer, and therefore the farmers repudiated the entire contract. In another case, the seller tried to abuse market shortage conditions of a product to impose an increase in the baseline prices.[141] When the buyer objected to the price increase, the seller replied that the buyer should look for another supplier. Additionally, the seller failed to deliver the products until and unless the buyer would have agreed with the price increase. As stated in the Official Comments, a buyer who reasonably believes that the seller's deliveries have become uncertain cannot safely wait for the due date of performance when they have been buying to assure themselves of materials for their current manufacturing.[142] In this situation, the buyer was absolutely entitled to demand assurance regarding future delivery of goods. Other case law illustrations of reasonable foundations for insecurity include: a seller who withheld producing the machines to be delivered under the contract,[143] goods similar to those contracted for by other buyers are delivered but fail to work as anticipated,[144] and where the seller announces that the contract price is too low to guarantee the fulfilment of their obligation.[145]

To determine what constitutes an adequate assurance, regard should be given to the minimum kinds of promises or acts on the part of the promisor that would

[140] (1999) Supreme Court of South Dakota, United States, 602 NW 2d 749. See also *Universal Builders Corp v United Methodist Convalescent Homes Inc* (1986) Appellate Court of Connecticut, 508 A 2d 819; *Validsa, Inc. v PDVSA Services Inc.* (2011) United States Court of Appeals, 11th Circuit, 424 Fed. Appx. 862.

[141] *BRC Rubber & Plastics, Inc. v Continental Carbon Company* (2020) United States Court of Appeals, 7th Circuit, 981 F.3d 618.

[142] UCC Official Comments, section 2-609, para 1.

[143] *AMF Inc v McDonald's Corp* (1976) United States Court of Appeals, 7th Circuit, 536 F 2d 1167, 1170: the prototype cash register did not perform adequately during one year trial, and the seller then stopped producing manufacturing the remaining machines.

[144] *Creusot-Loire International Inc v Coppus Engineering Corp* (1983) United States District Court, New York, 585 F Supp 45: the court confirmed that the buyer of precision parts has reasonable grounds for insecurity when he learns that his seller is conducting defective deliveries of such parts to other buyers with similar needs. See also *Remuda Jet One, LLC v Cessna Aircraft Co.* (2012) United States District Court, Massachusetts, 2012 WL 5866243; *Jabil Inc v General Electric Company* (2021) United States District Court, Georgia, Atlanta Division, 2021 WL 9347145.

[145] *Kaiser-Francis Oil Co v Producer's Gas Co* (1989) United States Court of Appeals, 10th Circuit, 870 F 2d 563: the seller had clearly reasonable grounds for insecurity as a matter of law, since the buyer of natural gas explicitly failed to carry on performing unless the seller agreed to modify 'take-or-pay' provision.

satisfy a reasonable merchant in the position of the buyer that their expectation of receiving due performance will be fulfilled.[146] Thus, the key factor for determining the adequacy of an assurance is whether the assurance provided by the promisor in light of all the circumstances can resolve the buyer's suspicion about future performance such that they would resume fulfilling their contractual duties.[147] The buyer's satisfaction must, however, be based 'upon reason and must not be arbitrary or capricious'.[148] This doctrine also begs for something that the seller would not otherwise be obliged to provide, something which is not contractually agreed by the parties.[149] An adequate assurance is wide-ranging, and could comprise a mere promise to perform or could entail the provision of a guarantee bond. It is not unreasonable if the buyer demands 'an extension of contractual guarantee' in light of the circumstances.[150] In *Louisiana Power & Light Co v Allegheny Ludlum Industries Inc*, the parties had known each other through the course of dealings for about five years, and, when a suspicion arose as to whether the supplier would fulfil their duties following the change of circumstances, the buyer demanded written assurances that the supplier would fully and properly perform as stated under the contract.[151] This was deemed by the court to be an adequate assurance. However, in most cases a reasonable demand may extend to a guarantee. For example, in *Hornell Brewing Co In v Spry*, the distributor did not provide documentation of the factoring agreement, leading to a reasonable ground for the supplier's insecurity regarding whether payment would be forthcoming.[152] The supplier then demanded a documented line of credit or similarly powerful guarantee as a form of adequate assurance, which in the court's view was reasonable. The buyer should, however, be cautious when demanding assurance, because, if the assurances

[146] UCC Official Comments, section 2-609, para 4; WD Hawkland, CS Bjerre, LR Rusch and LT Garry, *Hawkland's Uniform Commercial Code Series* (Thomson Reuters, 2023), section 2-609, para 3; *By-Lo Oil Co. Inc. v Partech Inc.* (2001) United States Court of Appeals, 6th Circuit, 11 Fed. Appx. 538; *Remuda Jet Five LLC v EMBRAER-Empressa Brasileira de Aeronautica, S.A.* (2012) United States District Court, New York, 2012 WL 1142296.

[147] Sargis (n 135) 113, 135. See also TM Quinn, *Quinn's Uniform Commercial Code, Commentary and Law Digest*, 2nd edn (Thomson Reuters, 2009) 430.

[148] *Richmond Leasing Co v Capital Bank, N.A* (1985) United States Court of Appeals, 5th Circuit, 762 F.2d 1303, 1309; see also *Cinicola v Scharffenberger* (2001) United States Court of Appeals, 3rd Circuit, 248 F. 3d 110, 120.

[149] JJ White and RS Summers, *Uniform Commercial Code*, 6th edn (Thomson Reuters, 2010) 198–200; see also *Pittsburgh- Des Moines Steel Co v Brookhaven Manor Water Co* (1976) United States Court of Appeals, 7th Circuit, 532 F 2d 572.

[150] *American Bronze Corp v Streamway Products* (1982) Court of Appeals of Ohio, 8th District, 8 Ohio App 3d 223.

[151] (1981) United States District Court, Louisiana, 517 F. Supp. 1319; see also *Norcon Power Partners LP v Niagara Mohawk Power Corp* (1997) United States Court of Appeals, Second Circuit, 10 F.3d 6.

[152] (1997) Supreme Court, New York County, 174, 664 N.Y.S.2d 698; see also *Precision Master Inc v Mold Masters Co* (2007) Court of Appeals of Michigan, 2007 WL 2012807; *QVC Inc v MJC America Ltd* (2011) United States District Court, Pennsylvania, 2011 WL 2790156; *Carolina Consulting Corp. v Ajax Paving Industries, Inc. of Florida* (2012) District Court of Appeal of Florida, Second District, 86 So.3d 502; *BRC Rubber & Plastics, Inc. v Continental Carbon Company* (2020) United States Court of Appeals, 7th Circuit, 981 F.3d 681.

sought are more than 'adequate' and the other party rejects to accede to the excessive demands, the court may rule that the buyer themselves were in repudiatory breach, thus entitling the other party to terminate the contract.[153]

B. CISG and UPICC

Similar to UCC section 2-609, CISG Article 72(2) states that 'if time allows, the party intending to declare the contract avoided must give reasonable notice to the other party in order to permit him to provide adequate assurance of [their] performance'. This Article should be read alongside CISG Article 72(1), concerning anticipatory breach of contract. UPICC has also provided for the right to adequate assurance in Article 7.3.4, which states that 'a party who reasonably believes that there will be a fundamental non-performance by the other party may demand adequate assurance of due performance and may meanwhile withhold [their] own performance'. UPICC Article 7.3.4 is largely similar to CISG Articles 71 and 72 and should thus be analysed together.

The seller, who has received a sufficient notice from the buyer indicating they will avoid the contract, may prefer to continue the contract. The seller is thus given the opportunity to address the buyer's doubt by providing adequate assurance of their performance. The concept of 'adequate assurance' is notoriously vague. CISG and UPICC have failed to provide necessary guideline. It is ambiguous what constitutes an acceptable adequate assurance and whether the assurance must guarantee performance by the due date or by later dates 'falling short of lateness amounting to a fundamental breach'.[154] These instruments would usually restore buyer's confidence in the proper performance of the contract and they can then continue to stay in the contract. If the seller provides an adequate assurance within a reasonable period, the buyer need not avoid the contract. This means that an adequate assurance should be afforded before the due date of performance to guarantee future performance.

There is a wide range of measures that may be adequately protect the innocent party's interests such as usual bank securities.[155] In general, 'adequate assurances are those which provide the [buyer] with reasonable security regarding the future performance by the other party'.[156] The UPICC Official Comments explains that it depends on the circumstances of each case as to what constitutes an adequate assurance of performance.[157] If adequate assurance is provided by the seller, the

[153] White and Summers (n 149) 199. See also *Erwin Weller Co. v Talon Inc.* (1980) Supreme Court of South Dakota, 295 N.W. 2d 172.

[154] Bridge (n 103) 681.

[155] Schlechtriem and Schwenzer (n 15) 1034.

[156] Kroll, Mistelis and Viscasillas (n 26) 961; see also R Koch, 'The concept of fundamental breach of contract under the United Nations Convention on Contracts for the International Sale of Goods (CISG)' in *Review of the Convention on Contracts for the International Sale of Goods (CISG)* (Kluwer Law International, 1999) 305.

[157] UPICC Official Comments, Article 7.3.4, para 2.

buyer 'regains the sense of security and the expectation that the contract will be honoured and can continue to perform; if the other party fails to respond to the notice, [the buyer] is likely to be in the position to avoid the contract'.[158] What is important is that the assurance guarantees performance of the contract or, alternatively, compensation of the loss that a fundamental breach, despite the given guarantee, would incur.[159] The assurance given does not need to compensate for additional losses that may occur due to the breach. Nor does it need to be so wide as to cover potential claims for damages, which may arise by the innocent party.[160] If the assurance is adequate from an objective viewpoint, the buyer must accept it and they lose their right to terminate the contract.[161]

C. SGA

While the doctrine of anticipatory breach of contract originated and developed in English law, it has remained rigid. As explained in the previous section, the modern regimes of UCC, CISG and UPICC supplemented this doctrine with the mechanism of adequate assurance, which is absent from English law. In this section, the possibility of adopting the novel mechanism of adequate assurance into English will be analysed.[162]

Legal certainty and predictability is arguably the most indispensable quality of mercantile contracts.[163] The parties must be able to conduct business with confidence in the legal repercussions of their actions. With this in mind, it is submitted that adequate assurance is a *logical corollary* of the doctrine of anticipatory breach of contract. As shown in the previous section, the latter doctrine shall be invoked when a repudiation is purported with utmost certainty. The buyer should demonstrate that the refusal to perform was unequivocal and absolute. The requirement of certainty is undermined when the seller shows inconsistent behaviour that may place the buyer in an ambiguous situation. Seller, who may not wish to breach but are unable to perform, may often exhibit thoroughly vague signals. For example, in the American case of *Hornell Brewing Co v Spry*, the distributor's failure to sell

[158] Kroll, Mistelis and Viscasillas (n 26) 959; For a counter argument see K Kryla-Cudna, 'Adequate assurance of performance under UN Convention on Contracts for the International Sale of goods and the Uniform Commercial Code' (2021) *International & Comparative Law Quarterly*. In this article, the author suggests that the adequate assurance mechanism under Article 72(2) aims solely to protect the interests of the promisor by giving them a chance to re-establish themselves and prevent the avoidance of a contract by the promise.

[159] Schlechtriem and Schwenzer (n 15) Article 72, para 30; see also Bridge (n 123) 405, 417.

[160] Vogenauer (n 107) Article 7.3.4, para 8.

[161] Schlechtriem and Schwenzer (n 15) 978.

[162] Please note that the longer version of this specific point can be found here: Beheshti (n 102) 276.

[163] *Bunge v Tradax* [1981] 1 WLR 711, 715; [1981] 2 Lloyd's Rep 1, 5. See also JH Merryman, 'On the convergence (and divergence) of the civil law and the common law' (1981) 17 *Stanford Journal of International Law* 357; EA Farnsworth, 'Developing international trade law' (1979) 9 *California Western International Law Journal* 461.

even a small fraction of the product led the supplier to have reasonable doubts about the distributor's ability to perform in the future.[164] In this case, the distributor did not manifest their intention or ability not to perform in an explicit manner, thereby placing the supplier in an uncertain situation. Such a breach thus puts the promisee or the buyer, who has perceived an apparent repudiation, in a difficult and risky dilemma. If the buyer avoids the contract and sues for breach based on an apparent repudiation, they are at risk of being found to have breached the contract themselves should the court rules that the perceived repudiation was not sufficiently clear to constitute an anticipatory breach. Not only is this unfair to the buyer, but it would cause economic inefficiency. Should the buyer mistakenly decide that repudiation has occurred and terminate the contract, any subsequent seller's performance before becoming aware of the buyer's decision may be partially or wholly wasted.[165] This issue occurred in the English case of *Gulf Agri Trade FZCO v Aston Agro Industrial AG*.[166] In this case, the seller had to ship 6,000 metric tonnes of Russian Feed Barley during the period 10 August to 10 October 2004. The seller had made no shipment by the end of September 2004. The buyer therefore sent a notice of default to the seller on 4 October, demanding an 'amicable settlement in order to close this file'.[167] The buyer stated that they considered the contract as defaulted and claimed an amount to be paid as compensation. Because the seller failed to purport any action showing their willingness or ability to perform the contract by the end of September, the buyer assumed that it would be impossible for the seller to ship the goods in a timely manner in accordance with the contractual arrangements. The buyer thus took action on the basis of an apparent repudiation of contract. However, as a matter of fact, when the buyer gave notice of default to the seller, the buyer could not have been reasonably certain that the seller 'could not or would not perform the contract'.[168] The default notice was therefore held to be premature and thus unjustified, which convinced the GAFTA Appeal Board to rule that '[the buyer] could not reasonably have concluded that [the seller] were in anticipatory breach of the contract through impossibility or renunciation'.[169] If the doctrine of adequate assurance was formally recognised in English Sale of Goods, the buyer with reasonable doubts could demand confirmation that contractual performance would be rendered by the seller. The buyer in this case relied on the seller's contractual undertakings, expected to receive those goods and, as such, they concluded contract with several sub-purchasers. Because the seller did not execute their obligations, the buyer had to pay damages for losses incurred to their sub-buyers. Having understood that the seller is unwilling or

[164] (1997) Supreme Court, New York County, 664 NYS 2d 698.

[165] Crespi (n 129) 179, 183; D DeNooyer, 'Remedying anticipatory repudiation- past, present, and future' (1999) 52 *Southern Methodist Law Review* 1787, 1790.

[166] [2009] 1 All ER (Comm) 991. See also *Fleming & Wendeln GmbH & Co v Sanofi Sa* [2003] EWHC 561 (Comm); [2003] 2 Lloyd's Rep 473.

[167] [2008] EWHC 1252 (Comm); [2008] 1 All ER (Comm) 991, para 5.

[168] ibid, 23.

[169] ibid, 23.

unable to perform the contract in due time, the buyer would have had the chance to notify their sub-buyers so that they could have started searching for alternatives with a reasonable amount of time, which could perhaps reduce the economic waste. This case strongly reinforces the suggestion that English law should introduce the doctrine of adequate assurance.

Another pertinent and controversial case is *Universal Cargo Carriers Corporation v Citati*, in which the owner of a vessel was accused of wrongful termination of contract, despite the apparent repudiation by the charterer.[170] The charterer was contractually obliged to furnish a cargo of 6,000 tons of scrap iron, to load it at the rate of 1,000 tons per day, and to complete the loading by 21 July. However, they did not provide any cargo by 18 July. On this day, the owner terminated the contract by rechartering the vessel to another charterer; because the original charterer failed to provide any cargo three days before the lay days were due to expire under the charterparty.[171] The owner justified this action by arguing that on or before 18 July the charterer had committed an actual or anticipatory breach of their obligations under the charterparty. They believed that on that day 6,000 tons could not possibly have been loaded in the lay time remaining. The issue was then whether the charterer's failure to load the goods on 18 July led to reasonable inference that there will be prospective fundamental breach of contract.[172] To convince the court, the shipowner had to demonstrate 'that on July 18 the charterer was unable to load a cargo within such a time as would not have frustrated the venture'.[173] While it is well settled that the obligation to load within the lay days is a warranty and its breach gives rise to a claim for damages only,[174] the injured party may terminate if the delay becomes so long that the breach is so serious as to go to the root of the contract.[175] It was a factual question to assess the delay to find out whether it constituted the frustration of charterparty. Devlin J stated that 'an anticipatory breach must be proved in fact and not in supposition'.[176] The doctrine of adequate assurance precisely operates to shed light on blurred factual situations, such as this case. If the doctrine were recognised in English law, the shipowner could employ it to justify their termination of contract. Although the charterer appeared willing to perform, they could not possibly load the goods due to the length of delay occurred until 18 July. For the shipowner to be entitled to terminate the contract, it should have been sure that the charterer's inability to perform was inexorable or sufficiently probable. Failing to furnish an adequate assurance by the

[170] [1958] 2 Lloyd's Rep 17; [1957] 2 QB 401.
[171] [1958] 2 Lloyd's Rep 17, 19; [1957] 2 QB 401, 420.
[172] [1958] 2 Lloyd's Rep 17, 20; [1957] 2 QB 401, 440.
[173] [1958] 2 Lloyd's Rep 17, 23; [1957] 2 QB 401, 450.
[174] *Thorpe v Fasey* [1949] Ch. 649.
[175] *Evera S.A. Commercial v North Shipping Co. Ltd* [1956] 2 Lloyd's Eep. 367. See also N Andrews, M Clarke, A Tettenborn and G Virgo, *Contractual Duties: Performance, Breach, Termination and Remedies*, 2nd edn (Sweet & Maxwell, 2017) 133.
[176] *Universal Cargo Carriers Corparation v Citati* [1958] 2 Lloyd's Rep 17, 23; [1957] 2 QB 401, 450. See also *Forslind v Bechely-Crundall* 1922 SC (HL) 173, 192.

charterer would have led to a reasonable anticipation that the charterparty will not be performed, thus providing a solid ground for the owner to rightfully terminate the charterparty.

In the more recent and similar case of *SK Shipping (S) Pte Ltd v Petroexport Ltd (The Pro Victor)*, the Commercial Court reached a different conclusion.[177] SK Shipping chartered to Petroexport for a voyage from Karachi, Pakistan carrying naphtha to Mailia, Taiwan. The charterparty provided that the vessel had to start loading by 27 August and the lay days were to last for three consecutive days. However, following the conclusion of the charterparty and before the vessel arrived in Karachi, the charterer faced some difficulties both in securing sufficient naphtha from their suppliers and finding a customer. As a result, the charterer ordered the vessel to slow steam. Furthermore, it never returned the copy of the charterparty sent by the owner for signature, which was required to procure freight text exemption. When the owner learned that the charterer experienced hardship in finding a buyer and might not proceed with the charterparty, it initiated a series of email exchanges to ascertain whether the charterer would perform the contract. The owner's emails were answered elusively.[83] Having received no persuasive confirmation, the owner sent a final email aiming at terminating the charterparty as a response to the charterer's alleged renunciation. The Commercial Court upheld the owner's decision to terminate the contract and recharter the vessel for another voyage on the basis that the charterer's words and conduct gave rise to the renunciation of the charterparty. Although the Commercial Court ruled in favour of the owner, it was unpredictable as to whether the charterer's conduct would lead to repudiation of performance, as indicated in their judgment that courts should take account of 'the totality of the relevant words and conduct relied upon, in the light of all the circumstances, including the history of the contractual relationship'.[178]

As shown above, the absence of the doctrine of adequate assurance in English law can lead to inconsistent decisions by courts or arbitral tribunals in broadly factually similar cases, which ultimately impairs certainty with regard to future similar cases. These decisions clearly demonstrate that English law lacks an effective mechanism by which the suspicious party can draw the inference that a prospective non-performance or fundamental breach is likely, on the balance of probabilities, to materialise at the time for performance. Such inference would be particularly difficult in blurred situations where the seller has behaved inconsistently, indicating that it lacks clearness of purpose or has insufficient understanding of markets which necessitate prompt and accurate compliance with obligations. The doctrine of adequate assurance can therefore function to alleviate the position

[177] *SK Shipping (S) Pte Ltd v Petroexport Ltd (The Pro Victor)* [2009] EWHC 2974 (Comm); [2010] 2 Lloyd's Rep 158.

[178] ibid, 88. See also *Maredelanto Compania Naviera SA v Bergbau-Handel GmbH (The Mihalis Angelos)* [1971] 1 QB 164, 210; [1970] 2 Lloyd's Rep 43; *BS & N Ltd (BVI) v Micado Shipping Ltd (Malta) (The Seaflower)* [2000] 2 Lloyd's Rep 37.

for the buyer, in that the failure to provide the assurance by the seller will make it safer and hence more certain to terminate the contract.[179]

To find out whether the doctrine of adequate assurance fits neatly into English law, the nature of this doctrine should be examined. As discussed before, adequate assurance has a promissory character, in the sense that the promisor pledges that their obligations will be fulfilled in future.[180] Assurances may consist of new undertakings, which may take the form of granting the insecure party the right to inspect the books of a suspect merchant to confirm ongoing solvency. To enforce the promisor's undertaking to furnish adequate assurance, a serious objection may arise from the rationale underlying the doctrine of consideration, as a complicated and multifarious body of rules, which limit the enforceability of agreements in English law.[181] The doctrine of consideration is founded on the idea of reciprocity, indicating that 'something of value in the eye of the law' must be provided in order for an enforceable contract to be constituted.[182] On this basis, adequate assurance may seem unlikely to be transplanted into English commercial law, because this doctrine requires the promisor to provide something showing their intention regarding future performance without receiving anything in return from the promisee. As a result, the promisee obtains the benefit of an assurance aimed at confirming the future performance of the promise. However, this objection is unlikely to be serious enough to stall efforts at reforming the current status of the doctrine of anticipatory breach of contract, for one important reason.

This reason is mainly concerned with sophisticated situations where the assurance involves more robust, substantive promises than a mere verbal affirmation of future performance, such as when the promisor furnishes a personal guaranty. It has been argued that perhaps consideration is rooted in the promisee's forbearance from suspending their performance.[183] However, it may be unclear whether and how exactly the forbearance is a benefit to the promisor ('in that he may receive value'[184]) or a detriment to the promise ('in that he may give value'[185]). At first blush, forbearance is likely to confer benefit to the promisor, in the sense that the promisee resumes performance of their contractual duties. It is logical to assume that the essential purpose of a contract between commercial men is actual performance and they do not bargain merely for a promise.[186] It can also be argued that, when the promisee withholds performance of contract, they are likely to embark

[179] The proposal to introduce the doctrine of adequate assurance was put forward by Scottish Law Commission. The proposal was ultimately not adopted. *Discussion Paper on Remedies for Breach of Contract* (Sc LC 109, 1999) para 9.2.

[180] See section 5(B).

[181] Beale (n 67), para 4.001.

[182] *Thomas v Thomas* (1842) 2 QB 851.

[183] Borden (n 135) 167, 184.

[184] *Currie v Misa* (1875) LR 10 Ex; *Bainbridge v Firmstone* (1838) 8 A & E 743; 112 ER 1019; *Gore v Van der Lann* [1976] 2 QB 31.

[185] *Modahl v British Athletics Federation Ltd* [2001] EWCA Civ 1447; [2002] 1 WLR 1192.

[186] UCC Official Comments, section 2-609, para 1.

a lawsuit against the promisor in due course, and furnishing adequate assurance induces the promisee to forbear from pursuing their claim.[187] Nevertheless, it cannot be easily determined the extent to which such forbearances confer benefit to the promisor or incur detriment to the promisee. There might be situations where it is pointless to 'imprison two parties in a long-term contract where there is absence of trust or the prospect of mounting, incremental losses', and that termination of contract is more beneficial for both parties.[188]

However, a fresh perspective may be able to effectively analyse the role of forbearance in satisfying the requirement of consideration. As shown above, the promisor or the seller enjoys freedom in granting an adequate assurance. When the promisor is faced with a demand for adequate assurance, it has presumably had the chance to engage in a cost-benefit analysis following the conclusion of contract, in that it is able to evaluate the costs of full performance of the contract versus paying damages in the event of repudiation due to new circumstances in the market. This means that the promisor's decision is likely to be informed by an assessment of whether it declines to provide an assurance, thus entitling the promise or the buyer to terminate the contract, as a result of which the former should pay damages to the latter. These costs could potentially be increased by the usual costs of concluding a new transaction with another party, especially when a commercial promisor is in urgent need of supplying their sub-buyers or other associated parties.[189] But when the promisor positively responds to the promisee's request by providing assurance to the effect of continuation of contract, thereby forcing the promisee to forbear from suspension, the promisor should have been convinced that the costs of contract performance do not outweigh the costs of non-performance, ie paying damages. This cost-benefit analysis conducted by the promisor shows that providing or declining to afford an adequate assurance confers in return a commercial advantage to it, which constitutes a good consideration. According to Kitchin LJ in the recent case of *MWB Business Exchange Centres Ltd v Rock Advertising Ltd*, since a practical benefit which offers a clear commercial advantage to the promisor is sufficient for enforcing a modification or variation promise.[190] Therefore, notwithstanding the lack of consideration moving from the promisee, the benefit, as enjoyed by the promisor, which results from their opportunity to conduct a financial assessment may constitute good consideration for the promise to afford adequate assurance.

[187] Forbearance to start a legal action is formally recognised by English courts as a good consideration: *Alliance Bank v Broom* (1846) 2 Dr & Sm 289; 62 ER 632.

[188] Bridge (n 18) 911, 915.

[189] See eg *Hess Energy Inc v Lightning Oil Co Ltd* (2002) United States Court of Appeals, 4th Circuit, 276 F 3d 646; *Brisbin v Superior Valve Co* (2005) United States Court of Appeals, 3rd Circuit, 398 F 3d 279.

[190] [2016] 2 Lloyd's Rep 391, 388; [2017] QB 604, 613. For further explanations regarding practical benefit see *Williams v Roffey Bros & Nicholls (Contractors) Ltd* [1991] 1 QB 1.

6. Evaluation

International sales of manufactured goods transactions are likely to require a great degree of collaboration between the parties so that parties' expectation interest can be achieved. One of the major issues parties may face in international trade, especially in the context of long-term supply of goods, is an unforeseen change of circumstances. As the recent global pandemic showed, we live in an uncertain world. Such unforeseeable events may cause serious obstacles for the parties in executing their obligations. Disrupting the equilibrium of the contract prior to the due performance date is an issue that should be carefully addressed by any appropriate legal regime. The doctrines and principles discussed in this chapter precisely provide legal solutions for such disruptive circumstances.

'Withholding performance' and 'request for adequate assurance' are considered informal, self-help remedies that permit the innocent buyer to unilaterally withhold their payment obligations. Self-help remedies are regarded to be a party's immediate and rational reaction to a perceived problem. Self-help actions refer to 'private actions taken by those interested in the controversy to prevent or resolve disputes without official assistance of a governmental official or disinterested third party'.[191] Recourse to courts as well as international tribunals have become fraught with difficulties: complex issues of jurisdiction and applicable law, unfamiliar civil procedural rules and inherent problems with enforcing judgments or awards. In other words, these formal dispute resolution mechanisms may be unfitted to tackle the parties' most significant needs, such as speed and efficiency. As a result, parties involved in complex international sale of goods transactions would prefer self-help remedies in case of breach of contract. Promoting self-help is not only desirable but necessary in international business transactions where prospects of the enforcement of courts' decisions and arbitral awards are often inconceivable. While suspension of performance may be invoked without any third party's interference, the suspending party is likely to face an official proceeding commenced by the other party. For instance, in the leading English case of *Agios Giorgis*, charterers made unjustified deductions to the hire and the owners, in turn, refused to unload cargo requesting payment of the balance.[192] While the hire was eventually paid, the charterers started a court's proceedings due to the delay in unloading.

As shown in previous sections, suspension of performance may be used in two occasions: first, the buyer faced by uncertainty regarding future performance by the seller; second, the buyer encounters a breach of contract, not serious enough to warrant termination. English law is the only legal regime, which does not explicitly and officially recognise withholding performance as a buyer's remedy in SGA. But it can be deduced that withholding performance is available as a

[191] Gergen (n 135) 1397, 1447; Taylor (n 4) 839, 852.

[192] *Steelwood Carriers Inc. of Monrovia, Liberia v Evimeria Compania Naviera S.A. of Panama*, (1976) 2 Lloyd's Rep 192 (the *'Agios Giorgis'*).

logical reaction to the seller's precarious behaviour. For instance, when the seller does not respond to the buyer's enquiries regarding upcoming deliveries or have failed to tender performance in comparable transactions, the buyer is entitled to withhold their payment duty. Other legal regimes have clearly incorporated this remedy within the range of remedies available to the buyer. The buyer would, therefore, enjoy sufficient certainty in invoking this remedy once faced with dubious circumstances. It appears that UCC provides greater flexibility, when it comes to the availability of this remedy. Under UPICC Article 7.3.4, a party is entitled to suspend performance and demand further assurances of performance where they have reasonable grounds to believe that the other party will commit a 'fundamental breach'. Similarly, CISG Article 71, which sets forth a right to suspend performance in case of anticipatory breach, speaks in terms of a party's potential failure to perform 'a substantial part' of their obligations. Such approach should be contrasted to that of UCC in section 2-609, which only requires that suspension of performance be 'commercially reasonable', when reasonable grounds for insecurity arises and the innocent party demands adequate assurance of due performance. In other words, UCC does not hold the suspension of performance on to the successful proof of fundamental breach or non-performance of a substantial part. Rather, the innocent party should only demonstrate a reasonable fear of future breach. CISG and UPICC have adopted the same standards of termination of contract for suspension of performance, whilst UCC has adopted a more lenient and commercially suitable standard of proportionality, focusing mainly on insecurity with respect to the other party's future performance.

In relation to the doctrine of adequate assurance, at first sight, it appears to be similarly set out under UCC, CISG and UPICC. At least the ways in which this mechanism is presented in these legal regimes are not very different. However, it might be noticeable that CISG Article 71(3) employs the term 'adequate assurance of performance', whilst UCC section 2-609 and UPICC Article 7.3.4 use 'adequate assurance of due performance'. Such difference in wordings is trivial. These provisions contribute significantly to economic efficiency in that it would reduce the probability that inefficient allocation of resources will be taking place by affording an innocent buyer with relative certainty that contract will be fulfilled. If adequate assurance is not provided, the buyer would have the chance of relocating their resources by exploring the market and finding another seller with similar goods. The adequate assurance mechanism under these regimes therefore seeks to restore the sense security and confidence that were shaken by the seller's behaviour.

However, despite UCC section 2-609, relevant CISG and UPICC principles do not stipulate the consequences of a failure to provide an adequate assurance. In relation to CISG Article 71(3), it can be inferred that the suspending buyer may continue with the suspension of performance until the grounds giving rise to suspension cease to exist. Similarly, UPICC Article 7.3.4 explicitly stipulates that when waiting for an adequate assurance, the aggrieved party may 'withhold their own performance'. Alternatively, the suspending party may invoke their right to avoid the contract should the requirements specified in CISG Article 72 and UPICC Article 7.3.3 be satisfied. What cannot be easily deduced is the consequences of the seller's failure to provide an adequate assurance, when buyer seeks to act on the basis of anticipatory breach. The UPICC Official Comments states that if adequate assurance of due performance is not given the other party may terminate the contract.[193] While this statement has clarified the situation and may enhance the parties' certainty interests, it does not seem to be accurate. It would rather be simplistic to argue that a party's failure to provide adequate assurance provides the certain ground for the other party to terminate the contract. The principle of *favor contractus* is one of the general principles underlying this legal instrument.[194] This principle seeks to preserve the contractual relation by restricting the situations in which the existence or validity of the contract is undermined or in which it can be terminated. The underlying idea is to keep the contract alive, notwithstanding deficiencies in the process of contract formation or the performance of the contract. Additionally, following Article 7.3.1, an aggrieved party can only terminate a contract where the fundamental breach is satisfied. Not providing an adequate assurance does not necessarily indicate future occurrence of fundamental breach.

CISG lacks official commentary and its *travaux préparatoires* may potentially provide a suitable answer. At the United Nations Conference on Contracts for the International Sale of Goods held in 1980, the delegates from Canada and Australia suggested an additional provision clarifying 'a failure to provide adequate assurance of performance within a reasonable period of time shall entitle the party requesting the assurance to avoid the contract'.[195] This joint proposal was quite similar to UCC section 2-609 part 2. The justification for this proposal was that one party's failure to give adequate assurance indicates their unwillingness to perform, the other party would thus be entitled to take fast action and escape the contract. The delegate from Canada argued that it should be clarified that if a party did not receive an adequate assurance of the other party's ability to perform, they were entitled to avoid the contract and not merely suspend performance.[196] Without this provision, the non-defaulting party would be in a position of intolerable uncertainty.[197] However, the joint proposal was not approved. The reason was

[193] UPICC Official Comments, Article 7.3.4 para 3.

[194] See eg N Kornet, 'Evolving general principles of international commercial contract, the Unidroit Principles and *favor contractus*' (2011) Maastricht Faculty of Law Working Paper Series 1,7; MJ Bonell, *An International Restatement of Contract Law. The Unidroit Principles of International Commercial Contracts*, 3rd edn (BRILL, 2005) 102; AG Doudko, 'Hardship in contract: the approach of the Unidroit Principles and legal developments in Russia' (2000) *Uniform Law Review*, 483, 491; MJ Bonell, 'The UNIDROIT Principles of International Commercial Contracts. Why? What? How?' (1995) *Tulane Law Review* 1121–47.

[195] See Official Records, A/CONF.97/19, 129.

[196] ibid, 377.

[197] ibid.

that CISG, quite identical to UPICC, generally entitles an innocent party to avoid the contract only when fundamental breach occurs and the 'exact circumstances' allowing avoidance 'should not be specifically defined in each article'.[198] It should thus be left to the adjudicators to decide whether the specific circumstances of a given dispute are sufficient to justify avoidance. Such circumstances include, for example, the probability of finding and obtaining substitute goods when the seller is no longer able to provide them,[199] while the seller initially indicates that they intend not to deliver the goods, they continued to negotiate with the buyer,[200] the seller's threat not to deliver the goods while insisting on amendment of the letter of credit.[201] These examples indicate that the courts or arbitral tribunals need to take into account the entire spectrum of the factual circumstances of each case to ascertain the probability that a fundamental breach will occur. As such, the seller's failure to provide adequate assurance may be considered as one such circumstances in the court's assessment that would make it 'clear' that they will commit a fundamental breach.

In terms of the first criterion of 'preservation of relationship', the doctrines concerning insecurity prior to performance analysed in this chapter, appear to be suitable legal instruments in contributing effectively to the long-standing contractual relationship between the parties. Anticipatory breach of contract recognised in these legal regimes complement the remedy of withholding performance. Both doctrines are mainly concerned with predicting whether there will be a breach and reflect an underlying policy to provide further protection to the innocent buyer.[202] The anticipatory breach of contract, if properly invoked, leads to the avoidance of contract prior to due performance date and can contribute to maintaining a fair balance between the interests of both parties, which may not be necessarily achieved through keeping the existing contract alive. Expecting the innocent buyer to perform their part where it is evident that the seller will not execute what was promised in return would cause a disparity in the level of protection that should be given to each party. Anticipatory breach of contract, running counter to the preservation of relationship, thus entitles such innocent buyer to escape the contract and pursue their interests elsewhere. However, doctrines of 'adequate assurance of

[198] ibid, 378; for a counter argument, which is in line with the UPICC Official Comments and suggests that the buyer may immediately avoid the contract should the seller fail to give adequate assurance within a reasonable time after receipt of notice, see Honnold and Flechtner (n 29) 737; LA DiMatteo, A Janssen, U Magnus and R Schulze, *International Sales Law, A Handbook*, 2nd edn (Bloomsbury Publishing, 2021) 555.

[199] *Royal Feinsprit 96% for Moscow case* (1997) Court of First Instance Saane, Switzerland, CISG-online 426.

[200] *Metal concentrate case* (1996), ICC International Court of Arbitration, Switzerland, CISG-online 1293.

[201] *Magellan International Corporation v Salzgitter Handel GMBH* (1999) United States District Court, Illinois, 99 C 5153, US District Court of Illinois, 76 F.Supp.2d 919.

[202] Kroll, Mistelis and Viscasillas (n 26) 919; UNCITRAL Digest of Case Law on the United Nations Convention on Contracts for the International Sale of Goods (2016) Article 72, para 2.

contract' and 'withholding performance' associated with the anticipatory breach do not disrupt the contractual arrangement and instead reinforce strict adherence to contractual promises.

The doctrines of 'adequate assurance of contract' and 'withholding performance' are directly facilitative of cooperative behaviour and result in the continuation of interdependence, as required for preservation of relations. When the buyer requests for an adequate assurance, they have to wait and suspend their performance until the seller responds. As such all benefits of withholding performance are carried by the doctrine of adequate assurance. A party facing with uncertainty regarding prospective performance does not make a capricious or irrational decision by suspending their own performance. Rather, this party reacts logically to this situation and employs a 'fillip' mechanism, which nudges the other party to clarify the situation promptly. This mechanism constitutes an intermediate step between the relatively drastic alternative of terminating all remaining performance and the commercially oriented remedy of damages. When the buyer withholds the payment, the seller, who may genuinely wish to maintain their relationship with the buyer and is keen to transform it into a flourishing long standing relationship would be encouraged to either perform the contract or cure their already rendered defective performance. Suspension of performance precisely provides an opportunity for the seller to reflect on their past and ongoing contractual relationships with the buyer and make up their mind on whether to perform the outstanding obligation, cure the defective performance or deciding to withdraw from the contract.

In addition, the self-help nature of 'withholding performance' and 'adequate assurance' doctrines provides the necessary flexibility in maintaining a long-term relationship, without rigid and formal interference from any third party. Relations cannot be preserved, nor conflict in relations harmonised, without adequate attention to the demands of change. In fact, relational norms necessitate flexibility to adjust relationships to supervening changes. Rather than resorting to formal proceedings that may deprive parties from constructive cooperation, withholding performance, and in particular request for an adequate assurance, may present parties with an opportunity to collaboratively resolve issues hindering proper performance.

In addition, when withholding the payment obligations and asking for assurance, the buyer notifies the seller of their concerns regarding prospective performance of contract. The notice requirement may function as a tool that encourages ambivalent parties to communicate. They can then identify and understand the effect of any change of circumstances on each other's performing abilities. This may afford parties with the very last opportunity to exchange ideas and identify solutions for preventing the contract from being terminated. When the contract is on halt, parties would enjoy the chance to renegotiate the terms and thus accommodate each other's needs. Since exercising the right to remedies of termination and damages for an anticipated failure to perform involves a risk of error, the instrument of adequate assurance would boost confidence in invoking such remedies. Providing an adequate assurance, as a suitable reaction to the buyer's broken trust by the seller's harmful conduct, can thus be an effective way of accommodating each other's needs and restoring sense of security in commercial transactions, which, in turn, induces parties' cooperation. Both doctrines, which are clearly set out in UCC, CISG and UPICC, will provide the parties with the necessary flexibility to address each other's needs through modifying contract terms. Having the option of modifying the terms and indeed varying the terms according to the new circumstances may lead to the preservation of their relationship without external interference. The parties may, however, choose to terminate the contract, should their negotiations fail. As shown in *Gulf Agri Trade*, the seller failed to constructively react to the buyer's legitimate concern, which stemmed from the seller's failure to make any shipment by the end of September.[203] This destructive behaviour could have been amended by a convincing response, by potentially offering an assurance, from the seller indicating their willingness to perform the contract.

The law is well settled in the four legal regimes, as reflected in their provisions and the relevant caselaw, which indicates that a buyer can take immediate action where anticipatory repudiation is established. Anticipatory breach would be beneficial to both parties, and it appears to be in line with the second norm of 'conformity of extended relations with commercial matrix'. Following the repudiation of the contract by the seller, the buyer is at liberty to be freed from any future performance of the contract, while retaining the right to claim for any damages they have suffered from the seller's breach. It would be a waste of resources for the innocent buyer to stay in such an insecure contract.[204] They should, rather, be able to immediately exercise their right to terminate and enter another transaction, which could potentially reduce further transaction costs.

In addition, the doctrine of 'withholding performance', which come into effect after the buyer's request for 'adequate assurance', may allow parties to figure out whether an extended relationship is economically sustainable and whether they should maintain such a relationship. First, it is presumed that maintaining a contractual relationship is likely to be economically justified. Rather than employing the drastic remedy of termination which ends contractual relationship, the buyer, by choosing suspension of performance as a conservatory and defensive remedy, effectively exerts pressure on the other party. The buyer preserves their interests by refusing to transfer payment to the seller so long as the latter's counter performance is not forthcoming. The buyer's pressure may lead to proper performance by the seller, thus holding the contract alive. As confirmed in a German court of appeal, provisions providing the right to suspend performance express the

[203] [2009] 1 All ER (Comm) 991.

[204] Saidov (n 35) 795, 798; JW Carter, A Phang and S-Y Phang, 'Performance Following Repudiation: Legal and Economic Interests' (1999) 15 *Journal of Contract Law* 100, 107–109, 121.

so called functional synallagmatic, which seeks to secure the claim and exert pressure on the seller to perform their obligations in due time.[205] A legal regime, which entitles parties to withhold performance subject to requirements being satisfied, discourages parties from terminating their contractual relationships, whenever changing circumstances adversely affect their interests in contractual performance. For instance, sellers would seek to terminate their contracts when market price of the goods are rising. Buyers likewise would wish to terminate when market price is dropping. Withholding performance aims to discourage opportunistic behaviours and reinforce the role of contracts as instruments of certainty and rational planning in commercial transactions.

Second, withholding performance may prompt parties to organise their relationship consistent with efficient contractual behaviour. Maintaining the contractual relationship will be less costly for the parties than entering a new contract. By preserving their contractual relationships, the parties will save the costs of initial planning, which includes negotiations essential to the mutual planning required in forming contracts. In addition, withholding performance and adequate assurance doctrines precisely underpin 'reciprocity' as a necessary norm for continuation of efficient relationship paying off the initial investment made by the parties. The relationship shall continue so long as each party's analysis concludes that continuance is more advantageous than ending the contract. Maintenance of relationship essentially requires that each party would be able to trust with confidence in the other party's efficient cooperation. This means that so long as parties reciprocate and satisfy each other's self-interest, the relationship would continue. The question in the background of long-term relationship is 'what has the seller done for buyer lately?'.[206] When contract is on halt due to the buyer's suspension of performance following their request for assurance, both parties would have the opportunity to assess whether enough value is tied up in their existing contract. The seller may take into account any estimate of how long it would take them to complete performance or whether they have an incentive to cure the defective goods already delivered. The seller's previous destructive behaviour could be amended by the convincing response of offering an adequate assurance, which indicates their willingness to perform. This cost-benefit analysis conducted by the seller shows that providing or declining to provide an adequate assurance confers in return a commercial advantage to it. The buyer can also consider their own benefits on whether the seller's non-performance or defective performance may incur additional costs. For instance, when the buyer reasonably doubts that the seller will not perform the contract, they can terminate the contract. In so doing, they avoid unnecessary costs and will have the opportunity to use their money elsewhere. For instance, in the *Rijn Blend oil* case, the buyer

[205] *Pesticides case I* (2008) Court of Appeal Cologne, Germany, CISG-online 1700; see also JW Carter 'Adequate assurance of due performance' (1996) 10 *Journal of Contract Law* 3, 10.

[206] IR Macneil, 'Contracting Worlds and Essential Contract Theory' (2000) 9 *Social & Legal Studies* 431, 432.

failed to take delivery of several instalments and withheld their payment obligations due to the increased level of mercury in the crude oil condensate.[207] This caused difficulties for the buyer in processing the condensate and selling the goods downstream. The seller's performance thus failed to satisfy the buyer's commercial interest. While suspending their performance, the buyer notified the seller that they would continue suspension until a solution for the mercury problems was found. If an adequate assurance was provided, the buyer should have stayed in the contract. The Tribunal decided that 'Rijn Blend' failed to meet the reasonable quality norm. No quality issues were occurred nor raised in the first years following the conclusion of contract and the buyer could, therefore, reasonably expect an appropriate quality level of 'Rign Blend'. It seems obvious that the buyer initially did not intend to terminate their long-term contracts with the seller and was willing to provide a chance for the seller to cure their breaches. While the seller failed to take necessary actions and the contract was eventually terminated, the buyer's suspension struck a fair balance between the interests of both parties. Suspension of performance was, therefore, employed precisely when the seller's poor performance failed to reciprocate the buyer's payment obligation and the buyer was left with no options but to terminate the contract.

[207] (2002) Netherlands Arbitration Institute, CISG-online 740.

3

Financial Incentives During Performance

1. Introduction

This chapter aims to analyse the law concerning price reduction and set-off. These remedies may be invoked during the lifetime of a contract and may provide a suitable opportunity for the parties to preserve a fruitful and efficient relationship. Both remedies seek to resolve the buyer's problem with money and the parties may also employ them as self-help solutions. The remedy of price reduction is not prescribed under SGA, UCC and UPICC. This exclusion will be explored in the chapter. There will also be analysis of the law of set-off under these regimes. In this book the doctrine of set-off is solely considered within the context of buyers' remedies in international sales transactions when it is used as a buyer's defence against the seller's claim for the contract price. Set-off is a defence in nature and is 'an immediate answer to liability'.[1] It is not a remedy as such, but it is closely connected to the remedy of damages, since the amount which the buyer is entitled to deduct is calculated by way of damages.[2] However, the legal regimes focused on in this book have provided the right to set-off in such a way that the buyer can employ it as an independent right. Thus, the comparison will be conducted between set-off and price reduction, as two substantive remedies of the buyer. First, the law of price reduction under CISG will be exposed. Second, there will be an attempt to identify and analyse the complex law of set-off within the other three legal regimes. Finally, the significant distinctions drawn out between damages along with set-off and price reduction will be assessed on the basis of the evaluative framework.

2. Price Reduction

A. CISG

The remedy of price reduction provides the buyer with the right to 'unilaterally alter the terms of the contract'.[3] Despite UPICC, which does not recognise price

[1] R Derham, *Derham on the Law of Set-off*, 4th edn (Oxford University Press, 2010) 70; see also C Fountoulakis, *Set-off Defences in International Commercial Arbitration* (Hart Publishing, 2011) 110.

[2] GH Treitel, *Remedies for Breach of Contract: A Comparative Account* (Oxford University Press, 1988) 107.

[3] S Kroll, L Mistelis and PP Viscasillas, *UN Convention on Contracts for the International Sale of Goods (CISG) Commentary* (Hart Publishing, 2011) 751.

reduction, this remedy is regulated in CISG Article 50. The doctrine of 'price reduction' is grounded on the *actio quanti minoris* of Roman law.[4] When a buyer becomes aware, following delivery of goods, of certain deficiencies which the seller did not declare and which, had the buyer had been aware of them at the time of sale would have induced them to pay a lesser price, they may reduce the purchase price.[5] This remedy is an efficient and practical reaction to the seller's breach, by which the buyer may keep the goods and adjust the price term of contract to the new situation: the price is reduced to reflect the less valuable goods actually delivered.[6] This self-help remedy provides the buyer with very valuable procedural strategic advantages. The remedy is not designed to protect a buyer's expectation, reliance, or restitution interests, such as damages or set-off.[7] It is calculated on the basis of 'the abstract relationship between the actual value of the goods delivered and the hypothetical value of conforming goods'.[8] This type of calculations is called 'proportionate'. The mathematical model for calculating the reduced price is as below:

[9]

$$\text{Reduced price} = \frac{\text{value of delivered}\left(\text{non-conforming goods}\right)}{\text{value of owed}\left(\text{conforming}\right)\text{goods}} \times \text{contract price.}$$

As stated in CISG Article 50, a buyer may exercise its right to reduce the price 'if the goods do not conform with the contract'. Non-conformity is defined in Article 35, and refers to defects as to quantity, quality, description and packaging.[10] Thus, breaches involving non-delivery or late delivery cannot be compensated by this remedy. What has remained unclear is whether defects in title is considered non-conformity. The Norwegian delegations proposed an amendment which expressly included such defect as a type of non-conformity to be recognised under Article 35. The amendment was neither accepted nor rejected due to a lack of time.[11] Eventually, the Vienna Conference decided that question of whether a defect in title constitutes a non-conformity in the goods should be resolved by the courts, presumably by reference to other applicable rules and regulations.

[4] For a detailed historical analysis of this remedy see Treitel (n 2) 107–111.

[5] EE Bergsten and AJ Miller, 'The remedy of reduction of price' (1979) *American Journal of Comparative Law* 255–77.

[6] E Sondahl, 'Understanding the remedy of price reduction – a means to fostering a more uniform application of the United Nations Convention on contracts for the International Sale of Goods' (2003) 7 *Vindobona Journal of International Commercial Law and Arbitration* 255, 259.

[7] R Beheshti, 'Price reduction versus damages: a battle without a winner' (2016) *Uniform Law Review* 216, 220.

[8] Treitel (n 2) 108.

[9] Kroll, Mistelis and Viscasillas (n 3) 759; see also P Schlechtriem and L Schwenzer, *Commentary on the UN Convention on the International Sale of Goods*, 5th edn (Oxford University Press, 2022) 1024.

[10] See UNCITRAL Digest of case law, Article 50, para 3; see also Kroll, Mistelis and Viscasillas (n 3) 752.

[11] JO Honnold, *Documentary History of the Uniform Law for International Sales: The Studies, Deliberations, and Decisions that Led to the 1980 United Nations Convention with Introductions and Explanations* (Kluwer Law and Taxation Publishers, 1989) 582.

This remedy may apply irrespective of the degree of non-conformity, seller's negligence and seller's exemption from liability regulated under Article 79.[12] For instance in the recent case of *China Railway No. 10 Engineering Group Co. Ltd. v Triorient LLC*, the seller, who was the Venezuela's state-owned company, had to deliver 33,000 metric tons of hot-briquetted iron (HBI) with a minimum of 85 per cent FeM.[13] The seller delivered those goods with 83.46 per cent of FeM. Due to this breach, although minor, the buyer withheld part of payment that was deduced from the original purchase price. The arbitral tribunal decided that the buyer was entitled to rely on this quality deficiency in the goods as a justification for exercising the remedy of price reduction.

Price reduction is an efficient remedy for two reasons. First, the buyer is not required to prove an actual loss, nor do they need to demonstrate fault or foreseeability on the seller's side. They just need to show the goods delivered are non-conforming. Second, price reduction can be exercised by the buyer without performing their duty to mitigate: CISG Article 50 is not subject to CISG Article 77, 'which imposes a duty on the buyer to mitigate [their] losses'.[14] However, there are some disagreements amongst the commentators of CISG about whether the buyer should be sanctioned for their failure to mitigate losses. Kritzer opines that the buyer's right to price reduction is not subject to the duty to mitigate under Article 77.[15] In contrast, Honnold argues that not only does the second sentence of Article 50 incorporate certain concepts of mitigation, but Article 77 should be read to apply to a wide range of remedies.[16] It seems that Kritzer's opinion is more accurate as price reduction does not aim to compensate the loss. This remedy operates to refine the original contract, with the aim of retaining the relative balance of the bargain struck by the parties. The buyer keeps the non-conforming goods by adjusting the contract price according to the lesser value of the goods.[17] Therefore, the rules with the aim of limiting the compensation of the loss such as 'duty to mitigate' or 'the test of foreseeability' should not be applied to this remedy.

However, the remedy of price reduction has limited application: it cannot be used for breaches consisting of late delivery and total non-delivery, as the price is reduced on the basis of delivered non-conforming goods being either defective in quality or quantity.[18] Price reduction only covers 'delivery of non-conforming

[12] UNCITRAL Digest of case law, Article 50, para 4.

[13] AAA – International Centre for Dispute Resolution (2020) CISG-Online 5639.

[14] Sondahl (n 6) 255, 256.

[15] AH Kritzer, *Guide to Practical Applications of the United Nations Convention on Contracts for the International Sale of Goods* (Kluwer, 1989) 377.

[16] JO Honnold and HM Flechtner, *Honnold's Uniform Law for International Sales under the 1980 United Nations Convention*, 5th edn (Wolters Kluwer Law and Business, 2021) 600.

[17] I Schwenzer and E Munoz, *Global Sales and Contract Law*, 2nd edn (Oxford University Press, 2022) 816; see also Bergsten and Miller (n 5) 255, 273.

[18] Kroll, Mistelis and Viscasillas (n 3) 752; see also *Calzaturificio Piceno di Roberto Catinari & Uvaldo Raccosta v Vivace Mode GmbH* (1996) District Court Dusseldorf, Germany, CISG-online 18[illegible]; *Elkay Manufacturing Co v Compania de Aguas Belnature, SL* (2000) Court of Appeal Navarra, Spain,

goods and delivery of an *aliud*' (totally different goods).[19] In addition, this remedy cannot be applied when the seller has remedied any lack of conformity either under Article 37 (cure in case of early delivery) or under Article 48 (cure after date for delivery).[20] Also, certain actions or inactions of the buyer can preclude their right to declare price reduction. The buyer needs to initially give timely notice of the non-conformity to the seller, before declaring price reduction.[21] The content of declaration 'must clearly and unambiguously state that the buyer wishes to reduce the purchase price but need not include the technical term of price reduction'.[22] In *Natural Stone* case, the buyer lost its right to reduce the price, notwithstanding the defective quality of goods delivered.[23] The buyer failed to give proper notice specifying the lack of conformity of the goods, which corresponds to the general rule established in CISG Article 39(1). This article stipulates that the buyer loses the right to rely on a lack of conformity of the goods if they do not notify the seller and specify the nature of non-conformity within a reasonable tome after the buyer has discovered or ought to have discovered it. However, CISG Articles 40 and 44 acting as 'safety valves' help the buyer use price reduction.[24] These two articles are particularly designed to benefit buyers from developing countries, who often buy complex machineries and lack the technical knowledge needed for an immediate examination of these goods.[25] These articles protect the buyer when the notice about the defect goods is not given within the reasonable time prescribed by CISG Art 39(1). CISG Article 40 provides that if the seller knew or could not have been unaware of the non-conformity of goods, they are not entitled to rely on the provisions concerning buyer's examination and notification. CISG Art 44 deals with exempting the buyer from their notification duty, provided that they could raise a reasonable excuse for failure to give the required notice.[26]

CISG-online 575; *Bevarage Dispending System case* (2002) District Court Innsbruck, Austria, CISG-online 2985; *Dutch Leather case* (2010) District Court Dordrecht, Netherlands, CISG-online 4956; *Carbomat N.V. v Pric Advies B.V.* (2020) Court of Appeal Arnhem-Leeuwarden, Netherlands, CISG-online 5495.

[19] Schlechtriem and Schwenzer (n 9) 1025; Kroll, Mistelis and Viscasillas (n 3) 752.

[20] Schlechtriem and Schwenzer (n 9) 1026.

[21] See CISG Articles 35(3), 38, 39, 40 and 44. These articles deal with examination and notification duties of the buyer. CISG Arts 40 and 44 deal with the circumstances exempting the buyer from giving a timely notice.

[22] Kroll, Mistelis and Viscasillas (n 3) 756; Schlechtriem and Schwenzer (n 9) 1026; *Furniture case II* (1992) Court of First Instance Locarno Campagna, Switzerland, CISG-online 68; *Cowhides case* (1994) ICC Arbitration Case No. 7331, Paris, France, CISG-online 106.

[23] (2000) District Court Stendal, Germany, CISG-Online 592.

[24] CB Andersen, 'Exceptions to the notification rule – are they uniformly interpreted?' (2005) 9 *Vindobona Journal of International Commercial Law and Arbitration* 20, 26.

[25] 1980 Vienna Diplomatic Conference, March 25, 1980, Summary Records of Meetings of the First Committee, 21st Meeting, ¶ 42 (Ghestin), U.N. Doc. A/CONF.97/5.

[26] ibid; see also *US Cars Technologies S.a.r.l. v Auto Global Trade AG* (2021) Court of Appeal, Paris, France, CISG-online 5625.

3. Set-off

In a paper prepared for the Working Group for International Commercial Contracts for the new International Institute for the Unification of Private Law ('UNIDROIT') set of rules, Professor Jauffet-Spinosi highlighted the confusion that parties face in the context of international commercial contracts:

> The development of international commercial trade has created an assortment of Contractual interrelationships. It is no longer unusual for a party to find himself being at the same time both the creditor and the debtor to another party. The question arises whether the debt owed and the debt owing should be considered independent of each other, with each debtor obligated to perform without taking into account the existence of the debt owed to him, or whether one may consider the two debts linked because of their reciprocal nature?[27]

Such confusion stems partly from the fact whilst the basic definition of set-off is relatively straightforward and it appears to be recognised by most legal systems, the legal understanding of this doctrine lacks uniformity and is plagued by national intricacies. It is not simple to provide a thorough definition of set-off due to its complex nature. On a general level closely connected to commercial contracts, it can be defined 'as the setting of money cross-claims against each other to produce a balance'.[28] In other words, when two parties have mutual obligations arising from a contract, each party is entitled to set-off its obligations against the other party's obligation. Mutual deductions lead to the discharge of both obligations up to the amount of the lesser obligation.[29] Set-off is concerned with money claims and operates as far as the mutual obligations coexist, provided that the requirements set by the applicable law are satisfied. The essence of set-off is thus the existence of cross-demands. Because it can simplify and expediate performance obligations, set-off has become central to international commerce. It can particularly accelerate payment obligations, since a debtor may set off the cross-claim owed to them against the main claim which they to their creditor, and instead of paying money through bank transfer or other usual methods, they use the claim owed to them to pay the claim they owe.[30]

In the context of international sale of goods and for the purpose of this book, set-off is normally employed as a defence by the buyer against the seller's claim

[27] C Jauffret-Spinosi, 'Set-off' (2000), Paper prepared for the Working Group for the International Commercial Contracts, Meeting of the Drafting Group in Freiburg, 17–20 January 2001, p 2, see www.unidroit.org/english/documents/2001/study50/s-50-071-e.pdf; for further analysis of set-off in international arbitration see also C Kee, 'Set-off in international arbitration – what can the Asian region learn?' (2005) 2 *Asian International Arbitration Journal* 141.

[28] Derham (n 1) para 1.01; see also P Pichonnaz and L Gullifer, *Set-off in Arbitration and Commercial Transactions* (Oxford University Press, 2014) para 2.02.

[29] UPICC Official Comments Article 8.1, para 1; see also Fountoulakis (n 1) 7–8.

[30] PR Wood, *Set-off and Netting, Derivatives, Clearing Systems*, 2nd edn (Sweet & Maxwell, 2007) para 1-004.

for a sum of money.[31] In a report on UNCITRAL deliberations in the field of international arbitration in 2000, it was explained that sometimes during an arbitral proceeding the defendant would invoke a claim that they have against the claimant, not as a counter-claim, but as a defence for the purpose of a set-off. Interestingly, the doctrine of set-off appears to be absent under CISG.[32] Set-off should be deemed inadmissible under CISG given that this regime does not completely govern problems related to set-offs and given that this issue was not addressed during the drafting process. CISG's failure to govern set-off is widely accepted by the courts and scholars.[33] The next sections will analyse the doctrine of set-off within the legal regimes focused in this book.

A. SGA

The term set-off in English law has no uniform meaning and is a ready source of confusion. Although there have been abundant arguments attempting to explore the nature of set-off, its nature remains ambiguous and needs clarification within the context of sale of goods.[34] Set-off under SGA is a form of transaction set-off, which can be exercised where both claims are for money, are mutual and are so closely connected that the defendant's cross-claim impeaches the claimant's claim.[35] Transaction set-off incorporates not only equitable set-off but also 'abatement', which is a common law right, and is not, strictly speaking, a set-off.[36] Abatement functions as a way of reducing the buyer's contractual liability due to the seller's breach. When a defence is raised by the buyer who seeks to 'establish that the [seller] is not entitled to the full, or perhaps any part the price' due to the defective performance of the contract, the common law principle known as 'abatement' is turned on.[37] The buyer who has been sued for the price of goods can plead in an

[31] D Harris, David Campbell and R Halson, *Remedies in Contract and Tort*, 2nd edn (Butterworths LexisNexis, 2002) 61.

[32] Kroll, Mistelis and Viscasillas (n 3) 82; F Ferrari, 'Scope of application: Articles 4–5' in F Ferrari, H Flechtner and RA Brand (eds), *The Draft UNCITRAL Digest and Beyond: Case, Analysis and Unresolved Issues in the U.N Sales Convention* (Sellier, European Law Publishers, 2004) 107.

[33] *High Pressure Filters case* (2003) District Court Mönchengladbach, Germany, CISG-online 813; *Roller Bearings case* (1999) ICC Arbitration Case No. 9448, Zurich, Switzerland, CISG-online 707; *VW Passat and Golf case* (1998) Court of Appeal Munich, Germany, CISG-online 339; see also P Huber and A Mullis, *The CISG, A New Textbook for Students and Practitioners* (Sellier, European Law Publishers, 2007) 30: set-off is not covered by the CISG and it is for the private international law to designate the applicable rule to set-off; AE Butler, *A Practical Guide to the CISG: Negotiations through Litigation* (Aspen Publishers, 2007) para 8.06.

[34] See Derham (n 1); Spinosi (n 27) 2.

[35] E McKendrick, *Goode and McKendrick on Commercial Law*, 6th edn (Penguin Books, 2020) 556; see also Wood (n 30) para 1-011.

[36] Pichonnaz and Gullifer (n 28) para 5.04; see also Fountoulakis (n 1) 101.

[37] 'Abatement applied only to matters which reduced the actual value of the work performed, or the goods sold'. *Mellowes Archital Ltd v Bell Projects Ltd* (1997) 87 BLR 26; see also *Bluestorm Ltd v Portvale Holdings Ltd* [2004] EWCA Civ 289, [2004] HLR 49; *Addax Bank BSC v Wellesley Partners LLP* [2010] EWHC 1904 (QB).

action by way of defence showing a diminution in the value of the subject-matter of the contract.[38] This indicates that the buyer can on its own initiative reduce the price claimed by the seller to reflect the real value of the goods received.[39] *Mondel v Steel* is the case that has established this common law right.[40] In this case, a ship was to be built for the buyer, but the seller failed to do so in accordance with the contractual specifications.[41] The buyer insisted that if the amount of compensation exceeded or equalled the contract price, they were entitled to a verdict; if less, then they were entitled to a deduction.[42] They buyer was awarded damages, which were calculated by reference to the difference between the actual value of the ship at the time of delivery and what it would have worth if built to the contractual standard. According to Parke B Justice, an abatement is a deduction from the agreed price according to the difference between the goods as were and the goods as they ought to have been according to the contract.[43] He then explained that the injured buyer in sale of goods cases may not set-off by a proceeding in a cross action the amount of damages incurred due to the breach.[44] Rather, the buyer faced with a claim for the price of the goods can defend themselves by demonstrating that the subject matter of the contract, due to a breach of contract, worth less than it would have been were the contract properly performed. This substantive defence is explicitly recognised in SGA section 53(1)(a),

> Where there is a breach of warranty by the seller, or where the buyer elects (or is compelled) to treat any breach of a condition on the part of the seller as a breach of warranty, the buyer is not by reason only of such breach of warranty entitled to reject the goods; but he may—
>
> (a) set up against the seller the breach of warranty in diminution of extinction of the price.

To exercise set-off under this section, three requirements must be satisfied: first, both obligations are for money: the seller claims the contract price and the buyer sets off the claim for price against the breach of warranty in diminution or extinction of price. Second, both claims are mutual, as mutuality means that 'the demands must be between the same parties and they must be held in the same capacity, or right, or interest'.[45] Third, both claims are closely connected, as they

[38] Derham (n 1) 248; see further DP Friedman, 'Set-off – avoiding the confusion' (2011) 27 *Construction Law Journal* 494, 496.

[39] Fountoulakis (n 1) 110; see also Treitel (n 2) 50–51.

[40] [1841] 8 M & W 858, [1841] 151 ER 1288; see also *Mellowes Archital Ltd v Bell Products Ltd* (1997) 87 BLR 26 (CA); *Multiplex Constructions (UK) Ltd v Cleveland Bridge UK Ltd, Cleveland Bridge Dorman Long Engineering* [2006] EWHC 1341 (TCC).

[41] [1841] 8 M & W 858, [1841] 151 ER 1288.

[42] ibid, 1292.

[43] ibid, 1292.

[44] ibid, 1292.

[45] Derham (n 1) 472; see also *Axel Johnson Petroleum AB v MG Mineral Group* [1992] 1 WLR 270, 272.

must have arisen from the same transaction.[46] In *Gilbert Gilbert-Ash (Northern) Limited v Modern Engineering (Bristol) Limited*, the House of Lords gave force to this common law right and argued that this remedy is available as of right and does not lie within the discretion of any court to withhold it.[47] This remedy is independent of the doctrine of equitable set-off developed by the Court of Chancery, which operates mainly as a procedural defence. As such, an injured buyer can invoke abatement to defend against the seller's action and reduce damages from the price payable. Contrary to general set-off, the scope of abatement is narrow and applies only to certain types of contracts, particularly, contracts for the sale of goods and construction contracts.[48] Finally, it only applies to cross-claims, which reduce the value of the performance including delay in delivery of the goods.[49] Consequential loss cannot thus be addressed by set-off.[50]

B. UCC

According to the American Uniform Commercial Code, acceptance of goods occurs when the buyer, who has received the goods, and following a reasonable opportunity to inspect the goods signifies to the seller that the goods are conforming or that they will retain them in spite of their nonconformity.[51] This buyer must pay for accepted goods at the contract rate, on the basis of UCC Section 2-607(1). Buyer's rejection thereafter would be inconsistent with the principle that the property in the goods is transferred from seller to the buyer. This means that the only practical remedies are either asking the seller to repair the goods, or offset damages due to the breach incurred against the contract price. In the significant case of *Southern Concrete Products Company v L.A. Martin*, the seller commenced a legal action against the buyer to recover contract price for the bricks sold and delivered to the buyer.[52] The buyer counterclaimed that certain amount of the bricks were defective and that they had suffered loss as a result. The buyer in their counterclaim sought to reduce the contract price requested to reflect the loss incurred due to the poor quality of materials received. The Court of Appeals decided that where

[46] McKendrick (n 35) 556.

[47] [1974] AC 689; see also *Hanak v Green* [1958] 2 QB 9.

[48] See SGA section 53(1)(a) although this section appears to be wider than the common law abatement, since it relates to any breach of warranty and not just one which results in diminution of value of the goods (see the minority view of Windeyer J in *Healing (Sales) Pty Ltd v Inglis Electrix Pty Ltd* (1968) 121 CLR 584, 618).

[49] *Hanak v Green* [1958] 2 QB 9: see also *Young v Kitchin* (1878) 3 Ex.D. 127; *Newfoundland (Government of) v Newfoundland Railway Co.* (1888) 13 App.Cas. 199.

[50] *Davis v Hedges* (1871) LR 6 QB 687; *Mellowes Archital Ltd v Bell Products Ltd* (1997) 87 BLR 26 (CA).

[51] UCC section 2-606; see *Kasper Global Collection & Brokers, Inc v Global Cabinets & Furniture Mfrs. Inc.*, (2013) United States District Court, New York, 952 F.Supp.2d 542.

[52] (1972) Court of Appeals of Georgia, Division No.3, 126 Ga. App. 534; see also *Ag Services of America, Inc v DeBruce Grain Inc* (2001) Court of Appeals of Kansas, 19 P.3d 188.

the buyer has accepted the goods and has notified the seller of any deficiency, they may recover as damages for any nonconformity of tender the loss incurred in the ordinary course of events due to the seller's breach, as determined reasonably.[53] The buyer in the trial showed a proper measure of damages, based on an expert witness. The court held that the buyer was entitled to reduce the damages from the contract price and the seller's claim for reduced payment was dismissed.

Similar to SGA, transaction set-off is also regulated in UCC. Section 2-717 establishes that 'the buyer on notifying the seller of his intention to do so may deduct all or any part of the damages resulting from any breach of the contract, such as delay in delivery or a deficient quantity, from any part of the price still due under the same contract.[54] 'Breach of contract' is not defined by the code. According to case law, it refers to the seller's failure to supply conforming goods.[55] Non-conformity includes any seller's failure to perform according to their obligations under the contract.[56] UCC thus allows the buyer to deduct from the contract price all or any part of the damages caused by a breach of the contract by the seller. Such relief available in UCC is not limited to cases of breach of satisfactory quality requirement and include also late delivery,[57] provided the seller's breach is of the same contract under which the price in question has to paid.[58] The burden of proof is on the buyer to demonstrate that the seller has breached the contract and show the amount of damages deduced from the contract price. The buyer typically measures damages to be deduced using the difference-in-value formula, under which the buyer reduces the amount of seller's demand by difference in value between the contract price and actual value of the goods at the time of acceptance.[59] The requirement of being in the 'same contract' is difficult to demonstrate. In *Travenol Laboratories Inc v Zotal Ltd*, the Massachusetts Supreme Judicial court dealt with a dispute between a manufacturer of medical products and its Israeli distributor.[60] The manufacturer terminated the distributorship agreement and requested the price of goods sold and delivered. The distributor counterclaimed that they had a right to set off for breach of the distributorship agreement. In this case, the buyer

[53] (1972) Court of Appeals of Georgia, Division No.3, 126 Ga. App. 534, 535.

[54] *Ohline Corp. v Granite Mill*, (1993) Court of Appeals of Utah, 849 P.2d 602; see also *Corono Oro Inc v Thompson* (2002) Court of Appeal, 6th District, California, WL 471679.

[55] *American Exploration Co. v Columbia Gas Transmission Corp* (1985) United States District Court, S.D. Ohio 443 F.Supp. 14; *Flick Lumber Co., Inc. v Breton Industries, Inc* (1996) SC, Appellate Division, NY, 223 A.D.2d 779.

[56] UCC Official Comments, section 2-714.

[57] While in *Ohline Corp. v Granite Mill*, (1993) Court of Appeals of Utah, 849 P.2d 602, the court held that losses incurred due to the delay could be offset under UCC section 2-717, in *Accent Commercial Furniture Inc v P Schneider & Associates PLLC* (2013) United States Supreme Court, Appellate Division, New York, 110 AD 3d 1415, the court adopted a strict view, dismissing the buyer's offset against the purchase price due to late delivery. The court held that the buyer failed to demonstrate how the delay in delivering furniture company rendered the office space unusable.

[58] UCC Official Comments, section 2-717, para 1; see also WD Hawkland, CS Bjerre, LR Rusch and LT Garry, *Hawkland's Uniform Commercial Code Series* (Thomson Reuters, 2023) section 2-717, para 1.

[59] UCC section 2-714(2).

[60] (1985) Supreme Judicial Court of Massachusetts, Middlesex, 474 N.E. 2d 1070, 1073.

tried to rely on the alleged breaches of distributorship agreement to justify their non-payment for the goods, which were properly conforming and properly delivered. However, the court held that the buyer's obligation to pay for goods delivered and accepted does not arise under the same contract as the alleged breach of the distributorship arrangement by the seller.[61] This shows that the asserted breach must go to the essence of the transaction under which the seller sues to recover their price. The buyer thus should only rely on those breaches being directly related to the goods themselves.

In addition, the buyer must notify the seller of their intention to withhold all or part of the price due to the non-conformity of the goods received. In line with the general policies under section 2-717, no formality of notice is required and any language which reasonably show the buyer's intention for withholding their payment is sufficient.[62] The notice of intention to reduce damages from the contract price is in addition to the notice of breach which UCC also requires.[63] However, there is no reason why both notices cannot be combined in one communication to the seller, and in fact, it may be more practical and efficient to combine both. The notice of breach must be rendered within a reasonable time after the buyer discovers or should have discovered the breach, otherwise the buyer is barred from invoking any remedy. When a notice is provided too late under UCC, the buyer may not be able to salvage its right to remedies by characterising it as a notice of intention to set-off damages against contract price.[64] Finally, it should be noted that UCC entitles the parties to stipulate a damages clause for the seller's breach under section 2-718. The US courts have consensually held that the buyer's right to deduction under section 2-717 does not restrict the buyer's ability to reinforce the contract clauses or other common law rights.[65]

C. UPICC

Set-off under UPICC has a payment function and offers an effective and simplified mechanism of discharging a party's obligation, thus preventing from overlapping

[61] ibid, 1078; see also *Devine v Town of Nantucket* (2007) Supreme Judicial Court of Massachusetts, Nantucket, 870 N.E.2d 591; *Commerce Insurance Company v Szafarowicz* (2019) Supreme Judicial Court of Massachusetts, Worcester, 131 N.E.3d 782.

[62] UCC Official Comments, section 2-717, para 2.

[63] UCC section 2-607 (3).

[64] *A & G Const. Co., Inc. v Reid Bros. Logging Co., Inc.* (1976) Supreme Court of Alaska, 547 P.2d 1207; *Cullman Ventures, Inc. v MSS Associates, Inc.* (1996) New York Supreme Court, New York County, 31 U.C.C. Rep. Serv. 2d 111.

[65] In *Magid Glove & Mfg. Safety Co., LLC v Tower Intern., Inc.* (2012) United States District Court, Michigan, Southern Division, WL 5821814, the court even held that parties' contract may broaden scope of set-off beyond what is provided in UCC section 2-717. See also *Biegas v Quickway Carriers Inc* (2009) United States Court of Appeals, Sixth Circuit, 573 F.3d 365; *North Alabama Fabricating Company Inc v Bedeschi Mid-West Conveyor Company LLC* (2018) United States District Court, Kansas, 2018 WL 2198638.

payment or performances.[66] In other words, set-off can be employed to reduce the buyer's liability to pay the contract price. The buyer, who intends to exercise the right to set-off, is required to notify the seller.[67] This shows that a buyer can unilaterally and without judicial approval diminish or extinguish their obligation of paying the contract price, when the seller has not properly performed his obligations. The set-off under UPICC is similar to the notion of set-off in German Civil Code (the BGB).[68] In the German Civil Code, 'the set-off is basically a voluntary act invoked at the discretion of a party who seeks to take advantage of it'.[69] The buyer needs to declare that their debt is extinguished or diminished by way of set-off.[70] The Official Commentary on the UPICC Articles have, however, suggested that judicial intervention may be necessary to figure out whether the conditions of set-off are in fact satisfied.[71] If the buyer claims that the seller has breached their obligations and thus is liable for damages, the adjudicators will have to intervene and decide whether the seller is liable. The right of set-off has been expressly prescribed under UPICC Article 8.1.

Under UPICC, there are four requirements for exercising the right of set-off. The first requirement is mutuality of obligations and capacity. This requirement, which is common to all legal systems, states that each party should be the obligor and obligee of the other in the same capacity or in the same right. This requirement lies partially in the original procedural nature of set-off, which indicates that the court or arbitral tribunal is unable to drag third parties in its decision applying the set-off defence. Set-off is thus not permissible if the one party has an obligation to the other party in its own name but is an obligee of the other party in another capacity, for example as the absolute shareholder of a company.[72] Notwithstanding the fact that it is the same person, the assets belong to separate patrimonies. Second, both obligations must be of the same kind or nature: monetary obligation may be set-off only against a monetary obligation.[73] There is no need for the obligations to be fungible. As illustrated in the Official Commentary, two obligations to deliver wine of the same vineyard but not of the same year can be characterised as the obligations of the same kind but would not be fungible.[74] In addition, the same kind must be construed broadly to mainly consider the object of the obligations, by disregarding their legal origins, whether they would be contractual, tortious or public law. Third, both obligations should have become due.[75] Fourth,

[66] UPICC Art 8.5.

[67] UPICC Art 8.1.

[68] Division 4 (Extinction of Obligations), Title 3, § 387–396 of German Civil Code (BGB) deals with set-off.

[69] Spinosi (n 27) 3.

[70] BGB § 388: 'Set-off is effected by declaration to the other party'.

[71] UPICC Official Comments, Article 8.1, para 7.

[72] UPICC Official Comments, Article 8.1, para 2.

[73] ibid, para 3; see also S Vogenauer, *Commentary on the UNIDROIT Principles of International Commercial Contracts*, 2nd edn (Oxford University Press, 2015) 1045–46.

[74] UPICC Official Comments, Article 8.1, para 3.

[75] ibid, para 4.

both obligations should have been ascertained both as to their existence and as to their amounts.[76] An obligation is ascertained when the obligation itself cannot be challenged. It may be based on a valid and executed contract or a final judgment or arbitral award, which is final and not subject to review or appeal.[77] However, if the obligations of two parties have arisen from the same contract, the buyer is allowed to set off their obligation, even if the seller's obligation is not ascertained as to its existence or to its amount.[78] For instance, seller's obligation to pay damages may be ascertained as to its existence but not as to its amount. However, one qualification needs to be observed. Where parties have stipulated a specific date for performance, set-off is not permitted prior to that date when the obligee is not yet entitled to receive performance.

4. Evaluation

It is questionable whether SGA allows the remedy of price reduction. It has been strongly suggested that common law systems do not provide for the remedy of price reduction, when defective goods are delivered.[79] The main reason is that damages are more readily available in common law systems than under many civil law systems, as most of these systems allow buyers to claim damages only when the seller is at fault for his breach. The common lawyers are thus reluctant in recognising the nature and utility of the remedy of price reduction.[80] However, it has been suggested that 'a general remedy of price reduction can be implied from sections 30 and 53 of SGA'.[81] With respect, this opinion does not seem to be correct. SGA section 53 deals merely with the remedy of set-off, which comes into effect when there is a breach of warranty. Set-off is calculated on the basis of loss incurred by the buyer. In contrast, price reduction does not consider the loss and it is calculated according to the abstract relationship of the delivered goods and conforming goods. Bridge has noted this difference: 'in English law, the position is somewhat different, though superficially similar.'[82]

[76] ibid, para 5.
[77] ibid.
[78] ibid, para 7: Even though one of the obligations is contested, the right to set-off can be exercised because all the relevant obligations capable of being set-off arise from the same contract and can therefore be easily identified.
[79] Treitel (n 2) 108; see also AE William, 'Forecasting the Potential Impact of the Vienna Sales Convention on International Sales Law in the United Kingdom' in *Pace Review of the Convention on Contracts for the International Sale of Goods (CISG)* (Kluwer Law International, 2000–2001) 9.
[80] Schlechtriem and Schwenzer (n 9) 1024; Kroll, Mistelis and Viscasillas (n 3) 749; Bergsten and Miller (n 5) 255, 272.
[81] PA Piliounis, 'The remedies of specific performance, price reduction and additional time (Nachfrist) Under the CISG: Are These Worthwhile Changes or Additions to English Sales Law?' (2000) 12 *Pace International Law Review* 1, 19.
[82] MG Bridge, *The International Sale of Goods*, 4th edn (Oxford University Press, 2017) 708.

Take the following example. The contract price of a quantity of goods is £100 and at the delivery date, the market price has risen to £ 120. The delivered non-conforming goods are worth £108 at the delivery date. Under SGA, the buyer recovers £12, the difference between the market price of the conforming goods and the actual value of the goods. If price reduction applies, the goods has lost one-tenth of the value they should have had at the delivery date (£12 over £120) and the buyer recovers one tenth of the price paid: £10. Here, the buyer has the goods with a value of £108, plus the amount of £10. Therefore, the results of applying set-off and price reduction are different.

Nevertheless, SGA section 30 is functionally equivalent to price reduction under CISG Article 50. Professor Treitel has suggested that SGA section 30(1) applies a principle very similar to price reduction, in the case of short delivery of goods.[83] This section provides that 'where the seller delivers to the buyer a quantity of goods less that he contracted to sell, the buyer may reject them, but if the buyer accepts the goods so delivered he must pay for them at the contract rate'. The contract price is reduced proportionately to reflect the amount which the shortage bears to the full quantity contracted for.[84] The reference to 'contract rate' under SGA is comparable to the 'proportional' calculations stated in CISG Article 50 If the parties have stipulated a contract rate for each contract item, that item determines the proportion of value that the goods delivered had to the conforming goods.[85] Therefore, when there is a short delivery of goods, SGA section 30 is likely to reach the same result as price reduction under CISG Article 50.

There are two significant differences between the doctrine of set-off and the remedy of price reduction. The first and most obvious one revolves around their method of calculation. In the case of set-off, the price is *prima facie* reduced on the basis of the difference between the market price and the actual value of the goods. In contrast, price reduction is not dependent on actual loss being suffered, but merely dependent on the abstract relationship between the actual value of the goods delivered and the hypothetical value of conforming goods. This divergence can be evaluated in three different situations to see whether and to what extent the buyer's interest can be protected more effectively. First, when the market price of the goods has remained the same as the time of contract and the time of delivery, there would be no difference in the amount that could be claimed as set-off versus a price reduction. For instance, if a car is sold to a buyer for £10.000, and, at the time of delivery, its motor is deficient so that the car is worth only £8.000. The amount awarded as damages is £2.000: the difference between the market value of the conforming goods (£10.000) and the delivered goods. The same amount is reduced under price reduction, which is shown in the following equation.

[83] Treitel (n 2) 110.

[84] ibid, 109.

[85] Piliounis (n 81) 1, 19; see eg *Behrend & Co Ltd v Produce Brokers Co Ltd* (1920) 3 KB 530 (KB); *Biggerstaff v Rowatt's Wharf Ltd* (1896) 2 Ch 93 (CA); *Oxendale v Wetherell* (1829)109 ER 143 (KB).

$$\text{Reduced price}\left(£8.000\right) = \frac{\text{value of delivered }\left(\text{non-conforming goods}\right)\left(£8.000\right)}{\text{value of owed }\left(\text{conforming}\right)\text{ goods }\left(£10.000\right)} \times \text{contract price}\left(£10.000\right).$$

Under set-off, the buyer is left with £10.000 in value: a car valued at £8.000 plus £2.000 as the loss. Under price reduction, the buyer will also recover £2.000 since the car has lost one fifth of the value it should have had at the delivery date (£2.000 over £10.000). The buyer is left with £10.000 in value: £2.000 as the reduced price plus the car valued at £8.000. Accordingly, price reduction set-off can equally satisfy the buyer's expectation interest.

The second situation occurs when there a falling market and the contract price is reduced at the time of delivery. In the example given above, the contract price of the car is £10.000, and its market price has dropped to £8.000 at the delivery date. The value of the defective car is now £6.000. By exercising set-off, the buyer can reduce £2.000 from the contract price. However, under price reduction, the buyer is able to recover one quarter (£6.000, which is the value of the delivered goods, over £8.000, which is the value of the conforming goods) of the contract price, which results in £2.500, as the price reduced from contract price.

$$\text{Reduced price}\left(£7.500\right) = \frac{\text{value of delivered }\left(\text{non-conforming goods}\right)\left(£6.000\right)}{\text{value of owed }\left(\text{conforming}\right)\text{ goods }\left(£8.000\right)} \times \text{contract price}\left(10.000\right).$$

£10.000 – £7.500 = £2.500.

Through set-off, the buyer is left with £8.000 in value: a car valued at £6.000 plus £2.000 as loss. Under price reduction, the buyer is left with £8.500 in value: a car valued at £6.000 plus £2.500 as the reduced price. This shows that price reduction is not only able to satisfy the expectation interest of the buyer, but it also puts them in a better position financially if the contract is performed.

The third situation is when the parties encounter a rising market, and the contract price is increased at the time of delivery. In the same example, the market price of car is increased to £12.000 at the delivery date. The value of the defective car is now £9.000. Under set-off, the buyer is able to recover £3.000 as the difference between the market value of the conforming goods and the delivered goods. Under price reduction, the buyer is permitted to recover only one fourth (£3.000 over £12.000) of the contract price, which is £ 2.500:

$$\text{Reduced price}\left(£7.500\right) = \frac{\text{value of delivered }\left(\text{non-conforming goods}\right)\left(£9.000\right)}{\text{value of owed }\left(\text{conforming}\right)\text{ goods }\left(£12.000\right)} \times \text{contract price}\left(£10.000\right).$$

£10.000 – £7.500 = £2.500.

Under price reduction, the buyer's contractual expectancy is not fully recovered when the market is rising, whilst the set-off can more effectively satisfy the buyer's interest.

Another distinction relates to the rules limiting the availability of these remedies. Price reduction is subject to the buyer's duty to notify the seller of non-conformity and declaration of price reduction as well as the seller's duty to cure and.[86] In other words, if the seller cures their defective performance or the buyer does not timely notify the seller about deficiency or does not declare price reduction, the buyer is precluded from exercising price reduction.[87] Set-off, as it stands under SGA, UCC and UPICC, is also subject to declaration duty of the buyer.[88] But contrary to price reduction, the buyer is not required to notify the seller about non-conformity of the goods, if they wish to defend themselves by set-off. However, the rules limiting damages and hence the defence of set-off, ie, the foreseeability test or force majeure defence and the duty to mitigate are not applicable to price reduction.[89] The reason is that the buyer's right to price reduction does not depend on their actual loss suffered as a result of the reduction in the value of the goods.

In terms of the first criterion of 'preservation of relationship', both price-reduction and set-off appear to be suitable legal doctrines in maintaining and promoting the long-standing contractual relationship between the parties. Price reduction is primarily concerned with preserving the bargain between the parties and being employed as a means of rebalancing the performance required by both sides. Preserving the bargain can be accomplished through 'reformation of the original contract which retains the relative balance of the bargain made by the parties'.[90] Because modification of contractual terms is perceived as normal business behaviour when one or both parties encounter unexpected difficulties or express concerns with the original contract, a party refusing a reasonable modification request risks harm to its reputation with other potential contractual parties in the relevant industries or information networks. When this remedy is exercised, the parties renegotiate with each other and adjust the contract to the new situation without any resort to the court. This can maintain the parties' relations. The process of exercising the right to price reduction can provide an opportunity for the parties to cooperate with each other and that might lead to preserving the relations. For instance, in the Swiss *Furniture* case, governed by CISG, the buyer

[86] CISG Articles 39, 37, 48.
[87] CISG Articles 48, 50.
[88] UPICC Articles 8.3, 8.4; However, this declaration requirement is not expressed under SGA section 53(1), but in *Mondel v Steel*, the buyer of the ship declared his intention of deducing the contract price due to the breach.
[89] *Mondel v Steel* [1841] 8 M & W 858, [1841] 151 ER 1288; MG Bridge (ed), *Benjamin's Sale of Goods*, 11th edn (Sweet & Maxwell, 2022), paras 17-049-51; Piliounis (n 81) 1, 15.
[90] Bergsten and Miller (n 5) 255, 273.

notified the seller about the non-conformity and declared their intention of reducing the price to the seller.[91] The seller sent one of its representatives to inspect the goods. The representative communicated effectively with the buyer and the parties had the chance to get to know each other and to preserve their relations. Also, in the American case of *Maxxsonics USA, Inc. v Fengshun Peiying Electro Acoustic Comp. Car Amplifiers*, governed also by CISG, the seller manufactured amplifiers for the buyer for two years.[92] However, one of the deliveries of amplifiers was defective and the buyer sought to reduce the price. The buyer notified the seller about the deficiency and that encouraged the presidents of the seller's company and the buyer's company to cooperate in order to solve the problem. However, it should be noted that reformation and modifications may become particularly burdensome in certain circumstances and inhibit the informality and flexibility governing long term contractual relationship.

In addition, the defence of set-off also provides opportunities for the parties to maintain and enhance their relationships. Similar to price reduction, set-off enables the parties to negotiate and hold their relations when the seller has not yet started the legal proceedings claiming for the purchase price. In other words, there is a possibility for the buyer to send a letter to the seller requesting damages without any resort to the court.[93] This might provoke a process of communication by which the parties' relationships are likely to be enhanced. The defence of set-off, similarly to price reduction, requires the buyer to declare the deduction of the price due to the incurred loss. Set-off facilitates cooperation between the parties by requiring the buyer to declare the deduction of the price, which can prompt the seller to adhere to. In the significant case of *Industrial Lumber v Cherry Tree* governed by UCC, the buyer, following delivery of the goods, discovered that the goods were defective and notified the seller.[94] The buyer claimed that the seller repeatedly promised to do whatever it takes to make it right. In the meantime, because the buyer did not pay the seller invoice for its losses in using the earlier defective wood products, the buyer offset its alleged losses from subsequent invoices from the seller. The significance of the case lies in the fact that despite

[91] *Furniture case II* (1992) Court of First Instance Locarno Campagna, Switzerland, CISG-online 68.

[92] (2012) U.S. District Court for the Northern District of Illinois, CISG-online 2372; see also *Tiberias Plast Ltd v Sandretto Industrie S.r.l.* (2016) Court of Appeal Turin, CISG-online 6031; *Salzgitter Flachstahl GmbH v Riveco Generalsider S.p.A.* (2022) Italian Supreme Court, CISG-online 6009; *Products and Related Fittings case* (2022) ICC International Court of Arbitration, Paris, France, CISG-online 5909.

[93] H Beale and T Dugdale, 'Contracts between businessmen: planning and the use of contractual remedies' (1975) 2 *British Journal of Law and Society* 45, 45; see also S Deakin, C Lane and F Wilkinson, 'Contract Law, Trust Relations and Incentives for Co-operation: A Comparative Study' in S Deakin and J Michie (eds), *Contracts, Co-operation and Competition: Studies in Economics, Management and Law* (Oxford University Press, 1997); C Mitchell, 'Behavioural Standards in Contracts and English Contract Law' (2016) 33 *Journal of Contract Law* 234; C Mitchell, 'Remedies and Reality in the Law of Contract' in D Campbell and R Halson, *Research Handbook on Remedies in Private Law* (Edward Elgar, 2019).

[94] *Industrial Lumber & Plywood, Inc v Cheery Tree Cabinets* (2010) Court of Appeals of Minnesota, WL 155370.

the seller's default in earlier deliveries, the parties maintained their contractual and business relationship, with the buyer ordering and the seller supplying wood products. Similarly, in *Mondel v Steel*, the buyer declared the amount of compensation to which he was entitled.[95] This declaration might be viewed as a way for the parties to further cooperate with each other and possibly maintain their contractual relations. Also, in *Adam Metal Supply, Inc v Electrodex, Inc*, the manufacturer notified the supplier about the nonconformity of aluminium within the reasonable time after discovery and thereby, they subtracted from the purchase price.[96] These cases illustrate that the process of exercising the defence of set-off provides an opportunity for the parties to cooperate and maintain their relationship, despite difficulties in delivering full performance. The parties were, indeed, able to reach a compromise settling their disputes without necessarily referring to the court and that might have led to preservation of their relationships.

In terms of the second criteria, both remedies can maximise the expected value of the contract for the parties. Both price reduction under CISG and set-off under SGA, UCC and UPICC amount to minimising transaction costs incurred to both parties. Set-off and price reduction are self-help remedies, indicating that they can be employed by the parties without involvement of any third parties, ie, courts or arbitral tribunal. The parties are thus not faced with extensive transaction costs. They may only incur negotiation, and modification or alteration costs. The parties are mainly faced with the post-breach re-negotiation costs. Modification, facilitated by these remedies, is normal business behaviour when one or both parties encounter unexpected difficulties or express concerns with the original contract.[97] The parties would therefore be spared from litigation, which causes trouble and annoyance. Litigation costs money, directly in the form of legal and other expenses and indirectly in the form of loss of parties' time and disruption of their normal business activities. In addition, litigation is risky and way more burdensome. None of parties can ever be sure that they can overcome any of these obstacles and secure their putative black letter rights. Even if a favourable judgment is made, there may be little chance of successful enforcement, especially in international commercial contracts where parties place of businesses and assets are scattered in different jurisdictions.

Parties in a long-term commercial contract would strive to avoid litigation and as much as possible settle their disputes by invoking self-help doctrines. As has been discussed before, price reduction is an adjustment of the contract to the new situation.[98] The price is reduced to precisely show that the subject matter of the contract had from the outset been the non-conforming. These costs should not

[95] [1841] 8 M & W 858, [1841] 151 ER 1288, 1289.

[96] *Adam Metal Supply, Inc. v Electrodex, Inc* (1980) District Court of Appeal of Florida, 386 So.2d 1316; see also *Shreve Land Co., Inc. v J & D Financial Corp* (1982) District Court of Appeal of Florida, 3rd Circuit, 421 So.2d 722.

[97] RE Scott, 'A relational theory of default rules for commercial contracts' (1990) 19 *Journal of Legal Studies* 604.

[98] Schlechtriem and Schwenzer (n 9) 1024; see also Bergsten and Miller (n 5) 255, 273.

be high, as the parties in international sales of manufactured goods have normally done a substantial amount of negotiation and it would not be costly for them to alter the contract terms. For instance, in the *Clothes* case decided by a German district court, the representatives of the buyer and seller communicated several times concerning delivery of the goods and method of payment.[99] The buyer could easily demand a price reduction of 20 per cent by modern online technologies such as fax, email and Skype as part of this communication process. Also, in the *Cobalt sulphate* case, the parties communicated several times concerning the inspection of the quality and the quantity of manufacturing the cobalt sulphate.[100] Under set-off, the parties are conducting a very similar procedure, but with a different formula. The buyer is also deducting from the purchase price based on the buyer's damages, which is normally calculated by reference to the market price rule. Under the defence of set-off, the buyer should notify the seller about such deduction, however, this duty has not been expressly highlighted under SGA, UPICC or UCC. Accordingly, before the start of litigation or arbitration, very similar procedures are followed by the parties under both set-off and price reduction and as such they are equally able to minimise post-breach renegotiation costs.

It should be noted that the defence of set-off minimises transaction costs more effectively than price reduction, when the seller has not yet started legal proceedings. Set-off, as provided under SGA, UCC and UPICC, does not require adjustment of the contract as price reduction does require. The buyer can merely deduct the purchase price on the basis of the calculation used in the remedy of damages.[101] In other words, the buyer defending themselves by invoking set-off and the seller claiming for the purchase price do not need to alter the contract terms by following the specific formalities established under price reduction, such as the duty to notify within a reasonable time and adjustment of the price to the new situation. Thus, set-off is likely to be more efficient than price reduction.

In *Mondel v Steel*, the buyer informed the seller by declaration about reduction of the price due to the alleged breach of contract, without any assistance from the court.[102] This shows that the defence of set-off operates closely to 'a self-help remedy exercised outside judicial proceedings'.[103] It has been strongly claimed that the self-help remedies 'lie entirely within the control of [buyer] and [they] need no assistance from the court or from any third party to affect them'.[104] However, it should be noted that the self-help remedies are not completely within the control

[99] (1995) District Court Kassel, Germany, CISG-online 370.

[100] *Cobalt Sulphate case*, (1996) Supreme Court, Germany, CISG-online 135.

[101] ibid.

[102] [1841] 8 M & W 858, [1841] 151 ER 1288.

[103] Fountoulakis (n 1) 111; see also Derham (n 1) 102.

[104] Harris, Campbell and Halson (n 31) 43; see further MP Gergen, 'A theory of self-help remedies in contract' (2009) 89 *Boston University Law Review* 1397; DI Brandon, ML Cooper, JH Greshin, AL Harris and JM Head, 'Self-Help: Extrajudicial Rights, Privileges and Remedies in Contemporary American Society' (1984) 37 *Vanderbilt Law Review* 845, 913.

of the buyer and it is only the pursuit of those remedies that lies outside the court's control. This can give the buyer a valuable procedural advantage, by which the buyer can exercise their right before the start of the legal proceedings. But the seller can always object to such exercise, and the adjudicators should decide about the case. Accordingly, a second variation occurs when the seller disagrees with the reduction of price and thus starts legal proceedings against the buyer for the purchase price. Even if the seller reacts in this manner, the litigation costs under price reduction would be lower than in the case of set-off. It has been claimed that 'price reduction does not require any affirmative action by a court' and that the court does not have to delve into subjective circumstances surrounding each individual case.[105] However, this statement does not seem to be entirely correct. The court needs to realise whether the price reduction was fulfilled properly and the buyer has carefully performed according to the mathematical formula. But the court does not need to explore the relevant doctrines limiting damages, ie, foreseeability and mitigation. For instance, in the *Wine Bottles*[106] and *GMS Modules*[107] cases the courts did not investigate whether the loss actually occurred and whether it was foreseeable and also whether the buyer has performed their duty to mitigate. In these cases, if damages were claimed by the buyer, the court should have examined whether all those requirements were satisfied, which could considerably increase litigation costs. Following a costly litigation, it would seem unlikely that the parties continue their contractual relationship. Their contractual relationship may only continue if the parties have properly calculated the expenditures during the process of litigation in comparison with the fruitful relationship they may enjoy in the future.

[105] Sondahl (n 6) 255, 260.
[106] (2006) Court of Appeal Koblenz, Germany, CISG-online 1408.
[107] (2007) Court of First Instance Canton Zug, Switzerland, CISG-online 1722.

4

Compensation

1. Introduction

This chapter aims to survey damages under the four legal regimes (SGA, UCC, CISG, and UPICC). It is not the purpose of this section to provide an exhaustive exposition of the doctrines of either regime. Instead, the focus will be on the central aspects of damages, such as the aim of damages and general rules governing the measure of damages. Additionally, there will be an exploration of those aspects of the law of damages that shed light on the degree to which the criteria of the evaluative framework are satisfied. The rules and doctrines governing damages under these four legal regimes will be examined on the basis of the evaluative framework, established in the first chapter. First, the law of damages under the four legal regimes will be outlined, with the central aspects being identified and explained in the context of those four legal regimes. The doctrines governing damages under CISG and UPICC will be described together, as the relevant provisions have considerable textual uniformity, whereas UCC and SGA are somewhat different and their provisions will be surveyed separately. In the second part of this chapter, the major differences between the laws of damages under these four legal regimes will be compared and evaluated.

2. Nature and Aim of Damages

A. SGA and UCC

Damages are the standard remedy in common law systems, including the UK and the USA. The action for damages is thus always available, as of right, when a contract is broken and causes loss to the buyer.[1] Loss is a general term in

[1] For English law see: SGA section 51(1); *Robinson v Harman* [1848] 1 Ex 850, [1848] 154 ER 363; *Lock v Furze* [1866] 144 ER 722; *Wertheim v Chicoutimi Pulp Co* [1911] AC 301; *Johnson v Agnew* [1980] AC 367 (HL); E Peel, *Treitel on The Law of Contract*, 15th edn (Sweet & Maxwell, 2020) 988; For US law see RA Lord, *Williston on Contracts*, 4th edn (Thomson Reuters, 2023) para 64:1; D Frisch, *Lawrence's Anderson on the Uniform Commercial Code*, 3rd edn (Thomson Reuters, 2013) para 1; JJ White and RS Summers, *Uniform Commercial Code*, 6th edn (Thomson Reuters, 2010) 293. More generally see: JN Adams, 'Damages in sale of goods: a critique of the provisions of the Sale of Goods

commercial law and includes any harm to the injured party's economic position, any diminution in this party's financial position as a result of breach or this party's failure to acquire the use or economic advantage of a physical object.[2] Pecuniary or financial loss takes two main forms: first, normal pecuniary loss occurred because of breach, such as loss of bargain.[3] Second, consequential or incidental loss is constituted of expenditure including loss of profit, which is over and above the loss of bargain or loss of diminution in the value of the delivered subject matter of the contract.[4] Non-pecuniary loss includes, but is not limited to, pain and suffering, physical inconvenience, loss of enjoyment and mental distress.[5] As this book deals with commercial sales of goods, the focus will be on remedies for pecuniary losses. Commercial actors normally make contracts in order to make profits and maximise their wealth. Therefore, they will seek to achieve a remedy that will put them in a same financial position they would be in if the expected benefit had flown from the contract and might ignore the ways for compensating their non-pecuniary losses.

Under both English law and American law, the aim of an award of damages for breach of contract is to compensate the injured party for their loss incurred as a result of breach. Parke B in the remarkable English case of *Robinson v Harman* set out the general purpose of damages in the common law: 'The rule of the common law is that where a party sustains loss by reason of a breach of contract, he is, so far as money can do it, to be placed in the same situation, with respect to damages, as if the contract had been performed.'[6] A very similar approach was adopted by US courts. For instance, in *Ambrogio v Beaver Road Associates*, the court held that damages, in general, are awarded to make the injured party whole.[7] In other

Act and Article 2 of the Uniform Commercial Code' (2002) 9 *Journal of Business Law* 553, 553–54; D Campbell, 'Market damages and the invisible hand' in L DiMatteo and M Hogg (eds), *Comparative Contract Law* (Cambridge University Press, 2015).

[2] Peel (n 1) 990; D Harris, D Campbell and R Halson, *Remedies in Contract and Tort*, 2nd edn (Butterworths LexisNexis, 2002) 75; United States Restatement (Second) of Contracts (1981) section 347.

[3] J Edelman, D Varuhas and S Colton, *McGregor on Damages*, 21st edn (Sweet & Maxwell, 2022) para 2-003; Also, Lord Denning stated in *Parsons (Livestock) Ltd v Uttley Ingham & Co Ltd* that 'economic loss includes loss of profit or loss of opportunities for gain in some future transaction'. [1978] QB 791 (CA) 802.

[4] E McKendrick, *Goode and McKendrick on Commercial Law*, 6th edn (Penguin Books, 2020) 133.

[5] ibid, 132.

[6] [2001] 154 ER 363, 365; see also *Golden Strait Corp v Nippen Yusen Kubishika Kaisha (The Golden Victory)* [2007] UKHL 12, [2007] 2 AC 353; *Alfred McAlpine Construction Ltd v Panatown Ltd* [2000] 3 WLR 946 (HL) 987; *Omak Maritime Ltd v Mamola Challenger Shipping Co Ltd* [2010] EWHC 2026 (Comm); *BPE Solicitors v Hughes-Holland*, [2017] UKSC 21, [2018] AC 599, paras 31–33.

[7] (2003) Supreme Court of Connecticut, 836 A.2d 1183; see also *Windt v Shepards/McGraw-Hill, Inc.* (1997) United States District Court, Pennsylvania, 1997 WL 698182; *Protectors Ins. Service, Inc. v U.S. Fidelity & Guar. Co* (1998) United States Court of Appeals, 10th Circuit, 132 F.3d 612; *Genencor Intern., Inc. v Novo Nordisk A/S* (2000) Supreme Court of Delaware, 766 A.2d 8; *U.S. Naval Institute v Charter Communications, Inc.*, (1991) United States Court of Appeals, 2nd Circuit, 936 F.2d 692; *OneWest Bank, F.S.B. v Association of Owners of Kumulani at Uplands At Mauna Kea*, (2020) Supreme Court of Hawai'i, 456 P.3d 178.

words, the injured buyer is entitled to the benefit of their bargain and should be placed, as nearly as is possible through an award of money damages, in the position they would have been in had the seller fully performed the contract. An award of monetary damages being reasonably calculated should be sufficient to enable such buyer to obtain the promised performance from another party, thus satisfying its legitimate expectation interest. In other words, a reasonably precise measurement of damages makes the injured buyer whole, neither more nor less; in the sense that any greater amount operates to punish the breaching seller, resulting in unwarranted windfall to the buyer, while any lesser amount rewards the seller for their wrongful conduct in breaching the contract, thus failing to provide the buyer with benefit of the bargain they made.[8] Burrows explains that the 'expectation measure is ... the natural measure of recovery, since it accords directly with the underlying morality of promise keeping'.[9] Damages, therefore, seek to achieve the essential function of exchange, which is to realise the legitimate expected benefit.

B. CISG and UPICC

Contrary to SGA and UCC, CISG and UPICC does not give primary importance to the remedy of damages.[10] The international instruments have been influenced by civil law traditions, in which the injured party's primary remedy is specific performance. However, many civil law countries are increasingly permitting the recovery of damages as the preferred remedy.[11] CISG provides the general right for damages under CISG Art 74. This article indicates that 'damages for breach of contract by one party consist of a sum equal to the loss, including loss of profit, suffered by the other party as a consequence of the breach'. This article 'gives the tribunal the authority to determine the aggrieved party's "loss suffered ... as a consequence of the breach" based on the circumstances of the particular case'.[12]

[8] *Community Health Choice, Inc. v United States* (2020) United States Court of Appeals, 970 F.3d 1364.

[9] A Burrows, *Remedies for Torts, Breach of Contract, and Equitable Wrongs*, 4th edn (Oxford University Press, 2019) 20; see also MG Bridge, *The Sale of Goods*, 4th edn (Oxford University Press, 2019) 640; Edelman, Varuhas and Colton (n 3) paras 1-021-22; HG Beale (ed), *Chitty on Contracts, vol 1*, 34th edn (Sweet & Maxwell, 2022), para 26-001; A Burrows, 'Legislative reform of remedies for breach of contract: the English perspective' (1997) 1 *Edinburgh Law Review* 155, 157; LL Fuller and WR Perdue, 'The reliance interest in contract damages' (1936–1937) 46 *Yale Law Journal* 52, 54; MG Bridge, *The International Sale of Goods* (4th edn, Oxford University Press 2017) 461; DH Vernon, 'Expectancy damages for breach of contract: a primer and critique' (1976) 2 *Washington University Law Review* 179, 180.

[10] See CISG Article 45.

[11] See Article 918 ABGB (Allgemeines Burgerliches Gesetzbuch) (Austria); Section 241 BGB (Burgerliches Gesetzbuch) (Germany).

[12] CISG Advisory Council, 'Calculation of damages under CISG Article 74' (2006) Opinion n 6, para 1.1; see also I Schwenzer and P Hachem, 'The scope of the CISG provisions on damages' in D Saidov and R Cunnington (eds), *Contract Damages, Domestic and International Perspective* (Hart Publishing 2008) 95.

However, this article fails to clarify when and how a guilty party can be discharged of a damages claim. It also fails to provide any suitable method of valuation of the loss incurred.[13] Such a general, 'brief but powerful'[14] approach, although criticised strongly by several scholars, may be functionally appropriate because a breach of contract can happen in infinite variety of situations.[15]

Similar to CISG, UPICC has also recognised the general right to damages under the UPICC Article 7.4.1, lays down a general framework for the measurement of damages, however, it leaves the details to be determined by adjudicators. The structure and content of this article resembles the provisions of CISG on damages. Under UPICC, the right to performance seems to have been expressed in stronger terms than those found in common law regimes. It is enough for the aggrieved party to simply prove the non-performance and there is no need to prove the fault of breaching party.[16] According to the UPICC Official Comments, the injured party may request damages either as an exclusive remedy, for instance, damages solely be sought for delay in performance or for defective performance, or in conjunction with other remedies.[17] Thus, when the buyer seeks to terminate the contract, they may be entitled to receive compensation for the loss arising from fundamental breach leading to termination of contract.

Damages seeks to fully compensate the injured buyer for all losses suffered as a result of the breach of contract.[18] The principle of full compensation adopted in CISG Article 74, follows the Anglo-American strict liability principle, stipulating that the promisor is liable for all losses arising from non-performance, irrespective of fault.[19] 'Full compensation' principle implies that damages are designed to place the injured buyer in the same financial position they would have been had the breach not occurred. In other words, damages seek to give the buyer the benefit of the bargain or its expectation/performance interest.[20] Moreover, this article aims to protect the reliance interest (ie expenditures made in reliance on the existence of

[13] UNCITRAL Digest of Case Law on the United Nations Convention on Contracts for the International Sale of Goods (2016) Article 70, para 4.

[14] JO Honnold and HM Flechtner, *Honnold's Uniform Law for International Sales under the 1980 United Nations Convention*, 5th edn (Wolters Kluwer Law and Business, 2021) 755.

[15] ibid.

[16] UPICC Official Comments Article 7.4.1, para 1; see further JY Gotanda, 'Using the UNIDROIT Principles to fill gaps in the CISG' in Saidov and Cunnington (n 12).

[17] UPICC Official Comments, Article 7.4.1, para 2.

[18] P Schlechtriem and L Schwenzer, *Commentary on the UN Convention on the International Sale of Goods*, 5th edn (Oxford University Press, 2022) 1000.

[19] See *Indian Glass Mosaic Tiles case* (2013) Austrian Supreme Court, CISG-Online 2398 ('fault is not a requirement for liability for damages under the CISG'); *Seat Belts case* (2012) Court of Appeal Linz, Austria, CISG-online 2444: ('the CISG does not recognize any discharge of liability by proving lack of fault'); *DSM Dyneema B.V. v Electromichaniki Kimis EPE* (2009) Multi-member Court of First Instance Athens, Greece, CISG-online 2228.

[20] S Kroll, L Mistelis and PP Viscasillas, *UN Convention on Contracts for the International Sale of Goods (CISG) Commentary* (Hart Publishing, 2011) 991; see also Schlechtriem and Schwenzer (n 18) 1000; JY Gotanda, 'Awarding Damages under the United Nations Convention on the International Sale of Goods: A Matter of Interpretation' (2005) 37 *Georgetown Journal of International Law* 95, 98.

the contract) too.[21] For instance, in *TeeVee Toons Inc & Steve Gottlieb Inc v Gerhard Schubert GmbH*, governed by the CISG, the contract goods, which were packaging systems, were improperly manufactured and the buyer claimed damages, including money paid to the seller for the system and money paid to technician for repairing the system.[22] The court decided that the buyer was entitled 'to seek damages determined, inter alia, by article 74'.[23] By awarding damages, the buyer would be placed in as good a position they would have been in as if the contract goods were properly manufactured by the seller. While the CISG offers compensation for losses suffered from a breach of contract, it fails to describe in greater detail what losses are recoverable. Recoverability should necessarily be determined in light of the overall objective of the CISG, which seeks to achieve full compensation in accordance with the particular purpose of the contract.[24] Especially in cross-border sales transactions, the damages provisions should enable the buyer to obtain alternative, similar performance to the original contract. When damages are properly measured, the buyer should be able to acquire either similar goods or repair the defective goods and thus be placed in a good financial position as if the contract was fully executed. As Trietel remarked in 1976 that the outcome of the principle that damages are compensatory is that 'an award of damages should not enrich the claimant: [they] cannot recover more than [their] loss'.[25]

Like CISG, UPICC Article 7.4.2 provides that a party to a contract who has been aggrieved by the other party's non-performance of their obligations has a right to compensation for the full amount of harm sustained as a result of the breach. UPICC does not explain what 'full compensation' actually means. Instead, Article 7.4.2 (1) insists that it includes the making good of losses suffered by the injured party. This is very similar to the first sentence of CISG Article 74. However, it appears that the UPICC's coverage of compensation is broader than CISG. UPICC Article 7.4.2.(1) has used the term 'harm' rather than loss or injury, covering a wider range of losses than financial loss only. 'Harm' includes both the infliction of loss and the deprivation of gain, which may include 'non-pecuniary' harm. Loss is not defined or described by UPICC, but the official comments states that 'the notion of loss must be understood in a broad sense'.[26] This indicates that 'loss' may cover a reduction in the injured party's assets or an increase

[21] Schlechtriem and Schwenzer (n 18) 1001.

[22] (2006) District Court, Southern District of New York, United States., CISG-online 1272.

[23] ibid, 8.

[24] See eg *Zweirad Technik Dieter Könemann v C. Reinhardt A/S* (2007) Danish Supreme Court, CISG-online 2014; *Brassiere Cups case* (2008) Court of Appeal Rennes, France, CISG-online 1746; *Indian Glass Mosaic Tiles case* (2013) Austrian Supreme Court, CISG-online 2398; *Steel Products* (2021) ICC International Court of Arbitration, Zurich, Switzerland, CISG-online 5831.

[25] GH Treitel, 'Remedies for Breach of Contract' in D von Mehren (ed), *International Encyclopedia of Comparative Law*, Vol VII (Mohr, 1976) 25.

[26] UPICC Official Comments Article 7.4.2. para 2; see also B Zeller, *Damages under the Convention on Contracts for the International Sale of Goods*, 3rd edn (Oxford University Press, 2018) para 14.47; JY Gotanda, 'Recovering lost profits in international disputes' (2004) 36 *Georgetown Journal of International Law* 61, 83.

in its liabilities occurred when, not receiving the performance by the promisor, must borrow money to meet their commitments. Equally importantly, harm is extended to cover 'any gain of which [they] have been deprived as a result of non-performance'.[27] The notable example of the deprivation of gain is the loss of profit, which is sometimes called consequential losses, and is described as the benefit, which would normally have accrued to the injured party if the contract had been properly performed. From this, it can be concluded that the damages provisions in UPICC seek to protect the injured party's expectation interest.[28] Therefore, under both of these international instruments, an injured buyer is entitled to recover any net gain not being realised due to the seller's failure to perform their contractual obligations. The principle of 'full compensation' is so well settled that it can be presented as a general rule of private international law.

3. Measure of Damages

A. SGA

The buyer's right to claim damages for non-delivery is laid down in SGA section 51, which states that where the seller wrongfully neglects or refuses to deliver the goods to the buyer, the buyer may maintain an action against the seller for damages for non-delivery. The precise obligation of the seller under the contract should be considered in order to determine the meaning of 'wrongfully'. For the sake of convenience and legal certainty, it must be assumed that the seller would perform, if entitled to do so under the contract, in the manner least favourable to the buyer. As demonstrated in several cases, a seller is not liable in damages for failing to do what they are not bound to do.[29] For instance, where the contract provides for '200 tons, 5 per cent more or less', the margin is interpreted at the seller's advantage and that damages are measured on the basis of failure to deliver 190 tons.[30]

[27] UPICC Official Comments Article 7.4.2. para 2.

[28] UPICC Official Comments Article 7.4.2. para 2; S Vogenauer, *Commentary on the UNIDROIT Principles of International Commercial Contracts*, 2nd edn (Oxford University Press, 2015) 980; B Borisova, 'Art-75 CISG- PECL' in J Felemegas, *An International Approach to the Interpretation of the United Nations Convention on Contracts for the International Sale of Goods (1980) as Uniform Sales Law* (Cambridge University Press, 2007) 220; B Zeller, 'Remarks on the Manner in Which the Unidroit Principles may be used to Interpret or Supplement Article 76 of the CISG' (2003) 1 *Nordic Journal of Commercial Law* 1, 8; A Anastasi, B Hayward and SP Brown, 'An Internationalist Approach to Interpreting Private International Law? Arbitration and Sales Law in Australia' (2020) 44 *Melbourne University Law Review* 1, 14.

[29] *Lavarack v Woods of Colchester Ltd* [1967] 1 QB 278, 293; *The Mihalis Angelos* [1971] 1 QB 164: the alleged contract-breaker had an option to avoid the contract; damages were then assessed on the basis that they would have exercised that option.

[30] *Abrahams v Herbert Reiach Ltd* [1922] 1 KB 477, 482; see also *Cockburn v Alexander* (1848) 6 C.B. 791, 814; *Bunge Corp New York v Tradax Export SA, Panama* [1981] 1 W.L.R. 711 HL; *Paula Lee Ltd v*

The minimum legal obligation of the seller is thus the basis for assessing damages to compensate the loss incurred.

The general measure of damages is reflected in SGA section 51(2): 'The measure of damages is the estimated loss directly and naturally resulting, in the ordinary course of events, from the seller's breach of contract'. This rule applies where there is no available market for the contract goods, or where the 'prima facie' rule in SGA section 51(3) is not applicable. For instance, in *Air Studios (Lyndhurst) Limited t/a Air Entertainment Group v Lombard North Central Plc*, the buyer intended to use the goods in a filming business.[31] The goods were unique, second-hand and finding an available market for them was almost impossible. It was established that there was no ready availability of an AMS Neve Gemini DFC system either in August 2011 or at all.[32] Alternatively, the buyer purchased similar goods, which could be used in their business. The court awarded damages, which was calculated as the difference between the contract price of £100,000 and the cost of obtaining the nearest equivalent second-hand equipment, together with interest.[33]

Due to a unique feature of SGA, rather than considering section 51(2), section 51(3) should be considered first.[34] This means where there is an available market, within a reasonable time after the breach, for the goods in question the prima facie rule is that damages is calculated on the basis of the difference between: (a) the market price of the relevant goods at the time fixed for delivery and at the place fixed for delivery; and (b) the contract price.[35] Lord Wilberforce in *Bremer Handelsgesellschaft mbH v Vanden-Avenne Izegem PVBA* clarified that the prima facie rule in SGA section 51 provide for damages to be ascertained by reference to the price as on the last day for performance.[36] The method of calculation for this prima facie rule is called the 'abstract' method.[37] SGA section 51(3), which

Robert Zehil & Co Ltd [1983] 2 All ER 390; *Dhanani v Crasnianski* [2011] EWHC 926 (Comm); [2011] 2 All ER (Comm) 799.

[31] [2012] EWHC 3162 (QB); [2013] 1 Lloyd's Rep 63; see also *Pagnan (R) & Fratelli v Corbisa Industrial Agropacuaria* [1970] 1 WLR 1306.

[32] [2012] EWHC 3162 (QB); [2013] 1 Lloyd's Rep 63, para 84.

[33] ibid, paras 104–106.

[34] SGA section 51(2) normally applies when there is no available market for the goods in question. One way to measure the 'value' of goods for which no substitutes are available is to consider the subjective or idiosyncratic value of the goods, see *Ruxley Electronics and Construction Ltd v Forsyth* [1996] 1 AC 344, 360; *Farley v Skinner* [2001] UKHL 49, [2002] 2 AC 732, 748; *Galtrade v BP Oil International Ltd ('The Pioneer')* [2021] EWHC 1796 (Comm), [2022] 1 Lloyd's Rep 129.

[35] SGA section 51(3); *Slater v Hoyle & Smith Ltd* [1920] 2 KB 11(CA) 12; see further *Rodocanachi Son & Co v Milburn Bros* [1886] 18 QBD 67; *British Westinghouse Electric& Manufacturing Co Ltd v Underground Electric Railways Co* [1912] AC 673 (HL); *William Bros v Ed T Agius Ltd* [1914] AC 510 (HL); *Kwei Tek Chao (t/a Zung Fu Co) v British Traders & Shippers Ltd* [1954] 2 WLR 365 (QB); *Johnson v Agnew* [1979] 2 WLR 487 (HL); *Air Studios (Lyndhurst) Ltd v Lombard North Central Plc* [2012] EWHC 3162 (QB); [2013] 1 Lloyd's Rep 63; *Bominflot Bunkergesellschaft fur Mineralole mbH & Co v Petroplus Marketing AG* [2012] EWHC 3009 (Comm); [2013] 1 All ER (Comm) 610; *BP Oil International Ltd v Glencore Energy UK Ltd* [2022] EWHC 499 (Comm).

[36] [1978] 2 Lloyd's Rep 109.

[37] GH Treitel, *Remedies for Breach of Contract: A Comparative Account* (Oxford University Press, 1988) 111.

highlights the market price rule, is premised on the assumption that the buyer refers to the market and purchases substitute goods with the difference between the contract price and the market price, thus satisfying their expectation interest.[38]

However, rather than market price rule, the compensatory principle was adopted in *Bence Graphics International Ltd v Fasson UK Ltd*.[39] In this case, the buyer contracted to purchase vinyl film on which they printed words and numbers and which they then sold to end users. The film supplied tended to degrade and the decals became illegible, but remarkably few end users actually sued. At first instance the buyer was held entitled to the difference between the value of the goods at the time of delivery and the value they would have had if they had fulfilled the warranty. But the Court of Appeal held that the market value rule would give the buyer 'more than his true loss'. Rather, the correct measure of damages was the actual loss suffered by the buyer and that damages would be based not on the difference between the value of the goods as delivered and warranted but on the buyer's liability to the subsequent or ultimate users of the product arising from the defects constituting a breach of the seller's warranty.[40] The buyer was thus entitled to actual loss from those that sued, which was limited to the nominal damages of £22,000 as the value of returned goods.[41] The buyer was awarded no damages in respect of the vinyl that were passed on to sub-buyers in the form of decals. However, the prima facie rule was favoured in *Slater v Hoyle & Smith Ltd*,[42] which has similar factual circumstances to *Bence* case. In *Bence*, the seller knew that the buyer would sell on to others after substantially converting the goods into another product, and the court ruled that the parties contemplated that the measure of damages for defects in the goods should be the extent of the buyer's liability to those others resulting from the defect.[43] Therefore, damages were measured on the basis of SGA section 53(2): 'the estimated loss directly and naturally resulting from the seller's breach of contract'. However, *Bence* is exceptional and should not be followed for an important reason. The implication of the reasoning in this case would be that a seller of deficient goods would be treated as being free from liability to the buyer if it happens that a subsequent sub-buyer, with whom the original seller has not dealings, does not complain of their quality. In other words, 'any windfall which the buyer may have obtained was obtained at the expense, or perhaps more accurately by the grace, of such of the users of the decals as made no claims against them'.[44] This sort of damages calculation requires a close scrutiny

[38] MG Bridge (ed), *Benjamin's Sale of Goods*, 11th edn (Sweet & Maxwell, 2022) para 17-004.

[39] [1998] QB 87 (CA); similar reasoning and decision was adopted in *Saipol SA v Inerco Trade SA* [2014] EWHC 2211.

[40] [1998] QB 87 (CA) 87; for further analyses about similar cases see MG Bridge, 'The market rule of damages assessment' in Saidov and Cunnington (n 12); MG Bridge, 'Markets and damages in sale of goods cases' (2016) 132 *Law Quarterly Review* 405.

[41] [1998] QB 87 (CA) 91.

[42] [1920] 2 KB 11 (CA).

[43] [1998] QB 87 (CA) 97.

[44] GH Treitel, 'Damages for breach of warranty of quality' (1997) 113 *Law Quarterly Review* 188, 194.

of subsequent contracts. The sub-buyer might also desist from any legal action for various reasons. There might be an exemption clause in the contract between the buyer and sub-buyer or the sub-buyer might merely refrain from starting any legal action, but they might change his mind at some future point.

The overriding compensatory principle was later reinforced by the court's decision in remarkable case of *Golden Strait Corp v Nippon Yusen Kubishika Kaisha (The Golden Victory)*.[45] The most crucial issue was that the charterer renunciated the contract by making it clear, by words or conduct, that they were no longer willing to perform their future obligations under the charter. The difficult and somewhat uncertain task was turned on when the owners sought to recover damages for the period between 17 December 2001 and 6 December 2005. Since the breach was anticipatory, the arbitrators had to speculate the amount of damages that would have placed the owners in a position as if no breach had occurred and the contract would have been fulfilled. The charterers maintained that damages should not be awarded beyond 20 March 2003, when the Second Gulf War started. At the time when the charterers' repudiation was accepted, war was far from inevitable. It was found to be no more than a possibility. There was indeed a clause in their contract that entitled the charterers to terminate the contract in the event of the outbreak of war or similar events. A majority of the House of Lords decided in the charterers' favour and held that the owners should not be given any damages after 20 March 2003, ie the outbreak of the war, as that contract clause would have entitled the charters not to perform after that date.[46] The House of Lords' decision, which departed from the market price rule, effectively holds that events subsequent to the breach should be considered in the assessment of damages. Despite the searing criticism of this decision that may impair the commercial certainty, the Supreme Court in *Bunge SA v Nidara BV*,[47] unanimously reaffirmed the compensatory principle upheld in *Golden Victory*. The Supreme Court thus made it clear that to satisfy the compensatory principle, the claimant's ability to perform should be taken into account when damages are to be assessed.[48]

B. UCC

As explained before, the fundamental principle underlying contract damages is that of compensation.[49] The injured buyer is thus generally entitled to damages in an amount reasonably measured to make them whole.[50] Damages are measured

[45] [2007] UKHL 12, [2007] 2 AC 353.
[46] ibid, para 22.
[47] [2013] EWCA Civ 1628 SC, [2015] UKSC 43.
[48] ibid, para 23.
[49] See section 2(A) above.
[50] Lord (n 1) para 64:1; see also *Tongish v Thomas* (1992) Supreme Court of Kansas, 840 P.2d 471; *United Vaccines, Inc. v Diamond Animal Health, Inc* (2006) United States District Court, Wisconsin, WL 1666271.

on the basis of the pecuniary losses incurred to the buyer, rather than on the basis of the benefits gained by the seller as a result of the breach. Of course, the parties enjoy freedom of contract to incorporate liquidated damages, invoked by the seller's breach, governed by sections 2-719 and 2-718.

UCC Article 2 prescribes two alternative methods for measuring damages: (i) the cover price set forth in section 2-712 and (ii) the market price as set forth in section 2-713. In light of this arrangement, UCC primarily encourages the injured buyer to make a substitute transaction as soon as reasonably possible prior to claiming for damages. It should be noted that the cover price method was not a recognised remedy under the Uniform Sales Act, the law prior to UCC.[51] Similar to English sales law, the law used to be the contract-market formula or the abstract method of damages calculation, which placed the buyer in the same position as performance would have, on the assumption that the buyer would purchase substitute goods. UCC section 2-712 seeks to achieve this goal with greater precision. UCC section 2-712(3) expresses the policy that cover is not a mandatory remedy for the buyer. The buyer thus enjoys the freedom to choose between making a substitute transaction and damages for no delivery under section 2-713. UCC section 2-712(1) states that following a breach, the buyer may cover by making, in good faith and without unreasonable delay, any reasonable purchase of or contract to purchase goods in substitution for those due from the seller. The next subsection, ie section 2-712(1) articulates the method of calculation of damages: 'the buyer may recover from the seller as damages the difference between the cost of cover and the contract price together with any incidental or consequential damages as hereinafter defined (section 2-715), but less expenses saved in consequence of the seller's breach'. The concept of 'cover' is flexible and necessarily encompasses a series of contracts or sales as well as a single contract or sale.[52] It even includes contracts for sale of the goods not identical with those agreed to originally but commercially usable as reasonable substitutes under the circumstances of the particular case. According to the Official Comments, the test of proper cover is whether at the time and place the buyer acted in good faith and in a reasonable manner and it does not matter that the method of cover used was proved to be the cheapest or most effective.[53] 'Cover' is intended to provide the buyer with the goods needed and to eliminate what may be a difficult task of determining the damages by the difference between the market price and the contract price.[54] In most of sale

[51] Uniform Sales Act section 67.

[52] UCC Official Comments, section 2-712:1, para 2; see also WD Hawkland, CS Bjerre, LR Rusch and LT Garry, *Hawkland's Uniform Commercial Code Series* (Thomson Reuters, 2023), section 2-712:1; *Jasmin v Ulyssese* (2006) Supreme Court, Appellate Term, New York, 13 Misc.3d 127(A); *Sun Pacific Marketing Co-op., Inc. v DiMare Fresh, Inc* (2011) United States District Court, California, WL 3568539; *Export Development Canada v Electrical Apparatus & Power, L.L.C.* (2008) United States District Court, New York, WL 4900557.

[53] UCC Official Comments, section 2-712:1, para 2.

[54] *McGinnis v Wentworth Chevrolet Co* (1983) Supreme Court of Oregon, 668 P.2d 365; *Cumberland County Improvement Authority v GSP Recycling Co., Inc* (2003) Supreme Court of New Jersey, Appellate

of goods cases, the operation of this section is straightforward. In *Laredo Hides co v H&H Meat Products Co*, after the seller's breach of contract was demonstrated, the court applied this basic formula and concluded that the buyer was entitled to the difference between the cover price and the contract price.[55] In addition, the buyer was awarded incidental damages for transportation costs and handling charges, incurred due to the cover purchase made by the buyer. For a cover transaction to be used to measure the buyer's damages, the cover must comply with the ambiguous requirements of 'good faith' and 'without unreasonable delay'. While good faith is a slippery and vague concept, it is not devoid of meaning. UCC section 1-201(b)(20) states that 'good faith means honesty in fact and the observance of reasonable commercial standards of fair dealing'. This section has thus established both a subjective standard for measuring good faith and an objective standard. As noted in the Official Comments, the buyer is given wide latitude to act reasonably under the circumstances and their focus should be on making a cover transaction in a way that the replacement goods are 'commercially usable as reasonable substitutes under the circumstances of the particular case'.[56] The terms of the substitute transaction also need not be identical with the terms of the original breached transaction. The presumption is that the buyer acts in good faith when making a cover transaction, unless they knowingly and without a legitimate reason avoid a less expensive market in favour of a more expensive one. A reasonable basis for choosing a more expensive cover might be that the goods are of higher quality, the goods would be delivered more immediately or the seller is more reliable. In *TVI, Inc. v Infosoft Technologies, Inc.*, although the replacement printers were purchased more expensively than the original contract price, the court found the cover was reasonable and in good faith.[57] In this case, the buyer made reasonable efforts by making enquiries to other dealers, had inadequate experience of purchasing used printers. They also needed the printers in a hurry.

If the substitute transaction is not complete or if it fails to qualify as cover, the buyer may still seek damages under UCC section 2-713.[58] This section established

Division, 818 A.2d 431; *Gulf Power Co. v Coalsales II, LLC* (2013) United States Court of Appeals, Eleventh Circuit, 522 Fed. Appx. 699.

[55] (1974) Court of Civil Appeals of Texas, 513 SW 2d 210.

[56] UCC Official Comments, section 2-712, para 2; see also *Hessler v Crystal Lake Chrysler-Plymouth, Inc.* (2003) Appellate Cour of Illinois, 788 N.E.2d 405; *Vitol S.A., Inc. v Koch Petroleum Group, LP*, (2005) United States District Court, New York, 58 U.C.C. Rep. Serv. 2d 545; *Sun Pacific Marketing Co-op., Inc. v DiMare Fresh, Inc.* (2011) United States District Court, California, 2011 WL 3568539; *Union Tank Car Company v NuDevco Partners Holdings, LLC* (2019) Appellate Court of Illinois, Second Division, 123 N.E.3d 1177.

[57] (2008) United States District Court, Missouri, 2008 WL 239784.

[58] *Turner v NJN Cotton Company* (2015) Court of Appeals of Texas, 485 S.W.3d 513; see also E Schneider, 'UCC § 2-713: a defence of buyer's expectancy damages' (1986) 22 *California Western Law Review* 233; RR Anderson, 'An overview of buyer's damage remedies' (1988) 21 *Uniform Commercial Code Law Journal* 28; RR Anderson, 'Damage remedies under the emerging Article 2- an essay against freedom' (1997) 34 *Houston Law Review* 1065; D Frisch, 'The compensation myth and UCC Section 2-713' (2014) 90 *Brooklyn Law Review* 173; RR Anderson, 'A look back at the future of UCC damages remedies' (2018) 71 *Southern Methodist University Law Review* 185.

the market price rule and provides that the measure of damages for non-delivery or repudiation by the seller is the difference between the market price at the time when the buyer learned of the breach and the contract price, together with any incidental and consequential damages provided in section 2-715, but less expenses saved in consequence of the seller's breach.[59] The formula offered in this section would yield approximately the same amount of damages in non cover cases against the seller as the previous section would have yielded had the buyer made substitute transactions. As stated by the Official Comments, the market price rule provides a remedy which is completely alternative to cover transactions and applies only when and to the extent that the buyer has not covered.[60] According to one critical scholar's view, this section is entirely hypothetical, implying that the buyer is not required to use the market and obtain substitute goods.[61] *Turner v NJN Cotton Company* confirmed that the buyer is entitled to recover damages based on the market price rule even if they have elected not to make a substitute transaction.[62] Finally, the place for calculating damages is the place of tender or the place of arrival if the goods are rejected, and the crucial time is when the buyer learns of the breach.[63]

C. CISG and UPICC

General measures of damages under CISG and UPICC are functionally the same. These legal regimes have provided similar mechanisms for calculating damages as well as comparable doctrines limiting damages. Damages are prima facie measured based on the substitute transaction actually concluded by the buyer following the breach of contract.[64] Under the so called 'concrete method' of calculation of damages, the buyer is expected to make a substitute transaction and the difference between the price under the original contract and the substitute contract constitutes the loss that can be recovered by damages.[65] If the buyer did not succeed in making a substitute transaction, they can recover the difference between the contract price and the current price at the time of termination of contract.[66]

CISG Article 75 and UPICC Article 7.4.5 have adopted similar principles. Following the seller's breach, the buyer is expected to make a reasonable substitute

[59] For detailed analysis of this section see R Childres, 'Buyer's remedies: the danger of section 2-713' (1977–1978) 72 *Northwestern University Law Review* 837.

[60] UCC Official Comments, section 2-713, para 5.

[61] R Childres, 'Buyer's remedies: the danger of section 2-713' (1977–1978) 72 *Northwestern University Law Review* 837, 842.

[62] (2015) Court of Appeals of Texas, 485 S.W.3d 513; see also *Jon-T Farms, Inc. v Goodpasture, Inc.* (1977) Court of Civil Appeals of Texas, 554 S.W.2d 743, 749.

[63] UCC Official Comments, section 2-713, para 1.

[64] CISG Article 75; UPICC Official Comments Article 7.4.5.

[65] CISG Advisory Council, 'Calculation of damages under CISG Articles 75 and 76' (2008) Opinion n 8, para 2.1; see also Schlechtriem and Schwenzer (n 18) 1029–30; Zeller (n 26) 141.

[66] CISG Article 76; UPICC Official Comments Article 7.4.6.

transaction and within a reasonable time in order to acquire similar goods. The 'concrete method' of measurement of damages crystallises the principle that the buyer should take reasonable steps in minimising the loss. Under both regimes, avoidance of the contract is required to conduct a substitute transaction. It is indeed the declaration of avoidance that terminates the rights of the parties under the contract and gives the aggrieved party the freedom to seek its performance elsewhere.[67] Identifying and making a substitute transaction will be particularly crucial when the parties have been in a long-term relationship and the goods have been specially manufactured or for some other reason are so unique that it will be difficult to establish a "current" price.[68] Parties in a long-term relationship may have already established a deep understanding of each other's business and interests. A commercial buyer in such a relationship may require and expect highly specific goods, which may then be difficult to be gained in a brand new, substitute transaction. The substitute transaction should be made in a reasonable time and in a reasonable manner. These requirements seek to avoid from unfairly imposing a liability on the guilty party for the loss which the injured party caused through malicious conduct.[69] The buyer is expected to act as a careful and prudent businessman and observe the relevant practice of the pertinent trade when making the substitute contract.[70] This indicates that whether a cover transaction is reasonable depends on the circumstances. It was suggested that an innocent buyer should make 'a cover purchase at the lowest price reasonably possible'.[71] However, a more accurate suggestion is that if the buyer makes a cover purchase with a price higher than the market price, they may have trouble in demonstrating that they had acted reasonably.[72] In certain situations, a reasonable cover transaction may entail purchasing over and above the market price. For example, in *Chicory Harvesting Machinery* case, the buyer who run an agricultural business contracted to purchase a self-driving harvesting machine.[73] The seller failed to deliver the machine. The buyer purchased a substitute machinery immediately to be used for harvesting season. While the purchase of this machinery was significantly higher in price than the originally ordered machine, it was the most favourable alternative on the

[67] CISG Advisory Council, 'Calculation of damages under CISG Articles 75 and 76' (2008) Opinion n 8, para 2.3.3; UPICC Official Comments Article 7.4.5, para 1; Vogenauer (n 28) 997.
[68] Honnold and Flechtner (n 14) 770.
[69] UPICC Official Comments Article 7.4.5. para 1; Vogenauer (n 28) 999.
[70] *Chemical Fertilizer case* (1995) ICC Arbitral Award, Basel, Switzerland, CISG-online 526; *Hewlett-Packard France v Matrox Graphics Inc* (2020) Superior Court of Québec, Cananda, CISG-online 4876. CISG Advisory Council, 'Calculation of damages under CISG Articles 75 and 76' (2008) Opinion n 8, para 2.3.1; UNCITRAL Digest of Case Law on the United Nations Convention on Contracts for the International Sale of Goods (2016) Article 75, para 10.
[71] Schlechtriem and Schwenzer (n 18) 1327.
[72] B Nicholas, 'The Vienna Convention on International Sales Law' (1989) 105 *Law Quarterly Review* 201, 231; see also HM Flechtner, 'Remedies under the New International Sales Convention: The Perspective from Article 2 of the U.C.C.' (1998) 8 *Journal of Law and Commerce* 53, 54.
[73] (2021) Switzerland Federal Supreme Court, CISG-online 5693.

market at the time. The court held that a higher price could be justified by the short amount of time available to conclude a replacement contract.[74]

Alternatively, the buyer may recover the difference between the terminated contract and the current price for the contract goods, if they have not made a substitute transaction, as stated in CISG Article 76 and UPICC Article 7.4.6. Conversely, where a substitute transaction has been made, concrete calculation of damages takes precedence. The market price rule is called the 'abstract' method of calculating damages, as the buyer does not actually need to make a new contract.[75] The concept of 'current price' is vague under these legal regimes. As indicated in the second part of UPICC Article 7.5.6, it can be argued that current price is functionally similar to the market price and should be understood as the price generally charged for goods of the same kind, traded in the same business under comparable circumstances at a particular location.[76] However, the requirement that a current price exists does not require that there be an official or unofficial market quotation for the goods in question.[77]

4. Remoteness of Loss and the Mitigation Principle

A. SGA

The buyer must show that their loss was directly caused by the breach and was not too remote or unforeseeable for the seller.[78] The necessity of foreseeability of damages is premised on the view that it is unfair to a seller, and imposes too great a burden, to be liable for losses that they could not have reasonably contemplated.[79] In addition, the remoteness test makes explicit what is implicit, that those losses are recoverable by damages that arise in the usual course of events and fell within the reasonable contemplation of the parties at the date of formation of contract. The latter requirement implies that the law aims to scrutinise the intention of parties at the time of conclusion of contract and objectively determine their

[74] ibid; see also *Chemical Fertilizer case* (1995) ICC Arbitral Award, CISG-online 526; *Jewellery* (2000) Austrian Supreme Court, CISG-Online 581; *Brassiere Cups case* (2008) Court of Appeal Rennes, France, CISG-online 1746.

[75] See section 2-2-5-1.

[76] See also Schlechtriem and Schwenzer (n 18) 1336; see also Kroll, Mistelis and Viscasillas (n 20) 1026–27; Zeller (n 26) 114–15; D Saidov, *The Law of Damages in International Sales, The CISG and Other International Instruments*, 2nd edn (Hart Publishing, 2022) 201; UPICC Official Comments 7.4.6, n 2.

[77] CISG Advisory Council, 'Calculation of damages under CISG Articles 75 and 76' (2008) Opinion n 8, para 4.3.1.

[78] *Hadley v Baxendale* [1854] 9 Ex 341, [1854] 156 ER 145; *Boys v Chaplin* [1971] AC 356 (HL); *Wroth v Tyler* [1974] Ch 30 (Ch); *Transfield Shipping Inc v Mercator Shipping Inc* [2008] UKHL 48, [2009] 1 AC 61; SGA section 51(2); see also Treitel (n 37) 151; Beale (n 9) 1626.

[79] Burrows (n 9) 76.

presumed business intention.[80] The courts should not thus merely concentrate on the literal analysis of the words as expressed in the contract, but they should also take account of purposive construction of the contract so that commercial certainty is served to a reasonable extent.[81] The rule of remoteness was stated in the leading case of *Hadley v Baxendale* to consist of two limbs.[82] The first limb has been reflected in SGA section 51 (2): 'The plaintiff would recover in respect of losses arising in the usual course of things.' The second limb is designed for unusual losses. To resolve the difficulty of contemplating unusual losses, this limb encourages the parties to exchange information regarding the particular needs or vulnerabilities of each other at the time of the contract.[83] For damages to be awarded to cover those losses depends upon the knowledge of the parties, particularly the party in breach, at the time of entry into the contract. The second limb has not been expressly adopted in the SGA. However, it is impliedly accepted by the wording of SGA section 54, which states that 'nothing in this Act affects the right of the buyer or the seller to recover … special damages in any case where by law … special damages may be recoverable'. The two rules identified in *Hadley v Baxendale* can be considered as, in fact, comprising a single rule, focusing on reasonable contemplation or, in other words, reasonable foreseeability.[84] The two limbs overlap to some extent rather than providing separate rules. The remoteness test under the SGA thus relies objectively on the knowledge of the parties at the time of the formation of the contract.

The approach taken by the House of Lords in *The Achilleas*[85] may be perceived as a departure from the test of remoteness established in *Hadley v Baxendale*.[86] *The Achilleas*, another significant charterparty case, is viewed as a modern decision on the law relating to remoteness of damage. In this case, the charterers claimed that the owners were only entitled to damages to be measured as the difference between the market rate and the charter rate for the period during which they were deprived of the ship. The Court of Appeal found that in commercial dealings the loss of a follow-on fixture was not unlikely.[87] The House of Lords, however, unanimously set aside the decision of the Court of Appeal on the ground that the large

[80] J Chuah, *Law of International Trade: Cross-border Commercial Transactions*, 5th edn (Sweet & Maxwell, 2013) 7–8.

[81] *River Wear Commissioners v Adamson* (1877) 2 App Cas 743.

[82] *Hadley v Baxendale* [1854] 9 Ex 341, [1854] 156 ER 145, 146.

[83] Harris, Campbell and Halson (n 2) 91.

[84] Burrows (n 9) 84–85; Bridge (n 9) 733. See also *C Czarnikow Ltd v Koufos* [1969] 1 AC 350; *The Pegase* [1981] 1 Lloyd's Rep 175, 182; *Victoria Laundry (Windsor) v Newman Industries* [1949] 2 KB 528 (CA) 539; *Kpohraror v Woolwich Building Society* [1996] 4 ALL ER 119 (CA) 127.

[85] *Transfield Shipping Inc v Mercator Shipping Inc* [2008] UKHL 48, [2009] 1 AC 61.

[86] See generally these journal articles: J Sundaram, 'Is the Court of Appeal decision in *The Achilleas* good law' (2008) 20 *The Denning Law Journal* 187; A Kramer, 'The new test of remoteness in contract'(2009) 7 *Law Quarterly Review* 408; Lord Hoffmann, '*The Achilleas*: custom and practice or foreseeability' (2010) 4 *Edinburgh Law Review* 47; VP Goldberg, '*The Achilleas*: forsaking foreseeability' (2013) 66 *Current Legal Problems* 107; A Gupta, 'The implications of *The Achilleas* on s.73 Indian Contract Act 1872' (2014) 6 *The Company Lawyer* 179.

[87] [2006] EWHC 3030 (Comm), para 109.

amount demanded by the owners as damages was caused by volatile and unstable market conditions being outside the parties' contemplation.[88] The charterers were thus not liable in damages for the owners' loss of profit. If a type of loss falls outside the sphere of the defendant's responsibility, the recovery by the way of damages will be denied 'even if the loss satisfies the probability standards of the remoteness of damages rule'.[89] This approach does not represent a substantial departure from the one adopted in *Hadley* and is unlikely to displace the orthodox remoteness rule. It is only in unusual cases that it may produce a different result to the test in *Hadley*.[90] The concept of assumption of responsibility is already embodied in both limbs of *Hadley* itself, as confirmed by the Singaporean Court of Appeal.[91] The first limb of *Hadley* clearly incorporates an implied undertaking or assumption of responsibility on the part of defendant, based on the premise that a reasonable person in the position of the defendant would be taken to have assumed responsibility for a loss that flowed naturally from the breach.[92] The notion of assumption of responsibility can also attribute to the second limb of *Hadley*, in the sense that the contract breaker is assumed to be responsible for unusual losses, for which they have been communicated special knowledge and hence have agreed to compensate them. *The Achilleas* does not therefore establish a substantially different rule as part of its ratio,[93] as confirmed by Sir David Keene's decision in *John Grimes Partnership Ltd v Gubbins*.[94]

Under English law, the buyer should take reasonable steps in mitigating their loss, which is so called 'the duty to mitigate'.[95] The underlying rationale of this rule is one of simple commercial fairness. The buyer owes no duty to the seller, but fairness requires that they should not ordinarily be allowed to rely on their own unreasonable and uncommercial conduct to increase the loss falling on the seller.[96] In addition, the duty to mitigate seeks to protect the buyer's 'expectation

[88] [2008] UKHL 48, [2008] 2 All E.R. (Comm) 753, para 60.

[89] Bridge (n 9) 733.

[90] Peel (n 1) 1060; A Robertson, 'The basis of the remoteness rule in contract' (2008) 28 *Journal of Legal Studies* 172, 176; *Supershield Ltd v Siemens Building Technologies FE Ltd* [2010] EWCA Civ 7, [2010] 1 Lloyd's Rep 349.

[91] *MFM Restaurants Pte Ltd v Fish & Co Restaurants Pte Ltd* [2010] SGCA 36, [2011] 1 SLR 140, 150.

[92] *Hadley v Baxendale* [1854] 9 Ex 341, [1854]156 ER 145, 151.

[93] For arguments supporting this point of view see Sir David Keene's decision in *John Grimes Partnership Ltd v Gubbins* [2013] EWCA Civ 37, [2013] BLR 126, 24.

[94] [2013] EWCA Civ 37, [2013] BLR 126, 24.

[95] English law: *Tucker v Linger* [1883] 8 App Cas 508 (HL); *Banco de Portugal v Waterlow & Sons Ltd* [1932] AC 452 (HL); *Macrae v Swindells (HG)* [1954] 2 All ER 260; *Garnac Grain Co Inc v HMF Fauré & Fairclough Ltd* [1968] AC 1130; *Tai Hing Cotton Mill Ltd v Kamsing Knitting Factory* [1979] AC 91. US Law: *Ron-Noc Industries, Inc. v Kenneth Schuck Trucking, Inc.* (1994) United States District Court, Pennsylvania, 1994 WL 665558; *Eazor Exp., Inc. v International Broth. of Teamsters, Chauffeurs, Warehousemen and Helpers of America* (1974) United States District Court, Pennsylvania, 376 F. Supp. 841; *Transoil (Jersey) Ltd. v Belcher Oil Co* (1992) United States Court of Appeals, 5th Circuit, 950 F.2d 1115; *Industries Magromer Cueros y Pieles SA v Louisiana Bayou Furs Inc* (2002) United States Court of Appeals, 5th Circuit, 293 F.3d 912.

[96] *Golden Strait Corp v Nippon Yusen Kubishika Kaisha (The Golden Victory)* [2007] UKHL 12; *Koch Marine Inc v D'Amica Società di Navigazione ARL (The 'Elena D'Amico')* [1980] 1 Lloyd's Rep 75.

interest', by requiring them to go to the market and acquire goods similar to the contract goods and accordingly put themselves in a financial situation as if the contract was performed. This duty implies that the claimant cannot recover for loss caused by the defendant's breach of contract where the claimant could have avoided or minimised the loss by taking reasonable steps, such as buying substitute goods in the market.[97] The rule of mitigation is related to the 'market price' rule that requires the innocent party to buy or sell immediately in an available market.[98] It may be argued that the market price rule in contracts for the sale of goods has departed from the ordinary rules of contract law concerning mitigation of loss. Thus, the concept of 'available market' relates exclusively to contracts for sale of goods and it therefore deserves further analysis.

English law has extensively used the concept of 'market price' for measuring damages, which may not be characteristic of other legal systems. The 'market price' rule reflects the buyer's duty to mitigate his loss by 'buying substitute goods in the open market'.[99] However, the vague concept of 'open' or 'available market' needs clarification. One may argue that the concept of market refers to a physical place where goods are bought and sold. Also, the availability of buyers and sellers, and their ready capacity to supply or to absorb the relevant goods, is the basic concept of an 'available market'.[100] Goode has adopted a more stringent approach by defining an available market as a market to which the buyer has reasonable access and in which they can procure goods of a description and quality comparable to those they have contracted to buy and at a price governed primarily by the market forces of supply and demand.[101] He provides three criteria. First, the test of fungibility: 'goods of which any one unit is considered in the locality or trade in question to be the exact equivalent of any other unit of the same grade, sample or description.'[102] Thus manufactured goods made to the buyer's special order are unlikely to satisfy this test.[103] However, Goode has stated that the buyer must still mitigate their loss if there is a reasonable access to a market in which the buyer can procure comparable goods to those they have contracted to buy.[104] Second, the test of sufficient quantity: 'the equivalent units must be available in sufficient quantities to meet all demands by would-be purchasers.'[105] This is obviously problematic with transactions involving unique goods which have no exact equivalent. Third, the

[97] *Roper v Johnson* (1872–73) LR 8 CP 167; *British Westinghouse Electric & Manufacturing Co Ltd v Underground Electric Railways Co of London* [1912] AC 673 (HL) 689; *Pilkington v Wood* [1953] Ch 770 (Ch); *Strutt v Whitnell* [1975] 1 WLR 870 (CA).

[98] Bridge (n 38) para 16-052.

[99] McKendrick (n 4) 452.

[100] Bridge (n 38) para 17-005.

[101] McKendrick (n 4) 451.

[102] ibid, 452.

[103] *Lazenby Garages Ltd v Wright* [1976] 2 ALL ER 770 (CA); *M&J Marine Engineering Services Co Ltd v Shipshore Ltd* [2009] EWHC 2031 (Comm).

[104] McKendrick (n 4) 452.

[105] ibid; see also *WL Thompson v Sullivan Ltd* [1955] Ch 177; *Hughes v Pendragon Sabre Ltd* [2016] EWCA Civ 18.

test of fluctuation of price: 'the price must be one which fluctuates with supply and demand.'[106] The same reasoning for the test of sufficient quantity of manufactured goods applies to this test as well; if goods are unique then it is highly unlikely that the price fluctuates according to supply and demand in the normal sense (ie in an abnormal sense, there will be price fluctuations in that there is no price without demand for unique goods, and a demand for such goods will necessitate the creation of a price). However, it has been submitted that if the contract goods are to be manufactured according to the specifications of the contract, there might be 'an available market in which the buyer could buy suitable substitute goods'.[107] But, it is likely that there will be no available market for unique manufactured goods, since 'the chance of buying such goods within a reasonable time after the breach is too limited and fortuitous'.[108]

In case-law, an early view was that 'an available market is some place (eg an exchange) where the goods in question can be sold'.[109] Upjohn J in *WL Thomson Ltd v R Robinson Ltd* has stated that an available market means 'a situation in the particular trade in the particular area is such that the particular goods could freely be sold'.[110] He then states that 'an available market in the subsection is not limited to a market such as the Baltic or Stock Exchange, but means that the situation in the trade in the area is such that the goods can freely be sold if a purchaser defaults'.[111] Another view is that it means 'a situation where the current price for the goods may fluctuate according to supply and demand'.[112] The case-law is inconsistent in dealing with the notion of available market for manufactured goods. For instance, in a recent case concerning second-hand goods, the court held that:

> New equipment cannot be regarded as being equivalent to 'the goods in question', which were second-hand goods and, although the availability of equivalent second-hand goods would have constituted an available market, it would have taken three months to source a similar console, which fell short of constituting an available market within the meaning of s.51(3).[113]

In that case, the court confirmed that there is an available market for the second-hand goods, although those goods have special characteristics conforming to the contract terms. In another case, the court rejected the available market for the contract goods by stating that an available market 'involves a reasonably available supply of the contract goods and a reasonably available source of demand for such goods, and there was no such market for the goods to be supplied by M&J'.[114]

[106] McKendrick (n 4) 452.
[107] Bridge (n 38) para 17-006.
[108] ibid, para 16-069.
[109] *Dunkirk Colliery Co v Lever* (1878) 9 Ch D 20 (CA) 25.
[110] [1955] Ch 177, 185.
[111] ibid, 187.
[112] *Charter v Sullivan* [1957] 2 QB 117 (CA) 128.
[113] *Air Studios (Lyndhurst) Ltd (t/a Air Entertainment Group) v Lombard North Central Plc* [2012] EWHC 3162 (QB), para 92, [2013] 1 Lloyd's Rep 63.
[114] *M&J Marine Engineering Services Co Ltd v Shipshore Ltd* [2009] EWHC 2031 (Comm) para 30.

B. UCC

American law provides damages for those losses that were reasonably foreseeable or contemplated by the parties at the time the contract was concluded as a probable result of a breach. Under American law, general losses are considered to flow naturally from a breach, that is, damages that 'would follow any breach of similar character in the usual course of events'.[115] Such losses are often described as the proximate or natural result of a breach and even sometimes called 'loss of bargain' damages, because they represent a failure on the seller's part to fulfil the bargain they made, or a failure of the promised or expected performance itself.[116] Because this type of loss is a natural and even necessary result of a breach, their occurrence is sufficiently predictable for the parties at the time of conclusion of contract.[117] The direct, necessary and immediate effects are thus always recoverable, because every person is presumed to foresee the direct and natural results of their acts. The Second Restatement of Contracts, reflecting the common law approach, states that 'loss may be foreseeable as a probable result of a breach because it follows from the breach (a) in the ordinary course of events, or (b) as a result of special circumstances, beyond the ordinary course of events, that the party in breach had reason to know'.[118] This approach to general losses has also been extended to UCC, in which the parties need not actually have considered the possibility of the occurrence of those losses, as long as they may fairly be supposed to have considered them.

On the other hand, consequential losses do not flow directly and immediately from the breach and they form some of the consequences or results of the breach.[119] To recover for this type of loss, the parties must meet the strict requirements of causation, certainty, and foreseeability. Those losses must have been

[115] Lord (n 1) para 64:16; see also JR Berryman, *A Treatise on the Law of Damages: Embracing an Elementary Exposition of the Law, and also Its Application to Particular Subjects of Contract and Tort*, 4th edn (Callaghan and Company, 1916) 170; L Horst, 'Two types of expectation interest in contract damages' (1989) 12 *University of New South Wales Law Journal* 98, 101; DE Barnes, 'The net expectation interest in contract damages' (1999) 48 *Emory Law Journal* 1143, 1152; T Arnold, A Dixon, M Sherill and M Gulati, 'The myth of optimal expectation damages' (2020–2021) 104 *Marquette Law Review* 141, 145; J Gustafson, J Kimpflen, SJT Necheles and KC Simmons, *Corpus Juris Secundum*, 25th edn (Thomson Reuters, 2023) damages section.

[116] *Sack Bros. v Great Plains Co-op., Inc* (2000) Supreme Court of Nebraska, 42 U.C.C. Rep. Serv. 2d 914; *Phipps v Skyview Farms, Inc* (2000) Supreme Court of Nebraska, 259 Neb. 492; *Gary's Implement, Inc. v Bridgeport Tractor Parts, Inc* (2005) Supreme Court of Nebraska, 702 N.W.2d 355; *BLB Aviation South Carolina LLC v Jet Linx Aviation LLC* (2015) United States Court of Appeals, 8th Circuit, 808 f.3d 389; *BRB Contractors Inc v Web Water Development Association Inc* (2021) United States District Court, South Dkota, 2021 WL 516545.

[117] *Lewis Jorge Construction Management, Inc. v Pomona Unified School District* (2004) Supreme Court of California, 34 Cal. 4th 960, 22 Cal. Rptr; see also *Lockwood Graders of Idaho, Inc. v Neibaur* (1958) Supreme Court of Idaho, 326 P.2d 675.

[118] United States Restatement (Second) of Contracts (1981) section 351(2).

[119] *CR-RSC Tower I, LLC v RSC Tower I, LLC* (2012) Court of Appeals of Maryland, 56 A.3d 170; *Caldwell Land and Cattle, LLC v Johnson Thermal Systems, Inc* (2019) United States District Court, Idaho, 452 P.3d 809; *Reid Hospital and Health Care Services, Inc. v Conifer Revenue Cycle Solutions, LLC.* (2021) United States Court of Appeals, 7th Circuit, 8 F.4th 642.

within reasonable contemplation of both parties at the time they entered into the contract, a common law principle generally adopted from *Hadley v Baxendale*, discussed earlier.[120] In the recent case of *Kreg Therapeutics, Inc. v VitalGo, Inc*, it was questionable whether losses suffered by medical supply company of future income and customer base was reasonably foreseeable by the manufacturer.[121] Their contract conferred exclusive distribution rights of a particular medical bed to the supplier in several regions. The manufacturer failed to deliver certain quantities of the goods to the supplier, according to the contract terms. Adequate evidence of the supplier's loss of exclusivity rights, future income and customer base were provided. The manufacturer argued that those consequential losses were not foreseen at the time of conclusion of the contract and were thus not recoverable. The New York law, as the applicable law to this scenario, takes a common-sense approach, which enquires the 'nature, purpose and particular circumstances of the contract'.[122] The court explained that during contract negotiations the supplier's representative made clear to the manufacturer that the supplier needed exclusive-distributorship protections to make the agreement worthwhile.[123] The medical beds, as the goods in question, were a new product at the time and exclusivity would offset the risks and investments the supplier had to make to establish a new business segment and develop a customer base. This factual background was sufficient to conclude that the manufacturer foresaw or should have foreseen the losses the supplier would suffer if goods were not delivered.

UCC Section 2-715 generally accords with the common law approach by allowing a recovery of consequential losses as long as the loss is proximately caused by the breach. This section states that consequential damages resulting from a seller's breach include:

(a) any loss resulting from general or particular requirements and needs of which the seller at the time of contracting had reason to know and which could not reasonably be prevented by cover or otherwise; and
(b) injury to person or property proximately resulting from any breach of warranty.

The Official Comments clarify that in the absence of merchant's excuse in failing to perform the contract, the seller is held liable for consequential losses in all cases where they are expected to know of the buyer's general or particular requirements at the time of contracting.[124] Particular needs of the buyer must generally be communicated and made known to the seller, while general needs must rarely

[120] *United States v Behan* (1884) Supreme Court of the United States, 110 U.S. 338 This is the first US case that cited *Hadley v Baxendale*; see also *Silver Creek Computers, Inc. v Petra, Inc.* (2002) Supreme Court of Idaho, 42 P.3d 672.
[121] (2019) United States Court of Appeals, 17th Circuit, 919 F.3d 405.
[122] ibid, 419.
[123] ibid, 420; see also *Kenford Co Inc v County of Erie* (1989) Court of Appeals of New York, 73 N.Y.2d 312; *Schonfeld v Hilliard* (2000) United States Court of Appeals, 2nd Circuit, 218 F.3d 164; *Bi-Economy Market Inc v Harleysville Inc Co of New York* (2008) Court of Appeals of New York, 10 N.Y.3d 187.
[124] UCC Official Comments, section 2-715, para 2.

be communicated to charge the seller with knowledge.[125] The most usual consequential damages in the context of commercial sale of goods are lost profits. The seller knows or is presumed to know that the buyer is in the business of resale, hence lost profits stemming from breach are foreseeable and normally recoverable. In the notable case of *National Farmers Organization, Inc. v McCook Feed & Supply Co*, the buyer was held entitled to recover lost profits as consequential losses under UCC section 2-715.[126] The buyer had contracted to buy 90,000 bushels of corn, however, the seller delivered less than 2,000 bushels. The buyer successfully showed that the seller knew at the time of contracting that the buyer intended to resell the corn in a place where a market existed. The buyer made an attempt to cover and obtain substitute goods, but it was unsuccessful. The question stressed as ultimately determinative in was whether at the time of conclusion of contract the seller who breached the contract knew that their breach would probably result in the kind of special losses claimed and thus could be considered to have foreseen them. If the seller knew or was presumed to have known, then they would be liable in damages for the consequential losses.

Similar to English law, the buyer must take reasonable steps to reduce the losses occurred due to the breach. Under American law, the buyer cannot simply recover those losses that they could have avoided by taking reasonable steps. In a recent American case, it was highlighted that in the context of claims for breach of contract, an injured party has a 'duty to mitigate', in the sense that an injured party may not recover 'damages which the plaintiff might have avoided with reasonable efforts without undue risk, expense, burden, or humiliation'.[127] Mitigation is thus a requirement conditioning the award of damages.

The principle of mitigation of loss has broad application and normally involves a determination whether the buyer has acted reasonably under the circumstances. Whether reasonable attempt is made by the buyer to reduce the losses after the seller's breach is a question of fact.[128] A buyer is not expected to take risky measures or even take steps that impose substantial expenditure over and above the expenditure incurred in performance of the particular contract. As explained in *S.A. Healy Co. v Milwaukee Metropolitan Sewerage Dist*, the duty to mitigate does not require a party to take unreasonable risk, subject itself to unreasonable inconvenience,

[125] ibid; see *English Whipple Sailyard, Ltd. v Yawl Ardent*, (1978) United States District Court, Pennsylvania, 459 F. Supp. 866: this is a key case in distinguishing between general losses and consequential losses.

[126] (1976) Supreme Court of Nebraska, 19 UCC Rep. Serv. 821; see also *Hawthorne Industries Inc v Balfour Maclaine International Ltd* (1982) United States Court of Appeals, 11th Circuit, 676 F.2d 1385; *Rowell v Voortman Cookies, Ltd.* (2002) United States District Court, Eastern Division, 2002 WL 31116640.

[127] *Universal Truckload, Incorporated v Dalton Logistics, Incorporated, 946* (2020) United States Court of Appeals, 5th Circuit, 946 F.3d 689; see also *The King v Taylor Chrysler-Plymouth, Inc.* (1990) Court of Appeals of Michigan, 457 N.W.2d 42; United States Restatement (Second) of Contracts (1981) section 350(1).

[128] *H & W Industries Inc v Occidental Chemical Corp.* (1990) United States Court of Appeals, 911 F.2d 1118.

incur unreasonable expenses or disorganise its business.[129] Interestingly, UCC does not employ the word 'mitigation' but the duty to mitigate can be inferred from section 2-715(2)(a) stating 'consequential damages resulting from the seller's breach include (a) any loss resulting from general or particular requirements and needs of which the seller at the time of contracting had reason to know and which could not reasonably be prevented by cover or otherwise'. This indicates that the buyer must show that the consequential loss could not reasonably be prevented by cover or otherwise. In other words, the seller is not held responsible for losses that the buyer could have reasonably avoided by proper action taken to reduce the loss after the seller's breach.[130] For instance, in *Steele v JI Case Co*, while the buyer did not take practically take steps in reducing losses, they were held entitled to consequential damages.[131] In this case, the manufacturer delivered three combines to be used in harvesting several farms.[132] The manufacturer knew that the combines were bought for use in harvest and was deemed to have known the urgency of harvest in the region where buyer's form was located. From the start, the combines failed to function properly and developed numerous mechanical deficiencies and breakages. In response to repeated complaints by the buyer, the manufacturer sent various employees and technicians to repair the machines, albeit with no success The court held that frequent assurances by the manufacturer of those machinery that they would remedy the defects, coupled with frequent attempts to repair them, were deemed to preclude the manufacturer's contention that the buyer failed to minimise their loss.[133] The buyer was therefore not barred from recovering their losses, including consequential loss.

C. CISG and UPICC

The principle of full recovery of losses suffered by the buyer is subject to a significant limitation. The second sentence of CISG Article 74 states that the amount of damages that can be awarded by the adjudicators 'may not exceed the loss which the party in breach foresaw or ought to have foreseen at the time of the

[129] *S.A. Healy Co. v Milwaukee Metropolitan Sewerage District* (1995) United States Court of Appeals, 7th Circuit, 60 F.3d 305; see also *Simeone v First Bank Nat. Ass'n* (1996) United States Court of Appeals, 8th Circuit, 73 F.3d 184.

[130] *H & W Industries, Inc. v Occidental Chemical Corp* (1990) United States Court of Appeals, 911 F.2d 1118; *Toshiba Machine Co., America v SPM Flow Control, Inc.* (2005) Court of Appeals of Texas, Fort Worth, 180 S.W.3d 761; *Federated Retail Holdings, Inc v Sanidown, Inc* (2010) United States District Court, New York, 2010 WL 5298113; *Packgen v Berry Plastics Corp.* (2015) United States District Court, Maine, 113 F.Supp.3d 371.

[131] (1966) Supreme Court of Kansas, 419 P.2d 902.

[132] See also *Little v Rose* (1974) Supreme Court of North Carolina, 208 SE2d 666; *Highmark Inc v Northwest Pipe Company* (2016) United States District Court, South Dakota, WL 884900.

[133] (1966) Supreme Court of Kansas, 197 Kan. 554, 564; similar decision was made in *Manouchehri v Heim* (1997) Court of Appeals of New Mexico, 941 P.2d 978, where the court confirmed that it was not unreasonable for the buyer to wait for the seller to attempt repairs of defective machine.

conclusion of the contract, in light of the facts and matters of which [they] then knew or ought to have known, as a possible consequence of the breach'.[134] Such a dual subjective/objective approach for remoteness test has also been adopted by UPICC in Article 7.4.4. The foreseeability targets the nature and extent of the loss as a possible consequence of the contractual breach, but not the contractual breach itself.[135] This means that the breaching party is not liable for just any loss; instead, their liability under these legal regimes is limited to the foreseeable loss. The foreseeability rule is widely considered as a necessary limitation to the strict liability regime adopted in both legal regimes, which is consistent with the wishes and expectations of the business community. The seller should thus be narrowly held liable for damages incurred and must not be considered the insurer of the buyer's contractual adventure. The foreseeability requirement is also associated with the very nature of the contract, in that not all the buyer's deprived benefits would fall within the scope of the contract. As mentioned by the UPICC's Official Comment, the non-performing party 'must not be saddled with compensation for harm which it could never have foreseen at the time of the conclusion of the contract and against the risk of which it could not have taken out insurance'.[136]

The foreseeability requirement adopted in these two legal regimes were heavily influenced by *Hadley v Baxendale*.[137] The first limb of this case corresponds with the objective test, enquiring whether a reasonable person in the position of the seller and aware of the circumstances at the time of the conclusion of the contract would have foreseen the loss. This can normally be satisfied by showing that the harm or loss flows naturally from the non-performance. In the notable case of *Delchi Carrier, S.p.A v Rotorex Corp*, an Italian manufacturer agreed to sell 10,800 compressors to an Italian buyer.[138] The buyer intended to use the compressor to produce air conditioners to be sold in the spring and summer of 1988. The seller sent the first shipment by sea on March 26 and Delchi paid for this shipment accordingly. While the seller sent a second shipment of compressors, the buyer founds out that the first lot failed to conform to the sample model and the agreed specifications. Those compressors did not pass the quality control checks since they had lower cooling capacity and consumed more power than the sample model and specifications. Following several unsuccessful attempts to rectify the defects in the compressors, the buyer requested the seller to supply new compressors but the seller failed to do so, claiming that the specifications were 'inadvertently communicated' to the seller. Because the buyer could not obtain goods in a timely fashion

[134] See eg *Cooling Machine case* (2002) Austrian Supreme Court, CISG-online 643; *Konsensus-Laomaailm AS v Rakvere Autobaas OÜ* (2008) County Court Viru, Estonia, CISG-online 4006; *Electronic Equipment case* (2011) Shanghai High People's Court, China, CISG-online 2318; *PVC Foil case* (2019) Court of Appeal Naumburg, Germany, CISG-online 4506.

[135] *DSM Dyneema B.V. v Electromichaniki Kimis EPE* (2009) Multi-member Court of First Instance Athens, Greece, CISG-online 2228.

[136] UPICC Official Comments, Article 7.4.4.

[137] Honnold and Flechtner (n 14) Article 4, para. 2.8; Kroll, Mistelis and Viscasillas (n 20) 968.

[138] (1995) United States Court of Appeals, 2nd Circuit, 71 F.3d 1024.

and was left empty handed, the buyer had to shut down its manufacturing operation for a few days, resulting in substantially detrimental production delay and incurred lost sales in the spring and early summer. It was, therefore, objectively foreseeable that the buyer would take orders for selling season, on the ground that the buyer was manufacturer of air conditioners and ordered a huge number of compressors. The loss incurred was a natural consequence of the seller's defective performance. The Court of Appeals decided in favour of the buyer and held that the seller liable for a large amount for consequential loss, which included loss of profits resulted from a diminished sales level, expenses that the buyer incurred in trying to remedy the non-conformity of the compressors and the costs of handling and storing the defective compressors.[139]

The second limb of *Hadley v Baxendale* corresponds with the subjective element of the foreseeability requirement, which basically supplements the objective element. As far as the subjective element is concerned, the seller as the party in breach would only be liable for those losses of which they had actual knowledge or foresight. This standard may rarely come into play, as the injured party should at the time of the conclusion of a contract consider that breach of the contract by the seller would cause them exceptionally heavy losses or losses of an unusual nature, which should be made known to the seller.[140] The result would be that if such special losses incur, damages recover them. However, when parties are engaged in a long-term relationship, they normally have adequate knowledge of each other's business and interests. The seller should thus be able to conduct a subjective risk evaluation and may be held liable for losses resulting from extraordinary uses.[141]

CISG and UPICC require the buyer to mitigate their losses by taking reasonable steps in minimising the loss resulting from the seller's breach of contract.[142] The mitigation principle safeguards the contractual equilibrium in these legal regimes. On the one hand, both regimes provide for a strict liability of the seller for their obligations and, on the other, both require the buyer, as the creditor, to act with due diligence when faced with the prospects of adverse consequences of the contract breach. A failure to reduce loss does not in fact attract a liability in damages; rather, the central approach underlying the principle of the duty to mitigate the loss is that the injured party cannot claim damages for those losses which they could avoid by taking reasonable steps.[143] The mitigation principle adopted in these legal regimes would mean that not all foreseeable losses are recoverable by damages. This duty,

[139] ibid, 1030.

[140] *Castel Electronics Pty Ltd v Toshiba Singapore Pte Ltd* (2011) Federal Court of Australia, CISG-online 2219; See UPICC Official Comments, Article 7.4.4, para 1; Vogenauer (n 28) Article 7.4.4. para 5.

[141] *Indian-Russian sales contract case I* (2004) (Tribunal of International Commercial Arbitration at the Russian Federation Chamber of Commerce and Industry (MKAC)), CISG-online 1188.

[142] CISG Article 77 & UPICC Official Comments, Article 7.4.8, para 1.

[143] D Saidov, 'Methods of Limiting Damages under the Vienna Convention on Contracts for the International Sale of Goods' (2002) 14 *Pace International Law Review* 307, 350.

which relies on the injured party taking appropriate measure to prevent the occurrence of further loss or to mitigate its extent, is viewed by civil law scholars as an expression of the general principle of good faith in international commerce.[144] This principle seeks to prevent the injured party from waiting passively for the loss to take place and then expecting the party in breach to compensate the loss that could have been minimised by taking reasonable steps.[145] Following reasonable measures taken by the injured party, they can recover any expenses reasonably incurred in attempting to reduce the harm.

The question of what steps are reasonable is difficult and uncertain. What is clear is that the injured buyer is not expected to take extraordinary or expensive measures. In general, possible measures to reduce losses are reasonable, where those measures could have been expected as a good faith conduct from a reasonable person in the position of the injured buyer under the circumstances.[146] When applying CISG, Article 8 is particularly helpful. It provides a guideline on how to determine the understanding of a prudent businessperson in light of all relevant circumstances of the case, including negotiations, any practices which the parties have established themselves, or any trade usages. This indicates that whether the injured buyer has taken appropriate measures to reduce the loss is a question of fact. For instance, an injured buyer failing to take steps to protect the goods in question from deterioration may be held to have failed to take reasonable steps. Making a replacement transaction by the buyer evidently illustrates the mitigation principle when they are faced with substantively defective performance that the goods could not be effectively cured. In *Vacuum Cleaners* case, the injured buyer had the chance to conclude a cover purchase, which could properly mitigate the loss.[147] The buyer argued that a substitute transaction was not possible to make because no local company could sell the goods during the relevant period. The court disagreed, ruling that since the seller was a foreign company, the buyer should have considered offers from foreign countries, at least from all Germany.

5. Evaluation

There are slight variations in the wording of the provisions governing the remoteness test in each of the legal regimes. One discrepancy lies in the fact that the loss under SGA and UCC should be within the contemplation of both parties, whereas

[144] L Vekas, 'The foreseeability doctrine in contractual damage cases' (2002) 43 *Acta Juridica Hungarica* 145; P Huber and A Mullis, *The CISG, A New Textbook for Students and Practitioners* (Sellier, European Law Publishers, 2007) 289.

[145] UPICC Official Comments, Article 7.4.8, para 1; see also Zeller (n 26) 74.

[146] *Propane Gas* case (1996) Austrian Supreme Court, CISG-online 224; see also Kroll, Mistelis and Viscasillas (n 20) 1018.

[147] *Vacuum Cleaners* case (1998) Court of Appeal Celle, Germany, CISG-online 506.

under CISG and UPICC, it suffices that the party in breach foresees the loss. However, this difference is of minor practical significance, as described by Treitel:

> The [injured party's] contemplation in such a situation may be necessary to establish the purpose for which he intended to use the subject matter and hence to show that his failure to obtain it actually led him to suffer the alleged loss. But it is foreseeability by the [party in breach] which is the crucial factor in determining whether the loss is too remote.[148]

There is another discrepancy which seems to be more significant, and it lies in the probability of the occurrence of loss that can be foreseen by the breaching party. English law and American law have adopted a similar approach, in that they speak of 'contemplated damages' by both parties as being the 'probable result' of the breach. CISG Article 74 makes it a condition of recoverability that 'the party in breach knew or ought to have known [that loss might occur] as a possible consequence of the breach of contract'. UPICC states that it depends on the harm having been 'likely to result from the non-performance of contract'. The meanings of the various terms of 'possible consequence', 'likely to result', 'probably result', have been the subject of much debate and scrutiny. 'Possible' is a very broad word.[149] It might extend the scope of a seller's liability for those losses that occurred as the result of breach. The difference between 'possible consequence' and 'probable result' was illustrated in *The Heron II*: 'suppose one takes a well-shuffled pack of cards, it is quite likely or not unlikely that the top card will prove to be a diamond: the odds are only 3 to 1 against. But most people would not say that it is quite likely to be the nine of diamonds for the odds are then 51 to 1 against.'[150] In this case, it was suggested that the words 'not unlikely' or some similar words denotes a much smaller degree of probability.[151] The foreseeability requirement in CISG Article 74 is much broader than the tests adopted in other legal regimes.[152] The CISG's wide approach may substantially expose a seller to increasing liability. However, the term 'in light of the facts and matters' used in that article would reduce what could otherwise indicate a potentially extensive liability. SGA, by using the words 'probable result', requires a higher degree of probability of occurrence of the loss than the CISG, which uses the term 'possible consequence'. UCC itself has not clearly prescribed the 'foreseeability requirement', but the restatement of contract and the case law rely mainly on the reasonable contemplation of both parties, informed

[148] Treitel (n 37) 159; for the counter argument see F Ferrari, '*Hadley v Baxendale* v Foreseeability under Article 74 CISG' in Saidov and Cunnington (n 12) 310–11.
[149] *Koufos v C. Czarnikow Ltd. ("The Heron II")* [1969] 1 AC 350, 390.
[150] ibid.
[151] ibid.
[152] See also JS Ziegel and C Samson, 'Report to the Uniform Law Conference of Canada on Convention on Contracts for the International Sale of Goods' (1981), see iicl.law.pace.edu/sites/default/files/bibliography/english2_0.pdf. For the same argument see Kroll, Mistelis and Viscasillas (n 20) 1003.

by the particular circumstances of the contract.[153] Nevertheless, the difference in wording between these legal regimes is not substantial.[154]

In addition, the modern development of the foreseeability requirement in English law demonstrates greater responsiveness to the context in which a contract is made and developed. This is particularly desirable where parties are involved in a relational contract, which requires higher attention to the parties' expectations and realism of their commercial dealings. Other legal regimes have remained rather static and rigid in this regard. As explained previously, the House of Lords in *The Achilleas* argued that liability for damages for breach of contract was founded upon the presumed intention of the parties and required the court to determine objectively what the common basis on which the parties had contracted.[155] The parties who have been in a relational contract may have established a shared understanding as to what each can and should expect from the contract, whether it is duly performed without breach on either side. The approach adopted in *The Achilleas* provides an opportunity for the adjudicators to examine more carefully the surrounding circumstances and general understanding in the relevant market to determine whether the seller could be held liable for loss. This is likely to be particularly the case in relational contracts, where the seller may be reasonably expected to have sufficient knowledge and understanding of buyer's interests and demands. Although *The Achilleas* does not establish a substantially distinctive rule from *Hadley v Baxendale*, it crucially recognises the context on which a contract is based and the extent to which parties have communicated special information for recovering losses arising in special circumstances.

The rules governing the calculation of loss and the duty to mitigate are almost the same in these legal regimes. However, when it comes to calculation of loss, English law again appears to be have been more capable of accommodating particular needs and interests of parties, by developing doctrines and principles founded on contextual background. Notwithstanding which method of calculation of loss is preferred in UCC, CISG and UPICC, they have trenchantly asserted the need for commercial certainty even at the expense of the compensatory principle. In these regimes, the buyers are entitled to be compensated for the value of what they had lost due to the breach 'on the date they had lost'. Damages are thus crystallised and measured at the date of termination. This method of calculation of loss fits neatly with discrete, one-off transactions, with little prospect of continuing the relationship between the parties. In contrast, English law has shown greater readiness to replace the prima facie market price rule in favour of the overriding compensatory

[153] See ch 4 section 4(B).

[154] See KS Cohen, 'Achieving a Uniform Law Governing International Sales: Conforming the Damage Provisions of the United Nations Convention on Contracts for the International Sale of Goods and the Uniform Commercial Code' (2005) 26 *University of Pennsylvania Journal of International Economic Law* 601.

[155] *Transfield Shipping v Mercator Shipping* [2009] 1 AC 61, 62.

principle. This principle may lead to the preservation of relationships and promote the solidarity required for a relational contract. Relational contracts, contrary to discrete, one-off contracts, are subject to fundamental changes of circumstances and thus require more dynamic and flexible legal principles representing the particular needs of commercial parties. In *The Golden Victory*, the court, applying a well-established principle that the court should not close its eyes to what in fact had happened by the date of assessment, took account of the outbreak of the war that had occurred, in which event the charterer would have cancelled the charter, had it still been on foot.[156] The decision established that to allow the injured party's claim following the outbreak of war would be inconsistent with the overriding compensatory principle on which awards of contractual damages ought to be based. The injured party would be provided with a windfall, which would infringe the compensatory principle. If the court were only to assume that the innocent party would have been able to perform, rather than to consider what was likely to have happened in the event that there had been no repudiation, the court might well place the innocent party in a financially better position than they would have been in had the contract been performed. The strict market price rule may thus unjustly burden one party with excessive payment of damages, which in turn provides the innocent party with a windfall. This would be hugely detrimental to the parties' relationship and the party in breach may lose its interest in maintaining its relationship with the innocent party and staying in such a contract.

The overriding compensatory principle highlights that the *ex ante* likelihood of the contingency or force majeure events should be taken into account, when evaluating damages for breach of contract. This implies that when parties are in a long-term and relational contract, English law has the capacity to discount damages to reflect the *ex ante* possibility of the contingency coming to pass. Not providing the innocent party with a windfall would mean that the party in breach is required to pay a reasonably proportional amount of damages reflecting the true loss incurred. The overriding compensatory principle considering the *ex ante* events thus fairly allocate financial responsibilities between the parties. Since the seller may need performance of their obligations over a lengthy period, the application of strict market price rule fails to take into account the possibility and consequence of any contingency, which may adversely affect the value of contractual performance. The market price rule, strictly applied in UCC, CISG and UPICC, is consistent with the traditional economic allocating mechanism of contracts. Such a mechanism seeks to make an isolationist decision, without considering future aspects of a contractual relationship. Therefore, the overriding compensatory principle reinforced in *The Golden Victory* suggests that the English law of damages have greater capacity in reinforcing the needs of parties involved in relational contracts.

[156] [2007] UKHL 12, [2007] 2 AC 353.

The market price rule may not be consistent with the second norm, ie conformity of extended relations with commercial matrix. The reason is that the market price rule functions mechanically on the basis of difference between the market price and contract price. Damages are designed to place the injured party in as financially good a position as they would have been in had the contract been performed. This can be achieved by giving the injured party the benefit of the bargain. On the analytical level, which concerns the law's normative structure, the expectation damages prices a breach of contract and such legal price is set to an amount to discourage breach of contract. The intrinsic normative value of contract law derives greatly from its commitment to the performance of contract. The market price rule, which operates on the basis of the difference between contract price and market price at the date of breach, assumes a frictionless and perfect market. This mechanical principle, which ignores the context of contractual relationships and the value of missed performance, would overprice the breach and undermine the very legal order it ought to establish and maintain. The market price rule would be most appropriate in a hypothetical situation in which all values would be preserved on a perfect market. This rule ignores the possibility of happening events, which would affect the value of performance. The result would be that the damages awarded provide the innocent party with a windfall, which fails to accurately reflect the loss incurred. A windfall of damages to one party means a huge financial loss to the other party, leading to an unsustainable and unstable economic situation. When an innocent party is overcompensated for the loss incurred, they would be placed in a financially better position than if the contract was performed. This better financial position is unaccounted for, and a portion of money awarded does not reciprocate to anything. In other words, the innocent party's gain from breach would exceed its gain from performance, which undermines efficient allocation of resources. This sort of damages calculation would hugely benefit one and harm the other and does fail to replicate the outcome of a fully performed contract. In contrast to the market price rule, the overriding compensatory principle, by accurately measuring the actual loss incurred, results in the optimal division of financial resources, and promote proper functioning of the market mechanism, which would be socially desirable too. This principle maintains the contractual equilibrium between the parties and is precisely in line with the reciprocity and mutuality required in a relational, long-term contract.

There is another significant distinction regarding calculating damages under these four legal regimes, which should be analysed. The 'abstract method' of calculation of damages is preferred in the SGA. The buyer presumptively goes to the market, finds a seller, and buys similar goods. Therefore, the injured buyer is treated as being entitled to the position it would have occupied if the contract was fully performed. If there is no available market for the goods in question, the buyer has the option to make a substitute transaction and claim damages on the basis of section 51(2) of the SGA. Thus, there is a mixture of the abstract and the concrete methods under the SGA.[157] The reason for preferring 'abstract rule' in English law might lie in the fact that in the capitalist economy individuals are considered rational maximisers of their own benefit, and as such they can effectively satisfy their needs and interests in the market available to them. Equally importantly, the market is so developed that it enables the parties to independently address their needs with no interference from authorities.[158] The other legal regimes (UCC, CISG and UPICC) prima facie determine the calculation of damages by reference to the substitute transaction made by the buyer following the breach of contract: damages then recover the difference between the contract price and the price paid in the substitute transaction. If the buyer was unsuccessful in securing such transaction, they will be protected by the rule based on the difference between the contract price and market price. This shows that there is also a mixture of the two methods in these legal regimes. These two approaches adopted under English law and the rest reflect the fact that the rules governing the duty to mitigate are almost the same; both methods require the buyer to minimise the loss by either 'making a substitute transaction' or 'referring to the market and making a contract' in order to protect and satisfy the performance interest of the buyer.

The distinction is likely to be significant only where there is a market, which there usually is for manufactured goods and where the goods are not too specific, and the substitute contract is actually made by the buyer. One system relies heavily on the market price rule and the others rely on the substitute transaction. This distinction merits an analysis. But if the buyer does not enter a substitute transaction or if the substitute transaction was not made reasonably, the same result is likely to be achieved under these legal regimes, because then the 'abstract method' is employed for calculation of damages. The CISG Secretariat Commentary has confirmed that if the resale is not made reasonably after the avoidance of contract, damages would be calculated as though no substitute transaction had taken place.[159]

It is almost self-evident that neither the abstract method nor the concrete method can contribute to maintaining long-term, relational contracts. These two methods are incapable of inducing cooperation and collaboration between the parties in keeping their relationship in order to settle their disputes. Damages, in principle, are awarded by the adjudicators and therefore the parties' contractual relations have already been disrupted, when referring to formal methods of dispute resolution. However, it could be argued that the abstract rule preferred under SGA

[157] Bridge (n 40) 405, 408.
[158] Campbell (n 1) 297.
[159] Commentary on the Draft Convention on Contracts for the International Sale of Goods, prepared by the Secretariat (UN Doc. A/CONF.97/5), in: *United Nations Conference on Contracts for the International Sale of Goods* (1980, Vienna) Official Records: Documents of the Conference and Summary Records of the Plenary Meetings and of the Meetings of the Main Committees, New York: United Nations (1991) para 6.

does not explicitly entail breaking the original contractual relationship; instead, the buyer is required to investigate the market price and recover the difference. Under the abstract method, 'there is no requirement, as a condition of recovering damages that the plaintiff enters into a substitute transaction after terminating the contract'.[160] In contrast, under the 'concrete method' preferred under other legal regimes, the buyer is required to terminate the original contract and make a new transaction in order to gain the equivalent goods.[161] The CISG Advisory Council has expressed the view that the language of Article 75 mandates that avoidance of the contract must take place in order for a party to recover damages under this provision.[162] This preferred method under UCC, CISG and UPICC clearly involves breaking the contractual relations, but worse than this, the buyer is mandated to enter into a contract with a *different* seller. Breaking the original contractual relationship, coupled with entry into a contract with another seller, who would most likely be the competitor of the original seller, destroys the prospect of maintaining a relationship and promoting cooperation between the parties. The search for, and entry into, a new transaction with a new supplier endangers the trust and confidence between the parties and frustrates the expectation of loyalty, which may not be legislated for in the express terms of the contract, but are implicit in the parties' understanding and necessary to give business efficiency to the parties' arrangement. For instance, in a case concerning the purchase of oranges, the German buyer entered into two substitute transactions, as the Spanish seller did not send the agreed goods in due time.[163] The buyer declared the contract avoided prior to making the substitute transactions. This method of calculation of damages has the capacity to end the contractual relations, which might otherwise have been continued for several years between the commercial actors. In contrast, there is a slight possibility of preserving the relations between the parties under the abstract method preferred under SGA. This is so, because this method, at least in principle, does not force the buyer to end the original contractual relations and that the parties might preserve their relationships. Because this method presumptively determines damages on the basis of the market price, it does not actually involve making a new contract with a competing seller. In fact, should the parties be cooperative, this method permits the buyer to sort out their disputes with the seller and calculate the loss based on the information available on the market. The parties would get the chance to communicate and collaboratively deal with the issue, even without any third party's involvement, and keep alive the prospect of continuing and developing their contractual relations. Thus, the abstract method prioritised

[160] MG Bridge, 'Defective goods and sub-sales' (1998) 3 *Journal of Business Law* 259, 259; see also Y Adar and M Gelbard, 'The role of remedies in the relational theory of contract' (2011) 7 *European Review of Contract Law* 399, 414.

[161] CISG Article 75; UPICC Official Comments, Article 7.4.5.

[162] CISG Advisory Council, 'Calculation of damages under CISG Articles 75 and 76' (2008) Opinion n 8, paras 2.3.2, 2.3.3, 2.3.4, 2.4.3.

[163] *Frischaff Produktions GmbH v Guillem Export, S.L* (2005) Appellate Court Valencia, Spain, CISG-online 1369; see also *Sunflower Seeds case* (2006) Court of Appeal Lamia, Greece, CISG-online 5924.

under the SGA might maintain the preservation of relations to a greater extent than the concrete method prioritised under other legal regimes.

The concrete method may not be consistent with the second norm either, ie conformity of extended relations with commercial matrix. As explained previously, neither the abstract method nor the concrete method may lead to the extension of relationship. Nevertheless, they can be analysed to determine which one is more efficient by reducing transactions costs faced by the parties. The concrete method preferred under UCC, CISG, and UPICC requires the buyer to make a new contract. This can increase transaction costs, as the buyer needs to search for a seller with similar goods, negotiate with them to reach satisfactory terms, and monitor the performance of contract by the new seller. These costs are absent under the abstract method prioritised under SGA, as there is no need for the buyer to enter a substitute transaction. In *Simancas Ediciones SA v Miracles Press Inc*, governed by CISG, when the originally agreed goods did not work properly, the Spanish buyer entered a new transaction with a Dutch company in order to acquire the substitute machine and then they claimed damages on the basis of such transaction.[164] The buyer was required to make this transaction in order to claim damages, as the machine was available in the market and if he did not make the transaction, the court could accuse them of not performing their duty to mitigate. If hypothetically SGA was the applicable legal regime, the buyer was not required to make a new contract and, as such, the costs of making a new transaction were absent.

Also, the abstract method minimises transaction costs at the stage of litigation of the dispute and can reduce the court's costs. Normally, a commercial buyer makes regular purchases after the non-performance of the seller in the original contract and it could be extremely difficult for the courts to determine which contract was intended as a substitute for the original contract.[165] In an Arbitral Award, the panel stated that damages could not be calculated under Article 75 because records from the aggrieved sellers' storage company were conflicting and otherwise insufficient to prove that wool, which was the subject of the avoided contract was used to fulfil a second sale.[166] In this case the aggrieved party was the seller but this kind of conflict between regularly transacting parties is likely to happen for the buyer as well. On the other hand, the market price rule looks primarily at the market price at time of breach and the adjudicators are not required to take account of several purchases that have been made after the breach of the main contract. This would lead to minimising the costs related to litigation, specifically those costs of investigating potential substitute transactions.

In addition, there is remarkable merit in the retention and promotion of the abstract method that discourages lengthy proceedings and renders it

[164] (2005) Appellate Court Palencia, Spain, CISG-online 1673.

[165] McKendrick (n 4) 457; Schlechtriem and Schwenzer (n 18) 1028.

[166] *Australian Raw Wool case III* (1999) China International Economic & Trade Arbitration Commission (CIETAC), CISG-online 1112.

comparatively straightforward to calculate the buyer's damages. One of the crucial benefits provided by this method lies in the way that it simplifies trials and leaves collateral issues, and even disputes, to be worked out on their own terms. The method preferred in English law exempts the buyer from demonstrating that the transaction was concluded reasonably. The adjudicators are also not required to investigate the reasonableness of such transaction. Conversely, it might be hard and expensive for the buyer to show that the price paid in the substitute transaction was reasonable.[167] For instance, it is required under CISG Article 75 that the substitute transaction should be concluded 'in a reasonable manner and within a reasonable time after avoidance'. In a case dealing with providing some chemical fertiliser by an Austrian seller, the buyer had to make a substitute purchase at a higher price in order to be able to perform the contract already concluded with the third party, as the seller did not properly perform their obligation.[168] The Tribunal investigated the substitute transaction meticulously and held that a transaction is reasonable if the buyer acted as a prudent and careful businessman and that the goods bought in replacement should be of the same kind and quality as the undelivered ones. Small differences in the quality of the goods are of no importance.[169] This decision shows that where the buyer has only made a single substitute transaction and wishes to cover the different price, they should show its reasonableness, which would increase the costs of enforcement. It is also costly for the courts to determine whether the substitute contract was made in a reasonable time and reasonable manner. It has been indicated by the Advisory Council that all the circumstances surrounding the substitute transaction will be evaluated.[170] This would make the process of litigation lengthy and hence expensive, as the courts or arbitral tribunals are required to consider all the subjective circumstances involved in the substitute transaction. In contrast, the abstract method exempts the buyer from demonstrating that the transaction was concluded reasonably. The adjudicators are also not required to investigate the reasonableness of such transaction. The abstract method can, therefore, effectively reduce the transaction costs.

[167] MG Bridge, 'The market rule of damages assessment' in Saidov and Cunnington (n 12) 439.
[168] *Ukrainian Chemical Fertilizer case* (1995) ICC Court of Arbitration, Basel, Switzerland, CISG-online 526.
[169] ibid, para 7.
[170] CISG Advisory Council, 'Calculation of damages under CISG Articles 75 and 76' (2008) Opinion n 8, para 2.3.1.

5

Performance-Directed Remedies

1. Introduction

This chapter seeks to analyse the law relating to the remedies directed at bringing about performance, including specific performance and cure, under the four legal regimes. Treitel has asserted that 'by enforced performance is meant, in its broadest sense, a process whereby the creditor obtains as nearly as possible the actual subject matter of [their] bargain, as opposed to compensation in money for failing to obtain it'.[1] Specific performance is a decree of the court which compels the defendant personally to do what he promised to do.[2] Burrows has also defined specific performance as 'an equitable remedy which enforces a defendant's positive contractual obligations: that is, it orders the defendant to do what he or she promised to do'.[3] Looked at in this way, it also includes the remedy of an injunction. A prohibitory injunction functions negatively, ie it orders the defendant not to do something, whilst a mandatory injunction functions positively, ie it orders the defendant to do something.[4] Although injunctions feature rarely in proceedings concerning contracts of sale, this chapter will treat injunctions as falling under the general umbrella of specific performance. First, the remedy of specific performance under the legal regimes will be scrutinised. There will be an attempt to identify and examine the significant differences regarding specific performance under the legal regimes. Second, the law relating to the buyer's right to cure will be explained and assessed under the regimes.

The international contract and sales law regimes dealt with in this book are considerably influenced by both common law and civil law and can be seen as a compromise of both legal families while SGA and UCC are, of course, an outgrowth

[1] GH Treitel, *Remedies for Breach of Contract: A Comparative Account* (Oxford University Press 1988) 43; D Harris, D Campbell and R Halson, *Remedies in Contract and Tort*, 2nd edn (Butterworths LexisNexis, 2002) 165; HG Beale (ed), *Chitty on Contracts, vol 1*, 34th edn (Sweet & Maxwell, 2022) para 30-15.

[2] G Jones and W Goodhart, *Specific Performance*, 2nd edn (Butterworths, 1996) 1; see also MG Bridge (ed), *Benjamin's Sale of Goods*, 11th edn (Sweet & Maxwell, 2022) para 17-096.

[3] A Burrows, *Remedies for Torts, Breach of Contract, and Equitable Wrongs*, 4th edn (Oxford University Press, 2019) 401.

[4] Burrows (n 3) 442; ICF Spry, *The Principles of Equitable Remedies: Specific Performance, Injunctions, Rectification, and Equitable Damages*, 9th edn (Thomson Legal & Regulatory Limited, 2013) 355; Harris, Campbell and Halson (n 1) 198; Justice Robert Sharpe, *Injunctions and Specific Performance*, 5th edn (The Carswell Company Ltd, 2017) 65.

of the common law.[5] As a general background to this chapter, it is worth discussing briefly the salient divergence of common law and civil law toward specific remedies. This outline can effectively contribute to identify the existing discrepancies between the four legal regimes and analyse them appropriately.

Both the English law and the US law, representing the common law, are generally perceived to be reluctant to compel a party in breach of contract to perform a non-monetary obligation.[6] In both jurisdictions, courts of equity refused to grant an injunction or issue a decree for specific performance when it was possible for the injured party to invoke an adequate remedy, normally damages, at law. As expressed famously by Holmes, the only accepted consequence of a legally binding promise under common law is that the law makes the promisor pay damages if the promised event does not come to pass.[7] In every case it leaves them free from interference until the time for fulfilment has gone by, and therefore frees to break their contract if they choose.[8] The reason for this approach partly lies in the historical origin of modern English contract law in the action of *assumpsit*. Such historical origin describes that the regular remedy for breach of a promise was payment of damages due to the wide availability of *assumpsit* as the principal remedy for the breach of contract in the sixteenth century.[9] The defendant who had made a promise and failed to honour it was conceived to have wronged the plaintiff and this wrong was considered trespass on their case.[10] Assumpsit was therefore a delictual remedy, by means of which the plaintiff was allowed to claim compensation in

[5] See generally JO Honnold and HM Flechtner, *Honnold's Uniform Law for International Sales under the 1980 United Nations Convention* (5th edn, Wolters Kluwer Law and Business 2021) 7; J Lookofsky, *Understanding the CISG, A Compact Guide to the 1980 United Nations Convention on Contracts for the International Sale of Goods*, 4th edn (Wolters Kluwer, 2012) 7-8-9; J Fitzgerald, 'CISG, specific performance, and the civil law of Louisiana and Quebec' (1996–1997) 16 *Journal of Law and Commerce* 291, 291; W Tetley, 'Mixed jurisdictions: common law *vs* civil law (codified and uncodified) (Part II)' (1999) 4 *Uniform Law Review* 877, 888.

[6] For English law see: Treitel (n 1) 63; E McKendrick, *Sale of Goods* (LLP Professional Publishing, 2000) 510; R Zimmermann, *The Law of Obligations: Roman Foundations of the Civilian Tradition* (Clarendon, 1996) 776; for US law see: MA Eisenberg, 'Actual and virtual specific performance, the theory of efficient breach, and the indifference principle in contract law' (2005) 93 *California Law Review* 975; RA Lord, *Williston on Contracts*, 4th edn (Thomson Reuters, 2023) para 67:1; D Frisch, *Lawrence's Anderson on the Uniform Commercial Code* (3rd edn, Thomson Reuters 2013) section 2-716, para 4.

[7] OW Holmes, 'The path of the law' (1897) *Harvard Law Review* 457, 462.

[8] OW Holmes, *The Common Law* (Harvard University Press, 1967) 301; see also OW Holmes, 'The path of the Law' (n 7) 457, 462; I Schwenzer and E Munoz, *Global Sales and Contract Law*, 2nd edn (Oxford University Press, 2022) 603.

[9] Zimmermann (n 6) 777; J Basedow, KJ Hopt and R Zimmermann, *The Max Planck Encyclopedia of European Private Law* (Oxford University Press, 2011) 1582; Jones and Goodhart (n 2) 6-7-8; C Szladits, 'The concept of specific performance in civil law' (1955) 4 *American Journal of Comparative Law* 208, 209; MG Bridge, 'Discharge for breach of the contract of sale of goods' (1982–1983) 28 *McGill Law Journal* 867, 873.

[10] GF Deiser, 'The origin of Assumpsit' (1912) 25 *Harvard Law Review* 428, 428; for further explanations regarding the historical origins of the action of assumpsit see JB Ames, 'The history of Assumpsit II, implied Assumpsit' (1888) 2 *Harvard Law Review* 53; JB Ames, 'The history of Assumpsit I. Express Assumpsit' (1888) 2 *Harvard Law Review* 1.

money for a wrong that had been done to them.[11] Assumpsit gradually acquired general recognition in the sixteenth century as the normal remedy for the breach of a simple promise.[12] However, on the other hand, an equitable relief of specific performance awarded by the English Court of Chancery was developed only in limited circumstances. Lord Hoffmann in *Co-operative Insurance* described that by the nineteenth century it was orthodox doctrine that the power to decree specific performance was part of the discretionary jurisdiction of the Court of Chancery to do justice in cases in which the remedies available at common law were inadequate.[13] The only type of goods that was considered unique per se was land, based on the assumption that since no two pieces of land are exactly alike, specific performance was truly the only satisfactory remedy. However, as will be explained in subsequent sections, both English law and US law gradually modified their closed-door positions regarding specific performance in the twentieth century. Apart from this historical explanation, two other reasons relevant to sales transaction are given for such approach. First reason deals with the problems associated with the courts' supervision on the specific performance order. The court has to conduct constant supervision to ensure that the order is executed completely and precisely. The principal difficulty with the courts' supervision is that the only means available to the court to enforce its order is the quasi-criminal procedure of punishment for contempt.[14] This powerful instrument would be unsuitable for adjudicating the disputes arisen over a business relationship. The reason might be that the prospect of jailing or fining one actor to enhance another actor's private gain is inharmonious with social norms concerning the appropriate use of the state's monopoly on force.[15] The second reason is that the order of specific performance may be in conflict with the buyer's duty to mitigate in sales transactions of manufactured goods.[16] The buyer is able to make a reasonable substitute transaction by referring to the market and acquire the goods similar to those contracted for. Such action by the buyer would not entail significant effort or attempt. A reasonably prompt action by the buyer would preclude further loss incurred to them. Incremental loss might actually happen, when the buyer waits for the courts' order of specific performance and its execution. Accordingly, those two reasons along with the underlying historical reason justify the common law approach about specific performance.

[11] Zimmermann (n 6) 777.

[12] Jones and Goodhart (n 2) 6.

[13] *Co-Operative Insurance Society Ltd v Argyll Stores (Holdings) Ltd* [1998] AC 1, 11.

[14] ibid, 12; see also *CH Giles & Co Ltd v Morris* [1972] 1 WLR 307, 316; A Phang, 'Specific performance-exploring the roots of "settled practice"' (1998) 61 *Modern Law Review* 421, 424; US Restatement (Second) of Contracts, section 366; *Crafts v Pitts* (2007) Supreme Court of Washington, 161 Wash.2d 16; *Woodruff v Thames* (2014) United States District Court, E.D. Arkansas, 143 So. 3d 54; Lord (n 6) para 67:2.

[15] Eisenberg (n 6) 977, 1020.

[16] Beale (n 1) para 30-006; E Peel, *Treitel on The Law of Contract*, 15th edn (Sweet & Maxwell, 2020) para 21-018; Bridge (n 2) para 17-095; S Herman, 'Specific performance: a comparative analysis: Part 1' (2003) 7 *Edinburg Law Review* 5, 20; Eisenberg (n 6) 975, 1022.

The English law and US law approaches are in stark contrast with the civil law approach, in which performance-directed remedies are considered primary remedies.[17] The idea that in the case of breach the promisor's primary obligation of performance is transformed into a secondary obligation to compensate the promisee by payment of damages is absent from civil law. Under Article 1221 of the French Civil Code 2016, the party towards whom the undertaking has not been fulfilled can compel the other to perform where performance is still possible.[18] Under the German Civil Code, the right to demand performance of the promise undertaken by the promisor in the contract is laid down in § 241(1) BGB: 'By virtue of an obligation an obligee is entitled to claim performance from the obligor. The performance may also consist in forbearance.' The buyer's right to cure has also been established under § 439 BGB: 'A seller who promised to deliver goods of a certain quality and has failed to do so is required by a regime of enforced performance to cure the defect or deliver conforming goods.' A widely accepted explanation for the centrality of specific remedies is the 'binding force of contracts', which lies in the doctrine of *pacta sunt servanda*: one must fulfil their promise.[19] The binding nature of promises arises out of the act of promise-making itself, which have a moral basis, as Fried has described that 'an individual is morally bound to [their] promises because he has intentionally invoked a convention whose function is to give moral grounds for another to expect the promised performance'.[20] What follows is the doctrinal analysis of specific performance under the four legal regimes, which illuminates whether they have adopted common law approach or civil law approach or a compromise of both approaches.

2. Specific Performance

A. SGA

i. Nature of Specific Performance

Specific performance is a secondary remedy under English law, which means that specific performance may only be awarded where damages are inadequate.[21]

[17] Article 1184 of Code Civile, 1804; see also Treitel (n 1) 56; Schwenzer and Munoz (n 8) 603; Szladits (n 9) 208, 212.

[18] F Terre, P Simler and Y Lequette, *Droit Civil, Les Obligation*, 7th edn (Dalloz, 1999) 615; B Nicholas, *The French Law of Contract*, 2nd edn (Oxford University Press, 1992) 211-212-216.

[19] Zimmermann (n 6) 576–77; see also BS Markesinis, H Unberath and A Johnston, *The German Law of Contract, A Comparative Treatise*, 2nd edn (Hart Publishing, 2006) 399.

[20] C Fried, *Contract as Promise: A Theory of Contractual Obligation* (Harvard University Press, 1981) 16.

[21] GH Treitel, 'Specific performance in the sale of goods' (1966) *Journal of Business Law* 211, 213–14; Peel (n 16) para 21-018; H Beale, B Fauvarque-Cosson, J Rutgers, D Tallon and S Vogenauer, *Cases, Materials and Text on Contract Law* (Hart Publishing, 2010) 848; R Zimmermann, *Roman Law,*

Damages are adequate where the buyer can acquire a satisfactory equivalent of what they contracted for from some other sources.[22] Thus specific performance is not generally ordered for example for the sale of commodities, or of shares, which are readily available in the market.[23] In fact, an order of specific performance in cases dealing with sale of commodities or shares would 'conflict with the mitigation requirement and be oppressive to the [seller]'.[24] The buyer would adequately be compensated by 'damages based on the difference between the cost (or market price) of the substitute, and the contract price'.[25] But where a substitute cannot be found, damages are considered to be inadequate. For instance, specific performance is almost invariably granted when there is a breach of sales contract of land: 'the traditional reasoning being that each piece of land is unique and cannot be replaced in the market'.[26]

However, it has been indicated that more recently English courts have tended to utilise the test of appropriateness of specific performance.[27] This test is not exactly whether damages are an adequate remedy, but whether specific performance will 'do more perfect and complete justice than an award of damages'.[28] This point has been shown in a case: 'the standard question in relation to the grant of an injunction, "are damages an adequate remedy?", might perhaps, in the light of the authorities of recent years, be rewritten: "is it just, in all the circumstances, that a plaintiff should be confined to [their] remedy in damages?"'.[29] In *Cavendish Square Holding BV v Makdessi*, Lord Neuberger mentioned that 'the minimum condition for an order of specific performance is that the innocent party should have a legitimate interest extending beyond pecuniary compensation for the breach'.[30] The courts exercise their discretionary power to determine the appropriateness of specific performance.

Contemporary Law, European Law, the Civilian Tradition Today (Oxford University Press, 2001) 145; *Co-Operative Insurance Society Ltd v Argyll Stores (Holdings) Ltd* [1998] AC 1, 11; S Rowan, *Remedies for Breach of Contract, A Comparative Analysis of Protection of Performance* (Oxford University Press, 2012) 17.

[22] Peel (n 16) para 21-020; Zimmermann (n 6) 779; E McKendrick, *Goode and McKendrick on Commercial Law*, 6th edn (Penguin Books, 2020) 144.

[23] Peel (n 16) para 21-020; see also Beale (n 1) para 30-025; for the sale of commodities see eg *Garden Cottage Foods Ltd v Milk Marketing Board* [1984] AC 130; for the sale of shares see eg *Re Schwabacher* [1901] 1 Ch 719; *Chinn v Hochstrasser* [1979] Ch 447.

[24] Beale (n 1) para 30-018.

[25] ibid.

[26] Burrows (n 3) 403; H Beale, B Fauvarque-Cosson, J Rutgers, D Tallon and S Vogenauer, *Cases, Materials and Text on Contract Law, Ius Commune Casebooks for the Common Law of Europe* 3rd edn (Hart Publishing, 2019) 940; see also *Sudbrook Trading Estate Ltd v Eggleton* [1983] 1 AC 444 478.

[27] It has been argued that this test is a reversion to the earlier approach taken by Court of Equity: Beale (n 1) para 30-018; *Beswick v Beswick* [1968] AC 58, 88-90-91; *Coulls v Bagots Executor and Trustee Co* [1967] ALR 385, 412; R Austen-Baker, 'Difficulties with damages as a ground for specific performance' (1999)10 *King's College Law Journal* 1, 4.

[28] *Tito v Waddell (No.2)* [1977] Ch. 106, 322; Peel opines that 'the test of appropriateness is generally more liberal than the test of inadequacy of damages': Peel (n 16) para 21-030.

[29] *Evans Marshall & Co. Ltd. v Bertola S.A* [1973] 1 WLR 349, 379.

[30] [2015] UKSC 67; [2016] AC 1172 at para 30; see also *Zinc Cobham 1 Ltd v Adda Hotels* [2018] EWHC 1025 (Ch); [2018] L. & T.R. 36 at para 48.

In other words, specific performance is less regarded as a secondary remedy and more as a kind of relief, being equally available as damages to an injured party. But this test does not seem to be significantly and practically different from the traditional test of the inadequacy of damages in general circumstances, as application of both tests to a case dealing with commodities or specific goods is most likely to yield the same result. In exceptional circumstances, however, they might diverge. For instance, in *Sky Petroleum Ltd v VIP Petroleum Ltd*, Goulding J ordered an interim injunction which had the effect of requiring specific performance of a contract to supply petrol.[31] The circumstances of the case were unusual, as the market for petrol was in a state of crisis in 1973, which made it almost impossible for the buyer to obtain alternative supplies.[32] In such exceptional circumstances, the test of appropriateness might expand the scope of the remedy by allowing the courts to examine the subjective circumstances of the case in order to find out which remedy can serve justice more effectively. More recently, this was endorsed by the Commercial Court in *VTB Commodities Trading DAC v JSC Antipinsky Refinery*, holding that in international sale of goods there is a strong presumption that specific performance should be confined to exceptional circumstances; for instance, where the goods are unique or the normal market is not functioning to enable the injured buyer find similar goods.[33] In contrast, the inadequacy test may imply that specific performance should not be awarded as the goods in question were commodities and the buyer could therefore obtain similar goods.

The discretionary power of the courts in relation to the order of specific performance signifies that the court is not mandated to grant it merely because the contract is valid at law and cannot be impeached on some specific equitable grounds such as misrepresentation or undue influence.[34] The discretion enjoyed by the courts is thus not an arbitrary discretion, but one to be governed as far as possible by fixed rules and principles.[35] It has been stated that 'specific performance depends upon a general discretion that should not be broken down into 'separate and distinct stages''.[36] Burrows opines that it is a misleading contrast to say that, unlike damages, specific performance is a discretionary remedy.[37] In fact, the description 'discretionary' makes the essentially insignificant point that, while there are no bars on damages, which are therefore available as of right for breach of contract, there are numerous, albeit clearly established, bars to specific performance.[38] SGA section 52

[31] [1974] 1 WLR 576, 578.

[32] [1974] 1 WLR 576; see also *Howard Perry Ltd v British Railways Board* [1980] 1 WLR 1375 (Ch).

[33] [2022] EWHC 2795 (Comm).

[34] *Stickney v Keeble* [1915] AC 386, 419; see also Burrows (n 3) 424; MG Bridge, *The Sale of Goods*, 4th edn (Oxford University Press, 2019) 710; Peel (n 16) para 21-031.

[35] *Lamare v Dixon* (1873) LR 6 HL 414, 423; see also *Co-operative Insurance Society Ltd v Argyll Stores (Holdings) Ltd* [1998] AC 1, 10-11-12.

[36] *CN Marine Inc v Stena Line A/B (No.2)* [1982] 2 Lloyd's Rep 336, 342; see also *VTB Commodities Trading DAC v JSC Antipinsky Refinery* [2020] EWHC 72 (Comm).

[37] A Burrows (n 3) 402.

[38] ibid.

gives the court discretion to order specific performance due to the breach of contract to deliver 'specific or ascertained goods'. This section provides:

> (1) In any action for breach of contract to deliver specific or ascertained goods the court may, if it thinks fit, on the plaintiff's application, by its judgment or decree direct that the contract shall be performed specifically, without giving the defendant the option of retaining the goods on payment of damages.
> (2) The plaintiff's application may be made at any time before judgment or decree.
> (3) The judgment or decree may be unconditional, or on such terms and conditions as to damages, payment of the price and otherwise as seem just to the court.

ii. Availability of Specific Performance

In this part, the grounds invoking and the factors limiting the availability of specific performance for the sale of manufactured goods will be considered. In order to do so, there will an analysis of the relevance of the type of goods and the concept of 'commercial uniqueness'. Also, the two significant factors limiting the availability of specific performance in sale of goods contracts, ie impossibility and severe hardship, will be surveyed.

Traditionally, English courts would only use their discretion to order specific performance in cases involving 'unique' goods, as these types of goods were not easily found in the market and the buyer could not replace them by using the money provided by an award of damages.[39] When the goods in question are unique in the sense that they possess significant physical characteristics and cannot be substituted in the market, an award of damages would therefore not adequately compensate the buyer.[40] Things like heirlooms, great works of art and valuable antiques are regarded as unique and they will be so regarded irrespective of the use to which the buyer intended to put them.[41] It has been said that 'where the article is not to be had upon the open market, this demonstrates a prima facie case for specific performance'.[42] But, in *Cohen v Roche* the court denied to order specific performance for a buyer of a set of Hepplewhite chairs, saying that they were 'ordinary articles of commerce and of no special value or interest'.[43] The buyer was an antique dealer purchasing the chairs for resale and he would treat the chairs as ordinary articles of commerce.[44] The fact that the buyer was purchasing the

[39] *Cud v Rutter* (1719) 1 P.Wms. 570; *Fothergill v Rowland* (1873) L.R. 17 Eq. 137; *Garden Cottage Foods Ltd v Milk Marketing Board* [1984] AC 130; *Pena v Dale* [2003] EWHC 1065; [2004] 2 B.C.L.C. 508; *Watson v* Watchfinder.co.uk *Ltd* [2017] EWHC 1275 (Comm); [2017] Bus L.R. 1309, see also V Mak, *Performance-oriented Remedies in European Sale of Goods Law* (Hart Publishing, 2009) 83.

[40] ibid; see also Burrows (n 3) 403–404.

[41] Treitel (n 21) 211, 214.

[42] *Eximenco Handels AG v Partredereit Oro Chief* [1983] 2 Lloyd's Rep 509, 521; see also *Swiss Bank Corp v Lloyds Bank Ltd* [1982] AC 584.

[43] [1927] 1 KB 169, 181.

[44] Ibid, 172.

chairs with a view to resale and not for personal use might have been relevant to the court's decision. In other words, the buyer did not expect to gain any special pleasure using the Hepplewhite chairs, which could not be acquired by other Hepplewhite chairs. The court's decision has been critiqued by Treitel stating that 'it is hard to see why specific relief was … refused in respect of a set of Hepplewhite chairs'.[45] This critique seems to be sensible, as the Hepplewhite chairs were rare, expensive antiques and not easily found on the market. Therefore, damages were not the appropriate remedy for compensating the buyer.

'Commercial uniqueness' is considered a specific application of the 'unique goods' test, under which specific performance may be ordered. Treitel has adopted a liberal view, which is more in favour of the buyer, of the term 'commercial uniqueness': 'although the goods may not be physically unique, buying substitutes would be so difficult or would cause such delay that the claimants' business would be seriously disrupted'.[46] The test of commercial uniqueness is therefore focused on the buyer's commercial situation and is particularly suitable for a commercial buyer who might have already sold the goods or might need the goods for use. This test was employed in *Sky Petroleum Ltd v VIP Petroleum Ltd*, in which an injunction was granted restraining the sellers from withholding supplies of petroleum to the buyers.[47] As explained before, the circumstances of the case were unusual, which makes it almost impossible for the buyer to obtain alternative supplies.[48] Bridge has stated that 'the remedy of specific performance or an equivalent form of relief has also been granted for more mundane objects which are difficult to acquire because no ready market exists'.[49] In *Behnke v Bede Shipping Co Ltd*, the ship (the *City*) bought by a German buyer had new boilers and engines which made her particularly suitable to the buyer's requirements as they were in accordance with certain German regulations.[50] Wright J stated that 'the *City* was of peculiar and practically unique value to the plaintiff' and that the buyer needed the ship immediately for the purposes of [their] businesses'.[51] However, in *Societe des Industries Metallurgiques SA v Bronx Engineering Co. Ltd.*, the buyer's request for specific performance was refused on the basis of 'commercial uniqueness' test.[52] This was so despite the fact that the goods in question was a complex machine to be manufactured by the seller and the buyer needed to wait for a long period of time in order to obtain a similar machine from another seller.[53] Specific performance was,

[45] Treitel (n 21) 211, 214.
[46] Burrows (n 3) 405; see also Austen-Baker (n 27) 1, 8.
[47] [1974] 1 WLR 576, 578; see also *Howard E Perry & Co Ltd v British Railways Board* [1980] 2 All ER 579.
[48] See section 3-2-1-1.
[49] Bridge (n 34) 714; see eg *Hart v Herwig* [1873] LR 8 Ch. App. 860; *Zegluga Polska SA v TR Shipping Ltd* [1996] 1 Lloyd's Rep 337; *The Oro Chief* [1983] 2 Lloyd's Rep 509.
[50] [1927] 1 KB 649.
[51] Ibid, 661.
[52] [1975] 1 Lloyd's Rep 465.
[53] ibid.

however, ordered on a different ground: the buyer had faced an impossible task in proving their loss in damages at trial.

SGA section 52 gives the court discretion to order specific performance in an action for breach of a contract to deliver 'specific or ascertained' goods.[54] This section, however, does not 'carefully set-out the circumstances in which specific performance is available'.[55] It only states that the remedy *may* be granted where the goods are specific or ascertained. 'Specific goods means goods identified and agreed on at the time a contract of sale is made, and includes an undivided share, specified as a fraction or percentage, of goods identified and agreed on as aforesaid.'[56] Ascertained goods have not been defined in the SGA. Treitel has opined that 'if the commercial man wants to find out what ascertained means he will have to go outside the [Act]'.[57] Ascertained goods signify the goods 'identified in accordance with the agreement after the time a contract of sale is made'.[58] It has been held that ascertained goods in section 52 'means that the individuality of the goods must in some way be found out, and when it is, then the goods have been ascertained'.[59]

The limiting factor of impossibility deals with the fact that specific performance will not be ordered where the performance is physically impossible and is based on the consideration that 'there is no sense in ordering the defendant to do something that he simply cannot do'.[60] For instance, the courts refuse to order specific performance against a person who has agreed to sell land which they do not own and cannot force the owner to convey to them.[61] Also, if the seller never receives the goods from its suppliers, the factor of impossibility implies that specific performance will not be decreed.[62] Impossibility is also applied when the performance of contract has become unlawful. For instance, if export of a specific type of goods becomes unlawful in a country after conclusion of a contract of sale, specific performance is not awarded due to the unlawfulness of performance.

In addition, the court is likely to avoid ordering specific performance when it will cause severe hardship to the seller. In *Patel v Ali*, the court's refusal to order specific performance was based on the ground of hardship suffered by the seller of land after the date of contract.[63] This hardship did not deal with financial difficulty and related mainly to the general health situation of the seller, as she had

[54] Peel (n 16) para 21-025; Bridge (n 2) para 17-100.
[55] Treitel (n 21) 211, 223.
[56] SGA section 61.
[57] Treitel (n 21) 211, 223.
[58] *Re Wait* [1927] 1 Ch 606, 630.
[59] *Thames Sack and Bag Co Ltd v Knowles & Co Ltd* (1918) 88 LJKB 585, 588.
[60] Mak (n 39) 97; see also Burrows (n 3) 430–31; Peel (n 16) 1109; *Forrer v Nash* [1865] 55 ER 858.
[61] See eg *Castle v Wilkinson* [1870] 5 Ch App 534; see also *Wroth v Tyler* [1974] Ch 30; *Warmington v Miller* [1973] QB 877.
[62] *CTI Group Inc v Transclear SA (The Mary Nour)* [2007] EWHC 2070 (Comm), [2008] 1 All ER (Comm) 192.
[63] [1984] Ch. 283; see also *Wedgwood v Adams* [1843] 8 Beav 103, [1843] 49 ER 598.

developed bone cancer and lost a leg.[64] Although this case does not involve the commercial buyer of manufactured goods, it can be considered to identify the general court's attitude regarding impossibility of performance in sales transaction, which is the sort of contract this book is particularly looking at. In terms of economic hardship, Goulding J has confirmed that 'mere pecuniary difficulties … afford no excuse from performance of a contract'.[65] In other words, specific performance will not be discharged solely due to financial difficulties.[66] It has been noted that hardship is a factor which the courts will consider alongside other factors but it is unlikely on its own to have sufficient weight to justify a decision to refuse to make an order for specific performance.[67] For instance, in *Co-operative Insurance Society*, the court's denial of granting specific performance was – amongst other reasons – on the ground that it would compel the defendants to run a business at loss, which would be financially ruinous for them to comply with the order.[68] Other reasons were that specific performance would be a potential instrument of oppression and the covenant terms lacked sufficient clarity.[69]

B. UCC

i. Nature of Specific Performance

Similar to English law, the US courts used to grant specific performance limitedly for unique chattels, such as works of art, heirlooms, vessels, and valuable documents. The rationale for such restrictive approach was that in the majority of sale of goods cases, monetary damages calculated on the basis of the market price rule, would enable the buyer to purchase the substitute goods, thus placing the injured party in as good a financial position as the enforcement of contract.[70] Nevertheless, for over a century, legal scholars were calling for a liberalisation of the availability of specific performance in general.[71] Although the courts remained

[64] [1984] Ch. 283.

[65] [1984] Ch. 283, 288; see also Mak (n 39) 98.

[66] Burrows (n 3) 431.

[67] E McKendrick, *Contract Law*, 10th edn (Oxford University Press, 2022) 909.

[68] [1998] AC 1, 7.

[69] ibid, 5–6.

[70] *i.Lan Systems, Inc. v Netscout Service Level Corp.* (2002) United States District Court, Massachusetts, 183. F.Supp.2d 328; *Barnes v Diamond Aircraft Industries, Inc* (2005) United States District Court, S.D. Florida. F.Supp.2d 131163; *Warehouse Technology, Inc. v Lift Inc* (2006) Court of Common Pleas of Pennsylvania, Philadelphia County, 2006 WL 224271; *Robins v Zwirner* (2010) United States District Court, New York, 713 F. Supp.2d 367; see also James White and Robert Summers RS, *Uniform Commercial Code*, 6th edn (Thomson Reuters, 2010) 313; WD Hawkland, CS Bjerre, LR Rusch and LT Garry, *Hawkland's Uniform Commercial Code Series* (Thomson Reuters, 2023), section 2-716, para 1; Frisch (n 6) section 2-715, para 4.

[71] J Pomeroy, *A Treatise on the Specific Performance of Contracts*, 3rd edn (1926); W Walsh, *A Treatise on Equity* (*Callaghan and Company*, 1930); EA Farnsworth, 'Legal remedies for breach of contract' (1970) 70 *Columbia Law Review* 1145; see also IA Elliott, 'Specific Performance' (1960) 1 *University of Illinois Law Forum*, 72; AT Kronman, 'Specific Performance' (1978) 45 *University of Chicago Law*

reluctant to grant specific performance, a buyer was able to recover the goods from non-delivering sellers by means of 'replevin', a form of legal action for the recovery of possession of chattels wrongfully withheld from a party entitled thereto.[72] The action was grounded on the passage of title of the goods, which led to the right of possession.[73] Thus, a buyer, who had paid the purchase price of identified goods, acquired title and was entitled to maintain the action. Following the filing of an appropriate claim form by the buyer seeking possession, an order would be issued and a sheriff would execute it by seizing the goods and delivering them to the buyer.[74] As such the right to replevin was inherently a possessory right, not a right concerning the enforcement of contracts. However, the elusive nature of the requirements for a decree of specific performance begged for codification of this remedy, which could more simply be employed in the emerging commercial world.

Williston, as the main drafter of the Uniform Sales Act being adopted between 1907 and 1941 in 36 States and the District of Columbia, was in favour of wider availability of 'specific performance', freed from the constraints of equity and thus added section 68.[75] This section provided that 'where the seller has broken a contract to deliver specific or ascertained goods, a court having the powers of a court of equity may, if thinks fit, on the application of the buyer, by its judgment or decree direct that the contract be performed specifically, without giving the seller the option of retaining the goods on payment of damages'.[76] Williston explained that this section would perhaps dispose courts to enlarge the number of cases where specific performance is allowed.[77] This section did not stray immediately from the previously developed common law principles. It failed to offer a general allowance of specific performance and only sought to broaden the conditions under which a court could order specific performance. Courts were of course given discretion to grant specific performance when they 'thought fit'. What was certainly implied in this codification was the idea that the common law requirement of an inadequate remedy at law was no longer a hard and fast rule. This meant that even if monetary damages were deemed adequate and ascertainable, a court could order specific performance in case it 'thought fit'. By the 1950s, the US courts started to recognise publicly the impact of section 68 of the Uniform

Review 351; EA Farnsworth, 'Problems of Non-performance in Contract' (1981) 17 *New England Law Review* 249; TR Lewis, MK Perry and DEM Sappington, 'Renegotiation and Specific Performance' (1989) 52 *Law and Contemporary Problems* 33.

[72] H Greenberg, 'Specific Performance under Section 2-716 of the Uniform Commercial Code: "a More Liberal Attitude" in "Grand Style"' (1981) 17 *New England Law Review* 321, 325.

[73] R Shinn, *A Treatise on the American Law of Replevin and Kindred Actions for Getting Possession of Chattels: Being a Complete Statement of the General Principle* (Gale, Making of Modern Law, 2010) 125.

[74] ibid, 127.

[75] S Williston, *The Law Governing Sales of Goods at Common Law and Under the Uniform Sales Act* (Baker, Voorhis & Company 1924) 996.

[76] Uniform Sales Act section 68.

[77] Williston (n 75) 997.

Sales Act and welcomed the growing tendency to liberalise the requirements for specific performance.[78] A significant example of how courts appeared to become less stringent in granting specific performance is found in *Poltorak v Jackson Chevrolet Co*, in which a sale of a new black Chevrolet was agreed between the parties.[79] The buyer traded in his old car and received $714.22 as a credit. While the seller could have sold the car to the buyer, they simply decided they would not. The court, ruling in favour of the buyer, reasoned that specific performance should be ordered where the buyer demonstrated that he was unable to procure a subject substantially similar to the one which he contracted to buy, due to the nature of the subject, the conditions of the market, or other circumstances.[80] In addition, delay, expense and difficulties associated with procuring such a subject would cause serious inconvenience, loss or hardship and that manifest justice would not be achieved unless performance is decreed. The same reasoning was given in favour of the buyer in *Hogan v Norfleet*, where a Florida appellate court was concerned with a suit to compel specific enforcement of a contract to sell a franchised bottled gas business.[81] The court ruled that where personal property is of peculiar character and value, specific performance will be granted.[82] Additionally, when the value of the property in question is uncertain or not readily identifiable in the market, or if losses resulting from the breach of the contract are too uncertain or indefinite, specific performance will be ordered. Rather than being concerned with the seller's ability to perform the contract, the test employed by the courts in these cases was whether damages for the breach were the equivalent of the promised performance. In other words, the key question was whether the injured buyer was able to find a replacement in order to cover and then claim for the adequate remedy of damages. Despite what Greenburg expressed, that UCC Section 2-716 was written so that 'liberalization of the availability of specific performance in sale of goods cases could be achieved in the "Grand Style of the Common Law"',[83] section 69 Uniform Sales Act and the line of cases that emerged, had already embarked on the trend toward liberalisation of specific performance and laid the groundwork for the new codification of specific performance under the UCC. This historical account of the early codification of specific performance under the Uniform Sales Act is a necessary introduction for understanding the new codification of this remedy under the UCC.

[78] J DuBay, 'Some problems in specific performance of timber sale contracts' (1960–1961) 38 *University of Detroit Law Journal* 324, 332; M Handler, 'Specific performance under section 2-716 of the Uniform Commercial Code- what other proper circumstances' (1971) 33 *University of Pittsburgh Law Review* 243, 246.

[79] (1948) Supreme Judicial Court of Massachusetts, 79 N.E.2d 285.

[80] ibid, paras 1, 2.

[81] (1959) District Court of Appeal of Florida, 113 So.2d 437.

[82] ibid, para 5.

[83] Greenberg (n 72) 321, 323.

ii. Availability of Specific Performance

UCC, which was drafted with the intention to modernise commercial law, sets forth a liberal approach to specific performance under section 2-716. The first subsection provides that 'specific performance may be decreed where the goods are unique or in other circumstances'. The Official Comment states that in drafting the first subsection, the drafters aimed to achieve two apparently inconsistent goals: on one hand, to continue the general prior policy as to specific performance; on the other, to further a more liberal attitude than some courts have shown in relation to the specific performance of contract of sale, without intending to impair in any way the exercise of the court's sound discretion in the matter under the general prior policy.[84] Such liberalisation was achieved, when the first sub-section codified the common law 'uniqueness test', as well as making specific performance available, and 'the other proper circumstances' test, which replaced the 'think fit' doctrine of section 68 under Uniform Sales Act.[85] This indicates that specific performance is no longer restricted to goods which are already specific or ascertained at the time of contracting. The test of 'uniqueness' must be fulfilled in light of the total circumstances surrounding the contract. Uniqueness is thus no longer the only ground for granting this remedy and is intended to be wider than the concept of 'heirlooms or priceless works of art'. For instance, in *Barnes v Diamond Aircraft Industries Inc*, the Court ruled that the goods in question, which was an aircraft, was not so unique to merit an order of specific performance.[86] In addition, there was lack of certainty regarding the individualised specifications concerning the goods and that damages would clearly be adequate to compensate the buyer. Similarly, in *DiabloSport, LLC v Granatelli Motor Sports, Inc*, the District Court of Florida decided that the manufactured goods in question, while being a very specific product that could not readily be obtained from other manufacturers, was not unique and specific performance was not granted.[87] On the other hand, in *Montanile v Botticelli*, the court argued that specific performance is addressed to the reasonable and sound discretion of the court.[88] The court ordered specific performance, since the goods in question were the baseball cards, being rare, highly unique and specialised ones. Also, in *Jet Experts, LLC v Asian Pacific Aviation Ltd*, it was found that the buyer of specialised aircraft had no adequate remedy at law, when the seller found a higher bidder and terminated the contract with the buyer.[89] The court explained that the specific performance remedy was mainly

[84] UCC Official Comments, section 2-716, para 1.

[85] Hawkland, Bjerre, Rusch and Garry (n 70) section 2-716, para 1; Frisch (n 6) section 2-716, para 4; see also *Tom Doherty Associates Inc v Saban Entertainment Inc* (1995) United States Court of Appeals, 60 F.3d 27; *Robins v Zwirner* (2010) United States District Court, New York, 713 F.Supp.2d 367.

[86] (2007) United States District Court, Florida, 499 F.Supp.2d 1311.

[87] (2005) United States District Court, Florida, WL 2465019.

[88] (2009) United States District Court, Virginia, Alexandria Division, WL 2378684.

[89] (2022) United States District Court, New York, 602 F.Supp.3d 636.

imposed when there was no satisfactory, easier remediation at hand, such as the delivery of an equivalent article or payment of money.[90] While aircrafts were not generally considered unique goods, this aircraft was not replaceable, since it was unique in its characteristics and ability to serve the buyer's purpose of organ transportation and ambulatory patient transport. The buyer was thus granted specific performance. These cases show that although the UCC section 2-716 appears to have adopted a more liberal approach toward specific performance, the concept of 'uniqueness' is still at the heart of judicial decision making and the characteristics of the goods in question as well as the overall circumstances should be taken into consideration. Therefore, it seems the US courts still follow the classical, common-law approach toward specific performance and are still hesitant in granting this equitable remedy more readily.

In addition to specific performance, subsection 3 of section 2-716 provides the conditions under which the buyer is entitled to replevy the goods which are the subject of sale. In addition to the requirement that the goods must be identified, one of these two conditions should be present: (i) the buyer being unable to effect cover or the circumstances showing the buyer will be unable to effect cover, or (ii) the goods having been shipped under reservation and the buyer tendering the amount of the security interest granted by section 2-505.[91] The right to replevin is available to the buyer in addition to the buyer's right to recover the goods under section 2-502 or the ability to obtain specific performance under subsection 1 of section 2-716. While there is certainly an overlap between this right and the remedy of specific performance due to their focus on the buyer's ability to cover, the right to replevin is considered a legal remedy, which would be more readily available should a court be unwilling to order the equitable remedy of specific performance.

C. CISG and UPICC

i. Nature of Specific Performance

Under both CISG and UPICC, the buyer's right to require performance has priority over any other legal remedy, which comes close to the civil law tradition, as explained previously. Requiring performance is not a discretionary remedy. This means that to choose and exercise this remedy, the buyer does not need to show

[90] ibid, 641; see also *Coastal Aviation, Inc. v Commander Aircraft Co* (1996) United States District Court, New York, 937 F.Supp. 1051; *Aviation Development Co. PLC v C&S Acquisition Corp* (1999) United States District Court, New York, 1999 WL 46630.

[91] UCC Official Comments, section 2-716, para 3; Hawkland, Bjerre, Rusch and Garry (n 70) section 2-716, para 2; Frisch (n 6) section 2-716, para 4; see also *Tatum v Richter* (1977) Court of Appeals of Maryland, 373 A.2d 923; *Putnam Ranchers Inc v Corkle* (1973) Supreme Court of Nebraska, 203 N.W.2d 502; *Robert Reish v Phoenix Heliparts, Inc* (2018) United States Bankruptcy Appellate Panel of the Ninth Circuit, WL 2107796.

that damages are inadequate in compensating their loss. However, it should be noted that these regimes represent a middle ground between the common law and civil law systems.[92] While these regimes establish the right to performance as a rule, they have included numerous exceptions, which in practice considerably restrict the right, thus resembles the approach of the common law.

The buyer's right to specific performance has been provided under the CISG Article 46 (1), which states that 'the buyer may require performance by the seller of [their] obligations unless the buyer has resorted to a remedy which is inconsistent with this requirement'. In a similar tone, UPICC Article 7.2.2 states that 'where a party who owes an obligation other than one to pay money does not perform, the other party may require performance …'. Both regimes fail to employ the term 'specific performance'; instead, they speak of a party 'requiring' performance by the other. CISG requires a clear declaration that the buyer requests the performance of a contractual obligation.[93] The buyer needs to fulfil this duty in accordance with the principles of Articles 26 and 27. UPICC Article 7.2.2(e) has also set out the similar requirement that the buyer should request performance within reasonable time.

Generally, the right to perform emerges in cases of non-performance if the obligation due, as indicated in UPICC Article 7.1.1. According to this article, non-performance covers various circumstances, such as partial or defective performance.[94] CISG Article 45(1)(a) more specifically and with greater detail explains that 'if the seller fails to perform any of [their] obligations under the contract or this Convention, the buyer may exercise the rights provided in articles 46 to 52'. The seller's failures are: the failure to deliver the goods within the prescribed period (Articles 30, 31, 33); to provide the documents required by the contract or usage (Article 30, 34); and to transfer unencumbered property in the goods (Article 41) or other contractually accepted obligations.[95] It thus follows that clear

[92] See MJ Bonell, 'The UNIDROIT principles and transnational law' (2000) 5 *Uniform Law Review* 199, 201; H Lutz, 'The CISG and common law courts: is there really a problem?' (2004) 35 *Victoria University of Wellington Law Review* 711, 712; ED Lauson, 'Construction and application of United Nations Convention on Contracts for the International Sale of Goods' (2005) 200 *American Law Reports ALR Federal*, para 14[c]; V Heutger, Janwillem and Oosterhuis, 'Specific performance within the hierarchy of remedies in European contract law' in J Smits, D Haas and G Hesen (eds), *Specific Performance in Contract Law: National and Other Perspectives* (Intersentia, 2008) 148; U Magnus, 'The Vienna Sales Convention (CISG) between civil and common law – best of all worlds?' (2010) 3(1) *Journal of Civil Law Studies*, 67, 76.

[93] UNCITRAL Digest of Case Law on the United Nations Convention on Contracts for the International Sale of Goods (2016) Article 46, para 10; see also *Coil Winding Machine Case* (2002) Appellate Court Karlsruhe, Germany, CISG-online 817; *Storage Tanks of a Fruit Processing Plant case* (2017) Austrian Supreme Court, CISG-online 3043; *PET Rolls case* (2020) Court of First Instance Canton Zug, CISG-online 5926.

[94] S Vogenauer, *Commentary on the UNIDROIT Principles of International Commercial Contracts*, 2nd edn (Oxford University Press, 2015) 831; see also GH Jones and P Schlechtriem, 'Breach of Contract' in A von Mehren (ed), *International Encyclopedia of Comparative Law, vol VII: Contracts in General, ch 15* (JCB Mohr (Paul Siebeck), 2008) paras 136–137.

[95] P Schlechtriem and L Schwenzer L, *Commentary on the UN Convention on the International Sale of Goods*, 5th edn (Oxford University Press, 2022) 965; S Kroll, L Mistelis and PP Viscasillas,

cases are where there has been no delivery at all; where the seller has delivered the goods at a place different from what was required; where the seller has failed to transfer the property in the goods to the buyer; where the seller has failed to provide correct documents.[96] An obscure situation arises where the contract is for the sale of goods with specific descriptions and the seller fails to deliver the goods with those specific descriptions but another one with the exact same function. The question is whether this is a case of the delivery of non-conforming goods or whether it should be construed as a delivery of something completely distinctive and should hence be considered as a non-delivery case governed by Article 46(1). Examining several cases shows that this situation is normally regarded as a case of non-conformity based on Article 35, which covers delivery of an aliud.[97] Non-conformity breaches are dealt with under Article 46(2),(3), referring to the seller's right to cure.

ii. Availability of Specific Performance

Under CISG, the buyer is generally entitled to require performance of the contract, unless they have resorted to inconsistent remedies with specific performance.[98] While such restriction is not explicitly found in UPICC, it would be logical for any adjudicator to take them into account when deciding whether the seller should be ordered performance of the contract. One of the obvious, inconsistent remedies is avoidance, which immediately discharges the seller from their original obligations and the contract is actually terminated (Articles 49, 81).[99] The other is price reduction, which aims to adjust the seller's obligations to the performance under way or already made (Article 50).[100] By invoking price reduction, the buyer either indicates the abandonment of any right to substitute goods in fundamental breach

UN Convention on Contracts for the International Sale of Goods (CISG) Commentary (Hart Publishing, 2011) 688; Herman (n 16) 194, 195; CM Bianca and MJ Bonell, *Commentary on the International Sales Law, The 1980 Vienna Sales Convention* (Giuffre, 1987) 335.

[96] Schlechtriem and Schwenzer (n 95) 941.

[97] *Mower case* (1993) Local Court Cloppenburg, Germany, CISG-online 85; *Intel Pentium II/300 Processors case* (2001) Austrian Supreme Court, CISG-online 652; *Cerámica Tudelana S.A. v Wassmer Gruppe Spezialmaschinen GmbH* (2014) Court of First Instance No.3 of Tudela, Spain, CISG-online 2527; *F.P.S.P.A V Hamburger P.S.* (2015) District Court Lodz, CISG-online 5295; *N.K. v P.K.S* (2016) Swedish Supreme Court, CISG-online 4088; *Cesaretti Iribarren y Asociados S.A. de C.V. v Bodegas Silvano García, S.L.* (2017) Court of Appeal Murcia, Spain, CISG-online 2901.

[98] UNCITRAL Digest of Case Law on the United Nations Convention on Contracts for the International Sale of Goods (2016) Article 46, para 7; *Officine Maraldi S.p.A. v Intessa BCI S.p.A.* (2009) Tribunale di Forlì (District Court Forli) CISG-online 1780; JS Ziegel, 'The Remedial Provisions in the Vienna Sales Convention: Some Common Law Perspectives' in M Bender, *International Sales: The United Nations Convention on Contracts for the International Sale of Goods* (Galston & Smit edn, 1984); Schwenzer and Munoz (n 8) 606.

[99] Schlechtriem and Schwenzer (n 95) 958; Kroll, Mistelis and Viscasillas (n 95) 690; Bianca and Bonell (n 95) 336; P Huber and A Mullis, *The CISG, A New Textbook for Students and Practitioners* (Sellier, European Law Publishers, 2007) 191.

[100] Bianca and Bonell (n 95) 336.

cases or the buyer signifies a desire to retain the non-conforming goods along a reduced purchase price corresponding to lost value, which largely reflects the cost of repair. In *Automated Pasta Production Lines*, the parties entered into the purchase contract of a second-hand automated line for the production of pasta.[101] The expert report indicated that the automated line failed to comply with the quality guarantees promised by the seller. The buyer did not request the seller to conduct another examination, nor to correct the defects within a reasonable period of time. Rather the buyer purported to reduce the purchase price, which proportionately corresponded the value of the goods actually delivered against the value of conforming goods at the time of the delivery. Another inconsistent remedy is the claim for damages due to failure to perform.[102] When the buyer requests damages for an impairment of their performance interest, which is calculated on the basis of difference between the contract price and the market price, specific performance will not be ordered, as both remedies aim to compensate the same interest.[103]

In addition, the buyer's right to specific performance has been seriously undermined by CISG Article 28, which, essentially, places a limitation on the remedies available to a non-breaching party to a transaction.[104] Such an article is absent in UPICC. It seems that this article seeks to bridge the differences between the continental European legal system and the English and American legal system on the issue of the right require performance. More precisely, this provision is a concession to Anglo-American legal systems, where damages is the primary remedy and specific performance is considered an exceptional, equitable remedy. This article provides a discretionary power to courts facing with a request for performance by a party who is entitled to this remedy under CISG, by setting out that 'a court is not bound to enter a judgement for specific performance unless the court would do so under its own law in respect of similar contracts of sale not governed by this Convention'. The term of 'its own law' refers to 'the authoritative law, [as] the domestic law of the forum State, excluding conflict of laws'.[105] This article thus explicitly allows the courts to refer to its own domestic law in order to decide about the remedy of specific performance. This means that buyer's right to require performance is unenforceable if the court appealed to would not issue a judgment of specific performance in case of similar contracts of sale according to its own law.[106] It is not necessary to determine the applicable law on the basis of the

[101] (2011) Federal Arbitrazh Court of North Caucasus Area, Krasnodor, Russia, CISG-online 2518.
[102] Schlechtriem and Schwenzer (n 95) 958.
[103] Kroll, Mistelis and Viscasillas (n 95) 690; Treitel (n 1) 45.
[104] I Schwenzer, C Fountoulakis and M Dimsey, *International Sales Law, A Guide to the CISG*, 2nd edn (Hart Publishing, 2012) 181; S Walt, 'For specific performance under the United Nations Sales Convention' (1991) 26 *Texas International Law Journal* 211, 218; PA Piliounis, 'The remedies of specific performance, price reduction and additional time (Nachfrist) under the CISG: are these worthwhile changes or additions to English Sales Law?' (2000) 12 *Pace International Law Review* 1, 8.
[105] Schlechtriem and Schwenzer (n 95) 659.
[106] ibid, 960.

principles of private international law.[107] For example, if a Belgian buyer brings an action against an English seller in English courts, English law will be applied to decide on the admissibility of the right to require performance. However, in a case of referring the dispute to an arbitral tribunal, the 'own law' situation is not entirely clear. It has been suggested that the arbitrators should resolve the issue by referring to the 'substantive law of the state, to whose *lex arbitri* (arbitration law) the arbitral tribunal is subject', which means 'the law determined by the seat of the arbitral tribunal'.[108] The apparent general right to specific performance under CISG is therefore seriously restricted by this article, as the courts of those jurisdictions restricting the availability of specific performance might decline to grant specific performance to the buyer. Nevertheless, this article has limited practical significance, as normally the buyers in international trade agreements seek to exercise their right to performance only if they are certain of unproblematic enforcement of the adjudicator's ruling. It may therefore be more convenient for the commercial buyers to achieve their desirable result by making cover transactions for the goods in question and claiming damages instead.

In addition to Article 28, impossibility of performance and hardship are the other limiting factors to the performance claim CISG.[109] These two factors are also considered the main limiting factors in UPICC. In this legal regime, the seller is exempt from performance of the contract if performance is impossible in law or fact. The reason is that demanding performance in such circumstances serves no purpose.[110] UPICC, however, has failed to clearly define when performance is considered impossible, nor what kinds of 'impossibility' are covered under this notion.[111] It has been suggested that 'the exception of impossibility covers all kinds of impossibility, ie objective and subjective impossibility, initial and subsequent impossibility, and partial and full impossibility'.[112] Rather than using the term 'impossibility', CISG Article 79 states that if the failure to perform is caused by an impediment for which the seller can claim exemption, the buyer is not entitled to require performance. However, it is clear that 'impediment' refers generally to impossibility of performance.[113] Although CISG Article 79 (5) states that 'nothing in this article prevents either party from exercising any right other than to claim damages under this Convention', it is illogical to hold party liable when performance is barred by an impediment.[114] 'Impossibility' consists of permanent

[107] ibid.

[108] ibid; see also Schwenzer and Munoz (n 8) 614.

[109] Huber and Mullis (n 99) 193; Schlechtriem and Schwenzer (n 95) 652; Kroll, Mistelis and Viscasillas (n 95) 691.

[110] Vogenauer (n 94) 888.

[111] ibid.

[112] ibid.

[113] Kroll, Mistelis and Viscasillas (n 95) 678.

[114] See eg Honnold and Flechtner (n 5) 568; see also L DiMatteo, A Janssen, U Magnus and R Schulze, *International Sales Law, A Handbook*, 2nd edn (Beck, Nomos, Hart, 2021) 608; Schlechtriem and Schwenzer (n 95) 961; Schwenzer and Munoz (n 8) 606; J Rimke 'Force majeure and hardship: Application in international trade practice with specific regard to the CISG and the UNIDROIT

(when the specific goods has been destroyed) and temporary impossibility (during the period of impediment the purchased item has been stolen).[115]

Hardship is a controversial limiting factor under CISG. Hardship refers to situations where 'performance may still be objectively possible but that the seller faces serious obstacles that he would have to overcome in order to make performance'.[116] An example of hardship is where the supply of a material needed to manufacture certain goods unexpectedly becomes dramatically reduced and excessively inflated in price that only a very few manufacturers would be able to continue in production. Such situation recently occurred during the global coronavirus pandemic, which significantly affected supply chains and rendered performance of contract impossible for manufacturers who were not able to procure the materials needed to produce goods they had contracted to sell. A recent CISG Advisory Council's opinion has clarified that Article 79 governs hardship situations.[117] As stated in the opinion, hardship can be considered as a special type of 'impediment', which should be outside of a party's sphere of control and could not have been reasonably taken into account by that party at the time of the conclusion of the contract.[118] Prior to the publication of the Opinion, it was ambiguous when and in what conditions the seller's failure to perform exempted them from the buyer's right to require performance. CISG Articles 79 failed to provide a clear yardstick governing hardship situations. The Opinion has offered a multifactorial approach, which can assist the parties ensuring whether a hardship satisfying the impossibility of performance criterion does exist in their situation.[119] Nevertheless, it has remained unclear to what extent those factors should be satisfied and inevitably the factual circumstances of an individual case should be examined.

While the concept of 'hardship' is recognised in UPICC Article 6.2.1, Article 7.2.2 governing specific performance and exceptions to this remedy has failed to use this concept. Perhaps the drafters of UPICC intentionally did not refer to hardship in order to avoid the difficulties and uncertainties associated with this concept.[120] Instead, this article states that where 'performance or, where relevant, enforcement is unreasonably burdensome or expensive', the buyer's right to require performance will be excluded.[121] The Official Commentary has clarified that in

Principles of International Commercial Contracts' 217 in *Pace Review of the Convention on Contracts for the International Sale of Goods* (Kluwer 1999–2000) 197–243; AM Garro, 'Comparison between provisions of the CISG regarding exemption of liability for damages (Art. 79) and the counterpart provisions of the UNIDROIT Principles (Art. 7.1.7)' in J Felemegas, *An International Approach to the Interpretation of the United Nations Convention on Contracts for the International Sale of Goods (1980) as Uniform Sales Law* (Cambridge University Press, 2007) 239.

[115] Schlechtriem and Schwenzer (n 95) 962.

[116] Kroll, Mistelis and Viscasillas (n 95) 691; see also Honnold and Flechtner (n 5) 579.

[117] CISG Advisory Council, 'Hardship under the CISG' (2020) Opinion n 20, para 2.2.

[118] ibid, para 4.5.

[119] ibid, para 7.

[120] For an analysis of distinction between unreasonably burdensome and hardship see Vogenauer (n 94) 895; I Schwenzer, 'Specific Performance and Damages According to the 1994 UNIDROIT Principles of International Commercial Contracts' (1999) 1 *European Journal of Law Reform* 289, 295.

[121] UPICC Article 7.2.2.

exceptional cases, particularly when there has been a dramatic change of circumstances after the conclusion of a contract, performance, although still possible, may have become so onerous that it would run counter to the general principle of good faith and fair dealing to require it.[122] In other words, the right to performance is excluded where chance of circumstances would lead to an unreasonable burden or performance would be unreasonably expensive for the non-performing party. Performance may still be feasible but has become so economically burdensome that it would be inconsistent with the principle of good faith to require it.[123]

3. Cure

A. SGA

The SGA lacks specific provisions concerning the buyer's right to cure for commercial buyers and has confined this remedy to consumer-buyers, under part 5A. These new remedies designed for consumers are pursuant to the EC Directive on Consumer Goods and Associated Guarantees of 1999 and are currently available through the Consumer Rights Act 2015, which falls outside the remit of this book.[124] In light of the UK Supreme Court's decision in *Res Cogitans*,[125] it has been re-emphasised that SGA is not a complete code and that the common law should be explored to see whether the seller's right to cure is present in English law. It is true that while still a remarkable number of commercial disputes are settled amicably, with the goods being repaired or replaced, it remains unclear under the present law whether, or to what extent, the buyer can insist on repair or replacement, following delivery of defective goods. The Law Commission of England and Wales alluded that under general common law doctrines, a seller may be entitled to repair or replace defective goods in certain circumstance and to require the buyer to accept the repaired or replacement goods.[126] Any right to cure would have to be exercised either before the contractual delivery date, where time is or has been made of the essence of the contract,

[122] Para 3.b.
[123] Vogenauer (n 94) 894.
[124] Bridge (n 2) para 12-073.
[125] *PST Energy 7 Shipping LLC v OW Bunker Malta Ltd (Res Cogitans)* [2016] UKSC 23, [2016] AC 1034.
[126] The Law Commission (Working Paper No. 85) and the Scottish Law Commission (Consultive Memorandum No. 58) on Sale and Supply of Goods (1983) para 2.38; see also A Apps, 'The right to cure defective performance' (1994) *Lloyd's Maritime and Commercial Law Quarterly*, 525, 531; WCH Ervine, 'Cure and retender revisited' [2006] *Journal of Business Law* 799, 805; V Mak, 'The seller's right to cure defective performance – a reappraisal' [2007] *Lloyd's Maritime Commercial Law Quarterly* 409, 412.

or within a reasonable time following the conclusion of contract. A number of cases, concerning tender of goods without the appropriate documents, demonstrated that when the buyer is correct in rejecting an invoice, failing to represent the contract goods, the seller is not prevented, if they have time within which to do so, from tendering another parcel of goods, which accord with the contractual specifications.[127] In the well-known case of *Borrowman Phillips & Co v Free & Hollis*, the buyers had correctly rejected a cargo of maize abroad a ship, because the shipping documents had not been tendered with it.[128] When the buyer rejected these goods before the expiry of the delivery date, the seller tendered another cargo with appropriate documentation. The Court of Appeal in a commercially sensible judgment held that since the buyer had rejected the goods, the seller was at liberty to tender another cargo in conformity with the contract. The buyer must therefore accept and pay for this cargo.

However, it has remained unclear whether the English courts would be prepared to extend the right to cure to breach of an express or implied condition concerning quality of goods delivered. When the contract is for the sale of specific goods, the right to cure the defect seems to be limited to repair and that the seller is not entitled to replace defective goods without the buyer's consent.[129] In the recent remarkable case of *J & H Ritchie Ltd v Lloyd Ltd*, a point concerning the possibility of repair or cure in a sale of goods contract was raised before a Scottish court, prior to being appealed at the House of Lords.[130] In this case, a piece of agricultural machinery, a seed drill and power harrow, as a specific goods was sold. When the buyer received the machinery and started using it, they noticed a serious problem with the drive train of the harrow. This issue was proved to be a breach of the terms of satisfactory quality and fitness for purpose implied by SGA section 14. The seller offered to take the harrow to its workshop for inspection and to provide a temporary replacement. It is not exactly clear from the facts whether the buyer agreed to a repair by the seller. However, Lord Hamilton from an Extra Division of the Scottish Court of Session argued that 'it is a reasonable inference that the buyer was content that, in light of what might be found on inspection, the respondent would be free, at its own expense, to effect any repair which be called for'.[131] At the seller's premises, it was discovered that two bottom bearings were missing from the harrow. These were ordered immediately from the manufacturer, fitted by the seller and the buyers were informed that the repairs had been

[127] See *E. E. & Brian Smith Ltd v Wheatsheaf Mills Ltd* [1939] 2 K.B. 302; *Empresa Exportadora De Azucar v Industria Azucarera Nacional SA (The Playa Larga and Marble Islands)* [1983] 2 Lloyd's Rep 171, 185.

[128] (1878) 4 QBD 500.

[129] The Law Commission (Working Paper no. 85) and the Scottish Law Commission (Consultive Memorandum no. 58) on Sale and Supply of Goods (1983) para 2.38.

[130] [2007] UKHL 9.

[131] [2005] 1 S.C. 155, para 32.

carried out and that the harrow was available for collection. The harrow was then conforming to the contract. However, when the buyer asked about the nature of the defect in the harrow, the seller did not cooperate and failed to disclose it. The buyer, being anxious about the state of the repaired machine, rejected the goods. The key question was whether in the circumstance the buyer was still entitled to reject the goods following the repair by the seller. The seller argued that where a buyer did not exercise a right to reject and the breach was remediable, it remained open to the seller to attempt to cure the defect and that if this was done and the goods re-tendered, a buyer who had not yet rejected them was obliged to accept them. The buyer, however, did not accept the repaired goods. Such disagreement between the parties and the complexity caused lies on the ambiguous scope of section SGA section 35(1). This section asserts that 'the buyer is deemed to have accepted the goods (a) when he intimates to the seller that [they] have accepted them, or (b) when the goods have been delivered to [them] and [they] do any act in relation to them which is inconsistent with the ownership of the seller'.

Under the previous version of SGA, it could be argued that the right to reject had been lost either because permitting a repair may amount to an act inconsistent with the ownership of the seller, or the delay incurred could have led to the loss of the right to reject due to the expiry of a reasonable time. SGA has also failed to insert any provisions dealing with the situation where a dispute arises about the quality of repair and whether the buyer would still be entitled to reject the goods even if the repair is properly conducted. In *J & H Ritchie Ltd*, when the buyer, following delivery of the goods and noticing the defect, declined to terminate the contract, the contract was perceived to be in existence.[132] Since the contract remained alive, the parties' duties to deliver and to accept the goods continued to be incumbent on the parties. This meant that, so long as the buyer refrained from rescinding the contract and the seller delivered the conforming goods, the buyer was bound to accept them. In addition, through the insertion of SGA section 35(6)(a), the buyer is now able to safely ask for or agree to repairs, without running the risk of losing the right to reject, should the repair not be carried out by the seller. This section provides that 'the buyer is not by virtue of this section deemed to have accepted the goods merely because (a) he asks for, or agrees to, their repair by or under an arrangement with the seller'. As suggested by the Law Commission, if a satisfactory repair is carried out the buyer would normally be willing to accept the goods.[133] It can even be suggested that when the seller retenders the goods in a state which conforms to the contract prior to termination of contract, the buyer is obliged to accept them. This case clearly shows that informal attempts at curing defects in goods are not only allowed, but also encouraged, despite the lack of formal provisions on the seller's right to cure the goods.

[132] [2005] 1 S.C. 155, 161.

[133] The Law Commission (no. 160) and the Scottish Law Commission (no. 104), Sale and Supply of Goods (1987) para 05.29.

B. UCC

Despite the English sales law, UCC has explicitly provided for the seller's right to cure in section 2-508. However, UCC has failed to exactly determine what 'cure' means or entails. In fact, there is no provision concerning the right to make repairs or adjustments under this instrument. However, it seems reasonable to argue that any attempts by the seller in removing the non-conformity of the goods can be characterised as 'cure'.[134] It should be noted that UCC retains the perfect tender rule. Section 2-106(2) states that goods conform to a contract when they are in accordance with the obligations under the contract. Section 2-601 then authorises a buyer to reject the whole 'if the goods or the tender of delivery fail in any respect to conform to the contract'. The perfect tender rule constitutes a powerful weapon for the buyer who can use to terminate the contract and end their contractual relationship. To reduce the harshness of the perfect tender rule, the UCC has set out provisions for revocation of acceptance and cure. It has even been claimed that section 2-508 is a liberalisation of the seller's obligations and the seller should strictly comply with the procedures stated in the provisions in order to obtain its benefit.[135] This indicates the UCC's increased willingness to allow the seller to cure its breach for delivering defective goods, which would provide a unique opportunity for the parties to resolve their conflicts without resorting to litigation or arbitration.[136] This approach is consistent with the code's underlying liberal approach and policy to incorporate and respect commercial practices and customs.[137]

Both sub-sections of 2-508 are arguably the most significant UCC provision in striking a right balance between the interests of buyers and sellers with a view to keeping the parties' deal alive.[138] Section 2-508 not only affords a seller with an absolute right to cure a nonconforming delivery before the expiry of the time for performance under the contract, but also gives a seller, who failed to deliver conforming goods and rejected by the buyer, another chance even beyond the time for performance under the contract to cure the defect.[139] This section has no antecedent in the Uniform Sales Act.

[134] Frisch (n 6) section 2-508, para 35.

[135] ibid, 5.

[136] *T.W. Oil, Inc. v Consolidated Edison Co. of New York, Inc* (1982) Court of Appeals of New York, 57 N.Y.2d 574; *Web Press Servs. v New London Motors*, (1987) Supreme Court of Connecticut, 525 A.2d 57; RA Hillman, 'Keeping the deal together after material breach – common law mitigation rules, the UCC, and the Restatement (Second) of Contracts' (1976) 47 *University of Colorado Law Review* 553, 587; WL Lawrence, 'Cure under Article 2 of the Uniform Commercial Code: practices and prescriptions' (1988) 21 *Uniform Commercial Code Law Journal* 138, 139.

[137] See UCC sections 1-102 (1) and 1-102 (2)(b).

[138] H Foss, 'The seller's right to cure when the buyer revokes acceptance: erase the line in the sand' (1991) 16 *Southern Illinois University Law Journal* 1, 3; see also GM Travalio, 'The UCC's three R's rejection, revocation, and (the seller's) right to cure' (1984) 53 *University of Cincinnati Law Review* 931, 933.

[139] *Dunleavey v Paris Ceramics USA, Inc.* (2002) Superior Court of Connecticut, 47 Conn. Supp. 565.

The first subsection provides that where any tender or delivery by the seller is rejected due to non-conforming and the time for performance has not yet expired, the seller may seasonably notify the buyer of their intention to cure and may then within the contract time make a conforming delivery.[140] What is a reasonable time for the notification depends of course upon the circumstances, such as the buyer's need for the goods and whether the buyer has attempted, in good faith, to obtain substitute goods.[141] The seller is thus entitled to rectify its performance, even where the seller has taken back the non-conforming goods and refunded the purchase price.[142] The seller can benefit from this opportunity and make a good tender within the contract period. However, the closer the performance to the contract, the greater the necessity for utmost promptness on the seller's part in notifying of their intention to cure, should such notification be considered 'seasonable' under this subsection. This section does not entitle the seller to cure if the buyer has not rejected the seller's tender.[143] Absent an agreement otherwise, once the buyer accepts the goods, the seller loses the right to cure to forestall the buyer's revocation of acceptance recognised under section 2-608.[144]

The seller's right to cure under this section is not an obligation to cure so that if the seller fails to exercise its right, the buyer is not entitled to force the seller to cure. The rationale behind such a narrow right to cure is that a buyer should not be allowed to reject or cancel merely because of a defective early delivery as long as the seller gives prompt notice of their intention to cure and does actually cure by the prescribed performance date. Additionally, the notice requirement by the seller seeks to free the buyer from an unreasonable period of uncertainty and economic paralysis, while the seller makes up its mind.[145] This indicates that UCC strives to accommodate the buyer's need for exact performance by allowing rejection only where there is a failure to conform 'in any respect' with the buyer's needs, by entitling the seller to cure defects within the time for performance. The logical inference of this subsection is that if the seller cures the breach following the requirements set out in the provision, the seller is presumed to have performed its obligations and the buyer must then perform their obligation, otherwise they

[140] See eg *Marine Mart Inc v Pearce* (1972) Supreme Court of Arkansas, 480 S.W.2d 133; *Central Dist. Alaram Inc v Hal-Tuc, Inc* (1994) Missouri Court of Appeals, Eastern District, Division Three, 886 S.W.2d 210; *Midwest Mobile Diagnostic Imaging, L.L.C. v Dynamics Corp. of America* (1997) United States District Court, Michigan, 965 F.Supp.1003; *H.A.S. of Fort Smith LLC v J.V. Mfg., Inc.* (2004) Court of Appeals of Arkansas, 2004 WL 2102009.

[141] UCC Official Comments, section 2-508, para 1.

[142] UCC Official Comments, section 2-508, para 1; *Murray Hill Apparel, Inc. v Yunsa,* (2008) Civil Court, New York, 856 N.Y.S.2d 499.

[143] *Bonebrake v Cox* (1974) United States Court of Appeals, 8th Circuit 499 F.2d 951, 957; *Jensen v Seigel Mobile Homes Group* (1983) Supreme Court of Idaho, 668 P.2d 65; see also Hawkland, Bjerre, Rusch and Garry (n 70) section 2-508, para 1.

[144] *Gappelberg v Landrum,* (1984) Supreme Court of Texas, 666 S.W.2d 88; *Bowen v Foust* (1996) Missouri Court of Appeals, 925 S.W.2d 211.

[145] Foss (n 138) 1, 6.

would be in breach of contract. For instance, in *Terrell v R & A Mfg. Partners Ltd*, a buyer received delivery of a trailer lacking controls but refused to return the trailer to the shop that installed the controls.[146] The court held that the buyer was precluded from maintaining an action against the manufacturer for breach of its express warranty, not least because the manufacturer was not given an opportunity to remedy the defect. Conversely, in *Ramirez v Autosport*, the buyer purchased a camper van, which had some defects.[147] The buyer thus purported to cancel the contract and claimed for damages. While the buyer returned the goods in question and gave the seller ample time to correct the defects, the seller failed to effect cure and demonstrated that the van conformed to contract. The buyer was therefore entitled to reject the goods and terminate the contract.

The second subsection normally operates in situations when the seller has performed its obligation at the agreed date and there is no longer any time to conduct a cure pursuant to section 2-508(1). Thus this subsection extraordinarily permits a seller to cure beyond the date set for performance.[148] In other words, it aims to protect the seller against a 'surprise rejection' of the goods based on the sudden technicality on the buyer's part, which the seller had reasonable grounds to believe would be acceptable.[149] According to the Official Comments, such reasonable grounds depend on prior course of dealing, course of performance or usage of trade as well as in the particular circumstances surrounding the conclusion of contract.[150] The seller is presumed to have commercial knowledge of any factors in a particular contractual situation which require them to comply strictly with their obligations under the contract, such as conformity of documents in an overseas shipment.[151] The surrounding circumstances may signify that it would be reasonable for the seller to think that a nonconforming delivery would be acceptable if the seller provided for a money allowance or may signify that the seller did not believe that the goods were nonconforming, and thus would be acceptable to the buyer. Courts are generally concerned with the reasonableness of the seller's belief and understanding that the goods would be acceptable, rather than with the seller's pretended knowledge or lack of knowledge of the defect.[152] In *TW Oil Inc v Consolidated Edison Co*, a seller, acting in

[146] (2002) Court of Civil Appeals of Alabama, 835 So.2d 216; see also *Mercury Marine v Clear River Const. Co., Inc.* (2003) Supreme Court of Mississippi, 839 So.2d 508; *Inter-Americas Ins. Corp., Inc. v Imaging Solutions Co.* (2008) Court of Appeals of Kansas, 39 Kan. App. 2d 875.

[147] (1982) Supreme Court of New Jersey, 88 NJ 277; see also *Lile v Kiesel* (2007) Court of Appeals of Indiana, 871 N.E.2d 995.

[148] Frisch (n 6) section 2-508, para 13; Hawkland, Bjerre, Rusch and Garry (n 70) section 2-508, para 3.

[149] UCC Official Comments, section 2-508, para 2.

[150] ibid.

[151] ibid.

[152] *Sinco, Inc. v Metro-North Commuter R. Co*, (2001) United States District Court, New York, 133 F.Supp.2d 308; *Allied Semi-Conductors Intern., Ltd. v Pulsar Components Intern., Inc* (1995) United States District Court, New York, 907 F.Supp. 618; *Wilson v Scampoli* (1967) District of Columbia Court of Appeals, 228 A.2d 848.

good faith and without knowledge of any defect, had acquired a cargo of fuel oil from another trader.[153] The seller sold and delivered the cargo, which was not conforming to the contractual specifications. The buyer rejected the delivery of the cargo and also rejected the seller's reasonable and timely offer to cure. The buyer argued that the cure under section 2-508(2) is restricted to situations where a seller *knowingly* made a nonconforming tender which the seller had reason to believe the buyer would accept. However, the court decided that the only real question was whether the seller should be viewed as having had reasonable expectations that the initial nonconforming tender would be acceptable. It was found that such seller, upon giving seasonable notice, can avail themself to cure the defect within a reasonable period beyond the time when the contract was to be performed.[154]

In addition, if the defect is immaterial so that the inconvenience or loss incurred to the buyer is minor, the seller may reasonably expect that the buyer would retain the goods with some financial adjustments or a quick cure.[155] Strictly speaking, the phrase 'with or without money allowance' used in the second subsection is concerned with determining whether the seller has a right to cure and does not seek to classify 'money allowance' as a cure.[156] This may be against the business practice in which price adjustments aiming to recompense the buyer for deficiency in quantity or quality is a common form of cure. In *Continental Forest Products Inc v White Lumber Sales Inc*, parties contracted for sale of 20 carloads of plywood.[157] The contract was subject to the rules and standards of US Products Standard, which permitted a variance of 5 per cent from specifications, and if variations exceed above 5 per cent, the buyer was only allowed to reject the nonconforming plywood but was not allowed to cancel or reject the entire shipment. Following an inspection, the first carload of plywood found to have a variance of 9 per cent. The remaining carloads were within the permitted variance range. As a result, the buyer sought to cancel the entire contract. The court found that the seller, who deduced the price for nonconformity, made an effective cure in relation to the minor defects in the first instalment. Nevertheless, price adjustment as a permissible method of cure had been agreed between the parties. This case exceptionally held that the remedy of 'cure' under section 2-508 does not entail price adjustments. However, more recent case law allows price adjustment as a method of cure.[158]

[153] (1982) Court of Appeals of New York, 57 N.Y.2d 574.

[154] ibid, 586.

[155] *Western Sky Industries, LLC v ColtTech, LLC*, (2009) United States District Court of Kansas, WL 2168914.

[156] White and Summers (n 70) 443; Hawkland, Bjerre, Rusch and Garry (n 70) section 2-508, para 3.

[157] (1970) Supreme Court of Oregon, 256 Or.466.

[158] *Superior Derrick Services, Inc. v Anderson*, (1992) Court of Appeals of Texas, 831 S.W.2d 868; *Abraham & Company, Inc. v Mansour Rahmanan & Company, Inc* (1998) Court of Appeals of Texas, WL 93743; *Inova Renovations, L.L.C. v Jones* (2014) Court of Appeals of Texas, WL 7204497.

C. CISG and UPICC

i. Buyer's Right to Cure

The cure regime under CISG is complex. On one hand, the seller can remedy at their own expense a failure to perform their obligations, even after expiry of the date for delivery. On the other hand, the buyer can require the seller to repair or replace the goods, as part of performance directed remedies under Article 46. Generally, the remedy of cure seeks to give the buyer the very performance that they contracted for. CISG Articles 46(2) and 46 (3) as well as UPICC Article 7.2.3 pursue the aim of respecting and fulfilling the contract (*pacta sunt servanda*), following delivery of non-conforming goods. Unlike CISG, UPICC has failed to provide necessary details as to when exactly the buyer's right to cure can be invoked. UPICC Article 7.2.3 provides that 'the right to performance includes in appropriate cases the right to require repair, replacement, or other cure of defective performance'. It is clear from the wordings of these provisions that the buyer's right to repair and replacements are regarded as sub-forms of the general right to specific performance, indicating that the buyer's right to cure operates under similar principles to performance.[159] Thus, the exceptions to specific performance, such as resorting to inconsistent remedies, Article 28, impossibility and hardship are also applicable to this remedy. CISG Article 46(2) gives the buyer the right to request the seller to deliver substitute goods in case of delivery of non-conforming goods. However, the buyer is able to do so only if the lack of conformity constitutes a fundamental breach of contract and their request complied with the notice requirement under Article 39. It is worth noting that the notification requirement of the buyer is subject to their duty to examine the goods. In other words, the law relating to the examination duty effectively guides the buyer to notify the non-conformity, so that they can invoke the suitable remedies. CISG Article 38 (1) provides that 'the buyer must examine the goods, or cause them to be examined, within as short a period as is practicable in the circumstances'. If the buyer fails to provide the timely notice required under CISG Article 39, 'their rights are reduced to damages and price reduction'.[160]

[159] Mak (n 39) 120; it has been stated that '[the right] to repair and replacement are special application of performance': Vogenauer (n 94) 904.

[160] Schlechtriem and Schwenzer (n 95) 868; Kroll, Mistelis and Viscasillas (n 95) 695; see *Window Frames case II* (2023) District Court Midden, Netherlands, CISG-online 6413; *China Railway No. 10 Engineering Group Co. Ltd. v Triorient LLC* (2020) American Arbitration Association – International Centre for Dispute Resolution (AAA/ICDR) CISG-online 5639; For further explanation on examination and notification duty see CISG Advisory Council, 'Examination of the Goods and Notice of Non-Conformity: Articles 38 and 39' (2004) Opinion n 2.

It appears from case law that the courts tend to adopt a strict approach toward application of the doctrine of fundamental breach, which therefore reduces the buyer's chance to demand substitute goods.[161] The concept of non-conformity has been defined by CISG Article 35.[162] This article states that 'the seller must deliver goods which are of the quantity, quality and description required by the contract and which are contained or packaged in the manner required by the contract'. This definition, however, does not involve all non-conformities such as when the seller has tendered the goods at another place (CISG Article 31), or when the seller has made an incorrect tender of documents required (CISG Article 30).[163] Two special types of non-conformity of the goods, ie discrepancy in quantity and defects in title, are not governed by this article.[164] CISG Article 51 provides that 'if the seller delivers only a part of the goods or if only a part of the goods delivered is in conformity with the contract, articles 46 to 50 apply in respect of the part which is missing or which does not conform'. If there is short delivery, CISG Article 46(1) is applicable in respect of that missing part, as 'there is a simple failure to perform within the meaning of [CISG Article 46(1)]'.[165] The cases of delivery of too many goods are governed specifically by CISG Article 52(2), which provides, 'if the seller delivers a quantity of goods greater than that provided for in the contract, the buyer may take delivery or refuse to take delivery of the excess quantity. If the buyer takes delivery of all or part of the excess quantity, he must pay for it at the contract rate'. In terms of defects in title, it has been indicated that 'third party rights and claims' are not covered under CISG Article 35.[166] The reason is that '"the term non-conformity" is used in a technical sense, covering only cases falling [under CISG Article 35] and so excluding 'third party rights and

[161] For instance, the Swiss Federal Court stated: 'The term "fundamental breach" under article 25 CISG is to be interpreted narrowly. If it is doubtful whether or not a breach may qualify as fundamental, it should generally be assumed that no fundamental breach is existent.' *Filling and packaging plant case* (2009) Swiss Federal Supreme Court, CISG-online 1900.

[162] For further explanation see Schlechtriem and Schwenzer (n 95) 965; Kroll, Mistelis and Viscasillas (n 95) 489; see also *Geiger v Nord Tractors Sàrl* (1997) Court of Appeal Canton Valais, Switzerland, CISG-online 328; *Expoplast CA v Reg Mac s.r.l* (2001) District Court Busto Arsizio, Italy, CISG-online 1323; *Seilfabrik Ullmann AG v Lift-Tex Industrie B.V.* (2019) Court of Appeal Arnhem-Leeuwarden, CISG-online 3935; *America Latina Agrisciences S.A. v Hefei Longchuan Chemical Technology Co., Ltd. II* (2018) Higher People's Court Anhui Province, China, CISG-online 4787; *Shenzen Synergy Digital Co., Ltd. v Mingtel, Inc.* (2023) US Court of Appeals, 5th Circuit, CISG-online 6392.

[163] CISG Article 30: The seller must deliver the goods, hand over any documents relating to them and transfer the property in the goods, as required by the contract and this Convention. CISG Article 31: If the seller is not bound to deliver the goods at any other particular place, his obligation to deliver consists: (a) if the contract of sale involves carriage of the goods – in handing the goods over to the first carrier for transmission to the buyer.

[164] Schlechtriem and Schwenzer (n 95) 963.

[165] ibid.

[166] ibid.

claims' [governed by CISG Articles 41, 42]'.[167] The cases of defect in title are solely governed by CISG Article 46 (1).[168]

Like the right to require delivery of substitute goods, the buyer's right to repair established in Article 46(3) is one particular aspect of the general right to require performance and accordingly it is linked to the preconditions of application of that general right.[169] The buyer's right to repair is subject to three requirements of non-conformity, reasonableness and timeliness. In addition to non-conformity, the seller is under obligation to conduct repairs only if doing so is reasonable for them, taking all circumstances into account. The request for repair should also be within the same time limit as the claim for delivery of substitute goods. The word 'unless' in this article indicates the seller's obligation to repair the goods and that it is for the seller to prove the unreasonableness.[170] To determine the reasonableness of the repair, the buyer's interest in repair can be weighed against the seller's expenses.[171] However, there is no clear yardstick for such determination. In an attempt to provide a yardstick, it has been proposed that 'the relationship between repair costs and purchase price is generally irrelevant, and the decision is made solely on the relationship between repair and delivery of substitute goods'.[172] Also, it has also been proposed that the reasonableness of repair is based on 'the idea that the buyer must not aggravate the seller's circumstances'.[173] Nevertheless, the reasonableness of repair is to be determined objectively on the basis of the circumstances of each case.[174] For instance, a request for repair is deemed unreasonable if the buyer could easily repair the goods themselves and the seller remains liable for the costs of such repair.[175] Also, if efforts to repair cause unreasonable expenses,

[167] ibid; CISG Article 41: The seller must deliver goods which are free from any right or claim of a third party, unless the buyer agreed to take the goods subject to that right or claim. However, if such right or claim is based on industrial property or other intellectual property, the seller's obligation is governed by article 42.

CISG Article 42(1): The seller must deliver goods which are free from any right or claim of a third party based on industrial property or other intellectual property, of which at the time of the conclusion of the contract the seller knew or could not have been unaware, provided that the right or claim is based on industrial property or other intellectual property:

(a) under the law of the State where the goods will be resold or otherwise used, if it was contemplated by the parties at the time of the conclusion of the contract that the goods would be resold or otherwise used in that State; or
(b) in any other case, under the law of the State where the buyer has his place of business.

[168] Schlechtriem and Schwenzer (n 95) 963; Kroll, Mistelis and Viscasillas (n 95) 688.
[169] Schlechtriem and Schwenzer (n 95) 971; Kroll, Mistelis and Viscasillas (n 95) 699.
[170] Kroll, Mistelis and Viscasillas (n 95) 699.
[171] Schlechtriem and Schwenzer (n 95) 972; Kroll, Mistelis and Viscasillas (n 95) 699; *Diesel Generator case* (2006) China International Economic & Trade Arbitration Commission, CISG-online 1454.
[172] Schlechtriem and Schwenzer (n 95) 972; see also Kroll, Mistelis and Viscasillas (n 95) 699.
[173] Bianca and Bonell (n 95) 333–41.
[174] Schlechtriem and Schwenzer (n 95) 720.
[175] UNCITRAL Digest of Case Law on the United Nations Convention on Contracts for the International Sale of Goods (2016) Article 46, para 19.

in relation to value of the goods, due to travel expenses, asking a seller to repair would be unreasonable and against good faith in international trade.

ii. Seller's Right to Cure

CISG Articles 37 and 48 provide extensive provisions for the seller to rectify at their own expense a failure to perform their obligations. They have been labelled as seller's right to cure, in a similar manner to UCC. These two articles have similar functions as those concerning buyer's right to cure, and it is questionable why the CISG has included both sets of remedies, when the outcomes of their applications would be very similar. Similarly, UPICC Article 7.1.4 has provided general right to cure by non-performing party, notwithstanding whether the deadline for performance has passed or not.

CISG Article 37 is concerned with the situation where the seller has delivered defective goods and they attempt to cure the breach before the delivery date. Such deficiency may be in relation to the quantity or quality of goods delivered. Even the seller is entitled to deliver goods in replacement of any non-conforming goods delivered. In *Sunrise Foods International, Inc. v Ryan Hinton Inc.*, Sunrise sold and delivered Hinton a few thousand tons of certified organic corn.[176] The contract period started from 1 October 2015 and ended on 30 September 2016. Because the buyer was in the business of selling the corn to dairy farmers to be used as cattle feed, the contract specified the vomitoxin level of maximum two part per million. In December 2015, the buyer was notified that some of the corn delivered by the seller had unknown levels of vomitoxin. The buyer, who then became very concerned about this situation, failed to take delivery of remaining goods. The seller offered the buyer certified organic corn that could replace the previously delivered corn, but the buyer failed to cooperate and rejected any attempts by the seller. The court held that on the basis of Article 37, the seller had the option to cure and offer conforming goods prior to the expiration of the contract term.[177] Thus, the seller's right to cure a defect can be exercised in relation to any non-conforming within the ambit of Article 35.[178] The last part of Article 37 stipulates that the buyer retains their right to damages under Article 74, which is relevant to those losses which cannot be cured even by subsequent performance. These losses include any expenses that the buyer is incurred in relation to the seller's curative performance, such as costs incurred in returning the goods to the seller.[179]

In addition, CISG Article 48 generally entitles a seller to perform the contract even after the expiry of the date for delivery. This article effectively enables the seller to deliver the goods and cure their breach of contract. Although this right to cure

[176] (2019) US District Court for the District of Idaho, CISG-online 4522.
[177] ibid, para 27; see also *Bravo Barros v Martínez Gares* (2007) Argentina National Commercial Court of Appeals, CISG-online 1517.
[178] Schlechtriem and Schwenzer (n 95) 847.
[179] Schlechtriem and Schwenzer (n 95) 847.

is subject to Article 49 dealing with the buyer's general right to avoid the contract. buyer's right to terminate is quite restricted and as such the seller's right to cure may effectively pre-empt buyer's access to their remedies. The CISG's adherence to the principle of *favor contractus* shows that the seller is given all chances to perform the contract and the buyer's right to terminate the contract is the last resort.[180] If the breach is so serious that satisfies the requirement of fundamental breach under Article 25, of course the buyer would have to decide whether the contract should be avoided and that the buyer may exercise the right to terminate without restrictions from the seller's right to cure.[181] The buyer's right to decide when a breach is fundamental is also supported by Article 48(2), stating that the seller must ask for the buyer's consent for cure. Thus, the buyer who is entitled to avoid the contract need not wait first for cure and may declare the contract avoided at once.

However, the rule of entitling the seller to cure any deficiency may imply that in each case the seller must be given an opportunity to cure before the buyer can terminate the contract.[182] In the case of *Inflatable Triumphal Arch*, three arches were delivered to be used in a race. As soon as they were located, the arches collapsed.[183] The court did not allow the buyer to terminate the contract in pursuance of Article 49. Even though it was established that a serious breach had happened, the court decided that the seller should be offered the chance to remedy the defect in the first instance. So long as the seller shows willingness and ability to cure any defects, the buyer may not terminate the contract. However, the rule should have been more accurately formulated to enhance the certainty of when exactly the seller should use their last chances of rectifying the defect. It is submitted that the rule should be redrafted to suggest that the seller should be entitled to cure only *remediable* defects so long as they have willingness and ability to perform such a cure. In the case of *Inflatable Triumphal Arch*, when the arches collapsed and the materials were destroyed, it was hard to envisage how the seller would be able to cure such a serious deficiency and may not be commercially satisfactory to impose the seller's new attempt on the buyer, who may be able to conveniently and immediately obtain suitable alternative arches from other suppliers.

The seller's right to cure under both Articles 37 and 48 can only be granted if the seller's breach can be corrected without unreasonable inconvenience to the buyer. 'Unreasonable inconvenience' refers primarily to the disturbances that cure would inflict on the buyer's business, eg, noise, dirt, disruption of business.[184] This means

[180] B Zeller, 'Article 48 CISG – confusion or sound drafting?' (2022) 22 *Internationales Handelsrecht* 7, 7.

[181] However, in *The Italian Cloth case I* (1998) District Court Regensburg, Germany, CISG-online 514, the German court decided that even if the seller had delivered non-conforming goods and even if the buyer had followed Article 39(1), the buyer was not entitled to avoid the contract under Article 49. This decision was incorrect and had been criticised.

[182] See Official Records of the United Nations Conference on Contracts for the International Sale of Goods, Vienna, 10 March-11 April 1980 (United Nations publication, Sales No. E.81.IV.3), 41, paragraph 6 ('in some cases').

[183] (2002) Commercial Court Canton Aargau, Switzerland, CISG-online 715.

[184] Kroll, Mistelis and Viscasillas (n 95) 698.

that the seller's right to correct defects is not excluded by mere inconvenience, but rather only if the inconvenience is unreasonable. In the case of Article 48, the seller should strive to cure without unreasonable delay and without uncertainty that the seller will compensate any costs the buyer may have incurred. For instance, in *Computer Hardware* case, these conditions were satisfied where defective products could easily be cured in a short time and at minimal costs.[185] However, in *Hungarian Injection Moulding Tools* case, the seller's attempt to remedy defects failed to satisfy these conditions.[186] In this significant case, the buyer who was itself a supplier of car parts to the automotive industry entered into a sale contract with a seller who was a manufacturer of highly specialised tools needed for the manufacture of car parts. The parties had an ongoing relationship for around four years. However, in the final year of their contract period, a dispute arose regarding the last delivery orders. The buyer claimed that the tools delivered in the last instalment were deficient. The court found that those tools were not in conformity with the contract under CISG Article 35.[187] The seller failed to notify the buyer of its intention to remedy the defects within a reasonable period of time. Rather, the seller announced in a letter that they would first compile a plan of action for all the tools supplied in order to overhaul them with the buyer's cooperation. The seller's attempt to cure caused unreasonable delays and inconvenience. The buyer was threatened by damages claims from their own customers since the seller, apparently acting unprofessionally, had repeatedly but hopelessly attempted to remedy the defects. The buyer was able to remedy the defects themselves and claim damages for the costs incurred.

4. Evaluation

The remedial scheme under CISG and UPICC, as opposed to SGA and UCC, signifies that these legal regimes seek to keep the parties' contractual bond alive insofar as possible, to reserve avoidance as a remedy of last resort and encourage the parties to insist on literal contractual performance rather than resorting to a claim for damages. The main distinction between these legal regimes is that under CISG and UPICC, the buyer is entitled to require the performance of the contract. In contrast, under SGA, this remedy is considered secondary, discretionary, and not generally available as of right. In other words, the buyer under SGA has been given greater freedom not to preserve the contractual relation and instead claim damages in lieu of performance. At first sight, UCC may not neatly fit into either of these two categories. As indicated in the Official Comments, section 2-716 of this instrument seeks to continue the general previous common

[185] (1995) Arbitration Court of the International Chamber of Commerce, Paris, France, Arbitral Award n 7754, CISG-online 834.

[186] (2014) German Supreme Court, CISG-online 2545; see also *Tetracycline HCL case* (1995) Local Court Munich, Germany, CISG-online 368.

[187] (2014) German Supreme Court, CISG-online 2545, para 20.

law policy in relation to specific performance and also to encourage a more liberal approach toward availability of specific performance.[188] Nevertheless, the US cases analysed in this chapter indicate that while section 2-716 sought to liberalise specific performance from restrictive principles of equity, the courts appear to be still in favour of confining specific performance to situations where damages are not an adequate remedy.[189] It makes perfect sense to still include the UCC in the same league as SGA.

In terms of the buyer's right to cure under UPICC and CISG, which are absent under SGA and UCC, there are some essential differences in the availability of this right that deserve analysis. These differences are particularly significant in situations when the buyer requires the seller to replace the goods due to non-conformity. Under CISG, the buyer is faced with two hurdles. The first one is to prove fundamental breach of contract.[190] This hurdle is absent under UPICC.[191] However, it seems that the requirement of 'fundamental breach' of contract might operate as functionally equivalent to the requirement of 'replacement transaction' under UPICC.[192] In other words, the hurdle of fundamental breach of contract has been designed, amongst other reasons, to avoid delivery of substitute goods, in cases where the defective goods are easily reparable [193] Under UPICC, the buyer is debarred from requiring delivery of substitute goods when they may reasonably obtain performance from another source. In the *Saltwater Isolation Tank case*, governed by CISG, the buyer alleged that the container leaked and as a result its property was damaged by water.[194] The court rejected the claim for delivery of substitute goods and mentioned that the seller's failure to perform their obligation was probably not a fundamental breach as the damage concerned was easily repairable.[195] According to the court's order, the buyer could find a local technician to fix this damage rather than asking for a substitute delivery. If UPICC was the applicable legal regime, the same result was likely to be reached, as UPICC Article 7.2.3 requires the buyer to reasonably obtain performance from another source.

The second hurdle facing the buyer requiring delivery of substitute goods relates to their duty to return the original goods to the seller.[196] CISG Article 82(1) 'presupposes that the buyer who claims substitute delivery will be under a duty to make

[188] UCC Official Comments, section 2-716, para 1.

[189] See section 2(B).

[190] See CISG Article 46(2).

[191] UPICC Article 7.2.3.

[192] See section 3(C)(i).

[193] UNCITRAL Digest of Case Law on the United Nations Convention on Contracts for the International Sale of Goods (2016) Article 46, para 4.

[194] (1995) Commercial Court Canton Zürich, Switzerland, CISG-online 248.

[195] ibid; see also *Rheinland Versicherungen v Atlarez s.r.l* (2000) District Court Vigevano, Italy, CISG-online 493; *Van Oers BV v Turbo's Hoet Truckcenter Productie NV* (2004) Court of Appeal Ghent, Belgium, CISG-online 986; *Ecogen Holding B.V. v Isolcell Italia S.P.A.* (2009) District Court Bolzano, Italy, CISG-online 2344.

[196] CISG Article 82(1).

restitution of the (non-conforming) goods that had originally been delivered'.[197] UPICC has provided no details concerning 'who has to bear the costs of returning the goods', which can lead to uncertainty.[198] However, there are other principles concerning the restitution of the goods that can be used for clarifying who is under the obligation to take back the goods. UPICC Article 3.2.15(1) provides that 'on avoidance either party may claim restitution of whatever it has supplied under the contract, or the part of it avoided, provided that the party concurrently makes restitution of whatever it has received under the contract, or the part of it avoided'. Also, UPICC Article 7.3.6 states that 'on termination of a contract to be performed at one time either party may claim restitution of whatever it has supplied under the contract, provided that such party concurrently makes restitution of whatever it has received under the contract'. In these two principles, either party *may* claim restitution of whatever he has supplied. This means that the party who supplied the goods has the right to request returning the goods and the other party who received the goods has the duty to return the goods. It can be, therefore, inferred from these principles that the seller has the right to claim back the goods under the remedy of the buyer's right to require substitute delivery, as the seller has supplied the goods under the contract, and that the buyer undertakes to take back the goods. Nevertheless, this vagueness still remains and that there is a need for legislative clarity.

As expressed by Lord Hoffmann in the remarkable case of *Co-Operative Insurance Society Ltd. Respondents v Argyll Stores (Holdings) Ltd*, requiring a party to perform is not only waste of resources but also locks the parties together in a continuing hostile relationship and the court's order for specific performance prolongs the battle.[199] In other words, it would make more economic sense if parties are able to more easily end such a futile and hostile contractual relationship and find suitable alternatives by dedicating their financial resources, for which they can claim damages. As shown in previous sections, CISG and UPICC have given priority to performance directed remedies over damages and that the buyer has to allow the seller implement their right to cure even after their defective performance.[200] In contrast, the right to cure (for commercial sales) is not explicitly stated in SGA, even though case law appears to be supportive of such a right.[201] The Law Commission of England and Wales expressed the view that informal attempts at curing defects in goods should be encouraged and if the seller willingly conducts repair, they should carry that out cooperatively and share clear information concerning their curative efforts with the buyer.[202] However, if a dispute concerning breach of contract eventually

[197] Huber and Mullis (n 99) 201; see also Schlechtriem and Schwenzer (n 95) 1432.
[198] Vogenauer (n 94) 907.
[199] *Co-Operative Insurance Society Ltd. Respondents v Argyll Stores (Holdings) Ltd* [1998] AC 1 (HL) 16.
[200] See CISG Article 48; UPICC Article 7.1.4.
[201] See section 3(A).
[202] The Law Commission (Working Paper no. 85) and the Scottish Law Commission (Consultive Memorandum no. 58) on Sale and Supply of Goods (1983) para 4.53.

ends up in courts, the very informality of such arrangements may make the legal analysis of the situation quite elusive. Rather, one should turn to analyse damages, as this remedy operates as functionally equivalent to performance-directed remedies, as the buyer will usually seek substitute performance from a third party, which can be as close as possible to the performance which they hoped to obtain from the seller.[203] In other words, the buyer can freely either fix the goods themselves, or have them fixed by a third party or acquire sufficiently similar substitutes from a third party, and claim damages to compensate them for the cost of such 'self-help'. It can be submitted that damages given priority under SGA and UCC might lead to the preservation of relations more effectively than specific performance under CISG and UPICC. Damages may also be economically more advantageous than specific performance, as *Robinson v Harman* establishes two principles of contract damages: protection of the claimant's expectation, with protection in such a way as to minimise the contracting parties' expenses.[204] The latter principle gives an opportunity to the buyer to show solidarity and cooperate with the seller. The buyer can deal with the seller's problem underlying the non-performance of contract by accepting the breach of contract and referring to the market obtaining the substitute goods in a cover transaction in order to comply with their duty to mitigate. The buyer will normally accept the breach and make a cover purchase 'in the knowledge that the seller will compensate lost net expectation'.[205] This shows that the buyer can actually help such sellers when they are not at fault and are seeking only to avoid serious loss by accepting breach of contract.[206] The seller, who has been helped by the innocent buyer in a drastic situation, might be willing to keep their relationship with such buyer so that their relationships are likely to be continued. It should also be noted that one aspect of such parties' cooperation is that it makes legal action unnecessary when compensation is adequate.[207] In other words, expectation damages may form the basis of an out-of-court settlement. This might happen when the seller does not have any objection to the buyer's performance of the duty to mitigate in making a cover transaction and they are ready to compensate the buyer's loss. Such self-help way of settling a legal dispute might more effectively lead to the continuing of the parties' relationship, compared with when the buyer seeks specific performance. This is so because the commercial parties can more readily cooperate with each other than when the courts or arbitrators paternalistically intervene in the parties'

[203] Harris, Campbell and Halson (n 1) 114; see also Austen-Baker (n 27) 1, 5–6.

[204] D Campbell, 'The relational constitution of remedy: co-operation as the implicit second principle of remedies for breach of contract' (2004–2005) 11 *Texas Wesleyan Law Review* 455, 466; see also D Campbell and D Harris, 'In defence of breach: a critique of restitution and the performance interest' (2002) 22 *Journal of Legal Studies* 208, 210.

[205] Campbell (n 204) 455, 468.

[206] S Macaulay, 'Renegotiations and settlements: Dr. Pangloss's notes on the margins of David Campbell's paper' (2007–2008) 29 *Cardozo Law Review* 261, 279.

[207] Campbell (n 204) 455, 469.

relationships to order specific performance.[208] Such a paternalist intervention might undercut the parties' willingness to settle the disputes by themselves and as such it might debar the parties from further cooperation leading to the maintenance of the relationship.

As explained previously, the cure regime under CISG is complex.[209] Underlying the right to cure in any legal regime is the recognition that parties should be encouraged to communicate with each other and resolve their own problems. In other words, the right to cure encourages parties to amicably resolve their own problems without resorting to adjudicators. The seller's right to cure can precede the buyer's right to cure under CISG and UPICC, although such priority has not been explicitly asserted in these regimes.[210] For instance, if the buyer demands delivery of substitute goods and the seller offers to repair the goods, the seller's offer prevails. The seller has the right to choose how they will remedy the defect.[211] In other words, 'the decisive factor is that the defect is completely remedied. How the seller achieves this success is [their] own affair'.[212] At first sight, it appears that the cure regime established in CISG Articles 37 and 48 would enable the parties to maintain and extend their relationship, as the seller would be able to correct its breach of contract and persuade the buyer to stay in the contract. A commercial view may also hold that the contract should be kept afoot as long as possible when parties can cooperate in fulfilling their duties. Great emphasis on the seller's right to cure and prioritising it over buyer's remedies would seek to maintain the contractual relationship between the parties, creating opportunities for the parties to resolve any tensions caused by breach of contract. The sellers, who are also manufacturers, are normally in a more suitable place than anybody else when it comes to curing manufactured goods. A cure can be conducted by supplementing a short-delivery, substituting conforming for non-conforming goods or repairing or altering the goods, as appropriate. Deploying the chance of curing deficiencies in the goods would probably reinstate the buyer's confidence in seller's skills. If the buyer was allowed to immediately seek repair or replacement from a third party and charge the costs to the seller as damages pursuance to Article 45 (1)(b), the parties' relationship may be easily broken and could no longer be healed, since the parties would not get the chance of resolving the issue internally.

[208] Campbell (n 204) 455, 476; see also Macaulay (n 206) 261, 280.

[209] See section 3(C).

[210] A Gärtner, 'Britain and the CISG: The Case for Ratification – A Comparative Analysis with Special Reference to German Law' in *Pace Review of the Convention on Contracts for the International Sale of Goods (CISG)* (Kluwer Law International, 2000–2001) 70; EC Schneider, 'The seller's right to cure under the Uniform Commercial Code and the United Nations Convention on Contracts for International Sale of Goods' (1989–1990) 7 *Arizona Journal of International and Comparative Law* 69, 77.

[211] Schlechtriem and Schwenzer (n 95) 741; see also JO Honnold, *Documentary History of the Uniform Law for International Sales: The Studies, Deliberations, and Decisions that Led to the 1980 United Nations Convention with Introductions and Explanations* (Kluwer Law and Taxation Publishers, 1989) 324; C Liu, 'Cure by Non-Conforming Party: Perspectives from the CISG, UNIDROIT Principles, PECL and Case Law' (2005) *Pace Law School Institute of International Commercial Law*, para 4.1.

[212] Schlechtriem and Schwenzer (n 95) 988.

However, CISG's unnecessary insistence on the seller's right to cure may lead to conflict between the parties. An innocent buyer may want substitute goods but the seller may insist on repair or adjustment, which would imbalance their interests as well as causing tension and hostility between the parties. The seller is legally allowed to manoeuvre the buyer into a situation which the latter would have no choice but to admit the seller's curative attempts. While Article 48 appears to assume that a proper form of cure may require the buyer's cooperation in conducting cure, curing a breach by the seller has a concessionary nature and provides the seller a chance to redeem itself.[213] In addition, the tone of the wording of Article 48(2) is permissive and it is unclear whether the seller must strictly follow the procedure in order to affect a cure.[214] In other words, the seller may perform a cure without necessarily waiting for the buyer's communication as to whether the buyer accepts performance. In addition, during the cure by the seller, the buyer is effectively paralysed and debarred from resorting to any remedy which is inconsistent with performance by the seller. However, realistically, the buyer should have equally enjoyed the opportunities to explore the market and seek alternative suppliers, when the buyer reasonably entertains doubts concerning the seller's capability or commitment to cure. Rather than imposing a legislative solution on parties, which might convey a paternalistic approach and would disturb the contractual balance, the parties should be trusted to work towards following their own practical and commercial instincts. The legislative framework of cure established in CISG Article 48 as well as Article 37, which allows the seller to cure the breach before the delivery date, places the seller in a stronger position. When one party enjoys an upper hand, the equality required for maintaining and growing the relationship can easily be broken, since the stronger party would impose its own decision on the other party, who has limited choice.

The necessary maintenance of balance between the parties is better achieved under UCC and SGA. There is a particular advantage flowing from the absence of the buyer's right to cure under SGA and UCC over its presence in other legal regimes. Under CISG and UPICC, the seller has to determine whether the goods are substantially defective and how they can be either repaired or replaced. This in itself involves some expenditure of time. For the seller to then perform this duty to replace or repair, there are costs of transporting the goods and/or a technician to the buyer's location. In addition to these costs for the seller, there might also be some costs for the buyer, as they would have to wait until the complete performance by the seller and there might be some delays and flaws in such performance. These difficulties might incur some costs on the buyer as a result of the buyer's defective performance of their sub-contract with other buyers and

[213] MG Bridge, 'Curing a seller's defective tender or delivery of goods in commercial sales' in A Bucheler and M Muller-Chen (eds), *Private Law – National-Global-Comparative* (Intersentia, 2011) 231, 233.

[214] ibid; see also Zeller (n 180) paras 16–21; T Maier-Lohmann, 'Buyer's self-repair of non-conforming goods vs. seller's right to cure, under Article 48 CISG' (2019) *Uniform Law Review* 58, 62.

the losses arising therefrom.[215] This type of loss refers to loss of use by the sub-buyer(s), 'based on the normal use made of such [goods]'.[216] In addition to this loss, the buyer might miss commercial opportunities, which could be achieved by entering into contracts with other business and as a result incur loss of business.[217] Loss of business and therefore loss of profits refer to profits where 'the buyer would have made from use of the goods during the period after the goods should have been delivered until the actual date of delivery'.[218] These losses and hence these costs are absent under the SGA, as the buyer can freely and promptly obtain sufficiently equivalent substitutes from another source in the market or fix them or hire a reliable person to fix them in their location.

In order to fulfil the realities of the more impersonal business world of the current time, UCC in particular, provides for the liberal construction of its remedial provisions,[219] so that the 'observance of reasonable commercial standards of fair dealing' is the rule rather than the exception in trade.[220] Contrary to CISG, UCC appears to have taken an approach which strikes a better balance between the competing interests of the parties, following a breach. UCC section 2-508 has been designed to act as a meaningful restriction on the absolutism and harshness of the traditional perfect tender rule, under which the buyer was allowed to reject the goods and terminate the contract for any imperfection. No room was thus left for the doctrine of 'substantial performance'.[221] Section 2-508 tempers such an absolute right of termination. The outcome of applying this section is that the buyer is not allowed to terminate the contract as long as the seller can reasonably cure the non-conformity. A significant issue concerning cure in section 2-508 is marked out in paragraph 2, which indicates that the seller should have reasonable grounds to believe that the tender would be acceptable with money allowance. The idea is to protect the seller from a surprise rejection of the goods by the buyer. In addition, UCC has the potential to maintain and develop a collaborative and efficient venture between the parties, following a breach of contract by seller. In *Bonekrake v Cox*, when the buyers of bowling equipment did not reject goods but accepted them despite their defects, the buyers were not required to give detailed notice of such defects to seller in order to preserve their right to claim that contract had been breached.[222] However, sufficient notice was given when

[215] Bridge (n 2) para 17-040.

[216] Bridge (n 2) para 17-040; *Contigroup Cos Inc v Glencore AG* [2004] EWHC 2750 (Comm); [2005] 1 Lloyd's Rep 241.

[217] *Victoria Laundry (Windsor) v Newman Industries* [1949] 2 KB 528 (CA) 530; Bridge (n 2) para 17-040.

[218] Bridge (n 2) para 17-040; see also *Satef-Huttenes Alberns SpA v Paloma Tercera Shipping Co SA (The Pegase)* [1981] 1 Lloyd's Rep 175 (QB).

[219] UCC section 1-102.

[220] UCC section 2-103.

[221] *Mitsubishi Goshi Kaisha v Aron & Co* (1926) United States Court of Appeals, Second Circuit, 16 F.2d 185, 186.

[222] (1974) United States Courts of Appeals, 499 F.2d 951.

the buyers communicated that pinspotters were not installed according to the contract and that the pinspotters needed repairs. The buyers proceeded to repair the defects and when sued by the seller for the balance of the purchase price, the buyers counter-claimed for the cost of the repair. The Court of Appeal, deciding in favour of the buyer, explained that in accordance with section 2-508 a buyer who has accepted nonconforming goods is under no duty to accept an offer of cure by the seller.[223] This indicates that the seller's right to cure does not restrict the buyer from self-repairing deficient goods. If a buyer has access to reliable, local sources for repairing the goods already delivered, the buyer is given the chance to repair them and claim costs from the seller, rather than waiting for the seller to cure those defects. Also, the words 'a further reasonable time to substitute a conforming tender' in UCC 2-508 (2) seek to protect the buyer, which would provide the right balance between the competing interests of parties following a breach.[224] What is a 'reasonable time' depends upon the attending circumstances. In other words, the UCC shows much needed sensitivity to the buyer's situation. It takes account of whether incurring delay on the part of the seller causes mounting losses for the buyer and whether the buyer has to expend time and energy to cooperate with the seller when there is other business for the buyer to attend to. The buyer may thus be keener in cooperating with the seller and maintaining the contract when their interests are respected by the applicable legal regime.

In terms of the second norm of 'conformity of extended relations with commercial matrix', performance remedies prioritised under CISG and UPICC should be contrasted with damages prioritised under SGA and UCC. The latter regimes may be more efficient than the former ones by allowing the efficient breach of contract, where the seller is tempted to breach the contract when they gain more from performance of the contract, even after payment of expectation damages to the buyer.[225] Expectation damages as a routine remedy for breach of contract gives an option to the seller either to perform the contract, or breach the contract, and pay the compensation satisfying the buyer's expected valuation from the performance of contract.[226] In contrast, under CISG and UPICC, the seller is obliged to perform the contract either through specific performance or cure, even if the breach is more advantageous.[227] It has been claimed that 'if [the theory of efficient breach] were

[223] ibid; see also *Audio Visual Artistry v Tanzer* (2012) Court of Appeals of Tennessee, United States, 403 S.W.3d 789; *NTA Graphics South, Inc. v Axiom Impressions, LLC* (2019) United States District Court, Alabama, Southern Division, 413 F.Supp.3d 1164.

[224] UCC Official Comments, section 2-508, para 3.

[225] D Campbell, 'The defence of breach and the policy of performance' (2006) 25 *University of Queensland Law Journal 271*, 272; see also D Campbell and R Halson, 'The irrelevance of the performance interest, a comparative analysis of "keep-open" covenants in Scotland and England' in LA DiMatteo, Q Zhou, S Saintier and K Rowley, *Commercial Contract Law, Transatlantic Perspectives* (Cambridge University Press, 2013) 467.

[226] R Cooter and T Ulen, *Law and Economics*, 4th edn (Pearson Addison Wesley, 2007) 254; D Friedman, 'The efficient breach fallacy' (1989) 18 *Journal of Legal Studies* 1, 2; Campbell (n 204) 455, 460.

[227] RJ Scalise, 'Why no efficient breach in civil law? a comparative assessment of the doctrine of efficient breach of contract' (2007) 55 *American Journal of Comparative Law* 721, 726–27.

correct it would provide a rationale for placing narrow limits on specific performance, because that remedy prohibits breach'.[228] The following paragraphs will compare these two situations – where the efficient breach is allowed under the SGA and UCC and where it is not allowed under CISG and UPICC- from the efficiency standpoint in the context of the international sales of manufactured goods.

First, the theory of efficient breach of contract should be elaborated. Economic efficiency can be achieved if resources are allocated to their highest-valued uses while minimizing the cost of reallocation.[229] If a legal regime seeks to serve efficiency, it should specify a remedy that 'will lead to ownership of the [goods] by the person who values it the most, and should attempt to reach this result at the lowest possible resource cost'.[230] Based on this argument, a theory of efficient breach of contract has been developed in which the seller is given an option to breach the contract as long as they are prepared to pay the plaintiff their expectation damages, that is, a sum necessary to make the plaintiff indifferent between the performance of the contract and the damages so paid.[231] A typical example of efficient breach is that a seller sells a buyer the goods for £20, which is valued at £15 by the seller and £25 by the buyer. The contract brings them £ 5 profits respectively. But, after the conclusion of the contract, a third party offers £30 for the goods that is valued at £35 by them. The seller is allowed to efficiently breach the contract by selling the goods to the third party, and then compensates the buyer £5. The breach generates £15 profits to the seller and £5 profits to the third party and makes the buyer no worse-off than if the contract was performed. In such instances, the efficient breach theory states that not only should the law not punish breaches of contract but it ought to encourage them.[232] There may be a trade-off between the costs involved in specific performance recognised under CISG and UPICC, and damages under the SGA. Although the superiority of damages over specific performance might effectively encourage the seller's efficient breach of contract, there are some costs involved in damages that might decrease its efficiency, which will be analysed.

One crucial problem with damages, which can be costly, is to determine what the innocent party's expected profit was at the time that the contract was formed.[233] In other words, the courts are required to satisfy the consumer's surplus protected by the expectation damages.[234] It may be difficult to realise how best to measure

[228] Eisenberg (n 6) 975, 997.

[229] TS Ulen, 'The efficiency of specific performance: toward a unified theory of contract remedies' (1984–1985) 83 *Michigan Law Review* 341, 342.

[230] Ulen (n 229) 341, 345; see also Scalise (n 227) 721, 722–23.

[231] Friedman (n 226) 1, 2; see also RW Brooks, 'The efficient performance hypothesis' (2006) 116 *Yale Law Journal* 568, 571; RA Posner, *Economic Analysis of Law*, 6th edn (Aspen Publisher, 2003) 253; IR Macneil, 'Efficient breach of contract: circles in the sky' (1982) 68 *Virginia Law Review* 947, 948–49; G Klass, 'Efficient breach' in G Klass, G Letsas and P Saprai, *Philosophical Foundations of Contract Law* (Oxford University Press, 2014) 363.

[232] Scalise (n 227) 721, 722.

[233] Ulen (n 229) 341, 361.

[234] ibid; see also Harris, Campbell and Halson (n 1) 169.

the buyer's subjective value of performance.[235] In order to satisfy the buyer's expectancy, the adjudicators must calculate the amount the seller is required to pay in order to fully compensate the buyer, which is equal to the amount the buyer requires to obtain an appropriate substitute.[236] Such an accurate calculation demands sufficient information regarding 'the relevant terms of contract, the market for the goods in question, the believability of each party's evidence on its expectancy, and so on'.[237] 'It would be very difficult and expensive for a court to acquire the information necessary to make these determinations'.[238] However, it seems that the problem of calculation of the buyer's expectancy has been exaggerated and the common law can effectively alleviate this problem by imposing the remoteness test and the duty to mitigate. The remoteness test implies that the profit must have been reasonably foreseeable by the breaching party. Such constraint guides the adjudicators to determine the scope of the buyer's profit which could have been obtained by the performed contract. The duty to mitigate implies that the buyer will usually try to find substitute performance from a third party which is as close as possible to the performance which he hoped to obtain from the seller. This means that the transaction made in a market can effectively address the reasonable expectation of the promisee, which can be satisfied by damages. Such cover transactions made in the market determines the ease with which a court may accurately estimate the expectation of the promisee.[239] This shows that the satisfaction of the buyer's expectancy would be difficult when the goods are scarcely available. It can be argued that in many situations, the law on remedies can safely ignore the problem of determining and valuing the consumer surplus expected by the buyer, especially when they can obtain a substitute in the market which will give them virtually the same surplus.[240] Thus, this problem is not significant when commercial parties are dealing with manufactured goods which their substitutes are normally available in the market.[241] This kind of problem is, however, absent in specific performance. The court merely decrees the performance of contract, regardless of the subjective valuation of the buyer at the time of conclusion of contract and the costs of determining various parties' valuations of performance are borne by those parties in voluntary negotiations.

There are, however, two types of enforcement costs in the remedy of specific performance in the international sales of manufactured goods. First, there are

[235] Eisenberg (n 6) 975, 990–1003.

[236] Kronman (n 71) 351, 360; see also N Khouri, 'Efficient breach theory in the law of contract: an analysis' (2000–2003) 9 *Aukland University Law Review* 739, 748–50.

[237] Ulen (n 229) 341, 369.

[238] Kronman (n 71) 351, 360; see also Harris, Campbell and Halson (n 1) 167.

[239] LA Kornhauser, 'An introduction to the economic analysis of contract remedies' (1985–1986) 57 *University of Colorado Law Review* 683, 715; see also Eisenberg (n 6) 975, 991.

[240] Harris, Campbell and Halson (n 1) 169.

[241] See eg *Sony Computer Entertainment UK Ltd and another v Cinram Logistics UK Ltd* [2008] EWCA Civ 955; *Air Studios (Lyndhurst) Limited t/a Air Entertainment Group v Lombard North Central Plc* [2012] EWHC 3162 (QB), [2013] 1 Lloyd's Rep 63.

costs of post-breach negotiations and transportation of the goods, which are borne by the parties.[242] These costs are minimal when damages are awarded. Specific performance is understood as an instruction to the litigating parties to use the market, rather than the court, to solve their dispute and the parties are likely to begin negotiations regarding the performance of the contract.[243] These negotiations might be particularly costly in the international sales of manufactured goods due to the geographical distance of the parties, which might make the parties' communications difficult. However, it can be counter argued that in general, post breach negotiation costs are likely to be minimal among the parties in such transactions, as the parties are likely to have established a relationship before the breach, which can facilitate the parties' further negotiations regarding the performance of contract. In contrast, these costs are absent in damages, as the courts simply order the seller to pay the amount of money compensating the buyer, with which there is less likely to be a need for the parties to negotiate about its implementation and thus damages are more efficient from this standpoint. The costs of transportation of the goods in specific performance are likely to be high. This is so because normally the seller's location is geographically far from the buyer's location and that the seller has to arrange transportation of the goods in question.[244] In order to prevent such an uneconomical outcome, the buyer can instead find the substitute goods in a market near to their location and claim damages. Such costs are, therefore, minimal in damages. Thus, damages are likely to effectively decrease transportation costs.

Second, there are costs associated with litigation and settlement of international sales disputes. Particularly, there are costs to the adjudicators in supervising the performance of contract, which are absent in damages.[245] As famously stated by Kronman, 'it is ancient dogma that specific performance necessarily means increased judicial involvement in the enforcement and supervision of contractual duties.'[246] A pertinent example of high supervisory costs arises when there is high probability of noncompliance, owing, perhaps, to the seller's having forcefully and convincingly indicated their refusal to comply. However, these costs are present mainly in contracts for personal services in which the courts need to oversee the adequacy of performance.[247] But, these costs should be minimal in the specific performance of the commercial sales of manufactured goods, in which the

[242] Ulen (n 229) 341, 385–401.

[243] Kronman (n 71) 351, 369.

[244] Schwenzer and Munoz (n 8) 614; Fitzgerald (n 5) 291, 303; for further explanation on transportation of the goods in international sales see CISG Art 31; CB Andersen and FG Mazzotta and B Zeller, *A Practitioner's Guide to the CISG* (JurisNet LLC, 2010) 459.

[245] AW Katz, 'Remedies for breach of contract under the CISG' (2005) 25 *International Review of Law and Economics* 378, 383; H Lando and C Rose, 'On the enforcement of specific performance in Civil law countries' (2004) 24 *International Review of Law and Economics* 473, 481; *Co-Operative Insurance Society Ltd v Argyll Stores (Holdings) Ltd* [1998] AC 1 (HL) 12.

[246] Kronman (n 71) 351, 373.

[247] S Shavell, 'Specific performance versus damages for breach of contract' (2005–2006) 84 *Tulane Law Review* 831, 845.

property of goods in question is conveyed. Two reasons can be provided for this view: first, it only requires the relevant court locates the property in question and uses its powers to achieve compliance. Second, realising whether compliance is adequate would normally not be an issue, for whether property has been conveyed is typically self-evident. These reasons, therefore, demonstrated that the factor of supervisory costs is not substantively incurred in implementing specific performance for the sales of goods.

6

Termination

1. Introduction

This chapter focuses on termination under the four legal regimes. Termination investigated in this chapter is available as a remedy to the buyer who has not received or will not receive the promised performance thus entitling them to end a contract otherwise concluded properly. Amongst various remedies available to the buyer for breach of international sale of goods contract, termination is the most drastic measure. In what grounds and circumstances the buyer can terminate is a perennial question, which should be addressed by reference to the circumstances of a contract. As indicated by Treitel, the most obvious reason, which a buyer has for terminating the contract is the hardship which they may suffer in receiving a performance different from that for which they bargained.[1] But the right to terminate can be asserted for different reasons. One such reason, which holds good in many legal regimes, is that termination is a faster remedy than a suit for performance or damages, in the sense it does not require the judgment of a court or an arbitral award, though such a judicial decision may still be required to work out the effects of termination. Another, and perhaps the most important practical, reason for invoking termination is that this remedy may yield a more favourable financial result. This will be so where the buyer's bargain turned out to be a bad one due to the market movements, even if the contract had been duly performed; or where the financial loss, which they have suffered, is wholly or partly irrecoverable, eg because it is unforeseeable. It is worth noting that CISG employs the term 'avoidance' and UCC employs the term 'cancellation', instead of termination, but it will be shown that these terms have the same function as termination under other legal regimes. This chapter will mainly focus on the grounds for terminating a contract to realise the extent to which those legal regimes can promote the relational normative framework. Significant differences in the principles governing termination of contract will be identified and will be evaluated on the basis of this evaluative framework. The effects of termination will also be described in the introduction. This chapter will then analyse the grounds for termination of contract under these legal regimes.

[1] GH Treitel, *Remedies for Breach of Contract: A Comparative Account* (Oxford University Press, 1988) 321–22.

Termination should be distinguished from rescission *ab initio*. Rescission *ab initio* places the parties in the position they occupied before entry into the contract, whereas termination brings the contract to a premature end without unwinding it.[2] Lord Wilberforce in *Johnson v Agnew* has clearly explained this distinction:

> [T]his so-called rescission [i.e. termination] is quite different from rescission *ab initio*, such as may arise, for example, in cases of mistake, fraud or lack of consent. In those cases, the contract is treated in law as never having come into existence. In the case of an accepted repudiatory breach the contract has come into existence but has been put to an end or discharged.[3]

What appears to be generally accepted in these legal regimes is that termination of contract, if elected by the buyer, operates only prospectively in the sense that it does not affect the accrued rights and liabilities of the parties.[4] It is accurately explained that the prospective effect of termination is 'to relieve both parties (guilty as well as innocent) of their primary duties of performance and their primary right to demand performance'.[5] Upon discharging the parties from their primary obligations to perform the contract, those primary obligations are transformed into an obligation on the party in breach to pay damages for their breach.[6] It is worth analysing in depth whether termination of contract might also operate retrospectively under these legal regimes. Treitel has stated that there are some common law discussions supporting the view that termination may have certain retrospective effects, particularly when it is said that the purpose of termination is to place each party in the position in which they would have been if the contract had never been made.[7] This issue will be evaluated comparatively against CISG and UPICC.

[2] MG Bridge, *The Sale of Goods* (4th edn, Oxford University Press 2019) 588; MG Bridge, *The International Sale of Goods* (4th edn, Oxford University Press 2017) 483.

[3] [1980] AC 367 (HL) 393.

[4] For English law see: E McKendrick, *Goode and McKendrick on Commercial Law* (6th edn, Penguin Books, London 2020) 428; Treitel (n 1) 383; R Bradgate, 'Termination for breach' in J Birds, R Bradgate and C Villiers, *Termination of Contracts* (John Wiley & Sons, 2005) 24; Bridge, *The International Sale of Goods* (n 2) 483. For UCC see: UCC section 2-106(3); WD Hawkland, CS Bjerre, LR Rusch and LT Garry, *Hawkland's Uniform Commercial Code Series* (Thomson Reuters, 2023), section 2-106 para 4; D Frisch, *Lawrence's Anderson on the Uniform Commercial Code*, 3rd edn (Thomson Reuters, 2013) section 2-106, para 3. For CISG see: CISG Article 81(1); UNCITRAL Digest of Case Law on the United Nations Convention on Contracts for the International Sale of Goods (2016) Article 81, para 4; *Partition Panels case* (1999) Austrian Supreme Court, CISG-online 483; CISG Advisory Council, 'Consequences of Avoidance of the Contract' (2008) Opinion n 9, para 3.2; Bridge, *The International Sales of Goods* (n 2) 697; P Schlechtriem and L Schwenzer, *Commentary on the UN Convention on the International Sale of Goods*, 5th edn (Oxford University Press, 2022) 1102; S Kroll, L Mistelis and PP Viscasillas, *UN Convention on Contracts for the International Sale of Goods (CISG) Commentary* (Hart Publishing, 2011) 1110; MG Bridge, 'Avoidance for fundamental breach of contract under the UN Convention on the International Sale of Goods' (2010) 59 *International & Comparative Law Quarterly* 911, 912. For UPICC, see UPICC Article 7.3.5; S Vogenauer, *Commentary on the UNIDROIT Principles of International Commercial Contracts*, 2nd edn (Oxford University Press, 2015) 956; UPICC Official Comments, Article 7.3.5, n 1; R Zimmermann, 'The unwinding of failed contracts in the UNIDROIT Principles' (2011) 16 *Uniform Law Review* 563, 573.

[5] McKendrick (n 4) 159.

[6] Bradgate (n 4) 24; see also Bridge, *The International Sale of Goods* (n 2) 404.

[7] Treitel (n 1) 383.

2. Grounds for Termination of the Contract

A. SGA

At common law, termination is always a matter of election. While in *MSC Mediterranean Shipping Co SA v Cottonex Anstalt*, the English Court of Appeal held that termination was automatic in circumstances where the promisor's breach frustrated the commercial purpose of the contract, a breach having that significant impact does not discharge the promisor analogous to an automatic discharge under doctrine of frustration.[8] A sales contract can be terminated on three grounds. First, when the term broken is a condition, in which case any breach of this term entitles the buyer to terminate.[9] Second, where the term broken is not a condition but an intermediate term, in which case a right to terminate arises if the breach in the circumstances goes to the root of the contract or, which amounts to the same thing, depriving the buyer of substantially the whole benefit of the contract.[10] Third, when there is an anticipatory breach of contract, which was examined in chapter two of this book.[11] These grounds will be analysed. At the outset, there will be an analysis of the doctrine of fundamental non-performance under English law in order to find out whether this doctrine still exists to the extent that it exists and is implemented in other legal regimes, ie, CISG and UPICC. Also, time obligations under English law and their importance will be taken into account.

i. Fundamental Non-performance of Contract

The doctrine of fundamental breach was developed by the courts partially in order to limit the operation of exemption clauses, the purpose being that a party who has fundamentally breached the contract would be precluded from relying upon an exemption clause contained in the contract.[12] This was indicated in *Karsales (Harrow) Ltd v Wallis*: 'the general principle [is] that a breach which goes to the root of the contract disentitles the party from relying on the exempting clause.'[13] Fundamental breach corresponded to the breach of the fundamental term of a contract, which 'went to the core or substance of the contract'.[14] In *Karsales*, a

[8] [2016] 2 Lloyd's Rep 494, 505.

[9] Bridge, *The International Sale of Goods* (n 2) 484.

[10] ibid.

[11] See ch 2, section 4(A).

[12] HG Beale (ed), *Chitty on Contracts, vol 1*, 34th edn (Sweet & Maxwell, 2022), para 14-020; see *Sze Hai Tong Bank Ltd v Rambler Cycle Co Ltd* [1959] AC 576, 587–89; *Yeoman Credit Ltd v Apps* [1962] 2 QB 508 (CA) 520; *Charterhouse Credit Co Ltd v Tolly* [1963] 2 QB 683 (CA) 710; *Astley Industrial Trust v Grimley* [1963] 1 WLR 1468 (CA) 1470.

[13] *Karsales (Harrow) Ltd v Wallis* [1956] 1 WLR 936 (CA) 941; see also *J. Spurling Ltd v Bradshaw* [1956] 1 WLR 461 (CA) 465.

[14] *Alderslade v Hendon Laundry Ltd* [1945] K.B. 189, 192; *Smeaton Hanscomb & Co v Sassoon I Setty Son & Co (No.1)* [1953] 1 WLR 1468 (QB) 1470; see also Beale (n 12) para 24-042.

car sold to the buyer was 'in a deplorable state and would not go', whereas the car, which was shown to the plaintiff before signing the contract, was in excellent condition and would go.[15] It was considered a fundamental term of contract to 'provide a functioning car which could be used on the roads' and accordingly it is a fundamental breach, when 'a car was in unusable, unroadworthy and unsafe condition'.[16] However, the House of Lords ruled that the principle of fundamental breach does not constitute a rule of law.[17] Lord Reid stated: 'General use of the term fundamental breach is of recent origin, and I can find nothing to indicate that it means either more or less that the well-known type of breach which entitles the innocent party to treat as repudiatory and to rescind the contract'.[18] Although this doctrine was ruled out by the House of Lords, the understanding behind this doctrine still exists in English law, as it has been indicated that 'the general principle is that any [deficiency in quality or quantity] must attain a certain minimum degree of seriousness to entitle the injured party to terminate'.[19] In other words, the seller must have been guilty of a substantial failure to perform. This will be explained.

It is, however, difficult to discover when a failure in performance is sufficiently serious to entitle the buyer to terminate the contract. The courts should consider the consequences of the breach of the contract to determine whether a substantial failure has happened.[20] In order to reduce the uncertainties and difficulties inherent in such process, English law has classified contractual terms into conditions, warranties, and innominate terms. The result would be that if a term is considered to be a condition, there is no need to weigh the gravity of the factual consequences of the breach, which can effectively serve certainty. This is mainly because the breach of this term affects 'the substance and foundation of the adventure' and the range of possible consequences flowing from the breach of this term is normally so serious that the term should be regarded in law as a condition.[21] Therefore, all consequences of a breach of condition are deemed to be sufficiently serious to justify termination. The practical application of recognising particular terms as conditions reflects the rationale underlying termination rights, in that termination is permitted if a breach goes to the root of the contract. As such, the classification of terms as conditions has been part of an attempt to restrict the right of termination to the cases in which the breach is sufficiently substantial.

[15] [1956] 1 WLR 936 (CA) 941.

[16] *Yeoman Credit Ltd v Apps* [1962] 2 QB 508 (CA) 509.

[17] *Suisse Atlantique Société d'Armement SA v NV Rotterdamsche Kolen Centrale* [1967] 1 AC 361 (HL); see also *UGS Finance v National Mortgage Bank of Greece and National Bank of Greece SA* [1964] 1 Lloyd's Rep 446 (CA) 450.

[18] [1967] 1 AC 361 (HL) 397.

[19] E Peel, *Treitel on The Law of Contract*, 15th edn (Sweet & Maxwell, 2020) para 7-018; see also Bridge, *The Sale of Goods* (n 2) 587.

[20] Peel (n 19) para 7-018.

[21] Bridge, *The Sale of Goods* (n 2) 587; see also JW Carter, *Carter's Breach of Contract*, 2nd edn (Hart Publishing, 2020) 151–52; C Twigg-Flesner and R Canavan, *Atiyah and Adams' Sale of Goods*, 14th edn (Pearson Education Limited, 2020) 417.

ii. Breach of Condition

Traditionally, the terms of a contract were classified as being either conditions or warranties.[22] The difference between them is that any breach of a condition entitles the innocent party to treat himself as discharged from further performance under the contract, and in any event to claim damages for loss sustained by the breach.[23] Warranty is a minor promise within a contract. SGA section 61 describes 'warranty' as an agreement 'with reference to goods which are the subject of a contract of sale, but collateral to the main purpose of such contract, the breach of which gives rise to a claim for damages, but not to a right to reject the goods and treat the contract as repudiated'. SGA has provided examples of implied terms which are classified as warranties, namely, the seller's obligations regarding quiet possession (SGA section 12(2b)) and freedom from encumbrances (SGA section 12(2 a)). But 'condition' has not been defined by the SGA. It has been suggested that '[a] condition is a term central to the main purpose of the contract'.[24] In order to ascertain whether a contractual term is condition, regard should be firstly had to the construction of a contract.[25] 'Construction' refers to the process by which a court determines the meaning and legal effect of a contract.[26] Devlin opines that 'the best known definition or pointer is that of Bowen L.J [that says] make up your mind whether the intention of the parties would best be carried out by treating the provisions as a warranty or as a condition'.[27] To ascertain the intention of the parties, Bowen LJ explains that 'there is no way of deciding that question except by looking at the contract in the light of the surrounding circumstances'.[28] The essential point is that the inquiry regarding whether a term is condition should be conducted on an *a priori* basis: 'The Court believed that the answer was to be found in the true construction of the contract taken as a whole'.[29] It is, however, difficult to determine the intention of the parties. Treitel has suggested that when the intention of the parties has not been discoverable from the words used in their contracts, 'the courts relied secondly on the general requirement of substantial failure in performance'.[30] In furtherance of this

[22] Beale (n 12) para 27-013; McKendrick (n 4) 113.

[23] Beale (n 12) para 12-019.

[24] R Bradgate and F White, 'Rejection and termination in contracts for the sale of goods' in J Birds, R Bradgate and C Villiers, *Termination of Contracts* (John Wiley & Sons, 2005) 57.

[25] *Glaholm v Hays* [1841] 2 Man 257, [1841] 133 ER 743, 746; *Tradax Export SA v European Grain & Shipping Ltd* [1983] 2 Lloyd's Rep 100 (QB).

[26] Beale (n 12) para 16-003; see also *Trump International Golf Club Scotland Ltd v Scottish Ministers* [2015] UKSC 74, [2016] 1 WLR 85 at para 35; *Bou-Simon v BGC Brokers LP* [2018] EWCA Civ 1525, [2019] 1 All E.R. (Comm) 955 at para 13; *Bates v Post Office Ltd (No.3: Common Issues)* [2019] EWHC 606 (QB) at para 690; *Wells v Devani* [2019] UKSC 4, [2020] AC 129 at paras 28 and 59.

[27] L Devlin, 'The treatment of breach of contract' (1996) 24 *Cambridge Law Journal* 192, 195–96.

[28] *Bentsen v Taylor, Sons & Co. (2)* [1893] 2 QB 274 (CA) 280–81.

[29] *Bettini v Gye* [1876] 1 QBD 183 (QB) 187.

[30] Peel (n 19) para 18-045; see also Carter (n 21) 120; MG Bridge (ed), *Benjamin's Sale of Goods*, 11th edn (Sweet & Maxwell, 2022) para 10-026; AM Shea, 'Discharge from performance of contract by failure of condition' (1979) 42 *Modern Law Review* 623, 624; *Photo Production Ltd v Securicor Transport Ltd* [1980] AC 827 (HL) 849.

suggestion, he has referred to a leading dictum explaining that if 'performance of the stipulation [went] to the very root … of the contract', then the stipulation was treated as a condition.[31] Fletcher Moulton L.J has described conditions as obligations 'so essential to its very nature that their non-performance may fairly be considered by the other party as a substantial failure to perform the contract at all'.[32] This indicates that English law has the general commitment of allowing termination when the breach is sufficiently fundamental.

Apart from the construction of the contract, conditions have been introduced in the SGA. Sections 12 to 15 of the SGA 'prescribe a set of seven implied terms in favour of the buyer', namely the buyer's right to sell (SGA s 12(1)), correspondence with description (SGA s 13(1)), quality (SGA s 14(2)), fitness for purpose (SGA s 14(3)) and correspondence with sample (SGA s 15).[33] Of these statutory implied terms, five (title, correspondence with description, quality, fitness for purpose and correspondence with sample) are labelled conditions, whereas the remaining two (freedom from charges and encumbrances, and quit possession) are considered warranties.[34] The statutory classification of terms as conditions can be explained on the ground that they promote certainty. Once a condition is broken, the buyer can safely terminate the contract, 'without having to consider the often difficult question whether the breach amounted to a substantial failure in performance'.[35] However, this does not mean that the general commitment to allowing termination only in cases when there is fundamental failure of performance has been abandoned. The decision to classify these particular terms as conditions shows that the breach must still be fundamental enough to allow the buyer terminate the contract, as it has been observed that 'the breach of such terms might have caused serious prejudice, irrespective of the question whether it actually did so'.[36] The Law Commission has asserted that 'breach of an implied condition is presumably a breach of material part of the contract'.[37] In other words, in order to demonstrate the requirement of substantial failure allowing termination, the law has implicitly assimilated a clear undertaking of correspondence with description, to the terms having no obvious consequences of their breaches, such as fitness and satisfactory quality. The breach of the duty to supply goods with the contract description is clearly a factual and express undertaking, the breach of which 'is not

[31] *Glaholm v Hays* [1841] 2 Man & G 257, [1841] 133 ER 743, 746; see also *Heyman v Darwins Ltd* [1942] AC 356 (HL) 397.

[32] *Wallis, Son and Wells v Pratt and Haynes* [1910] 2 KB 1003 (CA) 1012.

[33] For further explanation see McKendrick (n 4) 341–96.

[34] Bradgate and White (n 24) 58.

[35] Peel (n 19) para 18-050.

[36] ibid; see also *Lombard North Central Plc v Butterworth* [1987] Q.B. 527, 535; *Sanko SS Co Ltd v Kano Trading Co Ltd* [1978] 1 Lloyd's Rep 156; *Reardon Smith Line Ltd v Hansen Tangen* [1976] 1 W.L.R. 989; *B.S. & N. Ltd v Micado Shipping Ltd* [2001] 1 Lloyd's Rep 341, 350, 353, 356; *PT Berlian Laju Tanker TBE v Nuse Shipping Ltd* [2008] EWHC 1330 (Comm), [2008] 2 Lloyd's Rep 246 at para 65; *C21 London Estates Ltd v Maurice Macneill Iona Ltd* [2017] EWHC 998 (Ch) at paras 70–72.

[37] Law Commission and Scottish Law Commission, *Sale and Supply of Goods* (Law Com No 160, 1987) para 2.30.

merely breach of party of contract but a total non-performance of it'.[38] Therefore, if those ambiguous conditions with no obvious consequences are breached, it is presumed that the requirement of substantial failure is satisfied and that the buyer can terminate the contract.

iii. Breach of Innominate Terms

However, the classification of contractual terms into conditions and warranties is not exhaustive. Breaches can be so divergent in their consequences that this 'black and white' test can be applied only to the minority of terms.[39] The majority of terms fall between condition and warranty and as such there was a need to introduce a new category which could cover the grey terms.[40] In order to do so, the courts have limited the right of discharge following from the classification of a term as a condition by the invention of another category of terms, adopting a more flexible approach to the consequences of breach.[41] This new category is called '*tertium quid*' or 'intermediate terms' or 'innominate terms' denoting that the parties have not chosen to classify them as either conditions or warranties.[42] This category looks at the nature and effect of the breach of the contractual term, in contrast with the traditional approach which looks at the nature of the contractual term.[43]

The new category of innominate terms was introduced in *Hong Kong Fir Shipping Co Ltd v Kawasaki Kisen Kaisha Ltd*.[44] This case involved the breach of a seaworthiness term in a two year charterparty contract in circumstances where the charterer had already lost five weeks and was likely to lose a further 15 days when he repudiated the contract.[45] The Court of Appeal ruled that their repudiation had no legal basis. The reason for such judgment was that many complex contractual undertakings, such as the duty to tender a seaworthy ship, can be breached in many diverse circumstances from a rusty nail in the deck to the broken-down state of the ship's engine. Due to such vagueness arisen from the possibility of different types of consequences, those undertakings could not be fitted into the traditional classification of terms. An assessment should thus have been conducted to examine whether the breach had substantially deprived the injured party from their expected contractual benefit in order to entitle them to terminate the contract.

[38] *Chanter v Hopkins* [1838] 4 M & W 399, [1838] 150 ER 1484; see also *Re Moore & Co and Landauer & Co* [1921] 2 KB 519 (CA) 523.
[39] Devlin (n 27) 192, 197; see also Bradgate (n 4) 33.
[40] Devlin (n 27) 192, 197.
[41] Beale (n 12) para 27-011; Peel (n 19) para 18-053.
[42] *Compagnie Generale Maritime v Diakan Spirit SA (The Ymnos)* [1982] 2 Lloyd's Rep 574, 583; *K/S Merc-Scandia XXXXII v Lloyd's Underwriters (The Mercandian Continent)* [2001] EWCA Civ 1275; [2001] 1 Lloyd's Rep 563 at para 13; *Koompahtoo Local Aboriginal Land Council v Sanpine Pty Ltd* [2007] H.C.A. 61, 233 C.L.R. 115 at para 109; MG Bridge, 'Discharge for breach of the contract of sale of goods' (1982–1983) 28 *McGill Law Journal* 867, 897.
[43] E Peel, 'The termination paradox' [2013] *Lloyd's Maritime and Commercial Law Quarterly* 519, 521.
[44] [1962] 2 QB 26 (CA).
[45] ibid, 27.

This Court used a stringent test focusing on the gravity or seriousness of the breach occurred. The test provides: 'Does the occurrence of the event deprive the party who has further undertakings still to perform of substantially the whole benefit which it was the intention of the parties as expressed in the contract that he should obtain as the consideration for performing those undertakings?'[46] Implementation of this test would actually 'reduce the availability of termination for relatively minor breaches of contract and thus, perhaps, of bad faith termination on economic grounds'.[47] This reinforces the general principle that termination is allowed only when there is substantial failure of performance.

However, *Hong Kong Fir Shipping Co Ltd* was not directly relevant to the sale of goods. *Cehave NV v Bremer Handels GmbH (The Hansa Nord)* was the case in which the doctrine of innominate terms was explicitly imported into the law governing sale of goods contracts.[48] This case concerned the sale of citrus pulp pellets for compounding into cattle food. A dispute started when a substantial proportion of a shipment of 3,400 tons had suffered heating damage.[49] A term of contract was 'shipment to be made in good condition' and the buyer argued that the goods were not of 'merchantable quality' (the contemporary standard; now 'satisfactory quality') under SGA s 14(2), as such they were entitled to terminate the contract due to the breach of condition.[50] When the cargo arrived at Rotterdam, the market price of the goods had fallen. The buyer rejected the whole cargo. The Court of Appeal held that 'the term was an intermediate stipulation and the breach did not go to the root of the contract'.[51] The reason might revolve around the flexibility and vagueness of the term of 'merchantable quality', breach of which might cause several distinctive types of consequences and that the court should assess their seriousness to determine whether termination was allowed. It was doubted whether the SGA recognised the doctrine of intermediate terms. The doubt arose from the fact that the wording of SGA s 11(3) requires that all stipulations be classified as condition or warranties and as such it 'put in place a comprehensive scheme of remedies leaving no room for a *tertium quid* in sale of goods law'.[52] But there are two sections in this legal regime, which can be construed to permit the application of this doctrine to the sales contracts. SGA section 62(2) preserves the common law rules and that it prevents the condition/warranty dichotomy from being exclusive. By virtue of this section, if a term does not fit into the statuary classification of terms, 'a more modern doctrine' expressed by the House of Lords can be applied.[53] Also, part

[46] ibid, 66; see also *Photo Production Ltd v Securicor Transport Ltd* [1980] AC 827 (HL) 849.
[47] Bradgate and White (n 24) 34.
[48] [1976] QB 44 (CA).
[49] ibid, 45.
[50] ibid.
[51] ibid, 84.
[52] Bridge (n 42) 868, 898.
[53] *Reardon Smith Line Ltd v Hansen Tangen (The Diana Prosperity)* [1976] 1 WLR 989 (HL) 998; see also *Bunge Corp v Tradax Export SA* [1981] 1 WLR 711, 715–716.

of SGA s 31(2) prescribes *ex post facto* assessment of the event occurred by the breach. This part provides:

> [I]t is a question in each case depending on the terms of the contract and the circumstances of the case whether the breach of contract is a repudiation of the whole contract or whether it is a severable breach giving rise to a claim for compensation but not to a right to treat the whole contract as repudiated.

This section is 'the only section in the Act' which explicitly allows the implementation of the approach introduced by the *Hong Kong Fir Shipping Co Ltd*. Therefore, according to these two sections, the doctrine of innominate terms can be applied to the sale of goods cases.

iv. Time Obligations

It is questionable whether the breach of time obligations allows termination of contract. It can be argued that a time stipulation will be regarded as of the essence in two different circumstances. First, if it is made so expressly by the parties, as the parties are at liberty to stipulate in the contract that time is to be of essence in relation to the seller's obligation to deliver within an agreed time.[54] This liberty has been recognised in SGA, as section 10(2) provides that 'whether any other stipulation as to time is or is not of the essence of the contract depends on the terms of the contract'. It has been held in *Lombard North Central Plc v Butterworth* that 'a clause making time of the essence and thus prompt performance a condition of a contract is not to be struck down merely because a breach of the obligation would not be sufficient on its own to constitute a repudiation'.[55] This indicates that a breach of an express time clause stipulated by the parties would entitle the buyer to terminate the contract, regardless of the seriousness or triviality of the consequence of such breach.

Second, where the surrounding circumstances of the contract or the nature of the subject-matter indicate that the fixed date must be exactly complied with. This circumstance occurs when there is no expressed stipulation regarding the time of performance, but the parties have fixed a time for the delivery of the goods. In such circumstance, it can be implied that time is of the essence by looking at nature of the contract and the character of the goods dealt with.[56] In commercial sale of goods, time clauses are normally construed as the essence of the contract.[57] In *Hartley v Hyman*, McCardie J has confirmed that '[i]n an ordinary commercial contracts for the sale of goods the rule clearly is that time is prima facie of

[54] Bridge (n 30) para 9-051; see also JE Stannard and D Capper, *Termination for Breach of Contract* (Oxford University Press, 2014) 15.

[55] [1987] QB 527 (CA) 528.

[56] Bridge (n 30) para 10-35.

[57] *Bunge Corp v Tradax Export SA* [1981] 1 WLR 711 (HL) 712; Bradgate (n 4) 38; F Reynolds, 'Discharge of Contract by Breach' (1981) 97 *Law Quarterly Review* 541, 542.

the essence with regard to delivery'.[58] A valid justification might be that time clause tends to 'provide certainty, which is such as indispensable ingredient' of such contracts.[59] Certainty might be achieved, if a time clause is treated as condition, which would therefore enable the buyer 'faced with a breach by the other party to make a prompt decision to terminate the contract and seek a substitute'.[60] In terms of the circumstances of contract, time clauses are of essence where the performance of other obligations is linked to that of the obligation in question.[61] This might happen especially in string contracts of commodities, in which the goods have been sold by the buyer before actually receiving them.[62] For instance, in *Toepfer (Hamburg) v Lenersan-Poortman NV (Rotterdam)*, it was held that '[the seller's] obligation to tender documents in time was a condition of the contract', as the commercial buyer might have sold the goods to sub-buyer and the goods needed to be delivered promptly.[63] Also, in *Bunge Corp*, it was set by the parties that the buyers shall give at least 15 days' notice of probable readiness of vessel and the last day for them to give notice was June 12.[64]

Endangering the buyer's ability to perform other contracts might also happen in commercial sales of manufactured goods, in which a buyer promptly needs the goods to use in their factory in order to supply goods to consumers or deliver to sub-buyers. Accordingly, if either of the above mentioned circumstances occurs, time obligations can be treated as conditions and the seller's delay in performance would entitle the buyer to terminate the contract. Otherwise, a time clause is merely an innominate or intermediate term, the breach of which gives right to the buyer to terminate only if the delay in delivery is so long as to deprive them of substantially the whole benefit which it was intended they should receive from the contract.

B. UCC

The principles governing termination under UCC are expressed in a unique manner. First, UCC does not classify contract terms into condition, warranty, and innominate terms analogous to English law. However, warranty is commonly employed in the sense given to condition under English law.[65] Second, there is no single section in UCC, which delineates the buyer's right to terminate the whole contract. Rather, from various sections one can gather the nature of such a right

[58] [1920] 3 KB 475 (KB).
[59] *Cie Commerciale Sucres et Denrees v C Czarnikow Ltd (The Naxos)* [1990] 1 WLR 1337 (HL), 1348; see also *Bremer Handelsgesellschaft v JH Rayner & Co* [1978] 2 Lloyd's Rep 73, 89 (QB).
[60] Bradgate (n 4) 38.
[61] ibid.
[62] Ibid.
[63] [1980] 1 Lloyd's Rep 143 (CA).
[64] *Bunge Corp v Tradax Export SA* [1981] 1 WLR 711 (HL) 712.
[65] Treitel (n 1) 364.

and how it can be exercised. Third, the term 'termination' is used differently in UCC from other legal regimes. As stated in UCC section 2-106, 'termination' happens when either party pursuant to a power created by agreement or law puts an end to the contract otherwise than for its breach. When a contract is terminated, all executory obligations are discharged but any right based on prior breach or performance survives. Whereas 'cancellation' happens when either party puts an end to the contract for breach by the other, and its effect is the same as that of 'termination', except that the cancelling party also retains any remedy for breach of the whole contract or any unperformed balance. What is our concern in this chapter is thus 'cancellation', which is available as a right to an injured buyer when breach occurs.

i. Perfect Tender Rule

The main ground for the buyer's right to cancel a contract lies in the 'perfect tender rule'. This rule, which is set forth in UCC section 2-601, holds that if the goods or the tender of delivery fail to conform to the contract 'in any respect', the buyer enjoys three options: either reject all of the goods, accept all of the goods despite the imperfect tender, or accept any commercial units or units and reject the rest of the goods. It thus appears that the buyer enjoys an unfettered and self-help right to cancel a contract if the seller fails to conform perfectly to its obligation.[66] It has been argued that perfect tender rule is rather a misnomer, since the goods or tender are not required to be perfect in the abstract and must be perfect in the sense that they comply fully to the contract terms.[67] This depends not only on the literal terms of the contract but also on 'commercial practices and other surrounding circumstances',[68] such as any course of dealing or course of performance between the parties, or any relevant and applicable usage of trade. In *Printing Center of Texas, Inc v Supermind Pub. Co., Inc*, the court held that the contract included more than the words used by the parties and it encompassed 'the bargain of the parties in fact as found in their language or by implication from other circumstances including course of dealing or usage of trade of trade or course of performance as provided in the UCC'.[69] It was noted by the court that once the contract between the parties is determined and established, the evidence must be considered to realise whether the right goods were tendered at the right time and place.[70] If the evidence does show nonconformity in some respect, the buyer is entitled to reject the goods in good faith.[71]

[66] JJ White and RS Summers, *Uniform Commercial Code*, 6th edn (Thomson Reuters, 2010) 415.
[67] RA Lord, *Williston on Contracts*, 4th edn (Thomson Reuters, 2023) § 40:6; see also Hawkland, Bjerre, Rusch and Garry (n 4) section 2-601, para 1; see also *Carando Gourmet Frozen Foods Corp., Inc. v Axis Automation, LLC* (2020) United States District Court, D. Massachusetts 458 F.Supp.3d 60.
[68] UCC Official Comments, section 1-303, para 1.
[69] (1984) Court of Appeals of Texas, Houston, 669 S.W.2d 779, para 11.
[70] ibid, para 13.
[71] ibid.

This indicates that the seller has a clear obligation to provide the goods that conform to the contract in every respect and 'substantial performance' does not discharge the seller from their contractual obligations. Quite recently, the Court of Appeals of Nebraska in *Albrecht v Fettig*, rejected the argument that the 'perfect tender rule has eroded over time and only stands for the proposition that buyers may reject a substantially nonconforming delivery'.[72] However, commercial practice indicates that the legal rules on cancellation are not always literally followed. Certain industries, such as basic raw commodity markets, have developed their own details provisions, which expressly limit the remedy of rejection and cancelation, and encourage the use of substitute, contract-preserving remedies such as price reduction.[73]

ii. Substantial Impairment

It should be noted that the appearance of the powerful weapon of the 'perfect tender' rule is rather deceptive. This rule is significantly hedged about by significant express provisions. One significant exception is the seller's right to cure, as a modern device limiting the buyer's right to terminate the contract, was discussed in chapter five. Another significant exception stems from the requirement of seriousness of breach. As Treitel argued, the appearance of the powerful weapon of the perfect tender rule is deception as the seriousness requirement is reintroduced by a number of sections, which must be read and implemented together with UCC Section 2-601.[74] UCC Section 2-612 provides that neither party may cancel an instalment contract unless the non-conformity or default substantially impairs the value of the whole contract', and that a buyer may reject an individual instalment only 'if the non-conformity substantially impairs the value of that instalment and cannot be cured'. In addition, UCC Section 2-608, adopting a substantial performance standard, allows a buyer to revoke acceptance of a lot or commercial unit only if the 'non-conformity substantially impairs its value to [them]'. These provisions signify that fundamental or material breach constitutes the major ground for cancellation of contract by a buyer. Professors White and Summers have even argued that 'the law would be little changed if UCC Section 2-601 gave the right to reject only upon 'substantial non-conformity''.[75]

[72] (2019) United States Court of Appeals, Nebraska, 932 N.W.2d 331, which cited these cases: *Maas v Schoboda* (1972) Supreme Court of Nebraska, 195.N.W.2d 491; *Meyer v Sandhills Beef, Inc* (1982) Supreme Court of Nebraska, 318 N.W.2d 863.

[73] Worth Street Textile Market Rules (came into effect in 1941), providing detailed provisions applicable to trade in cotton textiles setting out careful tolerances of quality. For instance, specifications F.F. at numerous points prescribe tolerances within which 'the buyer may claim and allowance in value … but may not reject or cancel because of such deficiency'; Basic Sales Provisions, National Retail Dry Goods Associations and Apparel Industries Inter-Association Committee (came into effect in 1948), its clause three provides 'return only for non-conformity with 'material provision', seller may replace returned merchandise within 5 days after last permissible delivery date.

[74] Treitel (n 1) 364.

[75] White and Summers (n 66) 357.

It was explained in *Horton v Horton* that 'a material breach is a failure to do something that is so fundamental to the contract that the failure to perform that obligation defeats an essential purpose of the contract'.[76] To determine substantial impairment of the value of the entire contract requires taking account of the entire circumstances of the transaction.[77] In fact, one must consider the cumulative effect of the beaching party's performance based on all the circumstances. For instance in *Technology and Supply Management, LLC v Johnson Controls Building Automation Systems, LLC*, the seller was responsible for manufacturing the two story shelters, packing their components into shipping containers, delivering the containers to the buyer's facility and training the buyer's personnel on assembling the shelters.[78] Following the contract, the seller learned that due to a possible supply shortage, the amount of a certain material necessary for production of the goods in question might not be available, and they informed the buyer that they use alternative materials in their production, for which final pricing should be revised, without amending the terms of contract. The buyer did not communicate as to whether they would be satisfied with the use of alternative materials in manufacturing the goods. Nevertheless, the seller decided to use the alternative materials in part of their production and delivered to buyer the containers of two-story shelters. The containers delivered deviated from the packaging requirements outlined in the contract. The materials used in shipments were not palletised or were insufficiently palletised, and as such were not sufficiently secured for the sea voyage to Kuwait, which caused damage to components. As a result, the buyer had to spend more time in Kuwait than would have otherwise been required for unloading, identifying, and sorting the materials that arrived in the containers. As a result of these non-conformities, the buyer sought to terminate the contract. The court held that the buyer did not effectively reject the goods but rather accepted the good by using them instead of returning them.[79] The seller substantially performed with respect to the two-story shelters and the buyer accepted that performance by using the materials of those goods. In other words, the seller's nonconforming performance did not constitute a material breach. The early defects in seller's performance did not defeat the essential purpose of the contract, thus the buyer was not entitled to cancel the contract and was only entitled to receive damages for those breaches.

[76] (1997) Supreme Court of Virginia, 487 S.E. 2d 200; see also *Ervin Const.Co. v Van Orden* (1993) Supreme Court of Idaho, 874 P.2d 506; *Cady v Burton* (1993) Supreme Court of Mantana 851 P.2d 1047; *Management Computer Services Inc v Hawkins, Ash, Baptie & Co.* (1996) Supreme Court of Wisconsin, 557 N.W.2d 67; *Bernstein v Nemeyer* (1990) Supreme Court of Connecticut, 570 A.2d 164.

[77] *L&M Enterprises, Inc v BEI Sensors & Systems Co* (2000) United States Court of Appeals, 231 F.3d 1284; *Phoenix Color Corp v Krause America, Inc* (2001) United States Court of Appeals, 25 Fed. Appx. 133; *ebmpapst Inc v AEIOMed, Inc* (2010) United States District Court, Minnesota, WL 4720848; *Rexing Quality Eggs v Rembrandt Enterprises Inc* (2018) United States District Court, Indiana, 360 F.Supp.3d 817.

[78] (2017) United States District Court, Virginia, WL 3219281.

[79] ibid.

The Restatement (Second) of the Law of Contracts has provided four considerations for determining whether the breach is fundamental: (1) the extent to which the buyer receives its expected benefit under the contract; (2) whether the defect can be compensated by damages; (3) the extent to which the seller will suffer a forfeiture if the breach is determined to be material; and (4) likelihood that the seller will cure its failure.[80] These criteria show that substantial impairment is quite similar to the English or common law standard of fundamental breach. While the US courts have employed both subjective and objective tests in identifying substantial impairment, it appears from the statutory provisions that the test for realising substantial impairment in UCC is more subjective, which seems to be true at least for UCC Section 2-608, which provides that the buyer can revoke the acceptance in whole or in party, if they can show that the non-conformity substantially impairs the value to '*them*'. In the famous case of *Allen v Rouse Toyota Jeep Inc*, the court applied a two-part test established in UCC Section 2-608.[81] The first part concerns the buyer's subjective reaction to the alleged defect, by taking account of the buyer's needs and circumstances. The second part concerns the objective reasonableness of this reaction, taking into account the goods' market value, reliability, safety, and usefulness for purposes for which similar goods are used. In other words, courts will have to first determine the particular buyer's conditions, and second decide whether the defect incurred as a result of breach could be viewed objectively as a substantial impairment of value, given those particular needs.[82] This great dependency on the buyer's conditions is then balanced out at the second stage where a loss incurred as a result of breach is examined objectively. The test is therefore a personalised objective test, referring to how a reasonable person would react if in the buyer's position and affected by the seller's breach.

iii. Good Faith Requirement

Another significant limitation on the perfect tender rule is that, since the rejection of goods is a matter of buyer's discretion, the buyer is mandated to act in good faith.[83] As indicated by Professor Lawrence, of all the so-called exceptions to the perfect tender rule, the good faith requirement is the most significant.[84] The recognition and application of the pervasive duty of good faith has been one of the most important doctrinal development in American contract law over the last 70 years.[85] Certainly the important impetus to the development of the good

[80] US Restatement (Second) of the Law of Contracts, section 241.

[81] (1990) Court of Appeals of North Carolina, 398 S.E.2d 64.

[82] See *JRM Hauling & Recycling Services Inc v Newark Group Inc* (2017) Superior Court of Massachusetts, WL 7663034.

[83] Another significant limitation on the perfect tender rule is that the seller must normally be given an opportunity to cure a nonconforming tender or delivery, which was discussed in ch 5.

[84] WH Lawrence, 'The Prematurely Reported Demise of the Perfect Tender Rule' (1987) 35 *University of Kansas Law Review* 557, 558 and 571.

[85] See sections 1-203 and 2-103(l) (b).

faith doctrine was its powerful codification in UCC Section 1-203, providing that 'every contract or duty within this Act imposes an obligation of good faith in its performance or enforcement'. The Code further contextualises good faith in the case of business transactions by setting out that this doctrine means 'honesty in fact and the observance of reasonable commercial standards of fair dealing in the trade'.[86]

The academic commentary on the doctrine of good faith has been both voluminous and impressively enlightening, however, this book does not intend to engage in those discussions.[87] Rather, this doctrine will be analysed in the narrow context of a buyer's right to reject and cancel a contract. This doctrine can impose some degree of equitable restraint on exercising the seemingly unwavering right to reject.[88] A buyer's insistence on rejection for a minor contract deviation to end an unfavourable bargain is an unfair use of buyer's rejection rights that can be effectively restricted through employment of the good faith obligation of the buyer. Professor Lawrence believes that a buyer whose true subjective reason for rejection is to escape a bad bargain is acting in bad faith, because their conduct fails the honesty requirement of good faith.[89] It is an inherently difficult task to determine the true subjective intention of a buyer. The modern contextualist approach, which to some extent helps adjudicators understand the true intention of the parties and thus determining the requirement of good faith, takes account of the circumstantial evidence and in particular reasonable business norms in a given context. As established in *Hubbard v UTZ Quality Foods*, the court held that a commercial buyer of potatoes, which the contract required to be within a certain colour range, did not reject in bad faith when they failed to detect the potatoes' colour with a machine before rejecting based on poor colour.[90] Even though the machine would have been much more accurate, it was reasonable within the potato industry to use visual inspections.[91] Similarly, in *Austrian Airlines Oesterre AG v UT Finance Corp*, the seller unsuccessfully argued that, notwithstanding the view that the aircraft failed to conform strictly to the agreement, the buyer

[86] UCC section 2-103(1)(b); see also *Neumiller Farms, Inc. v Cornett*, (1979) Supreme Court of Alabama, 368 So.2d 272.

[87] Two major contributors to the general discussion concerning good faith in general contract law and the law of sales have been conducted by Professors Robert Summers and Steven Burton. Summers undertook his seminal work immediately after the UCC was promulgated. See R Summers, '"Good Faith" in general contract law and the sales provisions of the Uniform Commercial Code' (1968) 54 *Virginia Law Review* 195. Burton wrote two important pieces in the early 1980s and one in 1994: SJ Burton, 'Breach of contract and the common law duty of perform in good faith' (1980) 94 *Harvard Law Review* 369; SJ Burton, 'Good faith performance of a contract within Article 2 of the Uniform Commercial Code' (1981) 67 *Iowa Law Review* 1; SJ Burton, 'Good faith in articles 1 and 2 of the UCC: the practice view' (1994) *William & Mary Law Review* 1533.

[88] JM Dressler, 'Good faith rejection of goods in a falling market' (2009) 42 *Connecticut Law Review* 611, 612.

[89] Lawrence (n 84) 557, 558; see also MA Schmitt and D Frisch, 'The perfect tender rule – an acceptable interpretation' (1981–1982) 13 *University of Toledo Law Review* 1375, 1378; CP Gillette, 'Limitations on the obligation of goods faith' (1981) *Duke Law Review* 619, 652.

[90] (1995) United States District Court, New York, 904 F.Supp.444.

[91] ibid, 448.

acted in bad faith when they disregarded industry custom and rejected Austrian's delivery of the aircraft.[92] The seller contended that one of the reasonable commercial standards of fair dealing in the air craft trade is adherence to a custom and practice of accepting aircrafts with minor nonconformities along with financial compensation for those shortcomings.[93] The defects to the plane included the lack of a required FAA Certificate of Airworthiness, without which the plane was useless. The buyer rightfully counterclaimed that the aircraft did not comply with the delivery conditions in many material respects and the law of New York, as the applicable law, recognises the perfect tender rule.

Several courts have contended that failing market conditions prior to the buyer's rejection may be used as a powerful circumstantial evidence that the buyer rejected in bad faith. A remarkable case is *Oil Country Specialists v Philipp Bros*, where a buyer rejected pipe that was required to comply with American Petroleum Institute specifications.[94] The court found that the seller's failure to perform its obligations substantially impaired the value of the exclusive sales contract to the buyer as there was sufficient evidence showing that substantial portion of oil well pipe inventory failed to meet industry specifications.[95] Such a breach did not only substantially impair the value of the contract itself, but also impaired the buyer's future as a distributor in the oil countries' tubular goods marketplace. However, there was clear evidence indicating that the declining prices in the oil market turned the prices agreed in the contract highly unfavourable to the buyer, who did not foresee such a result and as such the sale prices created unfavourable competition for the buyer. The jury and the court argued while there was material breach of contract, the buyer was entitled to reject the entire inventory and cancel the entire contract if they did so in good faith. Referring to *Printing Center of Texas Inc v Supermind Publishing Co*,[96] the Court of Appeal contended that a finding of bad faith rejection can be supported by circumstances showing that buyer's motivation and subjective intention were to escape the bargain, rather than to avoid acceptance of a delivery which in some respect impaired the value of the bargain to them. Therefore, 'rightful rejection' refers to rejection, which satisfies both the perfect tender requirement and the buyer's duty to act in good faith.

However, a more balanced approach was adopted in *Austrian Airlines v UT Finance*, where the seller failed to deliver a plane in perfect condition on time and the buyer rejected delivery and claimed that time was of the essence.[97] In fact, the plane failed to meet the delivery condition in a myriad of respects, even though the seller's attempts in enhancing the quality of plane had caused delay in delivery. The buyer's rejection denied the seller any chance to cure. However,

[92] (2008) United States District Court, 567 F.Supp.2d 579.
[93] ibid, 598.
[94] (1988) Court of Appeals of Texas, Houston, 762 S.W.2d 170.
[95] ibid, 173.
[96] (1984) Court of Appeals of Texas, Houston, 669 S.W.2d 779.
[97] (2008) United States District Court, New York, 567 F.Supp.2d 579.

the seller argued that the buyer's rejection was motivated by the turmoil on the airline industry and decreased value of the plane to the buyer, following the terrorist attacks of September 11. In other words, the buyer attempted to escape a bad bargain and hence their rejection was in bad faith. The court, unaffected by the seller's evidence, stated that while the buyer, quite understandably, was influenced by the decline in market value, the decision to reject the plan was not made in bad faith. They argued that the buyer's conduct was entirely reasonable since the presence of defects was now even more important to the buyer than in a normal market. The court upheld that in light of the sophistication of the parties, there was no reason not to give the buyer the benefit of its bargain. To a similar extent, a Californian court prohibited a seller from furnishing proof of an ulterior motive by the buyer when rejecting the goods. In *KCA Electronics Inc v Legacy Electronics Inc*, the court focussed strictly on the non-conformities, namely that 6 per cent of the small computer components lacked the necessary uniformity.[98] This was sufficient for the court to grant judgment in favour of the buyer. The divergence judicial approach in using the good faith doctrine can endanger the certainty interest of the parties and the courts may strive to produce rational and well-reasoned decision similar to *KCA Electronics Inc*, where the court did not allow extraneous discussions on why the seller thought the buyer had decided subjectively to reject the goods.

C. CISG and UPICC

Since these two regimes have laid down the principles concerning termination of contract in a very similar fashion and to avoid repetitions, the grounds for termination of contract under these regimes will be analysed together. There are three grounds for termination of contract under these two legal regimes: fundamental breach of contract, non-performance by the seller within the additional period of time fixed by the buyer and when there is anticipatory breach of contract.[99] The focus will be on the first two doctrines and the last one has already been analysed in chapter two.

i. Fundamental Breach of Contract

Fundamental breach is considered as 'the central requirement for avoidance of contract'.[100] Neither the UPICC articles, nor its Official Commentary provides any

[98] (2007) Court of Appeal, California, WL 2137959.

[99] CISG Article 49 and UPICC Article 7.3.1.

[100] U Magnus, 'The Remedy of Avoidance of Contract under CISG – General Remarks and Special Cases' (2005–2006) 25 *Journal of Law and Commerce* 423, 424; see also Bridge, *The International Sale of Goods* (n 2) 669; M Torsello, 'Substantive and jurisdictional aspects of international contract remedies: a comment on Avery Katz's "remedies for breach of contract under the CISG"' (2005) 25 *International Review of Law and Economics* 397, 403.

exhaustive definition of fundamental non-performance. The Official Commentary has only stated that a fundamental non-performance is 'material and not merely of minor importance'.[101] Instead, CISG Article 25 has described this breach and there is abundance literature clarifying this challenging doctrine. This article does not offer any remedy to the parties, but the legal definition of 'fundamental breach of contract' given in the article functions as a pre-requisite for several disruptive and dramatic remedies recognised elsewhere in CISG. This article is concerned with one of the most challenging issues in the law of sales, which is under what conditions a breach by one party can entitle the other party to unwind the contract and be free from their obligations to perform. This article is constituted of two tests, which should be satisfied to show that fundamental breach has occurred. The first test deals with whether the fundamental breach substantially deprives the aggrieved party of what they are entitled to expect under the contract. This test thus deals with the gravity of the consequences of the breach of contract and the emphasis is on the expectations of the injured party.[102]

The CISG Advisory Council has attempted to provide a clearer test ascertaining substantial detriment: regard should be first had to 'the terms of the contract'.[103] The contractual terms refer to what the parties consider to be of the essence of the contract. For instance, in the *Roll Aluminium Case*, the tribunal ruled that the breach was fundamental, as the parties had agreed about the central feature of the goods being the thickness of a roll of aluminium.[104] The buyer had informed the seller about the great significance of the quality of the roll aluminium and its thickness: if the roll aluminium did not meet the specification, the buyer's end user was unable to use it in its factory.[105] Second, consideration should be given to 'the purpose for which the goods are bought'.[106] This element comes into effect when there is no stipulation in the contract about what amounts to a fundamental breach. The decisive factor satisfying this test is whether the goods are improper for the use intended by the buyer.[107] For instance, in *Delchi Carrier SpA v Rotorex Corp*,

[101] UPICC Official Comments, Article 7.3.1, n 2.

[102] AH Kritzer, *Guide to Practical Applications of the United Nations Convention on Contracts for the International Sale of Goods* (Kluwer Law and Taxation Publishers, 1989) 206; see also Kroll, Mistelis and Viscasillas (n 4) 337; F Ferrari, 'Fundamental breach of contract under the UN Sales Convention – 25 Years of Article 25 CISG' (2006) 25 *Journal of Law and Commerce* 489, 496.

[103] CISG Advisory Council, 'The buyer's right to avoid the contract in case of non-conforming goods or documents' (2005) Opinion n 5, para 4.1; see also R Koch, 'The Concept of Fundamental Breach of Contract under the United Nations Convention on Contracts for the International Sale of Goods (CISG)' *Review of the Convention on Contracts for the International Sale of Goods (CISG)* (Kluwer Law International, 1999) 214–15; P Huber and A Mullis, *The CISG, A New Textbook for Students and Practitioners* (Sellier, European Law Publishers, 2007).

[104] (1991) China International Economic & Trade Arbitration Commission (CIETAC), CISG-online 842.

[105] ibid, 285; see also *Palletizing Robots case* (2017) Lyon Court of Appeal, CISG-online 2823; *Etablissements JR Maruani SAS v Inmed* (2017) Court of Appeal Versailles, France, CISG-online 4604.

[106] CISG Advisory Council (n 103).

[107] ibid, para 4.3.

the court held that the breach was fundamental; because the compressors, which were meant to be used in summer and spring, had low cooling capacity and as such they were not suitable for the buyer's specific intention.[108] Third, a fundamental breach is determined by 'the question of whether it is possible to remedy the defect'.[109] If the seller can repair the goods to deliver substitute or missing goods, without of course causing unreasonable delay or inconvenience to the buyer, fundamental breach cannot be invoked.[110] In the *Inflatable Triumphal Arch case*, the court held that non-conformity of the arches with the agreed purpose was not considered a fundamental breach, as it would have been possible to repair the defect.[111] It may be argued that 'here, due regard is to be given to the purposes for which the buyer needs the goods'.[112] This test does not really provide something substantially different, as there can be an overlap between this test and the second one concerning the buyer's purpose for which the goods are bought. Thus, to realise whether the substantial detriment has occurred due to the fundamental breach, one has to look at the contract terms, the purpose for which the goods are bought and whether the goods can be repaired.

The second test deals with the foreseeability of loss. The foreseeability requirement in CISG Article 25 is similar to the foreseeability requirement with respect to damages in CISG Article 74, which has been discussed in chapter four.[113] Lack of foreseeability and knowledge, which may preclude the buyer from invoking the doctrine of fundamental breach of contract, relates 'to the detriment caused by the breach of contract, and not the breach itself or its reasons'.[114] It appears from the respective wording of Article 25 that foreseeability is a cumulative question: the seller must both subjectively and objectively have predicted the result of the breach. To address the foreseeability requirement, the party in breach should both show that neither they themselves in no way anticipated the substantial detriment caused; nor a reasonable person in their place would have done so.[115] The burden of proof is thus on the seller. It has been claimed that 'the objective test cannot replace the subjective test, but complements it'.[116] However, it has been counter argued that the focus should be on the 'objective component', as it can be used as a safeguard against

[108] (1995) United States Court of Appeals, 2nd Circuit, CISG-online 140; see also *Globes case*, (2002) District Court München, Germany, CISG-online 654; *Brown & Root Services Corp. v Aerotech Herman Nelson Inc. et al* (2004) Court of Appeal of Manitoba, CISG-online 1000; *KVM Industrial Machinery A/S v Construction Acton Vale Lt* (2006) Danish Supreme Court, CISG-online 2630.

[109] CISG Advisory Council (n 103); see also Huber and Mullis (n 103) 180.

[110] CISG Advisory Council (n 103) para 4.4; see also Bridge (n 4) 911, 922.

[111] (2002) Commercial Court of the Canton of Aargau, Switzerland, CISG-online 715.

[112] CISG Advisory Council (n 103) para 4.4.

[113] See ch 4 section 4(C).

[114] Schlechtriem and Schwenzer (n 4) 561.

[115] CM Bianca and MJ Bonell, *Commentary on the International Sales Law, The 1980 Vienna Sales Convention* (Giuffre, 1987) 216–17; see also Huber and Mullis (n 103) 215; Ferrari (n 102) 489, 498; A Babiak, 'Defining " Fundamental Breach" under the United Nations Convention on Contracts for the International Sale of Goods' (1992) 6 *Temple International and Comparative Law Journal* 113, 120.

[116] Bianca and Bonell (n 115) 220.

the defence that the seller did not actually foresee the damage.[117] This signifies that the defence of lack of foreseeability is only valid when 'a reasonable merchant in the same circumstances of the seller' would not have foreseen the results of his breach.[118] Also, the foreseeability of loss should be 'assessed as of the date of the conclusion of the contract'.[119]

UPICC Article 7.3.1 has formulated fundamental breach quite similar to CISG Article 25. It has been argued that the substantial deprivation factor used in this article is 'a slightly abridged (and improved) version of the definition of fundamental breach under CISG Art 25'.[120] However, this claim regarding an improved version of fundamental breach under the UPICC is not accurate.[121] The only difference regarding definition of fundamental breach is that under the CISG, the breach must have resulted in a detriment to the buyer. This difference does not lead to an improved version and does not seem to have any practical significance. Should the aggrieved party be substantially deprived of what it was entitled to expect under the contract, this alone constitutes a detriment. This similarity suggests that when interpreting the fundamental non-performance under the UPICC, reference can be made to the rich experience regarding CISG Article 25 in case-law and scholarly materials. Also, the foreseeability requirement in this article is almost similar to its counter-part under CISG Article 25.

ii. Nachfrist: Fixing Additional Period of Time for Performance

Another ground for avoiding the contract is when the buyer gives a notice fixing an additional period of time. In reference to corresponding doctrine in German law, this mechanism is often called *Nachfrist*.[122] The fixing of an additional period of time paves the way for the avoidance of the contract.[123] However, this mechanism for avoiding the contract can only be employed in cases of non-delivery in its strict sense.[124] If the seller has either failed to perform within the additional time or declared within that time that they will not perform, the buyer is entitled to avoid the contract. CISG Article 47 and UPICC Article 7.1.5 have set out the buyer's right to fix additional period of time for performance. The buyer can actually benefit from fixing an additional curative

[117] Kroll, Mistelis and Viscasillas (n 4) 340–41.

[118] ibid, 341.

[119] Huber and Mullis (n 103) 216.

[120] Vogenauer (n 4) 923.

[121] See C Pauly, 'The concept of fundamental breach as an international principle to create uniformity of commercial law' (1999–2000) 19 *Journal of Law and Commerce* 221, 227; AM Garro, 'The gap-filling role of the UNIDROIT Principles in international sales law: some comments on the interplay between the principles and the CISG' (1994–1995) 69 *Tulane Law Review* 1149, 1185.

[122] Kroll, Mistelis and Viscasillas (n 4) 702.

[123] UNCITRAL Digest of Case Law on the United Nations Convention on Contracts for the International Sale of Goods (2016) Article 47, para 1; Bianca and Bonell (n 115) 343.

[124] UNCITRAL Digest of Case Law on the United Nations Convention on Contracts for the International Sale of Goods (2016) Article 47, para 1.

period for the seller's performance under this article.[125] This is so because the seller's failure to perform their obligation within the additional fixed period allows the buyer to avoid the contract with no need to demonstrate the fundamental breach of contract.[126] The *Nachfrist* can be set by the buyer's declaration. This declaration must clearly fix a reasonable time and demand performance of the seller's obligations.[127] The additional period of time fixed by the buyer must be of reasonable length, which is vague. In a case, governed by CISG, a period of two weeks for delivering printing machines was considered too short and that the buyer was not entitled to avoid the contract after that period.[128] However, in another case dealing with car, an additional period of one week for delivery was found to be reasonable.[129] Also, the buyer's declaration must clearly demand performance of the obligations by the seller. In the remarkable case of *Calzaturificio Piceno di Roberto Catinari & Uvaldo Raccosta v Vivace Mode GmbH*, the court did not recognise that the buyer had fulfilled the requirements of the *Nachfrist*.[130] This was because the buyer's telephone call was merely a reminder demanding prompt delivery and they did not fix a specific time for performance. The idea behind fixing an additional period of time is to keep the contract alive to the stage that there is a possibility to perform contractual obligations. This might overcome some of the problems of distance and expense being possibly exacerbated by further complications such as language, currency and law, which are particularly prevalent in international sales transactions.

3. Effects of Termination of the Contract

A. SGA and UCC

Under the common law systems of England and the United Sates, when an injured buyer is faced with the seller's material breach of contract, they have a choice of inconsistent remedial paths: (i) terminate the contract and obtain restitution of the benefits it has conferred, or (ii) affirm the contract and sue for damages for breach of contract, which was discussed in chapter four.[131] The existence of such choice

[125] ibid, para 4; HM Flechtner, 'Remedies under the new International Sales Convention: the perspective from article 2 of the UCC' (1988) 8 *Journal of Law and Commerce* 53, 71.

[126] Kroll, Mistelis and Viscasillas (n 4) 705; UNCITRAL Digest of Case Law on the United Nations Convention on Contracts for the International Sale of Goods (2016) Article 47, para 4.

[127] JO Honnold and HM Flechtner, *Honnold's Uniform Law for International Sales under the 1980 United Nations Convention*, 5th edn (Wolters Kluwer Law and Business, 2021) 552; Kroll, Mistelis and Viscasillas (n 4) 703.

[128] *Rotary offset printing press case* (1993) Court of Appeal Hamm, Germany, CISG-online 239.

[129] *Ford Escort Cabrio case* (1999) Appellate Court Naumburg, Germany, CISG-online 512.

[130] (1997) Appellate Court Düsseldorf, Germany, CISG-online 385; see also *Iron Molybdenum case* (1997) Appellate Court Hamburg, Germany, CISG-online 395; *Metal Springs case* (1997) Appellate Court Barcelona, Spain, CISG-online 442.

[131] See UCC section 2-270; Hawkland, Bjerre, Rusch and Garry (n 4) section 2-720, para 1; Bridge (n 42) 867, 885–906; Peel (n 43) 519, 525; Bridge (n 30) para 12-017; *Photo Production Ltd v Securicor*

indicates that a fundamental breach does not automatically terminate the contract and it only gives the injured buyer the option either to terminate the contract or to affirm it and to claim for damages or sue for performance. As explained in the introduction, there seems to be no distinction between these legal regimes in relation to prospective operation of termination, which essentially relieves both parties of their remaining primary rights and obligations. There is also a consensus that upon termination of contract, primary obligations to fulfil the contractual duties are converted into an obligation on the party in breach to pay damages for their breach. What is not adequately investigated in a comparative context is the retrospective operation of termination under these regimes, which will be examined in light of the normative relational framework.

There is an argument that termination of contract might also operate retrospectively. Treitel has stated that there are some common law discussions supporting the view that termination may have certain retrospective effects, particularly when it is said that the purpose of termination is to place each party in the position in which they would have been if the contract had never been made.[132] In support of this view, it can be argued that termination of a contract of sale necessarily entitles the seller to recover possession of the goods and the buyer to repayment of the price, which produces effects closely resembling those of rescission in the strict sense. Rescission leads to restitution: the surrender by each party of benefits received from the other.[133] It can thus be argued that termination and rescission *ab initio* by the buyer in a simple sale of goods transaction both have the factual outcome of returning the goods to the seller. This means that 'the effect of termination of the contract will be automatically to revest the property in the goods in the seller'.[134] For instance, in the English case of *Barber v NWS Bank Plc*, the buyer was entitled to terminate the contract and claim repayment of the deposits and the instalments paid, as the seller was not the actual owner of the car at the time of conclusion of the contract.[135] The term broken was a condition, which allowed the buyer to terminate the contract and claim for restitution of the money paid.[136] This indicates that restitution 'compels [the seller] to make a payment to divest him of the valuable benefit he has received in order to prevent his unjust enrichment'.[137] By pursuing restitution, the buyer 'avoids all the rules on contractual damages'.[138] This means that the buyer does not need

Transport Ltd [1980] AC 827(HL) 832; SGA s 11 (2); *Glencore Energy UK Ltd v Transworld Oil Ltd* [2010] EWHC 141 (Comm), [2010] 1 CLC 284, 285.

[132] Treitel (n 1) 383.

[133] Bradgate (n 4) 17; B Dickson, 'The law of restitution in the Federal Republic of Germany: a comparison with English law' (1987) 36 *International & Comparative Law Quarterly* 751, 754–58.

[134] Bridge, *The International Sale of Goods* (n 2) 668; *Tradax Export SA v European Grain & Shipping Ltd* [1983] 2 Lloyd's Rep 100 (QB) 107.

[135] [1996] 1 All ER 906 (CA).

[136] ibid.

[137] D Harris, D Campbell and R Halson, *Remedies in Contract and Tort*, 2nd edn (Butterworths LexisNexis, 2002) 231.

[138] ibid, 232.

to satisfy the rules on remoteness and mitigation. The buyer's right to restitution has been recognised by SGA section 54, which states: 'Nothing in this Act affects the right of the buyer or the seller ... to recover money paid where the consideration for the payment of it has failed'. This particular buyer's right is described as follows: '[the buyer] sues to recover money paid to [the seller] under a contract if [the buyer] has not obtained the benefit of the performance promised by [the seller] in return'.[139] When the buyer does not receive the performance from the seller stipulated by a transaction, 'there has been a failure of consideration and this may enable the claimant to bring a restitutionary claim'.[140] The relevance of failure of consideration to restitution has been explained 'as a general principle which underlies the existence of a number of particular grounds of restitution'.[141] Failure of consideration occurs when 'the contract may no longer be operative for a number of reasons, the most important being that it was discharged for breach'.[142]

Similar to English law, under UCC, a buyer in possession of delivered goods, who rightfully rejects or revokes acceptance, is under a duty 'to hold them with reasonable care at the seller's disposition for a time sufficient to permit the seller to remove them; but the buyer has no further obligations with regard to goods rightfully rejected' or revoked.[143] In other words, notwithstanding whether a buyer is a merchant or not, they have the obligation to take reasonable care of goods in their physical possession or control for the time necessary for the seller to return the good. Section 2-604 also states that the buyer should restore or ship the goods to the seller or resell the goods for the seller's account. However, UCC section 2-603 goes further and prescribes additional obligations for a commercial buyer in relation to rejected goods in certain circumstances. This section exclusively applies to a commercial buyer, who has possession or control of goods which the buyer rightfully and effectively rejected. The buyer's duty to resell under this section originates from commercial necessity and that it only applies if the seller has no agent or place of business at the market for rejection. If the requirements of this section are satisfied, the commercial buyer is mandated to follow reasonable instructions from the seller as to how to deal with the goods.[144] When the seller fails to give reasonable instructions, the commercial buyer is under a duty to engage in reasonable efforts to sell the goods only if the goods are perishable or threaten to decline

[139] Harris, Campbell and Halson (n 137) 233; BS Markesinis, H Unberath and A Johnston, *The German Law of Contract, A Comparative Treatise*, 2nd edn (Hart Publishing, 2006) 432.

[140] G Virgo, *The Principles of the Law of Restitution*, 2nd edn (Oxford University Press, 2006) 304; Bradgate (n 4) 29.

[141] Virgo (n 140) 304.

[142] ibid, 310.

[143] UCC section 2-602 2(b)(c); see also UCC section 2-608, concerning the effect of rightful revocation of acceptance; *Mextel Inc v Air-Sheilds Inc* (2005) United States District Court, E.D. Pennsylvania, 2005 WL 975291.

[144] See eg *J.F. Daley Intern., Ltd. v Midwest Container and Indus. Supply Co.*, (1993) Missouri Court of Appeals, Eastern District, 849 S.W.2d 260 (In this case, the instructions were considered unreasonable, when seller refused to pay for return shipping costs).

in value. The buyer is explicitly mandated to perform these duties in good faith in a sense that if they fail to make a salvage sale when their duty to do so has arisen are subject to damages.[145] If a buyer successfully sells the goods, they actually sell them for the seller's account and thus owe the proceeds to the seller.[146] If the buyer revokes acceptance of the goods or reject them, and there is a fundamental change in the condition of the condition of the goods, which is not a result of defects in the goods prior to revocation of acceptance or rejection, the right to revoke or reject is lost.[147]

B. CISG and UPICC

The effects of avoidance are comprehensively regulated in CISG Articles 81–84 as well as UPICC Articles 7.3.4 and 7.3.5. The primary consequence of avoidance is that both parties are discharged from their contractual obligations.[148] This means that avoidance operates prospectively. The seller's primary obligations include the obligations to make delivery and transfer ownership and the buyer's obligations are to pay the price and take delivery.[149] The second part of CISG Article 81 as well as UPICC Article 7.3.5(3) provide an exception to the general rule governing the prospective effect of avoidance. Such exception involves some clauses of contract for example those dealing with the settlement of disputes such as jurisdiction clauses and arbitration clauses which survive after the avoidance of contract.[150] Also, a penalty clause requiring payments from a seller who failed to delivery or a clause requiring the return of delivered goods still remains effective.[151]

Avoidance also has restitutionary consequences, which implies that avoidance has retrospective effect as well.[152] This effect has been described in CISG Article 81(2),

[145] UCC Official Comments, section 2-603, para 5.

[146] *Kysar v Lambert* (1995) United States Court of Appeals of Washington 887 P.2d 431.

[147] UCC sections 2-603 and 2-608.

[148] CISG Advisory Council, 'Consequences of Avoidance of the Contract' (2008) Opinion n 9, para 3.2; Bridge, *The International Sales of Goods* (n 2) 668; Schlechtriem and Schwenzer (n 4) 1102; Kroll, Mistelis and Viscasillas (n 4) 1110; L DiMatteo, A Janssen, U Magnus and R Schulze, *International Sales Law: A Handbook*, 2nd edn (Bloomsbury Publishing, 2021) 623; Bridge (n 4) 911, 912; see also *Marlboro Shoes case* (1991) Court of Appeal Frankfurt am Main, Germany, CISG-online 28; *South Korean Stainless Steel Wire case* (1997) German Supreme Court, CISG-online 277.

[149] CISG Articles 30 and 53; *Crude Metal case*, (1995) ICC International Court of Arbitration, Paris, France, CISG-online 844.

[150] CISG Advisory Council, 'Consequences of Avoidance of the Contract' (2008) Opinion n 9, paras 3.3 and 3.4; UNCITRAL Digest of Case Law on the United Nations Convention on Contracts for the International Sale of Goods (2016) Article 81, para 4; Kroll, Mistelis and Viscasillas (n 4) 1110–11.

[151] UNCITRAL Digest of Case Law on the United Nations Convention on Contracts for the International Sale of Goods (2016) Article 81, para 4; *Partition Panels case* (1999) Austrian Supreme Court, CISG-online 483.

[152] MG Bridge, 'The nature and consequences of avoidance of the contract under the United Nations Convention on the International Sale of Goods' (2008–2009) 10 *International Law Review of Wuhan University* 118, 118.

stating that 'a party who has performed the contract either wholly or in part may claim restitution from the other party of whatever the first party has supplied or paid under the contract. If both parties are bound to make restitution, they must do so concurrently'. With a similar tone, restitutionary effect of avoidance can also be found in UPICC Article 7.3.6. CISG Article 81(2) entitles each party to 'claim restitution of whatever it has supplied or paid under the contract'.[153] The restitution process seeks to reverse the other party's gain and not to compensate for the claimant's loss.[154] Avoidance transforms 'the original contractual relationship into a winding-up or restitutionary relationship' which brings new rights and duties.[155] These new rights and duties entail returning the price by the seller and the goods by the buyer. When the contract has been executed, restitution authorises 'either party to the contract who has performed in whole or in part to claim the return of whatever he has supplied or paid under the contract'.[156] In addition, the parties have to make mutual restitution of the fruits of performance, so the seller must repay the price with interest and the buyer must return the goods and also account for any benefits received from the goods in the buyer's hands.[157] UPICC does not contain any rule governing the benefits derived from the performance or interest that has been earned. The reason is said to be that 'in commercial practice it will often be difficult to establish the value of the benefits received by the parties as a result of the performance. Furthermore, often both parties will have received such benefits'.[158] However, if this reason was really persuasive and justifiable, CISG would have also avoided from setting out the rules governing benefits derived from the performance by the other party.

CISG Article 81(2) and UPICC Article 7.3.6 require the parties to make concurrent restitution of whatever they have received. The principle of concurrency means that 'each party has a type of security in not having to give credit to the other'.[159] This may signify that the concept of concurrent restitution leads to a right of suspension for both parties until the other party has agreed to make restitution. This means that 'the rules governing the suspension of the performance are applicable by analogy'.[160] The buyer can therefore refuse to return the goods if the seller does not offer to restitute the price by virtue of the principle that 'a party may suspend the performance of his obligations if … it becomes apparent that the other party will not perform a substantial part of his obligations'.[161] However, in cases

[153] Schlechtriem and Schwenzer (n 4) 1106.

[154] Kroll, Mistelis and Viscasillas (n 4) 1116.

[155] CISG Advisory Council, 'Consequences of Avoidance of the Contract' (2008) Opinion n 9, para 3.7; Official Comments on UPICC, Article 7.3.6, para 3; see also Bianca and Bonell (n 115) 605.

[156] UNCITRAL Digest of Case Law on the United Nations Convention on Contracts for the International Sale of Goods (2016) Article 81, para 8.

[157] CISG Article 84.

[158] Official Comments on UPICC, Article 7.3.6, para 6; see also Vogenauer (n 4) 946.

[159] CISG Advisory Council, 'Consequences of Avoidance of the Contract' (2008) Opinion n 9, para 1.3; see also Bridge, *The International Sale of* Goods (n 2) 698.

[160] Bianca and Bonell (n 115) 605.

[161] CISG Article 71.

where only one party has performed their duties, this principle is of 'no help to the party who is claiming its performance'.[162] It has been suggested that in such cases, 'the party entitled to claim restitution holds a claim for damages if restitution is unduly delayed and causes any loss to the innocent party'.[163]

Under CISG, restitution is possible only if the delivered goods still exists and that the return of substitute goods or similar goods does not constitute restitution.[164] This means that if full restitution of the goods is impossible, termination is generally excluded.[165] The injured buyer must, however, be capable of making restitution of goods *substantially* in the same condition as they received them in order to exercise their right to terminate the contract. Impossibility of making restitution refers to actual and objective impediment to restitution. The examples of impossibility are when the goods have been damaged, lost, destroyed or stolen.[166] The requirement of returning the goods substantially in the same condition in which the buyer received indicates that the goods do no need to be in the identical condition. CISG Article 82(1) fails to clarify when goods are in substantially the same condition as when the buyer received them. It has been suggested that substantiality can be determined 'according to the type of goods that are the subject of the contract and the type of trade or market in which they bought and sold'.[167] However, it has more accurately been stated that the term 'substantially' shows that the change in the goods 'must be of sufficient importance that it would no longer be proper to require the seller to retake the goods as the equivalent of that which he had delivered to the buyer'.[168] This means that the decisive factor is whether the seller can reasonably be expected to accept the returned goods. For instance, the absence of replaceable screws or hinges from the furniture is considered insubstantial changes which allow restitution of the goods.[169] If the goods have been changed substantially, the buyer loses their right of avoidance even though the seller had been in fundamental breach of the contract and that the goods should be retained by the buyer.[170] However, it should be noted that CISG Article 82(2) provides three exceptions to the general rule requiring the return of the goods to the seller. This article is 'designed to preserve, in some circumstances, the avoidance and substitute goods remedies of buyers even when they cannot return the goods in substantially the same condition in which the goods were received'.[171]

[162] Schlechtriem and Schwenzer (n 4) 1108.

[163] Schlechtriem and Schwenzer (n 4) 1108; see also Kroll, Mistelis and Viscasillas (n 4) 1118.

[164] UNCITRAL Digest of Case Law on the United Nations Convention on Contracts for the International Sale of Goods (2016) Article 81, para 5; CISG Advisory Council, 'Consequences of Avoidance of the Contract' (2008) Opinion n 9, para 3.8; Schlechtriem and Schwenzer (n 4) 1106; Kroll, Mistelis and Viscasillas (n 4) 1116; *Partition Panels case* (1999) Austrian Supreme Court, CISG-online 483.

[165] Magnus (n 100) 423, 429.

[166] Vogenauer (n 4) 961; Bridge, *The International Sale of Goods* (n 2) 697.

[167] Kroll, Mistelis and Viscasillas (n 4) 1134.

[168] UNCITRAL Digest of Case Law on the United Nations Convention on Contracts for the International Sale of Goods (2016) Article 81, para 3.

[169] *Danish Furniture case II* (1999) District Court Oldenburg, Germany CISG-online 3609.

[170] Kroll, Mistelis and Viscasillas (n 4) 1134.

[171] Honnold and Flechtner (n 127) 870; see also DiMatteo, Janssen, Magnus and Schulze (n 148) 643.

UPICC has adopted a different approach. While it is accepted that restitution may be expensive and inappropriate where the goods received have been sold and 'passed on to a third party [who] is only prepared to return it for an unreasonably high sum of money', it is not considered impossible.[172] In such instances, an allowance in money has to be made.[173] It has been suggested that the term 'if' used in UPICC Article 7.3.6(2) should be read as meaning 'insofar as'.[174] Therefore, when part of the performance received cannot be returned, the allowance should be calculated for that part only, while the remainder of the performance should be restored in kind. An allowance can be measured in principle by considering the market and determining objective value of the performance received. The relevant date for such measurement should thus be the time 'when restitution would have been due because this is the value which the other party would have received if restitution in kind had been made'.[175]

4. Evaluation

The grounds for termination of contract under these legal regimes are almost the same. CISG and UPICC have given a central role to fundamental breach or non-performance as the main factor triggering the right to terminate the contract. While the perfect tender rule enshrined in UCC section 2-601 appears to provide an unfettered right to terminate to the buyer for trivial breaches, it is now subject to various exceptions and limitations. The result is that there is little left of the rule in practical sense and in majority of commercial sale of goods cases a substantial or material impairment is required for termination of contract.[176] This requirement is similar to the notion of fundamental non-performance under SGA.[177] Substantial non-performance or breach, as the main requirement for termination of contract, is thus adopted in all these regimes with slight variations in its formulation. This requirement focuses on whether there has been a substantial deprivation of what the buyer was entitled to acquire from a contract.

As explained previously, one exception to the buyer's right to terminate under UCC is the good faith doctrine. Such doctrine is obviously absent in SGA, when terminating a contract. It is doubtful whether it is present and operates under CISG and UPICC in a similar fashion as UCC. Under the former international legal regimes, the good faith doctrine has mainly remained as a guiding, general principle. The good faith doctrine is mainly employed, when interpreting these international regimes.[178] It is thus doubtful whether the 'good faith requirement'

[172] Vogenauer (n 4) 958; UPICC Official Comments, Article 7.3.6, n 3.
[173] UPICC Article 7.3.6 (2); see also Zimmermann (n 4) 563, 571.
[174] Vogenauer (n 4) 960.
[175] ibid, 962; UPICC Official Comments, Article 7.3.6, para 3.
[176] See sections 6-3(i) and 6-3(ii).
[177] Bianca and Bonell (n 115) 212.
[178] CISG Article 7.

is directly applicable to the contractual relationship between the parties.[179] While UPICC has employed a stronger tone by stating that 'each party must act in accordance with good faith and fair dealing in international trade',[180] lack of guideline and scant case law and practice would suggest that the good faith doctrine has remained a general, prevailing rule, with no clear consequences when it is not complied with. In contrast, under UCC, the duty of good faith and fair dealing elucidates parties' contractual bargains by preventing one party from engaging in a conduct that frustrates the other party's rights to the benefits of the contract. As shown in the cases of *Oil Country Specialists v Philipp Bros*[181] and *KCA Electronics Inc v Legacy Electronics Inc*,[182] a key component of 'rightful rejection' is good faith, in the sense that not only a substantial breach should be proven by the buyer, but also, they are entitled to reject and cancel a contract if they do so in good faith. This indicates that the good faith doctrine is a functioning principle, which is employed to establish rights and 'additional' obligations outside the scope of contractual framework. The case law and commentaries of UCC provide good example in concretising the obligation to conduct in good faith and fair dealing. Such a difference between these regimes may make a distinction in how grounds for termination of contract can be invoked in ending contractual relationship.

In addition, as explained previously, under SGA and UCC, there is no requirement of foreseeability of the consequences of the fundamental breach, while under CISG and UPICC, it is required that the seller subjectively and objectively anticipate those consequences.[183] It has been indicated that the foreseeability requirement 'constitutes a further innovation of the [CISG]', which has been used in UPICC as well.[184] This requirement arguably has a clear effect on the availability of the buyer's right to terminate the contract. However, it is not a requirement in a sense that it has to be satisfied by the buyer proving that the detriment is foreseeable. It is solely on the seller to prove that the detriment is unforeseeable.[185] In other words, 'the breach is not fundamental if the party in breach did not foresee and a reasonable person of the same kind in the same circumstances would not have foreseen such a result'.[186] This indicates that 'material loss which the promisor did not foresee and could not have foreseen should not be his responsibility'.[187] In contrast, such requirement is absent under SGA and UCC.

[179] See Schlechtriem and Schwenzer (n 4) 142.
[180] UPICC Article 1.7.
[181] (1988) Court of Appeals of Texas, Houston, 762 S.W.2d 170.
[182] (2007) Court of Appeal, California, WL 2137959.
[183] See sections 2(A)(i) and 2(B)(ii) and 2(C)(i) above.
[184] Bianca and Bonell (n 115) 214.
[185] Honnold and Flechtner (n 127) 371; see also Schlechtriem and Schwenzer (n 4) 401; Bianca and Bonell (n 115) 214.
[186] Schlechtriem and Schwenzer (n 4) 411; see also LA DiMatteo, L Dhooge, S Greene, V Maurer, and M Pagnattaro, 'The interpretive turn in international sales law: an analysis of fifteen years of CISG jurisprudence' (2004) 34 *Northwestern Journal of International Law & Business* 299, 410.
[187] Schlechtriem and Schwenzer (n 4) 401.

Another significant difference is that the doctrine of an additional period of time is present under CISG and UPICC, whilst it is absent under SGA and UCC. This might indicate that the preservation of contractual relations is not of paramount importance under SGA and UCC and that the parties can more easily end their contractual relations. An additional period of time is the final opportunity for the seller to perform their obligations, so that the contract would be kept alive if the seller performs their duty. Thus, the legal regimes such as CISG and UPICC incorporating such doctrine in their provisions tend to preserve the contractual relations as far as possible. Also, UCC offers sellers the right to cure, following breach of contract, which can restrict the buyer's termination right. In contrast, SGA provides no formal legal opportunity for the seller to cure their performance and a contract is likely to be terminated more easily and quickly. However, time obligations under English law might operate as functionally equivalent as the doctrine of additional period of time, even though the origin and the underlying aim of these two principles are not similar. Their functional resemblance is particularly highlighted from the certainty viewpoint. First, both can remove the uncertainty about whether and when the seller will deliver. In other words, if the buyer fixes a time limit, either by a time clause under English law or an additional period of time under CISG and UPICC, the buyer's right to claim performance and the seller's right to deliver will be limited within a specified and fixed period. This shows the significance of the performance in that period so that if there is delay or non-performance, the buyer is able to terminate the contract. Second, an additional period for performance removes the uncertainty of whether non-delivery amounts to fundamental breach. When an additional period has lapsed, the buyer can terminate the contract with no need to prove fundamental breach of contract. This function is very similar to when there is a delay in commercial contracts under SGA, in which time is presumably of essence. Then mere delay or non-performance gives rise to the buyer's right to terminate and they are exempted from proving the substantial failure of performance.

The prospective effect of termination operates almost the same under these legal regimes: as explained, both parties will be relieved from their future obligations, but they will remain subject to their secondary obligations, ie, damages.[188] The retrospective effect of termination, concerning the risk allocation mechanisms following the restitutionary obligations, are also generally similar. Under CISG, the buyer's right to terminate is excluded 'wherever the person who wants to terminate the contract is supposed to carry the risk'.[189] This means that if the buyer is unable to restitute in kind, their right is generally excluded. However, this general principle under CISG has been restricted by the exceptions, which allow the buyer to terminate the contract with no need to pay the monetary value.[190] These exceptions have moderated the harshness of the general principle

[188] See sections 3(A) and 3(B) above.
[189] Zimmermann (n 4) 563, 574.
[190] CISG Art 82 (2).

which excludes the buyer's right to terminate. A different approach is adopted in UPICC, which allows the buyer to terminate the contract when the goods have been destroyed, but 'it imposes a liability on [the buyer] to make good the value of the object received'.[191] Such approach might render the termination of contract difficult, as the parties have to perform their restitutionary obligations in order to exercise the right to terminate. Under UPICC, if restitution in kind is not possible, the monetary value of performance should be rendered. However, such difference does not seem to be practically significant, however, it may theoretically be significant.

The approach adopted under CISG is broadly similar to the approach taken by UCC and English law. In the latter two regimes, the buyer must normally restore the goods, but this requirement does not apply where their inability to restore them is due to the very defect which has given rise to the right to reject: eg, if the goods were so defective that they disintegrated; or if they were taken away from the buyer because the seller had no title to them. Also, the buyer does not have to restore the goods, where restoration of the goods is made impossible by some external cause for which neither party was responsible. In a case governed by English law, the buyer was allowed to terminate the contract and recover the price paid on the basis that the goods were not in conformity with the contract, even though the buyer was unable to return the goods, due to their accidental destruction.[192] In these circumstances, the buyer has no duty to pay the monetary value of the destroyed goods. However, it should be noted that the requirement of total failure of consideration should be satisfied under English law to enable the parties to perform their restitutionary remedies.[193] In other words, the buyer can claim the whole money back 'only if he or she has received nothing in exchange for it, that is, only if there has been "a total failure of consideration"'.[194] This requirement does not affect the availability of the right to terminate the contract and comes into effect only if the buyer seeks to claim the whole purchase price. If the buyer wishes to claim the return of the whole purchase price, '[they] must return what he has acquired under the contract so as to affect a total failure of consideration and make good his restitutionary claim'.[195] In other words, the buyer's right to exercise their restitutionary remedies relates to whether there is a total failure of consideration. If the buyer was successful in showing that no benefits were conferred on them as a result of the seller's performance or non-performance, they can reclaim the contract price.[196] Contrary to English law, UCC requires a commercial buyer to act in good faith, when dealing with rejected goods. As explained already, the additional duties

[191] Zimmermann (n 4) 563, 575.
[192] *Head v Tattersall* (1871–1872) LR 7 Ex 7, [1871] 11 WLUK 69.
[193] Virgo (n 140) 304; A Burrows, *The Law of Restitution*, 3rd edn (Oxford University Press, 2011) 353.
[194] Dickson (n 133) 751, 754; see also *Fibrosa Spolka Akcyjna v Fairbairn Lawson Combe Barbour Ltd* [1943] AC 32 (HL); *Ebrahim Dawood Ltd v Heath (Est 1927) Ltd* [1961] 2 Lloyd's Rep 512 (QB).
[195] Markesinis, Unberath and Johnston (n 139) 436.
[196] Carter (n 21).

imposed on a commercial buyer include reasonable efforts in selling perishable goods or those which are on the verge of reducing value due to the market movements.[197]

The approach adopted by SGA is uncertain. First, there is no detailed guidance under SGA, compared with other legal regimes, ie, UCC and CISG, for a buyer who seeks to exercise their restitutionary remedy. They should inevitably refer to common law doctrines and case-law. There is only SGA section 54, which deals with the buyer's right to reclaim the purchase price. The second reason for the uncertainty revolves around the vague concept of 'total failure of consideration'. The buyer can only claim the whole money back, if they shows that no benefit was conferred on him by the performance or non-performance of the seller.[198] As it has been indicated, 'the key point is that consideration will not have failed totally if any part of the condition, by reference to which the claimant has transferred a benefit to the defendant, has been satisfied'.[199] It was, however, held by the House of Lords in *Stocznia Gdanska SA v Latvian Shipping Co* that 'in truth, the test is not whether the promisee has received a specific benefit, but rather whether the promisor has performed any part of the contractual duties in respect of which the payment is due'.[200] But this dictum cannot be considered as an exclusive definition of the requirement of total failure of consideration. This is so because 'in the contractual context, whether consideration has failed totally will depend on the terms of the contract'.[201] In other words, it depends on the courts' discretion to discover in each case whether the requirement of consideration has been satisfied by the seller in performing any part of his essential obligation under the contract. This might end up with inconsistent and hence unpredictable results. In *Fibrosa Spolka Ackyjna v Fairbairn Lawson Combe Barbour Ltd*, the buyer entered a contract with a manufacturer seller and made an advance payment.[202] The seller had started manufacturing the machinery and incurred some expenditure when the contract was frustrated by the war and that the buyer did not receive any of the machinery. The House of Lords held that the buyer obtained no benefit and he could recover the advance payment. In contrast, in a similar case a different decision was reached. In *Hyundai Heavy Industries Co Ltd v Papadopoulos*, the seller promised to build and sell the ships to the buyer, who agreed to pay in instalments.[203] The buyer declined to pay the second instalment and the contract was considered

[197] See 6.2.2 (iii).

[198] Virgo (n 140) 305; Burrows (n 193) 341, 353.

[199] Virgo (n 140) 305; see also *Dies v British & International Mining and Finance Corp Ltd* [1939] 1 KB 724; *Yeoman Credit v Apps* [1962] 2 QB 508 (CA).

[200] [1998] 1 WLR 574 (HL) 583; see also *Giedo van der Garde BV v Force India Formula One Team Ltd* [2010] EWHC 2373; *Persimmon Homes (South Coast) Ltd v Hall Aggregates (South Coast) Ltd* [2008] EWHC 2379 (TCC).

[201] Virgo (n 140) 315; *Stocznia Gdanska SA v Latvian Shipping Co* [2002] EWCA Civ 889, [2002] 2 All ER 768.

[202] [1943] AC 32 (HL).

[203] [1980] 1 WLR 1129 (HL).

discharged.[204] The buyer claimed for his first instalment on the basis of total failure of consideration, as he had not received any part of the ship. His claim was rejected on the basis that the seller had incurred expenditure in building the ship before the contract was discharged, even though the buyer had not recovered any benefit from his expenditure.[205] These different outcomes reveal the uncertainty inherent in the requirement of total failure of consideration. The buyer is therefore unable to predict the courts' decision, mainly because there is no unified test for determining total failure of consideration and as such it depends on the court's investigation on the nature of contractual terms in each case.

The relational normative framework can be particularly helpful in realising the extent to which a legal regime can restrict the buyer's termination right, for reasons that have little or nothing to do with the breach of contract. In terms of the 'preservation of relation', concerning the maintenance of commercial and contractual relationships, it should be noted that termination's inverse relationship with performance is itself potentially revealing of the extent to which performance is protected. The powerful nature of this drastic remedy is precisely contrary to the idea of maintaining contractual relationships whenever possible. If it is difficult for an injured buyer to terminate, this suggests a stronger commitment to ensuring that performance is rendered than where their exit from the contract is straightforward. The foreseeability requirement as part of fundamental breach of contract doctrine as well as the doctrines of additional period of time and good faith would make it difficult for the buyer to end the contractual relationship. As shown already, SGA is the single legal regime, in which those doctrines are absent when invoking termination by a buyer. This can strengthen the claim that English law confers a relatively broad right to terminate on the injured buyer.

Under UCC, the functioning doctrine of good faith would slow down the buyer in exercising its discretion to terminate the contract and thus limiting its chance of entering into a more favourable deal. This indicates that the parties may stay in their contracts and maintain their contractual relationships. The good faith doctrine may limit the likelihood of termination of a contract and enhance the solidarity between the parties when market prices are fallen. In other words, when the buyer wishes to exercise its cancellation right in good faith, following a substantial non-performance, they would be debarred of breaking off a contractual relationship if their real motivation appears to be escaping a bad bargain. For instance, in the well-known American case of *Neumiller Farms v Cornett*, small potato farmers contracted to sell potatoes suitable for 'chipping' at a price of $4.25 per hundred-weight.[206] The buyer, a commercial potato broker, accepted the first several shipments when the market value was $4.25 per hundred-weight, but when the market price fell to $2.00 per hundred-weight, the buyer started

[204] ibid.

[205] ibid, 1130.

[206] (1979) Supreme Court of Alabama, 368 So.2d 272.

rejecting delivery, arguing that the potatoes did not chip satisfactorily.[207] Upon hearing evidence from the seller's expert that the potatoes were suitable in all respects, the court ruled that the buyer had breached by rejecting delivery in bad faith. The court stated that the law requires such a claim of dissatisfaction to be made in good faith, rather than in an effort to escape a bad bargain, and as such the buyer's rejection was ineffectual.[208] When the doctrine of good faith is established and applied as a functioning principle, rather than a guiding and general principle, the buyer would have to be more cautious when terminating a contract and they should make sure that their decision to terminate a contract is solely influenced by a fundamental non-performance, rather than anything outside the contractual framework, such as market movements. If there is a fundamental non-performance alongside a surprising fall of market price following a conclusion of contract, the seller may always accuse the buyer of cancelling a contract in bad faith and thus limit the buyer's right to escape the bargain. This in turn indicates that the buyer cannot terminate the contract for any trivial, insignificant breaches. As shown in *Joc Oil USA v Consolidated Edison Co. of New York*, Joc Oil contracted to sell a large quantity of oil with a specified maximum sulfur content to Consolidated Edison.[209] When the oil arrived it contained too much sulfur. By the time the buyer rejected delivery the time for performance had passed, and although the seller offered to cure one day later, the buyer declined this offer. The seller's claim, which was accepted by the court was that the buyer had refused to accept the replacement delivery because foreign market forces had caused the value of the oil to decline and that the buyer was attempting to escape from a bad deal. The court found that the seller did have a reasonable basis to believe the oil would be accepted and therefore should have been given additional time for cure. This indicates that a commercial buyer is encouraged to work closely with a seller so that the non-conformity could be addressed. The buyer gives enough chance to the seller to cure the goods, and thus their contractual relationship may be sustained more effectively. In contrast, in other legal regimes where good faith is not explicitly recognised as a duty, such as English law, or merely recognised as a general, guiding principle, such as CISG and UPICC, the buyer may opportunistically terminate the disadvantageous contract. The buyer can more easily walk away from the transaction 'on occasion' of a contractual breach in order to free itself from the unfavourable bargain, even though the breach of contract in itself may have been trivial. English law, in particular, appears to allow such opportunistic contract terminations, by classifying many contractual undertakings as 'conditions', the breach of which gives rise to an event which relieves the party not in default of further performance of their obligations, notwithstanding the ulterior motive of the buyer.

[207] ibid, 273.

[208] ibid, 274; see also *Printing Center of Texas Inc v Supermind Publishing Co Inc* (1984) Court of Appeals of Texas, Houston 669 S.W.2d 779.

[209] (2010) United States District Court, New Jersey 2010 WL 1380750.

The foreseeability requirement under CISG and UPICC might more effectively lead to the continuation of the relationship, compared with SGA and UCC in which this requirement does not exist. The foreseeability requirement induces the parties to exchange information and creates a powerful incentive for the buyer to disclose information to the seller when they make the contract. The buyer has to reveal private (or asymmetric) information, which is unknown to the other party in order to enable the seller to anticipate the loss. Such revelations may create or sustain relationships. Parties will have an opportunity to know each other's sphere of business activities and they might find some common business grounds, which would lead to further cooperation. For instance, in *Delchi Carrier v Rotorex*, governed by the CISG, the buyer agreed to purchase a number of compressors for use in a line of portable room air conditioners.[210] During the contractual negotiations, the buyer gave details of their business to the seller, who was a manufacturer. The seller was informed of the buyer's intention to sell the air conditioners in the spring and summer.[211] The seller thus became aware of the sort of business the buyer was active in and the time when their business was running. This might effectively prolong the commercial relationship between the parties and the manufacturer seller would be likely to provide the buyer with similar goods and he would not need to greatly look for potential purchasers of their products. Also, in *Expoplast C.A. v Reg Mac s.r.l*, governed by CISG, the buyer purchased machinery to be used in recycling plastic bags for the packaging of food products.[212] It was demonstrated that at the time of conclusion of the contract, that the buyer conducted intense negotiations regarding the special features of the product, which they intended to recycle.[213] This special information enabled the seller to be aware of the special type of the buyer's business, which could work as a strong ground for further cooperation, expanding their relationship.

Also, the presence of an additional time doctrine in CISG and UPICC reveals that the drafters are loyal to preserving the contractual relationship between the parties. Although fixing an additional period of time is optional for the buyer, it indicates that the drafters encourage the buyer to give a second chance to the seller for complying with their obligations.[214] By fixing a Nachfrist of reasonable length, the buyer is able to emphasise on their claim and exert pressure upon a defaulting seller. The principle of an additional period of time 'compliments the right to require performance under article 46'.[215] In other words, 'the position is

[210] (1995) U.S. Court of Appeals (2nd Circuit), CISG-online 140.
[211] ibid.
[212] (2001) District Court Busto Arsizio, Italy, CISG-online 1323.
[213] ibid.
[214] J Lookofsky, 'The 1980 United Nations Convention on Contracts for the International Sale of Goods, Article 47 Nachfrist Warning: Buyer Fixing an Additional Performance Period' in J Herbots and R Blanpain, *International Encyclopaedia of Laws – Contracts* (Kluwer Law International, 2000) 119.
[215] UNCITRAL Digest of Case Law on the United Nations Convention on Contracts for the International Sale of Goods (2016) Article 47, para 1.

the same as for a claim for performance of an obligation that is not yet due'.[216] This view signifies that the performance of contract is best served through keeping the contract alive as long as there is a possibility to perform contractual obligations. In addition to serving the immediate interest of the buyer in receiving performance, the Nachfrist principle can be viewed as a fertile ground for enhancing parties' relationship. When an additional period is fixed, the buyer shows solidarity and empathy with a seller, who failed to comply with the strict contractual deadline. Rather than pursing classic and harsh remedies such as damages or specific performance, which could possibly more immediately yield optimal financial results, the buyer chooses to employ this mechanism and offers the seller a second chance for performance. When the additional period of time doctrine is invoked, the buyer modifies that originally agreed contract term, which proved to be difficult to fulfil by the seller. A newly fixed date may render performance of contract by the seller more convenient. The buyer should also wait and should not resort to any remedy for breach of contract, indicating that the buyer cannot pressurise the seller by referring to other remedial principles. If a seller is genuinely willing and able to perform the contract, such a mechanism exactly serves the interests of both parties, in that not only will the contract be performed and no drastic remedies need to be pursued, but also the parties are likely to maintain and develop their commercial relationship. Therefore, when the contract is preserved as far as possible by the existence of a foreseeability requirement and an additional period of time, the seller is likely to be effectively forced to perform their obligations properly, put the buyer in their expected situation of a performed contract, leading to continuation of relationships.

The different approaches regarding the buyer's restitutionary remedy may have different impacts particularly when the goods do not exist anymore. The approach adopted by UPICC might more effectively preserve the parties' relationship than other legal regimes.[217] This approach strives to maintain an acceptable level of reciprocity between the parties, as the buyer is required to pay the monetary value of the non-existing goods and in exchange receives the contract price.[218] In contrast, the level of reciprocity is very low under other regimes, as the buyer does not have to pay anything for the non-existing goods.[219] However, it should be noted this conclusion regarding the continuation of parties' relationship is essentially speculative based on doctrinal analysis, as there is no empirical evidence demonstrating that the parties' relationships have been sustained after termination of contracts governed by UCC, SGA and CISG.

In terms of the second norm of 'conformity of extended relations with commercial matrix', the foreseeability requirement, as well as the doctrines of good faith and additional period of time might actually lock the parties in a hostile relationship.

[216] Schlechtriem and Schwenzer (n 4) 730.
[217] See section 3(B) above.
[218] ibid.
[219] See sections 3(A) and 3(B) above.

These doctrines associated with the remedy of termination under CISG, UPICC and UCC would create a difficult task for an injured buyer to invoke their termination right and end the contractual relationship. These doctrines might 'imprison two parties in a long-term, loveless contract where there is an absence of trust or the prospect of mounting, incremental losses'.[220] This suggests that a legal regime without these hurdles would facilitate ending an embittered relationship by the parties and, as a consequence, would free them to 'seek their opportunities elsewhere, [which] might avoid economic waste and put their abilities and resources to a more productive use'.[221] In *Gregg & Co. (Knottingley) Limited, Allied Glass Containers Limited v Emhart Glass Limited*, governed by SGA, the court held that the buyer of machineries for manufacturing glass receptacles was entitled to reject the goods quickly after receiving them, as they were unfit for the purpose and of unsatisfactory quality.[222] There was no need for a rightful rejection of goods, entailing good faith conduct by the buyer, as required under UCC, nor was there a right of defence for the seller to show that the loss occurred was unforeseeable, as stipulated by CISG and UPICC. This indicates that the buyer could promptly terminate the contract and restore the purchase price, and consequently could find a suitable provider of that sort of machinery in order to activate their business of manufacturing the glasses. In contrast, if this case had been governed by other legal regimes, the hostile relationship between the parties would have been prolonged and have become unproductive, due to the lengthy and wasteful legal proceedings dealing those associated doctrines.

More specifically, the foreseeability requirement under CISG and UPICC would make termination of contract costly, compared with termination under SGA and UCC where this requirement is absent. This requirement would increase the costs in both stages of formation of contract and litigation. At the stage of formation of contract, the buyer has to actively negotiate with the seller to inform them of the importance of certain obligations. It has been indicated that it is primarily the responsibility of the parties to clearly specify in the contract the importance of certain qualities of the goods, so that the absence of such qualities would amount to a fundamental breach of contract by the seller.[223] This is crucial because 'the relevant time for determining the foreseeability issue is the conclusion of the contract'.[224] In other words, at the time of conclusion of the contract, the buyer has to deliver sufficient knowledge or information about those obligations in order to enable the seller to foresee the substantial detriment incurred due to the breach of those obligations.[225] This would be particularly difficult and therefore costly, when commercial parties are contracting internationally. For instance,

[220] Bridge (n 4) 911, 915.
[221] Bridge, *The Sale of Goods* (n 2) 579.
[222] [2005] EWHC 804 (TCC) para 3; see also *Clegg v Andersson (t/a Nordic Marine)* [2003] EWCA Civ 320, [2003] 1 All ER (Comm) 721; *Kanakaris v Furniture Land Ltd* [2006] CLY 3632.
[223] *Cobalt Sulphate case*, (1996) German Supreme Court, CISG-online 135.
[224] Vogenauer (n 4) 928; see also Schlechtriem and Schwenzer (n 4) 583.
[225] Schlechtriem and Schwenzer (n 4) 583.

in the *Cobalt Sulphate case*, a German company purchased cobalt sulphate from a Dutch company and it was agreed that the goods should be of British origin and that the seller should have provided certificates of origin and of quality.[226] However, the goods were made in South Africa and the buyer's claim for avoidance of contract was unsuccessful, as the goods were still useable by the buyer.[227] The main reason for this result was that the buyer did not sufficiently convey the importance attached by him to the description relating to the English origin of the goods. This happened partly because 'the parties did not conduct direct negotiations for the purchase contract, but acted through a broker'.[228] This shows that in international sales of manufactured goods, the parties might enter in a contract by a broker and that there is always risk of misconception or misunderstanding on important terms of contract. The buyer must ensure that the relevant information and the attached importance are properly delivered in order to enable the seller to foresee the substantial loss happened due to the breach of those important terms. This would be difficult and hence costly. In contrast, termination under the SGA is more efficient, as this costly requirement is absent and the buyer does not need to ensure effective communication of greater volumes of more complex information at the time of conclusion of the contract.

This requirement also brings about significant costs at the stage of litigation. These costs arise from the fact that 'anyone who has committed a breach of contract giving rise to major problems will hardly admit that he foresaw those problems, but most likely will insist that unfortunately he did not foresee'.[229] The seller has to convince the courts by proving that '[they] themselves in no way anticipated the substantial detriment caused; and second, that no reasonable person in his place would have done so'.[230] The seller has to show that they actually failed to foresee such result and also a reasonable merchant of the same kind was unable to foresee such result. This would be difficult and costly for the seller, as it has been indicated that 'it is obviously not always easy to establish conclusive evidence for a very personal point of view of the matter. But even if such proof succeeds, a merely subjective test hardly satisfies the necessities of international trade'.[231] This would be costly for the courts as well. The seller's knowledge should be evaluated by reference to CISG Article 74, ie in the light of the facts and matters of which he then knew.[232] The courts should thus consider subjective factors such as 'the [seller's] (in) experience, level of sophistication, and organisational abilities'.[233] Second, the courts should inquire in whether an average merchant 'with a reasonable degree of knowledge and experience in their trade' is able to

[226] (1996) German Supreme Court, CISG-online 135.
[227] ibid.
[228] ibid.
[229] Bianca and Bonell (n 115) 217.
[230] ibid, 216–17.
[231] ibid, 216.
[232] Bianca and Bonell (n 115) 217; CISG Art 74 has been analysed in ch 4: see ch 4 section 2(B).
[233] Babiak (n 115) 113, 121; see also Bianca and Bonell (n 115) 217.

foresee the loss.[234] To satisfy this test, the courts have to accomplish the demanding and lengthy process of taking into account varying situations, which entail 'the conditions on world and regional markets, to legislation, politics and climate, also to prior contracts and dealings and to other factors, in short: to a whole spectrum of facts and events at the relevant time'.[235] Accordingly, the foreseeability requirement renders termination under CISG and UPICC significantly inefficient compared with SGA and UCC.

In terms of the retrospective effects of termination under the legal regimes, the various approaches should be evaluated to determine which one is less costly and thus in line with the commercial matrix. The process of mutual restitution involves the performance of a reversal of the original contract and hence the mechanics of returning the goods and purchase price to their original places. This reversal entails specific costs associated with the mechanics of exchange, ie return of the contract price and the goods. In a scenario when the goods exist and the buyer must restitute in kind in order to terminate the contract, all regimes, except UPICC, strictly requires the buyer to restitute the goods. This strictness is likely to increase the costs of executing restitution, particularly in cross-border transactions which normally involve physical transportation of goods in a long distance. There are costs of shipping the goods, insuring them, taking the bill of lading and transferring to the seller against the repayment of the purchase price and also there might be 'certain transactional costs in negotiating the incidents' of this resale contract.[236] For instance, in the *Roll Aluminum case*, governed by CISG, the Chinese buyer had to return 120 tons of roll aluminium to the American seller, due to the fundamental breach of contract by the seller.[237] In this case, the buyer had to preserve the goods in a warehouse before transferring them, which incurred significant costs plus the costs associated with physical delivery of the goods. The same result might have been achieved if other legal regimes were applicable laws. However, the relevant principles concerning restitution under UPICC are more flexible and might allow the buyer to pay monetary remedies instead of physical restitution of the goods and avoid those costs. UPICC Art 7.3.6 provides that 'an allowance is further envisaged whenever restitution in kind would not be appropriate. This is so in particular when returning the performance in kind would cause unreasonable effort or expense'.[238] However, those flexible and vague terms used in UPICC, such as appropriateness, might increase litigation costs. It seems that when those costs associated with the physical delivery are unreasonably high, especially due to the high geographical distance between the parties, the approach adopted by UPICC

[234] Kroll, Mistelis and Viscasillas (n 4) 341.
[235] Bianca and Bonell (n 115) 218.
[236] Bridge (n 4) 911, 913.
[237] (1991) China International Economic & Trade Arbitration Commission (CIETAC), CISG-online 842; see also (2000) *Danish Furniture case II*, Court of Appeal Oldenburg, Germany, CISG-online 683; *German Sportswear case* (1995) District Court Landshut, Germany, CISG-online 193.
[238] UPICC Official Comments, Article 7.3.6, para 3.

is more efficient than other legal regimes, even if those litigation costs exist. It should be noted that under SGA, the requirement of total failure of consideration is likely to increase litigation costs. The courts have to factually examine each contractual context in order to find out whether consideration has totally failed. They have to specifically scrutinise whether any part of performance has been rendered by the seller or any benefit has been conferred on the buyer.[239] This investigation is likely to be costly. For instance, in *Yeoman Credit Ltd v Apps*, the buyer rejected the car due to the 'breach of a fundamental condition of the agreement, namely, to provide a functioning car which could be used on the roads'.[240] The buyer reclaimed the instalments he already paid. The court rejected his claim for the price paid, as the courts evaluated the facts and realised that the buyer had possessed the car for some time and took some use of it and as such the requirement of total failure of consideration was not satisfied.[241] In *Rowland v Divall*, a different decision was taken by the court, in which a buyer bought a car from a seller, who had no title to it.[242] Although the buyer 'had had the use of the car the consideration had totally failed, he was entitled to get the purchase money back'.[243] It was explained that the use of the car was no part of the consideration that the buyer contracted for.[244] These show that the SGA is the least efficient one, as the buyer's costs associated with the physical delivery of the goods will be aggregated to these litigation costs.

[239] See eg *Ebrahim Dawood Ltd v Heath (Est 1927) Ltd Oosman v Heath (Est 1927) Ltd* [1961] 2 Lloyd's Rep 512 (QB); *Kwei Tek Chao (t/a Zung Fu Co) v British Traders & Shippers Ltd* [1954] 2 QB 459 (QB).
[240] [1962] 2 QB 508 (CA) 509; see also *Garside v Black Horse Ltd* [2010] EWHC 190 (QB) para 82.
[241] [1962] 2 QB 508 (CA) 509–510.
[242] [1923] 2 KB 500 (CA).
[243] ibid.
[244] ibid.

7

Conclusion

This monograph has explored which legal regime has provided the most appropriate array of remedies available to an international commercial buyer contracted to purchase manufactured goods. It has conducted this task through a detailed analysis of the law of remedies under four significant legal regimes governing international sales transactions. The remedies investigated are monetary remedies (including damages, set-off, and price reduction), performance-directed remedies (including specific performance and the buyer's right to cure), and termination remedies. In addition, chapter two has dealt with insecurity prior to the performance date of the contract and examines the doctrines of withholding performance, anticipatory breach of contract and adequate assurance. The book has employed a comparative method to critically analyse similarities and differences between the provisions governing each type of remedy in the investigated legal regimes. To find out which remedial provision in which legal regime functions most appropriately, it was necessary to concentrate mostly on identifying the significant differences between central aspects of the law of each remedy. Those differences were examined against a novel normative framework inspired by the relational theory of contract. This framework essentially reinforced a normative analysis, which has aimed to examine the differences against suitable criteria and to identify flaws, weaknesses and strengths in a remedial provision.

This concluding chapter will, first, provide a summary of the findings of the last five chapters. Second, an overall conclusion will be drawn on the basis of those findings relating to each particular segment of remedies with the aim of determining the most appropriate legal regime for providing buyers' remedies.

Chapter two was concerned with the doctrines and principles dealing with insecurity prior to the date of performance. As the recent global COVID-19 pandemic revealed, we live in an uncertain world. Unpredicted events can disturb the contracting parties' plans and their performance duties may be ceased. The doctrines and principles, investigated in this chapter, seek to offer legal solutions in such disruptive situations. Three specific doctrines of suspension of performance, anticipatory breach of contract and adequate assurance were analysed. The outcome is that SGA has failed to satisfy the particular interest of commercial buyers reflected in the relational normative framework. In terms of suspension of performance, English law is the only regime which has failed to explicitly and officially recognise this remedy, even though this remedy may be employed logically in response to the seller's suspicious behaviour. As stated in *Channel Tunnel Group Ltd*, the doctrine of withholding performance is not yet established in English law.[1] This legal regime has adopted a dogmatic approach, whereby an innocent party, faced with the other parties' non-performance, has the binary choices of either confirming the contract or accepting the breach and terminating the contract. The all or nothing approach may bring about more certainty, but surely it leaves parties with limited choice, hence inconsistent with commercial reality. UCC, on the other hand, has provided this measure for a buyer in an accessible and flexible manner.[2] This regime permits an aggrieved buyer to suspend its own performance, with an acceptable excuse for any resulting necessary delay, until the situation has been clarified. UCC only requires the buyer to show a reasonable fear of future breach, while CISG and UPICC require the buyer to demonstrate that a substantial part of the contract will not be performed. Despite these differences, it seems that in practice the relevant provisions in these regimes will lead to similar outcomes. Although the doctrine of anticipatory breach of contract was originally developed in English law, it has not been modernised to meet the reasonable expectations of commercial parties. The doctrine of anticipatory breach of contract, as it currently stands in English law, does not provide a satisfactory solution for a buyer facing uncertain and dubious circumstances, since it lacks a solid instrument to determine objectively whether the seller will perform the contract. The doctrine of adequate assurance, which is present in other legal regimes, precisely offers such a buyer a mechanism to extricate itself from the risks and uncertainties involved in relying on an anticipatory breach of contract. This doctrine is supported by the mitigation policy, in that reasonable steps must be taken by an injured part to avoid or diminish loss. This doctrine is again set out more clearly under UCC, where it has stipulated the implications of a failure to provide an adequate assurance, while CISG and UPICC have failed to do so.

In terms of the first norm of the relational evaluative framework, SGA appears to be the weakest legal regime. The self-help doctrines of adequate assurance of contract and suspension of performance, which are well established in other regimes, facilitate cooperative behaviour between the parties, which may result in the continuation of commercial and contractual relationships. SGA and more broadly English law appears to have adopted a rigid approach by giving ultimate value to legal certainty at the expense of sacrificing the flexibility necessary in long-term commercial transactions. Suspension of performance, in particular, acts as a nudge, which prompts the seller to clarify the situation quickly. By doing so, the buyer would hesitate and be slow in invoking more drastic remedies of damages or termination. The seller would gain the chance to assess its relationship with the buyer and, should they genuinely intend to stay in the contract with the

[1] [1972] QB 656, 670.
[2] UCC section 2-609.

buyer and transform their relationship into a long-term cooperative one, would either perform the remaining obligations or cure its previously delivered defective performance. Additionally, adequate assurance of contract and suspension of performance are considered self-help remedies, in the sense that the buyer can invoke them without any third parties' involvement. Resorting to formal and rigid proceedings such as litigation and arbitration deprives the parties from constructive cooperation. The notice requirement at the heart of both doctrines can function as a measure encouraging parties to communicate. The parties can then appreciate the effect of any change of circumstances on each other's performance and work out a solution resulting in alteration of the contract terms and ultimately performance of contract.

It is doubtless that anticipatory breach of contract is economically advantageous for both parties and is aligned with the second norm of conformity of extended relations with commercial matrix. The buyer, who is confronted with a repudiation of a contract by a seller, would enjoy the opportunity to be freed from staying in such a contract. Rather than wasting its financial resources in a futile contractual relationship, the buyer can immediately take drastic action, terminate the contract and enter an alternative, profitable transaction. All regimes have provided this doctrine for the buyer. In addition, suspension of performance, either as a stand-alone remedy or when it comes into effect following the buyer's request for adequate assurance, provides the parties with a cooling off period to examine whether continuing the contractual relationship is economically justifiable. Preserving the relationship is generally viewed as more efficient than breaking it. Suspension of performance is seen as a conservatory and defensive remedy, in that the buyer seeks to exert pressure on the seller to perform. By employing this remedy, the buyer indicates that they do not wish to terminate the contract, as an immediate option. The buyer's pressure may result in the seller's performance, leading to the maintenance of the contractual relationship. These two remedies also support 'reciprocity' as a necessary norm for sustaining economically advantageous contractual relationships. The contract remains an economically viable instrument so long as parties reciprocate and meet each other's interests. When a contract is placed on halt due to the buyer's suspension of performance, the seller would gain the chance to examine whether sufficient value is tied up in their contract and whether they should stay in that relationship. Such an opportunity properly used, can avoid further loss in the future.

Chapter three dealt with two financial remedies of price reduction and set-off that could be employed during the lifetime of a contract. Since these remedies can be exercised without any third parties' assistance, they are particularly significant in maintaining the parties' contractual and commercial relationship. As shown, the remedy of price reduction does not have formal status under SGA, UCC and UPICC. This exclusion may suggest that set-off is functionally equivalent to this remedy and that they may result in very similar practical consequences. In fact, Professor Treitel opined that SGA section 30, concerning set-off, applies very similarly to price reduction, in the case of short delivery of goods.[3] CISG is the only legal regime which has a provision concerning price reduction, however, set-off is expressly excluded in this regime. Set-off is special in nature: it is not a separate remedy, but a defence in nature, and is considered an immediate answer to liability. This defence is closely connected to the remedy of damages and the amount which the buyer is entitled to deduct is calculated by way of damages. This may indicate that set-off is not a substantive and dependent entitlement and that it should not be separately compared with price reduction. However, in practice, set-off is used by commercial parties in reducing their liabilities against each other and deserves a comparative analysis with price reduction.

While these remedies are functionally similar, there are two differences analysed in this chapter. The first salient distinction concerns their method of calculation. As shown, in set-off, the price is prima facie reduced on the grounds of the difference between the market price and the actual value of the goods delivered. In price reduction, the actual loss incurred is not taken into account and the reduced amount is measured proportionately on the basis of the abstract relationship between the actual value of the goods delivered and the market value of conforming goods. This difference was evaluated in three different situations, based on the change of market price. The outcome revealed that when the market price does not change from the time of contract and the time of delivery, both remedies function identically with no difference in the reduced amount through set-off and price reduction. However, when the market price reduces from the time of the conclusion of contract, the buyer enjoys a more reduced amount than when exercising set-off. Price reduction hence places the buyer in a better financial position than set-off. However, when the market price increases from the time of conclusion of contract, set-off performs better and places the buyer in a stronger financial position than price reduction. Another difference concerns the rules and principles restricting the availability of these self-help remedies. The buyer can exercise price reduction if they notify the seller of non-conformity and make a declaration of price reduction as well as the seller's decision to cure. If the seller decides to cure the deficiency, the buyer is not allowed to reduce the price and shall wait until the seller's endeavour is finished. Under set-off, the buyer shall only declare their intention of exercising this remedy, without being required to notify the seller about the non-conformity of the goods. However, since set-off is closely associated with damages, the pertinent restricting principles, such as the foreseeability requirement and the duty to mitigate, are also applicable to set-off.

In terms of preservation of relationship, both remedies are appropriate in helping the parties keep and develop their contractual relationship. As shown, price reduction reforms the original contract based on the delivered performance and can thus maintain the relative balance of the bargain between the parties. When

[3] GH Treitel, *Remedies for Breach of Contract: A Comparative Account* (Oxford University Press, 1988) 110; see section 3-04.

this remedy is used, the parties try to renegotiate with each other and adjust the contract to the new situation without any resort to any third party. This can maintain the parties' relations. Set-off functions similarly, in that the buyer can retain the defective goods, and reflects such non-conformity in reducing the contract price. Set-off prompts the parties to communicate and negotiate so that the parties can make adjustments without resorting to court or any other third party. Thus both remedies create an opportunity for the parties to cooperate and make necessary adjustments to their liabilities to retain the contractual balance, leading to the preservation of their contractual relationship.

In terms of the second criteria, both remedies appear to equally satisfy the expected value of the contract for the parties. Since both remedies are self-help in nature, they can be used by the parties without any third party interference. When exercising these remedies, the parties only face the post-breach renegotiation costs, which would normally be minimal, compared to litigation costs. Litigation or even arbitration of international commercial contracts do not only cost significant money, due to the complexity of procedural and jurisdictional issues but would also cause parties trouble and annoyance, which is likely to negatively affect their relationship and may even end it. In contrast, the costs of renegotiations mainly conducted by the parties themselves should not be high, since the parties involved in the international sale of manufactured goods have normally spent to a considerable extent in negotiating and drafting the contract and the alteration of price terms, reflecting the non-conformity either through set-off or price reduction, would not be time-consuming and costly.

Chapter four analysed the law of damages under the four legal regimes. The differences identified were mainly concerned with the rules concerning the remoteness test and the quantification of damages. In terms of the remoteness test, the recent development of the foreseeability requirement in *The Achilleas* and its greater readiness to take account of the context in which a contract is concluded may suggest that this regime is more apt for developing parties' relational interest. The other legal regimes have remained less flexible in this regard. The view adopted by the UK House of Lords in *The Achilleas* would enable the adjudicators to consider the surrounding circumstances and general understanding more carefully in the relevant market to see whether the seller could be held liable for loss.

In terms of the calculation of loss and the duty to mitigate, these regimes appear to have adopted similar provisions. However, again, English law through the decision made in *The Golden Victory* has demonstrated to have been more accommodating of the especial needs of parties involved in a relational, long-term contract. In contrast to the static and rigid market price rule, as a preferred rule in other legal regimes, the prevailing compensatory principle in English law has the capacity to take account of the *ex ante* high possibility of disruptive events in long-term and relational contracts. English law has the ability to most accurately calculate damages based on the actual losses incurred, following the breach of contract. This principle would fairly allocate financial burdens between the parties, particularly when a force majeure event has rendered contract performance less valuable. Such a principle may, therefore, convince both parties to maintain their relationship. The compensatory principle is also aligned with the second norm of conformity of extended relations with commercial matrix. Accurate calculation of damages, reflecting the actual loss incurred, replicates the outcome of a properly performed contract and would enhance the healthy functioning of the market. This principle preserves the contractual equilibrium between the parties and satisfies the reciprocity and mutuality, as required in a long-term contractual relationship.

Another significant distinction identified was that SGA has given priority to the abstract method for measuring damages, whereas, the other legal regimes have prioritised the concrete method. Under SGA, the loss is solely calculated on the basis of market price, even if a substitute transaction has actually been made. The other legal regimes' quantification rules are in contrast with this approach: the focus is primarily on the substitute transaction, even if there is an available market for the contract goods, on the condition that the substitute transaction has been reasonably concluded, otherwise, the market price rule is utilised. While it is evident that neither the abstract method nor the concrete method may enable parties to maintain their relationship, the former method does not explicitly require the parties to end their contract. Quite contrary, the concrete method requires the injured buyer to terminate the contract and enter into a new one to acquire similar goods. Ending the contract with the original seller and entering into a new one with a potential competitor would most likely ruin the prospect of developing a long-term contractual relationship between the parties. In addition, the abstract method appears to be more aligned with the second norm. In particular, as shown, the concrete method increases the transaction costs incurred due to the requirement of breaking the original contract and making a new one. The absence of this requirement under the abstract method would be more efficient and less costly for the buyer. This method may also reduce the litigation costs, compared to the concrete method. The abstract method is more streamlined than the concrete method and may make trials relatively straightforward and less lengthy. Also, the courts will have to primarily consider the market price at the time of breach, without necessarily considering several purchases made by a commercial buyer following the breach of the original contract, as required by the concrete method.

Chapter five was concerned with the law relating to performance directed remedies, ie, specific performance and cure. The significant difference between these regimes lies in their different approaches toward specific performance. Under CISG and UPICC, the buyer can require the seller perform the contract, as a matter of right, while under SGA and UCC, this remedy is discretionary and not readily available. Under SGA, the buyer enjoys much more freedom than any other regime to terminate the contract and seek damages in lieu of performance. While UCC, as a more modernised version of common law, has not fundamentally departed from the English law's approach, its section 2-716 seeks to strike a balance between the general common law policy of reluctance toward specific performance and a more flexible availability of specific performance. However, in practice, the courts tend to still order specific performance in circumstances where damages are inadequate in compensating the buyer's loss.

In terms of the first criterion of the evaluative framework, at first blush, it seems that since CISG and UPICC have prioritised performance directed remedies over damages, they are better able to maintain the parties' contractual relationship than SGA and UCC. However, as was shown as the exact opposite in this chapter, in the context of international commercial sale of goods, the buyers are presumably well placed to deal with non-conformity of goods, by either fixing them or having them fixed by a third party, and then claim damages from the seller. This may result in keeping the relationship alive and even developing it, as the parties would have the chance to cooperate with each other and sort out the issues, without necessarily involving third party adjudicators, such as courts or arbitrators, to order a performance directed remedy. Thus, a regime which allows an injured buyer to choose between performance remedies and damages would be more satisfactory. In addition, CISG's too much emphasis on performance directed remedies, and in particular, insistence on the seller's right to cure and prevailing it over the buyer's remedies, may not only prevent parties from developing a long-term, fruitful relationship but may also cause tension and enmity between them. UCC, on the other hand, has sought to recognise the importance of the seller's right to cure as well as giving the right to the buyer to choose between asking the seller to cure deficiencies or claiming for damages, following repairing the goods. Such a balanced approach is certainly more in line with reasonable commercial standards and far from dogmatism that other legal regimes are suffering from.

In relation to the second norm, performance directed remedies prioritised under CISG and UPICC were contrasted with damages prioritised under SGA and UCC. Since damages are given priority in the latter regimes, they may thus allow the efficient breach of contract, by enticing the seller to breach the contract, pay compensation and deliver the goods already sold to another buyer, who was willing to pay more. It may, however, be difficult and expensive to calculate the buyer's expected profit, which was lost due to the breach, at the time of conclusion of the contract. To conduct this task, the courts or arbitrators need to have a good amount of information such as those concerning the content of the contract and the market for the goods in question. However, this is not an insurmountable task in the context of commercial sale of manufactured goods. The doctrine of remoteness test and the duty to mitigate, sufficiently guide the adjudicator to determine the buyer's expected profit, which could be achieved by a fulfilled contract. When it comes to performance directed remedies, there are certain costs associated with executing performance remedies, which are incurred by the parties. Due to the long distance between the parties' place of business, the costs of transportation of the goods, namely carriage of goods by sea or air and insurance, are likely to be high. These costs could be minimal in damages, as the seller will not be required to transport repaired or replaced goods to the buyer. In addition to these costs, there are also costs of post-breach negotiations, which are, however, likely to be minimal for the commercial parties contracting in international sales.

Chapter six concentrated on the law concerning termination of contract, as a dramatic remedy and last resort solution to the situations where the buyer faces substantive breach of contract. It was found that the grounds for termination of contract under these regimes are somewhat the same: termination is allowed when there is a fundamental breach of contract. However, UCC has stipulated the requirement of good faith when the buyer intends to terminate the contract. In contrast to other regimes, UCC has imposed on the buyer terminating the contract the obligation to conduct in good faith, which would make termination of contract more difficult. Another difference was that there is the requirement of foreseeability of the consequences of the fundamental breach under CISG and UPICC, which require the buyer to show that the seller subjectively and objectively anticipated those consequences. CISG Article 25 and UPICC Article 7.3.1 show that foreseeability is a cumulative question: the seller must both subjectively and objectively have predicted the result of the breach. Another difference was found to be that the doctrine of Nachfrist is absent under SGA and UCC, which may reveal that maintaining contractual relationships is not of high importance in these regimes. On the other hand, CISG and UPICC, by embedding this doctrine, entitle the buyer to give another chance to the seller to perform the contract, which may lead to the preservation of contract for a longer period of time. The effect of termination of contract was found to be broadly similarly dealt with under these regimes.

In terms of the first criterion, obviously the dramatic remedy of termination functions against the maintenance and development of a commercial relationship between the parties. The logical implication would be that if a legal regime makes termination of contract difficult by prescribing more requirements, it may have a stronger commitment to keeping contracts alive. As shown, SGA is the regime with the least requirements for terminating the contract. Other regimes require satisfaction of the foreseeability doctrine as well as complying with the good faith regime, which is absent under SGA. The doctrine of an additional period of time, which is not present in SGA and UCC, may also suggest that CISG and UPICC seek to preserve the contractual relationship as much as possible. In addition, UCC, in contrast to the regimes, requires the buyer to act in good faith when exercising its right to terminate the contract, which may function as a barrier to ending a contractual relationship. Such doctrine may actually solidify the relationship between the parties, as the buyer will not be able to easily end the contract due to market fluctuations only and should always request the seller in the first instance to cure any deficiencies. As such, UCC, more actively than other regimes, encourages parties to sort out the issues themselves without necessarily involving third parties.

In terms of the second norm, the stringent requirements for termination of contract may lock the parties in a sort of relationship, which has lost its profitability for the parties. The doctrines of additional period of time, good faith and the foreseeability requirement would make termination of contract difficult and hence the relationship may remain longer than when those principles do not exist in a legal regime. Ending an embittered relationship easily would mean freedom for the parties to find opportunities elsewhere, resulting potentially in avoiding financial costs. SGA scores the highest from this standpoint. UCC, by requiring the buyer to act in good faith, may seem to lock parties in a contentious relationship, but actually, this principle seeks to tackle the buyer's ulterior motives in escaping a bad bargain and ending the contract. Should there genuinely be a ground for termination, UCC permits the buyer to terminate the contract. In contrast, the foreseeability requirement, prescribed under CISG and UPICC, significantly increases the costs at both stages of formation of contract as well as litigation. These costs are absent under UCC and SGA, and thus termination of contract would be less costly in these two regimes.

It can be concluded that UCC is the most appropriate legal regime for the purpose of this book. This conclusion reinforces the fact that American commercial law is the product of commercial consciousness and pragmatism, so that it can effectively serve the legitimate interest of a buyer contracting in international sales. These interests have been addressed in the norms of the framework used in this book. Although SGA scored satisfactorily in some chapters, and in particular, it was found to be the most appropriate one in providing the law of damages in accordance with the norms of the relational theory of contract, it falls short in certain aspects. The reason lies in its rigid and formalistic approach towards commercial contracts and the lack of formal recognition of certain modern doctrines such as the seller's right to cure and adequate assurance of performance. Even though English common law may be able to accommodate these modern doctrines, their absence may render this regime unattractive for international commercial parties, who can access and get the benefit of those doctrines more readily under other regimes, such as UCC. Should lawmakers wish to maintain the tremendous position of English sale of goods in the realm of international trade, they should modify this regime and incorporate modern and practically important doctrines.

It was also expected that the international legal regimes, ie, CISG and UPICC, which are essentially designed to govern international contracts, have provided the best possible provisions regarding the buyer's remedies. But it was revealed that they fell short of satisfying the significant norms that could express the proper principle of the relationship of remedial provisions to the buyer's commercial utility. Their drafters should have designed the remedial provisions in a way that could not only lead to the preservation of fruitful relationships in an effective manner but also be cost-effective, by reducing the transaction costs to their lowest possible level. Commercial buyers attempt to raise their wealth and as such, they are unwilling to choose a legal regime incurring them some expenditure, which is likely to be avoided if they select a legal regime with more relatively efficient remedial provisions, such as UCC and SGA. The main part of this inefficiency lies in the ambiguities of the remedial provisions of these international legal regimes and the lack of sufficiently clear guidance on how a buyer can exercise their remedial rights. Furthermore, these provisions under CISG and UPICC should have had the capacity to target and serve the pure contractual interest of the parties. The provisions should have been written in a way that could support a disappointed buyer, who was outraged by the seller's non-performance. Such a disappointed buyer reasonably expects that the remedial provisions place them in a position very close to when the contract was properly performed. This could be fulfilled by giving enough liberty to the commercial buyer to obtain sufficiently similar performance from a well-developed market. Additionally, the remedial provisions should have also been formulated in a manner that they could provide opportunities for the parties to enhance and sustain their fruitful relationship so that their commercial needs could be accommodated more effectively. But as shown, those investigated remedial provisions are likely to lock the parties in a sort of worthless relationship, which may lead to hostility and bitterness. It is, therefore, submitted that UCC should be considered as a proper model for possible modifications in these legal regimes.

The findings of this book are useful for a wide range of legal actors, including contractual parties, legal practitioners, legal drafters, and adjudicators. The latter group might significantly benefit from this book. The book provided effective and detailed guidance at different levels. First, it has determined and explained key remedies for a commercial buyer. Second, the study illustrated their strengths and weaknesses in light of the comparative and normative discussions. Therefore, judges, arbitrators, and mediators are able to wisely decide what remedy would well satisfy the dominant interests of a commercial buyer.

BIBLIOGRAPHY

Books

Andersen, CB, Mazzotta, FG and Zeller, B, *A Practitioner's Guide to the CISG* (JurisNet LLC, 2010).

Andrews, N, Clarke, M, Tettenborn, A and Virgo, G, *Contractual Duties: Performance, Breach, Termination and Remedies*, 2nd edn (Sweet & Maxwell, 2017).

Basedow J, Hopt KJ and Zimmermann R, The Max Planck Encyclopedia of European Private Law (Oxford University Press 2011).

Beale, H, Fauvarque-Cosson, B, Rutgers, J, Tallon, D and Vogenauer, S, *Cases, Materials and Text on Contract Law, Ius Commune Casebooks for the Common Law of Europe*, 3rd edn (Hart Publishing, 2019).

Beale, HG (ed), *Chitty on Contracts, vols 1 and 2*, 34th edn (Sweet & Maxwell, 2022).

Beatson, J and Friedman, D, *Good Faith and Fault in Contract Law* (Oxford University Press, 1997).

Bender, M, *International Sales: The United Nations Convention on Contracts for the International Sale of Goods* (Galston & Smit edn, 1984).

Berryman, JR, *A Treatise on the Law of Damages: Embracing an Elementary Exposition of the Law, and also Its Application to Particular Subjects of Contract and Tort*, 4th edn (Callaghan and Company, 1916).

Bianca, CM and Bonell, MJ, *Commentary on the International Sales Law, The 1980 Vienna Sales Convention* (Giuffre, 1987).

Birds, J, Bradgate, R and Villiers, C, *Termination of Contracts* (John Wiley & Sons, 2005).

Bonell, MJ, *An International Restatement of Contract Law, The Unidroit Principles of International Commercial Contracts*, 3rd edn (Ardsley, Transnational Publishers, 2005).

Bridge, MG (ed), *Benjamin's Sale of Goods*, 11th edn (Sweet & Maxwell, 2022).

—— *The International Sale of Goods*, 4th edn (Oxford University Press, 2017).

—— *The Sale of Goods* (4th edn, Oxford University Press, 2019).

Bucheler, A and Muller-Chen, M (eds), *Private Law- National-Global-Comparative* (Intersentia, 2011).

Burrows, A, *English Private Law, Oxford Principles of English Law* (Oxford University Press, 2013).

—— *Remedies for Torts, Breach of Contract, and Equitable Wrongs*, 4th edn (Oxford University Press, 2019).

—— *The Law of Restitution*, 3rd edn (Oxford University Press, 2011).

Butler, AE, *A Practical Guide to the CISG: Negotiations through Litigation* (Aspen Publishers, 2007).

Calamari, JD and Perillo, JM, *The Law of Contracts*, 3rd edn (West Group, 1987).

Campbell, D and Halso,n R, *Research Handbook on Remedies in Private Law* (Edward Elgar, 2019).

Carter, JW, *Carter's Breach of Contract*, 2nd edn (Hart Publishing, 2020).

Chuah, J, *Law of International Trade: Cross-border Commercial Transactions*, 5th edn (Sweet & Maxwell, 2013).

Cooter, R and Ulen, T, *Law and Economics*, 4th edn (Pearson Addison Wesley, 2007).

Dannemann, G and Vogenauer, S, *The Common European Sales Law in Context: Interactions with English and German Law* (Oxford University Press, 2013).

Deakin, S and Michie, J (eds), *Contracts, Co-operation and Competition: Studies in Economics, Management and Law* (Oxford University Press, 1997).

Derham, R, *Derham on the Law of Set-off*, 4th edn (Oxford University Press, 2010).

DiMatteo, L and Hogg, M (eds), *Comparative Contract Law* (Cambridge University Press, 2015).

DiMatteo, L, Janssen, A, Magnus, U and Schulze, R, *International Sales Law: A Handbook*, 2nd edn (Bloomsbury Publishing, 2021).

DiMatteo, LA, Zhou, Q, Saintier, S and Rowley, K, *Commercial Contract Law, Transatlantic Perspectives* (Cambridge University Press, 2013).
Edelman J, Varuhas D and Colton S, *McGregor on Damages*, 21st edn (Sweet & Maxwell, 2022).
Felemegas, J, *An International Approach to the Interpretation of the United Nations Convention on Contracts for the International Sale of Goods (1980) as Uniform Sales Law* (Cambridge University Press, 2007).
Ferrari, F, Flechtner, H and Brand, RA (eds), *The Draft UNCITRAL Digest and Beyond: Case, Analysis and Unresolved Issues in the U.N Sales Convention* (Sellier, European Law Publishers, 2004).
Fountoulakis, C, *Set-off Defences in International Commercial Arbitration* (Hart Publishing, 2011).
Fried, C, *Contract as Promise: A Theory of Contractual Obligation* (Harvard University Press, 1981).
Frisch, D, *Lawrence's Anderson on the Uniform Commercial Code*, 3rd edn (Thomson Reuters, 2023).
Goode, R, Kronke, H and McKendrick, E, *Transnational Commercial Law: Text, Cases and Materials*, 2nd edn (Oxford University Press, 2016).
Gustafson, J, Kimpflen, J, Necheles, SJT and Simmons, KC, *Corpus Juris Secundum*, 25th edn (Thomson Reuters, 2023).
Halson, R and Campbell, D, *Research Handbook on Remedies in Private Law* (Edward Elgar, 2019).
Hayton, D (ed), *Law's Future(s): British Legal Developments in the 21st Century* (Hart Publishing, 2000).
Harris, D, Campbell, D and Halson, R, *Remedies in Contract and Tort*, 2nd edn (Butterworths LexisNexis, 2002).
Hawkland, WD, Bjerre, CS, Rusch, LR and Garry, LT, *Hawkland's Uniform Commercial Code Series* (Thomson Reuters, 2023).
Herbots, J and Blanpain, R, *International Encyclopaedia of Laws – Contracts* (Kluwer Law International, 2000).
Holmes, OW, *The Common Law* (Harvard University Press, 1967).
Honnold, JO and Flechtner, HM, *Honnold's Uniform Law for International Sales under the 1980 United Nations Convention*, 5th edn (Wolters Kluwer Law and Business, 2021).
Honnold, JO, *Documentary History of the Uniform Law for International Sales: The Studies, Deliberations, and Decisions that Led to the 1980 United Nations Convention with Introductions and Explanations* (Kluwer Law and Taxation Publishers, 1989).
Huber, P and Mullis, A, *The CISG, A New Textbook for Students and Practitioners* (Sellier, European Law Publishers, 2007).
Jones, G and Goodhart, W, *Specific Performance*, 2nd edn (Butterworths, 1996).
Justice Robert Sharpe, *Injunctions and Specific Performance*, 5th edn (The Carswell Company Ltd, 2017).
Klass, G, Letsas, G and Saprai, P, *Philosophical Foundations of Contract Law* (Oxford University Press, 2014).
Koch, R, 'The Concept of Fundamental Breach of Contract under the United Nations Convention on Contracts for the International Sale of Goods (CISG)' *in Review of the Convention on Contracts for the International Sale of Goods (CISG)* (Kluwer Law International, 1999).
Kritzer, AH, *Guide to Practical Applications of the United Nations Convention on Contracts for the International Sale of Goods* (Kluwer Law and Taxation Publishers, 1989).
Kroll, S, Mistelis, L and Viscasillas, PP, *UN Convention on Contracts for the International Sale of Goods (CISG) Commentary* (Hart Publishing, 2011).
Liu, Q, *Anticipatory Breach* (Hart Publishing, 2011).
Llewellyn, K, *The Common Law Tradition: Deciding Appeals* (Little Brown, 1960).
Lookofsky, J, *Understanding the CISG, A Compact Guide to the 1980 United Nations Convention on Contracts for the International Sale of Goods*, 4th edn (Wolters Kluwer, 2012).
Lord, RA, *Williston on Contracts*, 4th edn (Thomson Reuters, 2023).
Mak, V, *Performance-oriented Remedies in European Sale of Goods Law* (Hart Publishing, 2009).
Markesinis, BS, Unberath, H and Johnston, A, *The German Law of Contract, A Comparative Treatise*, 2nd edn (Hart Publishing, 2006).
McKendrick, E, *Contract Law*, 10th edn (Oxford University Press, 2022).
McKendrick, E, *Goode and McKendrick on Commercial Law*, 6th edn (Penguin Books, 2020).

McKendrick, E, *Sale of Goods* (LLP Professional Publishing, 2000).
Macneil, IR, *The New Social Contract: An Inquiry into Modern Contractual Relations* (Yale University Press, 1981).
Neyers J, Bronaugh R, and Pitel, S (eds), *Exploring Contract Law* (Hart Publishing, 2009).
Nicholas, B, *The French Law of Contract*, 2nd edn (Oxford University Press, 1992).
Peel, E, *Treitel on The Law of Contract*, 15th edn (Sweet & Maxwell, 2020).
Pichonnaz, P and Gullifer, L, *Set-off in Arbitration and Commercial Transactions* (Oxford University Press, 2014).
Pomeroy, J, A *Treatise on the Specific Performance of Contracts*, 3rd edn (1926).
Posner, RA, *Economic Analysis of Law*, 6th edn (Aspen Publisher, 2003).
Quinn, TM, *Quinn's Uniform Commercial Code, Commentary and Law Digest*, 2nd edn (Thomson Reuters, 2009).
Rimke, J, 'Force majeure and hardship: Application in international trade practice with specific regard to the CISG and the UNIDROIT Principles of International Commercial Contracts' 217 in *Pace Review of the Convention on Contracts for the International Sale of Goods* (Kluwer, 1999–2000).
Rowan, S, *Remedies for Breach of Contract, A Comparative Analysis of Protection of Performance* (Oxford University Press, 2012).
Saidov, D and Cunnington, R (eds), *Contract Damages, Domestic and International Perspective* (Hart Publishing, 2008).
—— *The Law of Damages in International Sales: The CISG and other International Instruments*, 2nd edn (Hart Publishing, 2022).
—— (ed), *Research Handbook on International and Comparative Sale of Goods Law* (Edward Elgar, 2019).
Schlechtriem, P and Schwenzer, L, *Commentary on the UN Convention on the International Sale of Goods*, 5th edn (Oxford University Press, 2022).
Schwenzer, I and Munoz, E, *Global Sales and Contract Law*, 2nd edn (Oxford University Press, 2022).
Schwenzer, I, Fountoulakis, C and Dimsey, M, *International Sales Law, A Guide to the CISG*, 2nd edn (Hart Publishing, 2012).
Schwenzer, I, Hachem, P and Kee, C, *Global Sales and Contract Law* (Oxford University Press, 2012).
Shinn, R, *A Treatise on the American Law of Replevin and Kindred Actions for Getting Possession of Chattels: Being a Complete Statement of the General Principle* (Gale, Making of Modern Law, 2010).
Smits, J, Haas, D and Hesen, G (eds), *Specific Performance in Contract Law: National and Other Perspectives* (Intersentia, 2008).
Spry, ICF, *The Principles of Equitable Remedies: Specific Performance, Injunctions, Rectification, and Equitable Damages*, 9th edn (Thomson Legal & Regulatory Limited, 2013).
Stannard, JE and Capper, D, *Termination for Breach of Contract* (Oxford University Press, 2014).
Tepper, PR, *The Law of Contracts and the Uniform Commercial Code*, 3rd edn (Cengage Learning, 2014).
Terre, F, Simler, P and Lequette, Y, *Droit Civil, Les Obligation*, 7th edn (Dalloz, 1999).
Treitel, GH, *Remedies for Breach of Contract: A Comparative Account* (Oxford University Press, 1988).
Twigg-Flesner, C and Canavan, R, *Atiyah and Adams' Sale of Goods*, 14th edn (Pearson Education Limited, 2020).
Twining, W, *Karl Llewellyn and the Realist Movement* (Weidenfeld & Nicolson, 1973).
Virgo, G, *The Principles of the Law of Restitution*, 2nd edn (Oxford University Press, 2006).
Virgo, G and Worthington, S, *Commercial Remedies: Resolving Controversies* (Cambridge University Press, 2017).
Vogenauer, S, *Commentary on the UNIDROIT Principles of International Commercial Contracts*, 2nd edn (Oxford University Press, 2015).
von Mehren, D (ed), *International Encyclopedia of Comparative Law, Vol VII* (Mohr, 1976).
Walsh, W, *A Treatise on Equity* (Callaghan and Company, 1930).
White, JJ and Summers, RS, *Uniform Commercial Code*, 6th edn (Thomson Reuters, 2010).
Williston, S and Lord, RA, *Williston on Contracts*, 4th edn (2020).

Williston, S, *The Law Governing Sales of Goods at Common Law and Under the Uniform Sales Act* (Baker, Voorhis & Company, 1924).
Wood, PR, *Set-off and Netting, Derivatives, Clearing Systems*, 2nd edn (Sweet & Maxwell, 2007).
Zeller, B, *Damages under the Convention on Contracts for the International Sale of Goods*, 3rd edn (Oxford University Press, 2018).
Zimmermann, R, *Roman Law, Contemporary Law, European Law, the Civilian Tradition Today* (Oxford University Press, 2001).
Zimmermann, R, *The Law of Obligations: Roman Foundations of the Civilian Tradition* (Clarendon, 1996).

Journal Articles

Adams, JN, 'Damages in sale of goods: a critique of the provisions of the Sale of Goods Act and Article 2 of the Uniform Commercial Code' (2002) 9 *Journal of Business Law* 553.
Adar, Y and Gelbard, M, 'The role of remedies in the relational theory of contract' (2011) 7 *European Review of Contract Law* 399.
Ames, JB, 'The history of Assumpsit I. Express Assumpsit' (1888) 2 *Harvard Law Review* 1.
—— 'The history of Assumpsit II, implied Assumpsit' (1888) 2 *Harvard Law Review* 53.
Anastasi, A, Hayward, B and Brown, SP, 'An Internationalist Approach to Interpreting Private International Law? Arbitration and Sales Law in Australia' (2020) 44 *Melbourne University Law Review* 1.
Andersen, CB, 'Exceptions to the notification rule – are they uniformly interpreted?' (2005) 9 *Vindobona Journal of International Commercial Law and Arbitration* 20.
Anderson, RR, 'A Look Back at the Future of UCC Damages Remedies' (2018) 71 *Southern Methodist University Law Review* 185.
—— 'An Overview of Buyer's Damage Remedies' (1988) 21 *Uniform Commercial Code Law Journal* 28.
—— 'Damage Remedies under the Emerging Article 2 – An Essay against Freedom' (1997) 34 *Houston Law Review* 1065.
Apps, A, 'The right to cure defective performance' (1994) *Lloyd's Maritime and Commercial Law Quarterly* 525.
Austen-Baker, R, 'Difficulties with damages as a ground for specific performance' (1999)10 *King's College Law Journal* 1.
Azeredo da Silveira, M, 'Anticipatory Breach under the United Nations Convention on Contracts for the International Sale of Goods' (2005) 2 *Nordic Journal of Commercial Law* 1.
Babiak, A, 'Defining "Fundamental Breach" under the United Nations Convention on Contracts for the International Sale of Goods' (1992) 6 *Temple International and Comparative Law Journal* 113.
Baron, G, 'Do the UNIDROIT Principles of International Commercial Contracts form a new lex mercatoria?' (1999) 2 *Arbitration International* 115.
Beale, H and Dugdale, T, 'Contracts between businessmen: planning and the use of contractual remedies' (1975) 2 *British Journal of Law and Society* 45.
Beheshti, R, 'Anticipatory Breach of Contract and the Necessity of Adequate Assurance under English Law and The Uniform Commercial Code' [2018] *Lloyd's Maritime and Commercial Law Quarterly* 276.
—— 'Price reduction versus damages: a battle without a winner' (2016) *Uniform Law Review* 216.
Bergsten, EE and Miller, AJ, 'The remedy of reduction of price' (1979) 27 *American Journal of Comparative Law* 255.
Bonell, MJ, 'The law governing international commercial contracts and the actual role of the UNIDROIT Principles' (2018) 23 *Uniform Law Review* 15.
—— 'The UNIDROIT principles and transnational law' (2000) 5 *Uniform Law Review* 199.
—— 'The UNIDROIT Principles of International Commercial Contracts. Why? What? How?' (1995) *Tulane Law Review* 1121.
Borden, MJ, 'The Promissory Character of Adequate Assurances of Performance' (2010) 76 *Brooklyn Law Review* 167.

Brandon, DI, Cooper, ML, Greshin, JH, Harris, AL and Head, JM, 'Self-Help: Extrajudicial Rights, Privileges and Remedies in Contemporary American Society' (1984) 37 *Vanderbilt Law Review* 845.

Bridge, MG, 'Avoidance for Fundamental Breach of Contract under the UN Convention on the International Sale of Goods' (2010) 59 *International & Comparative Law Quarterly* 911.

—— 'Issues arising under Articles 64, 72 and 73 of the United Nations Convention on Contracts for the International Sale of Goods' (2005–2006) *Journal of Law and Commerce* 405.

—— 'Markets and Damages in Sale of Goods Case' (2016) 132 *Law Quarterly Review* 405.

—— 'Avoidance for fundamental breach of contract under the UN Convention on the International Sale of Goods' (2010) 59 *International & Comparative Law Quarterly* 911.

—— 'Defective goods and sub-sales' (1998) 3 *Journal of Business Law* 259.

—— 'Discharge for breach of the contract of sale of goods' (1982–1983) 28 McGill Law Journal 867.

—— 'Discharge for breach of the contract of sale of goods' (1983) 176 *McGill Law Journal* 868.

—— 'Issues arising Under Articles 64, 72 and 73 of the United Nations Convention on Contracts for the International Sale of Goods' (2005–2006) 25 *Journal of Law and Commerce* 405.

—— 'Markets and damages in sale of goods cases' (2016) 132 *Law Quarterly Review* 405.

—— 'The nature and consequences of avoidance of the contract under the United Nations Convention on the International Sale of Goods' (2008–2009) 10 *International Law Review of Wuhan University* 118.

Brooks, RW, 'The efficient performance hypothesis' (2006) 116 *Yale Law Journal* 568.

Burrows, A, 'Legislative reform of remedies for breach of contract: the English perspective' (1997) 1 *Edinburgh Law Review* 155.

Burton, SJ, 'Breach of contract and the common law duty of perform in good faith' (1980) 94 *Harvard Law Review* 369.

—— 'Good faith performance of a contract within Article 2 of the Uniform Commercial Code' (1981) 67 *Iowa Law Review* 1.

Campbell, D and Harris, D, 'In defence of breach: a critique of restitution and the performance interest' (2002) 22 *Journal of Legal Studies* 20.

—— 'The defence of breach and the policy of performance' (2006) 25 *University of Queensland Law Journal* 271.

—— 'The relational constitution of remedy: co-operation as the implicit second principle of remedies for breach of contract' (2004–2005) 11 *Texas Wesleyan Law Review* 455.

—— 'The Right to Assurance of Performance under UCC § 2-609: Toward a Uniform Rule of Contract Law' (1982) 5 *Fordham Law Review* 1292.

Carter, JW and Courtney, W, '"Ready and willing to perform": discharge for breach and damages' (2020) 1 *Lloyd's Maritime and Commercial Law Quarterly* 251.

Carter, JW, 'Adequate assurance of due performance' (1996) 10 Journal of Contract Law 3.

Carter, JW, Phang, A and Phang, S-Y, 'Performance Following Repudiation: Legal and Economic Interests' (1999) 15 *Journal of Contract Law* 100.

Childres, R, 'Buyer's Remedies: The Danger of Section 2-713' (1977–1978) 72 *Northwestern University Law Review* 837.

Christie D, Saintier, S and Viven-Wilksch, J, 'Industry led standards, relational contracts and good faith: are the UK and Australia setting the pace in (construction) contract law?' (2022) 43 *Liverpool Law Review* 287.

Cohen, KS, 'Achieving a Uniform Law Governing International Sales: Conforming the Damage Provisions of the United Nations Convention on Contracts for the International Sale of Goods and the Uniform Commercial Code' (2005) 26 *University of Pennsylvania Journal of International Economic Law* 601.

Crespi, GS, 'The adequate assurance doctrine after UCC § 2-609: a test of the efficiency of the common law' (1993) 38 *Villanova Law Review* 179.

Cuniberti, G, 'The international market for contracts, the most attractive contract laws' (2014) 34 *Northwestern Journal of International Law & Business* 455, 459.

Dalhuisen, JH, 'Some realism about a Common European Sales Law' (2013) 24 *European Business Law Review* 299.

Deiser, GF, 'The origin of Assumpsit' (1912) 25 *Harvard Law Review* 428.
DeNooyer, D, 'Remedying anticipatory repudiation- past, present, and future' (1999) 52 *Southern Methodist Law Review* 1787.
Devlin, L, 'The treatment of breach of contract' (1996) 24 *Cambridge Law Journal* 192.
Dickson, B, 'The law of restitution in the Federal Republic of Germany: a comparison with English law' (1987) 36 *International & Comparative Law Quarterly* 751.
DiMatteo, LA, Dhooge, L, Greene, S, Maurer, V, and Pagnattaro, M, 'The interpretive turn in international sales law: an analysis of fifteen years of CISG jurisprudence' (2004) 34 *Northwestern Journal of International Law & Business* 299.
Doudko, AG, 'Hardship in contract: the approach of the Unidroit Principles and legal developments in Russia' (2000) *Uniform Law Review* 483.
Dressler, JM, 'Good faith rejection of goods in a falling market' (2009) 42 *Connecticut Law Review* 611.
DuBay, J, 'Some problems in specific performance of timber sale contracts' (1960–1961) 38 *University of Detroit Law Journal* 324.
Eisenberg, MA, 'Actual and virtual specific performance, the theory of efficient breach, and the indifference principle in contract law' (2005) 93 *California Law Review* 975.
Elliott, IA, 'Specific Performance' (1960) 1 *University of Illinois Law Forum* 72.
Ervine, WCH, 'Cure and retender revisited' [2006] *Journal of Business Law* 799.
Farnsworth, EA, 'Developing international trade law' (1979) 9 *California Western International Law Journal* 461.
—— 'Legal remedies for breach of contract' (1970) 70 *Columbia Law Review* 1145.
—— 'Problems of Non-performance in Contract' (1981) 17 *New England Law Review* 249.
Ferrari, F, 'Fundamental breach of contract under the UN Sales Convention – 25 Years of Article 25 CISG' (2006) 25 *Journal of Law and Commerce* 489.
—— 'What sources of law for contracts for the international sale of goods? Why one has to look beyond the CISG' (2005) 5 *Internationales Handelsrecht* 314.
Fitzgerald, J, 'CISG, specific performance, and the civil law of Louisiana and Quebec' (1996–1997) 16 *Journal of Law and Commerce* 291.
Flechtner, HM, 'Remedies under the New International Sales Convention: The Perspective from Article 2 of the U.C.C.' (1998) 8 *Journal of Law and Commerce* 53.
Foss, H, 'The seller's right to cure when the buyer revokes acceptance: erase the line in the sand' (1991) 16 *Southern Illinois University Law Journal* 1.
Friedman, D, 'The efficient breach fallacy' (1989) 18 *Journal of Legal Studies* 1.
Friedman, DP, 'Set-off – avoiding the confusion' (2011) 27 *Construction Law Journal* 494.
Frisch, D, 'The Compensation Myth and UCC Section 2-713' (2014) 90 *Brooklyn Law Review* 173.
Fuller, LL and Perdue, WR, 'The reliance interest in contract damages' (1936–1937) 46 *Yale Law Journal* 52.
Garro, AM, 'The gap-filling role of the UNIDROIT Principles in international sales law: some comments on the interplay between the principles and the CISG' (1994–1995) 69 *Tulane Law Review* 1149.
Gärtner, A, 'Britain and the CISG: The Case for Ratification – A Comparative Analysis with Special Reference to German Law' in *Pace Review of the Convention on Contracts for the International Sale of Goods (CISG)* (Kluwer Law International, 2000–2001).
Garvin, LT, 'Adequate Assurance of Performance: of Risk, Duress and Cognition' (1998) 69 *University of Colorado Law Review* 71.
Gergen, MP, 'A Theory of Self-help Remedies in Contract' (2009) 89 *Boston University Law Review* 1397.
Goldberg, VP, 'The Achilleas: forsaking foreseeability' (2013) 66 *Current Legal Problems* 107.
Gotanda, JY, 'Awarding Damages under the United Nations Convention on the International Sale of Goods: A Matter of Interpretation' (2005) 37 *Georgetown Journal of International Law* 95.
—— 'Recovering lost profits in international disputes' (2004) 36 *Georgetown Journal of International Law* 61.
Greenberg, H, 'Specific Performance under Section 2-716 of the Uniform Commercial Code: "a More Liberal Attitude" in "Grand Style"' (1981) 17 *New England Law Review* 321.
Gupta, A, 'The implications of The Achilleas on s.73 Indian Contract Act 1872' (2014) 6 *The Company Lawyer* 179.

Handler, M, 'Specific performance under section 2-716 of the Uniform Commercial Code- what other proper circumstances' (1971) 33 *University of Pittsburgh Law Review* 243.

Hayward, B, Zeller, B and Andersen, CB, 'The CISG and the United Kingdom- exploring coherency and private international law' (2018) 67 *International and Comparative Law Quarterly* 607.

Herman, S, 'Specific performance: a comparative analysis: Part 1' (2003) 7 *Edinburgh Law Review* 5.

—— 'Specific performance: a comparative analysis: part 2' (2003) 7 *European Law Review* 194.

Hillman, R, 'Keeping the deal together after material breach- common law mitigation rules, the UCC, and the Restatement (Second) of Contracts' (1976) 47 *University of Colorado Law Review* 553.

—— 'The Crises in Modern Contract Theory (1988) 67 *Tulane Law Review* 103.

Holmes, OW, 'The path of the law' (1897) *Harvard Law Review* 457.

Kamp, AR, 'Between-the-wars social thought: Karl Llewellyn, legal realism, and the Uniform Commercial Code in context' (1995) 59 *Albany Law Review* 325.

Katz, AW, 'Remedies for breach of contract under the CISG' (2005) 25 *International Review of Law and Economics* 378.

Kee, C, 'Set-off in international arbitration- what can the Asian region learn?' (2005) 2 *Asian International Arbitration Journal* 141.

Khouri, N, 'Efficient breach theory in the law of contract: an analysis' (2000–2003) 9 *Auckland University Law Review* 739.

Kornet, N, 'Evolving general principles of international commercial contract, the Unidroit Principles and favor contractus' (2011) 7 *Maastricht European Private Law Institute*.

Kornhauser, LA, 'An introduction to the economic analysis of contract remedies' (1985–1986) 57 *University of Colorado Law Review* 683.

Kramer, A, 'The new test of remoteness in contract'(2009) 7 *Law Quarterly Review* 408.

Kronke, H, 'The UN Sales Convention, the UNIDROIT contract principles and the way beyond' (2004) 9 *Uniform Law Review* 758.

Kronman, AT 'Specific performance' (1978) 45 *University of Chicago Law Review* 351.

Kryla-Cudna, K, 'Adequate assurance of performance under UN Convention on Contracts for the International Sale of goods and the Uniform Commercial Code' (2021) *International & Comparative Law Quarterly*.

Lake, S, 'An empirical study of the UNIDROIT principles – International and British responses' (2011) 16(3) *Uniform Law Review* 669.

Lando, H and Rose, C, 'On the enforcement of specific performance in Civil law countries' (2004) 24 *International Review of Law and Economics* 473.

Lauson, ED, 'Construction and application of United Nations Convention on Contracts for the International Sale of Goods' (2005) 200 *American Law Reports ALR Federal*.

Lawrence, WH, 'The Prematurely Reported Demise of the Perfect Tender Rule' (1987) 35 *University of Kansas Law Review* 557.

—— 'Cure under Article 2 of the Uniform Commercial Code: practices and prescriptions' (1988) 21 *Uniform Commercial Code Law Journal* 138.

Lewis, TR, Perry, MK and Sappington, DEM, 'Renegotiation and Specific Performance' (1989) 52 *Law and Contemporary Problems* 33.

Liu, C, 'Cure by Non-Conforming Party: Perspectives from the CISG, UNIDROIT Principles, PECL and Case Law' (2005) *Pace Law School Institute of International Commercial Law*.

Llewellyn, K, 'Some Realism about Realism-Responding to Dean Pound' (1931) 44 *Harvard Law Review* 1222.

—— 'Why We Need the Uniform Commercial Code' (1957) 10 *University of Florida Law Review* 367.

Lord Hoffmann, 'The Achilleas: custom and practice or foreseeability' (2010) 4 *Edinburgh Law Review* 47.

Lutz, H, 'The CISG and common law courts: is there really a problem?' (2004) 35 *Victoria University of Wellington Law Review* 711.

Torsello, M, 'Substantive and jurisdictional aspects of international contract remedies: a comment on Avery Katz's "remedies for breach of contract under the CISG"' (2005) 25 *International Review of Law and Economics* 397.

Macaulay, S, 'Renegotiations and settlements: Dr. Pangloss's notes on the margins of David Campbell's paper' (2007–2008) 29 *Cardozo Law Review* 261.
Macneil, IR, 'Contracting Worlds and Essential Contract Theory' (2000) 9 *Social & Legal Studies* 431.
—— 'Efficient breach of contract: circles in the sky' (1982) 68 *Virginia Law Review* 947.
Magnus, U, 'The Remedy of Avoidance of Contract under CISG – General Remarks and Special Cases' (2005–2006) 25 *Journal of Law and Commerce* 423.
Magnus, U, 'The Vienna Sales Convention (CISG) between civil and common law- best of all worlds?' (2010) 3(1) *Journal of Civil Law Studies* 67.
Maier-Lohmann, T, 'Buyer's self-repair of non-conforming goods vs. seller's right to cure, under Article 48 CISG' (2019) *Uniform Law Review* 58.
Mak, V, 'The seller's right to cure defective performance- a reappraisal' [2007] *Lloyd's Maritime Commercial Law Quarterly* 409.
Malcolm, WD, 'The Proposed Commercial Code' (1951) 6 *Business Law Journal* 113.
Merryman, JH, 'On the convergence (and divergence) of the civil law and the common law' (1981) 17 *Stanford Journal of International Law* 357.
Mitchell, C, 'Behavioural Standards in Contracts and English Contract Law' (2016) 33 *Journal of Contract Law* 234.
Nicholas, B, 'The Vienna Convention on International Sales Law' (1989) 105 *Law Quarterly Review* 201.
O'Malley, N and Nieuwveld, LB, 'The UNIDROIT Principles: are they law?' (2007) 11 *Vindobona Journal of International Commercial Law and Arbitration* 229.
Patterson, EW, 'Constructive Conditions in Contracts' (1942) 42 *Columbia Law Review* 903.
Pauly, C, 'The concept of fundamental breach as an international principle to create uniformity of commercial law' (1999–2000) 19 *Journal of Law and Commerce* 221.
Peel, WE, 'The termination paradox' [2013] *Lloyd's Maritime and Commercial Law Quarterly* 519.
Phang, A, 'Specific performance – exploring the roots of 'settled practice' (1998) 61 *Modern Law Review* 421.
Piliounis, PA, 'The remedies of specific performance, price reduction and additional time (Nachfrist) Under the CISG: Are These Worthwhile Changes or Additions to English Sales Law?' (2000) 12 *Pace International Law Review* 1.
Reynolds, F, 'Discharge of contract by breach' (1981) 97 *Law Quarterly Review* 541.
—— 'Warranty, condition and fundamental term' (1963) 79 *Law Quarterly Review* 534.
Robertson, A, 'The basis of the remoteness rule in contract' (2008) 28 *Journal of Legal Studies* 172.
Robertson, RJ, 'The right to demand adequate assurance of due performance: Uniform Commercial Code Section 2-609 and Restatement (Second) of Contracts section 251' (1988–89) 38 *Drake Law Review* 305.
Saidov, D, 'Anticipatory non-performance and underlying value of the UNIDROIT Principles' (2006) 11 *Uniform Law Review* 795.
—— 'Methods of Limiting Damages under the Vienna Convention on Contracts for the International Sale of Goods' (2002) 14 *Pace International Law Review* 307.
Sargis, NW, 'The Uniform Commercial Code Section 2-609: a Return to Certainty' (1980) 14 *John Marshall Law Review* 113.
Scalise, RJ, 'Why no efficient breach in civil law? a comparative assessment of the doctrine of efficient breach of contract' (2007) 55 *American Journal of Comparative Law* 721.
Schlechtriem, P, 'Interpretation, Gap-Filling and Further Development of the U.N. Sales Convention' (2004) 16 *Pace International Law Review* 279.
Schneider, E, 'UCC § 2-713: a Defence of Buyer's Expectancy Damages' (1986) 22 *California Western Law Review* 233.
—— 'The seller's right to cure under the Uniform Commercial Code and the United Nations Convention on Contracts for International Sale of Goods' (1989–1990) 7 *Arizona Journal of International and Comparative Law* 69.
Schwenzer, I, 'Specific Performance and Damages According to the 1994 UNIDROIT Principles of International Commercial Contracts' (1999) 1 *European Journal of Law Reform* 289.

Schwenzer, I and Hachem, P, 'The CISG – Successes and Pitfalls' (2009) 57 *The American Journal of Comparative Law* 457.

Scott, RE, 'A relational theory of default rules for commercial contracts' (1990) 19 *Journal of Legal Studies* 604.

Shavell, S, 'Specific performance versus damages for breach of contract' (2005–2006) 84 *Tulane Law Review* 831.

Shea, AM, 'Discharge from performance of contract by failure of condition' (1979) 42 *Modern Law Review* 623.

Silveira, MAD, 'Anticipatory breach under the United Nations Convention on Contracts for the International Sale of Goods' (2005) 2 *Nordic Journal of Commercial Law* 1.

Sondahl, E, 'Understanding the remedy of price reduction – a means to fostering a more uniform application of the United Nations Convention on contracts for the International Sale of Goods' (2003) 7 *Vindobona Journal of International Commercial Law and Arbitration* 255.

Speidel, RE, 'The Revision of UCC Article 2, Sales in Light of United Nations Convention on Contracts for the International Sale of Goods' (1996) 16 *Northwestern Journal of International Law & Business* 165.

Spinosi, CJ, 'Set-off' (2000) *Working Group for the Preparation of Principles of International Commercial Contracts* 2.

Stoljar, S, 'Some problems of anticipatory breach' (1974) 9 *Melbourne University Law Review* 355.

Strub, MG, 'The Convention on the International Sale of Goods: Anticipatory repudiation provisions and developing countries' (1989) 38 *International & Comparative Law Quarterly* 475.

Summers, R, '"Good Faith" in General Contract Law and the Sales Provisions of the Uniform Commercial Code' (1968) 54 *Virginia Law Review* 195.

Sundaram, J, 'Is the Court of Appeal decision in The Achilleas good law' (2008) 20 *The Denning Law Journal* 187.

Szladits C, 'The concept of specific performance in civil law' (1955) 4 *American Journal of Comparative Law* 208.

Taylor, CR, 'Self-help in contract law: an exploration and proposal' (1998) 33 *Wake Forest Law Review* 839.

Tettenborn, A, 'Absolving the underserving: shopping centres, specific performance and the law of contract' [1998] *Conveyancer and Property Lawyer* 23.

Tetley, W, 'Mixed jurisdictions: common law vs civil law (codified and uncodified) (Part II)' (1999) 4 *Uniform Law Review* 877.

Travalio, GM, 'The UCC's three R's rejection, revocation, and (the seller's) right to cure' (1984) 53 *University of Cincinnati Law Review* 931.

Treitel, GH, 'Damages for breach of warranty of quality' (1997) 113 *Law Quarterly Review* 188.

—— 'Specific performance in the sale of goods' (1966) *Journal of Business Law* 211.

Ulen, TS, 'The efficiency of specific performance: toward a unified theory of contract remedies' (1984–1985) 83 *Michigan Law Review* 341.

Vanwijck-Alexandre, M, 'Anticipatory breach and instalment contracts in the CISG' (2001) 3–4 *International Business Law Journal* 353.

Vekas, L, 'The foreseeability doctrine in contractual damage cases' (2002) 43 *Acta Juridica Hungarica* 145.

Vernon, DH, 'Expectancy damages for breach of contract: a primer and critique' (1976) 2 *Washington University Law Review* 179.

Walt, S, 'For specific performance under the United Nations Sales Convention' (1991) 26 *Texas International Law Journal* 211.

Webb, C, 'Performance and compensation: an analysis of contract damages and contractual obligation' (2006) 26 *Oxford Journal of Legal Studies* 41.

Whitman, J, 'Commercial Law and the American Volk: A Note on Llewellyn's German Sources for the Uniform Commercial Code' (1987) 97 *Yale Law Journal* 156.

William, AE, 'Forecasting the Potential Impact of the Vienna Sales Convention on International Sales Law in the United Kingdom' in *Pace Review of the Convention on Contracts for the International Sale of Goods (CISG)* (Kluwer Law International, 2000–2001).

Xing Tan, Z, 'Disrupting doctrine? Revisiting the doctrinal impact of relational contract theory' (2018) 39 *Legal Studies* 98.
Zeller, B, 'Article 48 CISG – confusion or sound drafting?' (2022) 22 *Internationales Handelsrecht* 7.
—— 'Remarks on the Manner in Which the Unidroit Principles may be used to Interpret or Supplement Article 76 of the CISG' (2003) 1 *Nordic Journal of Commercial Law* 1.
Zimmermann, R, 'The unwinding of failed contracts in the UNIDROIT Principles' (2011) 16 *Uniform Law Review* 563.
Zimmermann, R, 'The unwinding of failed contracts in the UNIDROIT Principles' (2010) 570, 571.

INDEX

www.ingramcontent.com/pod-product-compliance
Ingram Content Group UK Ltd.
Pitfield, Milton Keynes, MK11 3LW, UK
UKHW020807290926
15470UKWH00003B/1015

9 781509 940462